THE CRAFTSMAN

An Anthology

THE CRAFTSMAN

An Anthology

Edited by
Barry Sanders

Designed by Richard Firmage

Peregrine Smith, Inc.
SANTA BARBARA AND SALT LAKE CITY
1978

 For Raoul 

Library of Congress Cataloging in Publication Data
Main entry under title:

The Craftsman.

A collection of articles, photos, and drawings from the Craftsman.

1. The Craftsman—Illustrations. 2. Art industries and trade—United States. 3. Arts and crafts movement. I. Sanders, Barry. II. The Craftsman.
NK1141.C7 700
78-15909

ISBN 0-87905-029-2

Book design by Richard A. Firmage

Manufactured in the United States of America

TABLE OF CONTENTS

INTRODUCTION

I

A unique magazine appeared in the early years of the twentieth century, which rapidly became the principal journal for the dissemination of the Arts and Crafts philosophy in America. That magazine was named *The Craftsman.* It was founded, edited, and published by Gustav Stickley.

Although Gustav Stickley is relatively unknown today, he was a remarkably talented individual. He was an inventor, a well known designer, a writer, a respected publisher and editor, an incredibly successful businessman, a political thinker. He ran the first electric streetcar in America. He was chiefly responsible for formulating the philosophy behind the most important revolution in aesthetics in America, the Arts and Crafts Movement, which lasted from approximately 1876 to 1916; and for a part of that time Stickley managed to affect the appearance of homes, both inside and out, across the entire country. He is probably best known—when he is remembered at all—for his functional, straight-line furniture designs, called Mission or Craftsman. Outspoken, eccentric, defiantly egocentric, Stickley edited, printed, and distributed his own magazine, *The Craftsman,* as a way of educating the public about his Arts and Crafts philosophy.

Stickley made his philosophy immediately clear in the first issue of *The Craftsman,* which appeared October 1, 1901, in Eastwood, New York: "The United Crafts endeavor to promote and extend the principles established by [William] Morris, in both the artistic and the socialistic sense. In the interests of art, they seek to substitute the luxury of taste for the luxury of costliness; to teach that beauty does not imply elaboration or ornament; to employ only those forms and materials which make for simplicity, individuality and dignity of effect." Stickley, in fact, devoted the first issue to William Morris, the leader of the Arts and Crafts Movement in England. Morris was an important printer, changing the face of printing styles in nineteenth century England with his own Kelmscott Press. (The *Kelmscott Chaucer* is still one of the most beautifully produced books in the history of printing.) In the early issues of *The Craftsman,* Stickley borrowed Morris' gothic type faces and art work, and referred periodically to Morris' philosophy. Over the years, however, Stickley changed *The Craftsman*'s format, size, and graphics. Although Stickley's central commitment and informing vision remained Morris' "simplification of life," he greatly expanded *The Craftsman*'s interests.

Throughout its sixteen years (31 volumes), *The Craftsman* never abandoned what Morris called "the household arts": furniture design, copperwork, ceramics, leatherwork, glass, jewelry, and bookbinding; but it also carried articles on art, architecture, poetry, drama, politics, economics, history, gardening, city planning, and education. *The Craftsman* was also a practical magazine, publishing instructions on how to weave, hammer copper, build furniture, and tool leather. Stickley utilized drawings and epigrams to underscore his Arts and Crafts philosophy. Pages were illustrated with photographs of Rodin sculptures, Rembrandt etchings, Millet drawings, stencil designs, Hiroshigi and Hokusai prints—whatever Stickley felt was artistically valuable, from throughout the world, for his readers. In addition, Stickley supplied his readers with an overwhelming 221 plans for his Craftsman homes. There were times when *The Craftsman* even resembled today's *Whole Earth Catalog*—it provided information, for example, on where to buy the best stove or refrigerator; how to raise healthy chickens; the advantages of proper nutrition; and the health hazards of carpeting. But most important, the magazine provided the essential information on developments in the Arts and Crafts Movement.

In *The Craftsman,* the general reader could learn about important work done by virtually everyone connected with the Arts and Crafts, both in America and Europe. There were articles by or about architects Louis Sullivan, Charles and Henry Greene, Irving Gill, and George Grant Elmslie; philosophers William Morris and John Ruskin; designers Ernest Batchelder, Charles Voysey, and Harvey Ellis; metalsmiths Robert Jarvie and Elizabeth Burton; ceramicists Artus and Anne Van Briggle; bookbinder T. J. Cobden-Sanderson; jewelers René Lalique and Louis Comfort Tiffany. There were stories by Tolstoy, Gorky, and Hamlin Garland; poems by Robert Frost, Carl Sandburg, and Amy Lowell.

Indeed, so many different authors covered so many subjects that, for some readers, *The Craftsman* was not only exhaustive, but exhausting. Stickley, however, never seemed to tire. By volume twenty-five (the end of 1913), Stickley triumphantly proclaimed: "There seems to be no limit whatever to the things which the Craftsman Movement can accomplish." While maintaining a successful furniture business, he contributed an editorial practically each month on a variety of subjects, as well as periodically writing longer pieces. In 1915, one year before *The Craftsman*'s demise, Stickley proudly advertised, as a premium to subscribers, a collection of readings from eight separate categories which his magazine had seriously covered over the years: American Architecture and Homebuilding, Furniture and Furnishings, American Gardens, Modern American Art, American Crafts, Photographic Art the World Over, Bird Life in America, and New Ideas.

Since there is not room to include every article from *The Craftsman* that I would categorize "the best," I have presented a sample of the most well written, interesting, and informative pieces, both about *The Craftsman* itself and the Movement in general. Included also is a wide selection of incidental photographs, etchings, drawings, and epigrams. In *The Craftsman,* they supplemented the articles and offered a break from discursive essays. Here, they provide concrete examples of what *The Craftsman* actually looked like. The selections are arranged chronologically so that the reader can see how *The Craftsman* changed over the years. Specifically, articles became more sophisticated; they no longer extolled, they analyzed and criticized. Type faces and page sizes changed. And most important, as Stickley himself emphasized, the magazine greatly expanded its interests:

> When *The Craftsman* was founded it was with the intention of making it a magazine devoted almost solely to the encouragement of handicrafts in this country. We believed, then, as we believe now, in the immense influence for good in the development of character that is exerted merely by learning to use the hands. One needs only to look at any part of the history of handicrafts to realize how much strength, sincerity and genuine creative thought went into the work of the old craftsmen who were also such solid and substantial citizens. We have always felt that it is not the making of things that is important, but the making of strong men and women through the agency of the sound development that begins when the child learns to use its hands for shaping to the best of its ability something which is really needed either for its own play or for the comfort and convenience of others in the home.... But, as *The Craftsman* grew and step by step attained a wider outlook, the question of the study of handicrafts as an end in itself gradually sunk to a position of minor importance in the policy of the magazine. Our belief that in it lay the foundation of all growth was no less, but the field was so broad that the record and discussion of all constructive work in the larger affairs of life came gradually to take first place.
>
> As we began to design houses and to shape the idea of the Craftsman country home as we have here tried to describe it, we took up the subjects of architecture and interior decoration, doing our best to promote the establishment of the right standards and to offer all the aid in our power toward the development of a national spirit in our architecture. This naturally led to other forms of art, and *The Craftsman* became a magazine for painters and sculptures as well as for architects, interior decorators, and craftsmen. Along these lines it has always been progressive and rather radical, aiming always to discover and bring to the front any notable achievement that seemed to indicate the blazing of a new trail. The magazine has also taken the deepest interest in all social, industrial and political reforms and in the question of industrial education along practical lines that would fit any boy or girl to earn a living under any and all circumstances. In fact, taken altogether, *The Craftsman* has been

the outward and visible expression of the more philosophic side of the Craftsman idea, just as the houses and their furnishings have put into form its more concrete phases.*

II

The Craftsman: An Anthology reflects the same wide variety of concerns and broad range of names as *The Craftsman* itself. But since *The Craftsman* may be new for some readers, a brief comment on key articles included here may serve as a touchstone. *The Craftsman* initially concerned itself with the philosophy of William Morris and the possibilities of work reform through socialism. Irene Sargent, Professor of Art History and Romance Languages at Syracuse University, and guiding spirit for the magazine's early years, wrote the article "William Morris" (page 2) for the first issue. A. M. Simons, who wrote "The Economic Foundation of Art" (page 18) for the first issue, was the editor of the *International Socialist Review*.

Although Stickley himself came to abandon socialism, he remained political. He always thought of the Arts and Crafts Movement as a political one; he even talked about himself as a political revolutionary. The Arts and Crafts Movement was to be a "peaceful revolution" in the condition of the worker who, because he now both designed and produced his product, would no longer experience alienation. For an introduction to the Movement itself, the reader should first see "Thoughts Occasioned by an Anniversary" (page 112) which Stickley wrote on the occasion of the magazine's third birthday. Then read "The Arts and Crafts Movement in America" (page 213) by Ernest Batchelder, a California designer and ceramic tile maker, who presents an historical look at the Movement. In "The Craftsman Movement: Its Origin and Growth" (page 219), Stickley describes his own role in the birth and growth of the Arts and Crafts Movement. He discusses his attitude toward the machine in "The Use and Abuse of Machinery, and Its Relation to the Arts and Crafts" (page 186). The Arts and Crafts Movement in this country is sometimes seen as a reaction to certain extravagant, non-functional designs of the Art Nouveau style. Art Nouveau was generally deplored in *The Craftsman,* but Stickley invited Samuel Bing, the man who coined the phrase, to present his side in a significant article, "L'Art Nouveau" (page 84). Bing's article is followed by Art Nouveau designs by Alphonse Mucha, Eugène Grasset, and Georges Auriol.

***Craftsman Homes* (The Craftsman Publishing Company, 1909), pages 202-03.

For a short time, Stickley himself manufactured a line of furniture with inlaid designs that echoed Art Nouveau patterns. Harvey Ellis, a young artist, designed that inlaid furniture for Stickley, and wrote for *The Craftsman* from 1903 to his death in January 1904. He may have also prompted the Home-Builders' Club, a department in *The Craftsman* which printed plans for Stickley's Craftsman Homes. (The Home-Builders' Club was so successful that it was later expanded to include information on available real estate, and home construction techniques.) One of Ellis' house plans, "A Craftsman House Design," appears on page 72.

Although the Arts and Crafts Movement generally affected domestic architecture, the changes were most evident in Southern California. Warm weather permitted bold experiments in indoor/outdoor living, expressed mainly through the California bungalow. Two brothers, Charles Sumner Greene and Henry Mather Greene, mastered the design. Their architecture is examined in "California's Contribution to a National Architecture" (page 251). Another important California architect, Irving Gill, interesting for his small houses of sharp angles and circles, describes "The New Architecture of the West" on page 308.

Closely connected with the magazine's concern for architecture was its concern for city planning and city beautification. Many articles strongly advocated the reclaiming of vacant lots, the painting of neighborhood murals, planting of trees, and other related civic projects. I have selected one, "The Garden City Idea" (page 285), which outlines an ideal the magazine pursued its entire life—cooperative neighborhood living and governing.

Stickley not only envisioned a world in which people planned their own cities and built their own homes, he also wanted them to construct their own furniture. So he provided plans and lumber lists in *The Craftsman* for all the major pieces of his commercially manufactured furniture, in a department called "Home Training in Cabinet Work." I have included sections from two installments. This should be read carefully by anyone interested in duplicating Stickley's wood finishes: he explains here his unique "fuming' technique for coloring wood. The care he took in finishing his furniture reflected his general attitude toward all labor. In "The Truth About Work" (page 219), unsigned though certainly by Stickley, he argues for the proper attitude toward labor in order to create "permanent beauty." If man "understands the truth about beauty and then labors to express it," Stickley says, he will have found the secret of happy living. Ever didactic, Stickley wanted parents to raise their children according to this philosophy.

Education was a subject constantly explored in *The Craftsman.* A number of articles dealt specifically with the education of the manual worker, and the advantages of the manual arts in public school curriculum. They ranged from the grand, philosophical principles of Prince Kropotkin to specific, detailed classroom outlines. I have selected one example, "The

New Industrialism" (page 60) by an important figure from the Movement, Oscar Lovell Triggs. He was Professor of Literature at the University of Chicago, secretary for the Industrial Art League in Chicago, and the author of *Chapters in the History of the Arts and Crafts Movement.* Triggs urges the uniting of art, education, and labor, and chooses as his model the Rookwood Pottery Studios of Cincinatti, started by Maria Longworth Nichols, "a high-minded and philanthropic woman."

Women were generally permitted minor voices in the Arts and Crafts Movement. They were not architects or furniture designers. They organized crafts societies and guilds; and they were well known in ceramics, textiles, and leather—genteel areas in which they could find immediate acceptance. *The Craftsman,* however, treated women differently. From its inception, the magazine included women among its editors, contributors, and central concerns. Several articles make clear the magazine's efforts toward the liberation of women. Giles Edgerton's "Is There A Sex Distinction in Art? The Attitude of the Critic Toward Women's Exhibits" (page 209) is a remarkably enlightened look at a fairly delicate and unspoken subject in the early years of the twentieth century. "Three Acres and Chains" (page 230) is a fascinating day-by-day account of a woman who left the city to try small farming. Also included is a photograph by Frances Allen (page 145), and drawings by Frances Lea (page 191) and Pamela Coleman Smith (page 264). Finally, there is an important literary piece by Amy Lowell, the influential imagist poet, titled "Is There A National Spirit in 'The New Poetry' of America?," on page 316. She supported her article with one of her own poems as well as others by H. D., Jean Starr Untermeyer, and Robert Frost (pages 324-27).

Stickley not only encouraged women in *The Craftsman,* but others who were functionally excluded from American Society. Throughout the years, *The Craftsman* made people aware of arts and crafts produced by ethnic minorities in America: Jews, Negroes, Italians, Japanese, Chinese, Hungarians, Czechoslovakians, and especially American Indians. Stickley encouraged people to accent his Craftsman furniture with Indian baskets and rugs. I have selected a range of articles and photographs here on Negro music, Chinese and Japanese crafts and craftsmen, and Indian culture and crafts.

The life force of *The Craftsman* was Stickley himself. It was his magazine, and so his voice is heard more often than any other. In the articles included here, Stickley touches on most of his interests: the need for a democratic art, the preparation and finish of woods, his attitude toward machines, political corruption, big business, farming, the Arts and Crafts Movement, and a good deal more. Stickley's editorial column was called—in most issues of the magazine—*Als Ik Kan* ("If I Can"); and this phrase from the Dutch was either glued or stamped on or burned into virtually every piece of furniture he manufactured. I have included one of his earliest politi-

cal editorials, "Als Ik Kan" (page 192). Beginning around 1907, Stickley became overtly political.

Stickley was in fact always agitating for change: for example, he printed Tolstoy's letter on land ownership in Russia, "A Great Iniquity" (page 162). He also experimented in order to produce change. He attempted two major experiments. First, when Stickley began manufacturing his own furniture, his workshops were loosely modeled on the medieval guild system; this early effort in profit-sharing is sketched for us in "A Visit to the Workshops of The United Crafts" (page 44). Second, Stickley announced in 1908 that he had purchased six hundred acres in Morris Plains, New Jersey, to eventually open a summer home for boys to study handicrafts and farming.

Both experiments were, unfortunately, short lived.

III

The last issue of *The Craftsman* appeared December 1916, with no warning that it was discontinuing publication. Stickley was still listed as editor, and the magazine advertised that, for 1917, subscriptions were available in Holly Red, Delft Blue, or Craftsman Brown sheepskin covers. Circulation figures for 1915, the last available year, had never been greater: 22,500. But the fact is that by December 1916 Stickley was already out of business. Almost a year earlier, March 24, 1915, a petition of bankruptcy had been filed against Craftsman, Incorporated.

In part, Gustav Stickley was responsible for his own demise. When his Mission Furniture designs became popular, large firms like Sears, Roebuck and Company offered copies at prices substantially lower than Stickley's. Unwilling to compromise with the quality of his materials and the fine details of his handiwork, he was unable to, and probably uninterested in, lowering his prices. Surprisingly, his furniture still sold well, at the substantially higher prices, So well, in fact, that he became infatuated with his own success. He expanded beyond his means. He opened a huge showroom in New York, expanded his Craftsman operations into a home-finding service, real estate service, a department for educational information, landscape and home gardening services, and other areas, until his Arts and Crafts empire eventually toppled.

The major reason Stickley fell, however, was that the Modern Age had altered traditional styles of living. Less emphasis was placed on the family and home life, and more on entertainment outside the house. People in general became more mobile. They wanted lighter, less cumbersome furniture. Women were leaving the home to enter college and the work force. They too wanted furniture easier to clean and care for. And, after the First

World War, there were more wealthy people, and they wanted to display their wealth. A more dramatic display of wealth could be made with antiques, rather than with Stickley's stark designs. In short, Stickley was no longer considered modern.

The Craftsman merged in January 1917 with a magazine (published in New York under the auspices of The Art Society of America) called *Art World.* Its first issue pointed out that *The Craftsman* had been "for a number of years in other hands." I assume that the strongest of those hands belonged to Mary Fanton Roberts, associate editor and then later (around 1912) managing editor of *The Craftsman.* Although *Art World* began publishing Stickley's Craftsman Home plans because of what it called "persistent demand," the magazine did not at all resemble Stickley's—it was too academic and theoretical for *The Craftsman*'s general audience. The spirit of *The Craftsman* was actually contained in another monthly, *The Touchstone,* started in May 1917 by Mary Fanton Roberts and most of the former staff of *The Craftsman.* The inside cover of the first issue of *The Touchstone* carried a somber note of well-wishing from Stickley: "I believe there is a wide field for your Magazine, and wish you every success." He was never mentioned in the magazine itself; he died April 21, 1942, virtually unknown.

The Craftsman too is a fairly obscure name today—few libraries have a complete run; scattered issues sometimes appear in thrift shops. What is most striking about the magazine is the incredible force it exerted during the Arts and Crafts period. In 1915 alone, over twenty million dollars worth of homes were built along Craftsman lines, from Alaska to the Fiji Islands. And although *The Craftsman*'s circulation was a modest one—an average of 20,000—it did enjoy a fairly long life. Perhaps in Stickley's case the desire to reform American aesthetics ensured *The Craftsman*'s longevity; for the Craftsman Movement can be seen as part of the period's larger desire for political reform. The words honesty, simplicity, straightforwardness, integrity, appear both in the descriptions of Craftsman furniture, houses, and accessories, as well as in Theodore Roosevelt's speeches. They describe Stickley himself. They constitute the timber of the tough, outspoken American character.

To fully appreciate *The Craftsman*'s grand and impressive sweep, one must look at the whole of Stickley's magazine—every article, epigram, photograph, and drawing. But, still, you will have experienced only part of the man. If you are able, construct one of Stickley's chairs from his own plans. Or better, since it more vividly reveals the political base of Stickley's Arts and Crafts philosophy, rescue a Gustav Stickley chair from a thrift shop and restore it. You'll have to strip away layers of paint, reglue tired joints, scrape and sand, and finally renew the personality of the oak through fuming. You will be surprised, as I have been many times, by how solid and functional that chair is; by the honesty and integrity of its design; and

most unusual, for contemporary America, you will be delighted by the quality of the craftsmanship, evident in the meticulous construction and the sensitive matching of woods.

Stripping the chair can become a radicalizing experience. You will uncover the most important element missing from our daily lives: *quality.* At the same time you will have stripped away those familiar meanings of the word *craft*—skill, deceit, and so on—to arrive at its radical or root meanings: strength, force, power, and virtue.

When a man's personality, his life, and his work are all of the same honest piece, he stands a better chance of feeling strong and powerful, of knowing that his life is virtuous. For Stickley, honest work was done with the hands, in the arts and crafts, in education and farming. He tried to integrate the hand, the heart, and the head in his "peaceful revolution," the Arts and Crafts Movement. And he tried to educate others with his work and through his monthly magazine, *The Craftsman.* For a time Stickley was effective. But aesthetics in contemporary America have disintegrated since then: everything from our formica and naugahyde furniture to our cheesebox architecture—in short, most of our throw-away, disposable culture dates from the close of Gustav Stickley's workshops, and the death of his magazine, *The Craftsman.*

Barry Sanders

In the Middle Ages, that golden period of the arts and crafts, each master-workman adopted some device or legend which, displayed upon every object of his creation, came finally to represent his individuality as completely as did his face, or his voice; making him known beyond the burgher circle in which he passed his life, and, after his death, becoming a magic formula, by which to conjure up his memory, even though the years had multiplied into centuries.

Among the legends so employed, the one assumed by Ian van Eyck, the early Flemish painter, has retained its force and point down to our own day. *Als ich kanne* (if I can) appears written across the canvases of this fourteenth century *chef d'ecole*, placed there, without doubt, as an inspiration toward excellence in that art wherein van Eyck became an epoch maker. Appearing in the background of his masterful portraits, it has something of defiance and humor, as if offering a covert challenge to less skillful limners.

The *Als ich kanne* of van Eyck, like the *Quand meme* of Sarah Bernhardt, reflects that sentiment of courage, boldness and persistency which appeals to all truly virile natures. Thus when William Morris, in his early manhood, visited the Low Countries, and there grew fired with enthusiasm for the decorative arts, he found this legend and made it his own. He used it, in French translation, first in tapestries designed for his own dwelling, and finally it became identified with him; so that the *Si je puis* now recalls his memory as vividly as do the designs which speak to us from the hangings of our walls, the tiles of our floors, or the covers of the books which lie upon our tables.

The same legend in its modern Flemish form, *Als ik kan* has been adopted by the Master of the United Crafts. It here forms an interesting device with a joiner's compass, which is the most primitive and distinctive tool of the worker in wood. The legend is further accompanied by the signature of the Master of the Crafts, Gustave Stickley, which, together with the proper date, appears branded upon every object produced in the workshop of the Guild.

In this way, authenticity is assured, comparisons of progress are made possible, and every facility of information is afforded to the one who shall acquire the piece.

VOL. I October, MDCCCCI NO. 1

The Craftsman

"The lyf so short the craft so long to lerne"

WILLIAM MORRIS

Some thoughts upon His life: work & influence

Published on the first day of each month by THE UNITED CRAFTS at EASTWOOD, NEW YORK

Price 20 cents the copy

WILLIAM MORRIS

LTHOUGH the name of William Morris has long since become a household word throughout America, yet the personality of the man, as well as his great part in the world's work, is definitely known but to the few. His was a versatile genius, each phase of which appeals to a more or less extended public.

To students of literature he is an innovator in his art; one who introduced a new element into the Victorian age; a poet who, beginning his career as an Anglo-Norman mediaevalist, next drew inspiration from the Greek and Latin classics, and finally from widened reading, knowledge and travel, absorbed, at first hand, influences from the Scandinavians who peopled Iceland. In literature, William Morris is the enthusiastic student of Chaucer; he is the creator of "The Earthly Paradise;" the modern skald who, learned in language, legend and history, told to English-speaking folk the Great Story of the North, which, in his own opinion, "should be for all our race what the tale of Troy was to the Greeks."

For others, William Morris represents a most important factor in the progress of modern art. He was a member of that group of brilliant, earnest young Englishmen who, at the middle of the Nineteenth Century, revolutionized the national school of painting, and generated a current of aestheticism whose vibrations are still felt, not only in the parent country, but as well in America and in France. From his relations with the Pre-Raphaelite Brotherhood and from his own practical genius, Morris evolved a system of household art, which has largely swept away the ugly and the commonplace from the English middle-class home. He so became an expert in what he himself was pleased to call "the lesser arts of life." He was a handicraftsman, an artisan self-taught and highly skilled in the technical processes of a half dozen trades. He disdained no apprenticeship however humble, no labor however protracted, arduous and disfiguring, in order that he might become the practical master of his work. The attainments of his genius, of his careful and intelligent study remain as lasting witnesses to the impetus and direction given by him to the arts and crafts of his time.

Again, many who, through ignorance or prejudice, refuse to recognize the functions of literature and art in the economy of life, still regard

William Morris as a lost leader, friend and brother. For such as these, he is the man who, by the light of history and of his own conscience, distinctly saw the evils of society as it is at present constituted; who lent his energies, his fortune and his fame to remedy the wrongs of the oppressed masses, and to prepare the advent of the reign of natural law. In William Morris all socialists honor the unprejudiced man of wealth, culture and position, who plainly formulated the proposition that:

"It is right and just that all men should have work to do which shall be worth doing, and be of itself pleasant to do; and which should be done under such conditions as would make it neither over-wearisome nor over-anxious."

Finally, above and beyond each and all of these claims of William Morris to the present and future consideration of the world, there lies the memory of his great heart which so animated all enterprises into which he entered that, at his death, a co-worker wrote of him: "Morris was a splendid leader, a great poet, artist and craftsman, a still greater man, and, oh! such a friend to know and love."

The place of Morris among the Victorian poets has been exhaustively treated by critics and reviewers, and it is well known that, at the death of Tennyson, the honors of the Laureate would have been for him an easy victory. His accomplishments in the various arts and crafts to which he successively devoted himself, have been chronicled and criticised from time to time, and in various countries and languages. But it is not generally appreciated that his art and his Socialism were associated integrally with each other, or, rather, that they were but two aspects of the same thing. However, this fact becomes evident to any one who will follow his life which, in its intellectual aspects, although it was apparently subject to abrupt changes, was, in reality, a logical expansion of inter-dependent ideas.

It is as an artist-socialist that we will briefly consider him.

The traditions of his family surrounded him with conservatism. He was born of affluent parents whose wealth increased during his childhood and youth. His father, a London City banker, gaining a controlling interest in productive copper-mines, grew wealthy beyond his own expectations, and was thus able to afford his children the most desirable educational and social advantages, as also to secure to them, at his own death, a very considerable fortune.

William Morris, the eldest of five sons, was destined for the Church, and for that reason,

was entered, at the age of fourteen, at Marlboro College, there to be educated under clerical masters. Even in these early days, the characteristics of the future artist and thinker were most marked and singular. The boy was father to the man. The lax discipline, the weakness of the school organization acted in no unfavorable way upon the scholar whose moral and physical strength gave him a unique place among the student body. Rather, these conditions afforded him opportunity for cultivating his individual tastes and for developing his peculiar powers. The school library at Marlboro was rich in works upon archaeology and ecclesiastical architecture, and through these, with his remarkable power of assimilation, he ranged at will. He there acquired that accurate knowledge, which, further developed by minute examination of all existing monuments, constituted him a great authority upon English Gothic, and, at the same time, a protector of the mediaeval cathedrals and churches against the vandalism of so-called "restorations." A school-fellow at Marlboro describes Morris as one who, given to solitude and monologues, was considered "a little mad" by the other boys: a dreamer who invented and poured forth endless stories of "knights and fairies," in which one adventure rose out of another; the tale flowing on from day to day, throughout a whole term. Another peculiarity then noticeable in him was the restlessness of his fingers. The natural undeveloped craftsman sought an outlet for his manual activity in endless netting. While studying in the large school-room, he worked for hours together, with one end of the net fastened to a desk and his fingers moving automatically. Altogether, the impression made by Morris upon his associates of those days was that of a boy remarkable for his physical force and his intense love of nature, but whose scholarship was quite ordinary, barring his intimate acquaintance with English history and architecture.

Leaving Marlboro, Morris passed under the tutorship of a High Churchman of fine attainment and character, of wide sympathies and of cultivated tastes, which extended to the fine arts. Responsive to the new influences, the boy developed into a more than fair classical scholar, and received the inspiration of the strongly individual literary and artistic work of his future years. But the decisive moment of his life occurred in June, 1852, when on passing his matriculation examination for Exeter College, Oxford, he occupied a desk next to that of Edward Burne-Jones, who was destined to be his life-long and most intimate friend. Going into residence in what he himself called the most beautiful of the ancient cities of England, the atmosphere of Oxford

became for him a forcing-place for that peculiar quality of mediaeval thought and culture, which, in his mature years, permeated his personality and vivified every piece of work, intellectual and manual, proceeding from him. Concerning the gracious influences of the old university town, he wrote late in life:

"There are many places in England where a young man may get as good book-learning as in Oxford; but not one where he can receive the education which the loveliness of the grey city used to give us."

The impulse toward mediaevalism was further strengthened in Morris, during his undergraduate days, by a study tour through the cathedral towns of France,—notably Rouen and Amiens,—as well as by a course of reading which gained him an intimate acquaintance with Froissart and with the Arthurian legends: two wells of thought from whose inexhaustible depths he drew an endless chain of artistic *motifs.*

The development of his social and political ideas was slower and later than his advancement in literature and art. During his residence at Oxford, he saw no objection to the monarchical principle; but yet, in the abandonment of his purpose to take Holy Orders, we may see the beginning of his revolt against constituted authority. The secularization of his mind, the widening of his interests convinced him that art and literature were not mere handmaidens of religion, but rather interests to be pursued for their own sake; that they were no less than the means of realizing life. For a short period indeed, he had cherished the idea of founding a religious Brotherhood whose patron was to be Sir Galahad of the Arthurian legend, and whose rules should include both celibacy and conventual life. But the idea of a common organized effort toward a higher life, which had been planned by Morris and his group of associates—Burne-Jones, Faulkner and others—gradually changed from the form of a monastic to that of a social brotherhood. With the passage of years, this socialistic idea expanded in the mind of William Morris, until the feelings which he had first entertained toward a small circle of personal friends extended so as to embrace the world, its work and its interests. Then, he declared himself in revolt against existing authorities; demanding a condition of society in which there should be "neither rich nor poor, neither master nor master's man, neither idle nor overworked, in which all men should live in equality of condition, and would manage their affairs unwastefully, with the full consciousness that harm to one would mean harm to all: the realization at last of the meaning of the word: COMMONWEALTH."

Such an evolution of thought was a direct result of Morris's study of the art and citizenship of the Middle Ages, just as evidently as his first idea of a religious brotherhood proceeded from an ardent study of the story of the knights of the Round Table. The former fact he acknowledged during the course of a debate on Socialism, which occurred at Cambridge, in 1884. His statement is as follows:

"I have come thoroughly to understand the manner of work under which the art of the Middle Ages was done, and that it is the only manner of work which can turn out popular art; only to discover that it is impossible to work in that manner in this profit-grinding society. So on all sides I am driven toward revolution as the only hope, and I am growing clearer and clearer on the speedy advent of it in a very obvious form."

The successive steps of his study and the specific accomplishments which gave him claim to the recognition and gratitude of many sorts and conditions of men are interesting and significant. His individuality and fearlessness asserted themselves in his first choice of a profession; for having received his baccalaureate degree, he sorely disappointed his family by binding himself in apprenticeship to an Oxford architect. The gravity of this action can not now be appreciated except by reference to the spirit of the times. The wealthy upper middle classes regarded the men following artistic pursuits as Bohemians: the painters being lowest in the social scale, and the position of architects even being questioned.

At the present distance of time, and in default of documentary evidence, we can not determine whether it was the archeological, or the artistic faculty in Morris that led him to the choice of a profession. But it would seem to have been the instinct of the born decorator, who understands the relative values of construction and ornament, and who knows that he must first build and afterward beautify. It would seem also that in so choosing, Morris vaguely felt that by force of his commanding intellectual, moral and personal influence, he was destined to redeem and to elevate the then denationalized English decorative arts.

The apprenticeship of Morris as an architect lasted only nine months, but during that time, with the great gift of concentration which characterized him, he gained a knowledge of both principle and detail which would have required a long laborious application from an ordinarily gifted person. His attainments as a builder were never put to extensive practical use, and even on planning his first home, in 1859, the "Red House," at Upton, County Kent, he employed the services

of his friend and fellow-student in architecture, Philip Webb; although the latter did little else than to carry out Morris's directions, especially in the design of the interior and its furnishings. The Red House proved to be an epoch-making building. It is remarkable as being the first example of the revived artistic use of red brick in domestic architecture. "The Studio" has referred to it as "that wonderful red building which became the prototype of all the charming houses of the so-called 'Queen Anne' revival; although it may be said in passing, that it is almost entirely Gothic, with a strong French influence apparent." Finally, it is known that the household decorative arts for which England became so famous in the latter part of the nineteenth century, grew out of the desire of Morris to provide a suitable home for his lovely bride, and his avowed effort to make that home the most beautiful dwelling-place in the kingdom.

Through the exercise of his ingenuity in mural and ceiling ornamentation, in embroidery design, and in other artistic mediums, he acquired practical experience as a decorator. And from these beginnings grew the work which engaged him from that time forward until his death. The activity consequent upon the planning and furnishing of the "Red House" followed upon a mood of idleness, not infrequent in Morris's youth; but with the coming of the new interests, the tendencies of earlier years disappeared. The eagerness of the maker, the joy of craftsmanship seized him, never to relax their hold. And the dreams of a monastic Brotherhood which had been the constant accompaniment of his Oxford days, evolved into the definite idea of a company of artists pledged to produce beautiful things.

Such was the origin of the firm of Morris & Company, which, beside the chief who devoted to its success his extraordinary talents, his time and his fortune, included among its members other men of genius and great attainment: Madox Brown, whose high place in English painting stands to-day acknowledged; Dante Gabriele Rossetti, who united in himself the incongruous qualities of the idealist, the artist and the astute financier; Burne-Jones, who did most to perpetuate and ennoble the English Pre-Raphaelite tradition; Philip Webb, the builder, as we know, of the "Red House," the master of proportion and ornament, whether as applied to the larger masses of architecture, or yet to small objects of interior decoration; and finally Faulkner, less gifted artistically than the others, but who was a forthright craftsman, a valuable associate as an expert accountant, and whose loyalty and longing for his friends had drawn him from his mathematical tutorship at Oxford to take up the restless life of London.

It is certain that no other such firm has ever been organized; since it was composed of Oxford graduates of distinction, and artists of already high reputation; since, also, its commercial object was wholly subordinate to the interests of art. The main employment of the Company was, at first, ecclesiastical decoration, as the so-called aesthetic revival was then in progress among the London churches. This movement, which was entailed by the vigorous study of history made by the High-Church party, created a demand for mural decoration, stained glass, tiles, carving, metal work and altar-embroideries, all of which, by reason of the peculiar talents and tendencies of Burne-Jones, Morris, Brown and Faulkner, could be most intelligently supplied. In the decade 1860-1870, the Morris firm executed windows for Salisbury Cathedral, and for certain of the College churches at Oxford and Cambridge; which works are to-day objects of pilgrimage for those interested in the modern revival of one of the most beautiful of the arts of the Middle Ages. At the same time, very successful experiments in tapestry-weaving and cabinet-making were in progress, as may be learned from the report of the jury of awards at the International Exhibition of 1862. This report, referring to the objects of household art shown by the Morris firm, declares that "the general forms of the furniture, the arrangement of the tapestry, and the character of the details are satisfactory to the archeologist from the exactness of the imitation, at the same time that the general effect is excellent."

It is needless to trace the development of the Firm at length; since the results of its work may be measured by any one who has the means to compare the household art of England and America, as it stands to-day, with the ugliness and barrenness of the upper and middle class homes of those countries, forty years ago. But it must be remembered that to the Firm capital, invention and control were supplied practically by Morris alone. His architectural instinct, the quality in which lay his unique strength, built up the material fortunes of the Company from the merest financial nothing, at the same time that it assured the complete aesthetic success of the enterprise by carrying the arts of design to their highest form.

As the desire for beautiful surroundings spread from ecclesiastical into secular life, the call for increased and diversified production made heavy demands upon Morris's time, strength and financial resources. But his energies and his spirit of self-sacrifice never failed or flagged. He was always persistent, sagacious and industrious. In order to revive the arts and crafts which so beautified the otherwise strenuous life

of the Middle Ages, he made the most practical and costly experiments in dyeing, weaving and printing. In the exercise of the first of these crafts, he supplemented all that could be learned from books and from chemical tests in his own vats by a thorough apprenticeship among the dyers of Staffordshire. And the results of his labor justified the means which he so ungrudgingly employed; for he succeeded in raising to an unexpected degree of beauty, the art which, since the introduction of the anilines at about the middle of the nineteenth century, had fallen into deplorable decline. As a colorist, Morris takes rank among the great masters. He followed the best traditions of Oriental art; using but few elements and obtaining his effects by skilfully varied juxtaposition and contrast. His system of color has been somewhat misunderstood by both buyers and imitators; for the peacock-blues, olive-greens and rusty reds dominant in the stage setting of "Patience" and other satires upon the "Aesthetic Craze," were simply provisional colors used during the early years of the Firm, and set aside by the establishment of the Morris dye-house, where full frank hues of indigo blue, madder red and weld yellow were perfected, and employed in the production of the beautiful Hammersmith carpets and Merton tapestries and chintzes.

In textile fabrics the progress made by Morris was no less sure and rapid than in the art and craft which we have just considered. His appreciation of necessities and how to accomplish them was alike in all fields of practical work. His attainments in the weaving of tapestry are especially remarkable and characteristic. He criticised the Gobelins Factories as having degraded a "fine art" into a mere "upholsterer's toy," and therefore set himself to revive the craft. In default of any existing instance where the actual weaving process might be observed, Morris gathered details, as best he might, from an old French official handbook, published prior to the Revolution. He caused a handloom to be set up in his own bedroom at Kelmscott House, Hammersmith, and, in order that the new interest should not interfere with his ordinary occupations, he was accustomed to practise weaving in the early morning hours. He so gradually became an expert workman, and even devised technical improvements upon the French historical system. Indeed, he may be said to have restored the splendid and almost extinct art of the fifteenth and sixteenth centuries. This statement is justified by the beautiful works in arras: "The Star of Bethlehem," and the series illustrating "The Quest of the San Graal," designed for the great dining-room of Stanmore Hall, near Harrow.

A third art,—that of printing,—to the practice of which Morris devoted much time during the later years of his life, would seem at first to be removed from the sphere of the pure decorator. But we find the secret of this devotion in the words of the artist himself: "The only work of art which surpasses a complete mediaeval book is a complete mediaeval building." And hence we realize that here again the architectural instinct provided impulse and energy. As Morris had realized early in life the impossibility of raising buildings worthy to compare with mediaeval structures, and had found the cause of such impossibility to lie in the adverse circumstances under which the modern workman is compelled to labor, deprived of pleasure in the work of his hands, so the great-hearted reformer and artist set himself to remedy the wrong, and to restore the lost pleasure to the worker. His architectural studies led him to Socialism, and when his hopes of effecting great improvements in the economic conditions of his country passed away, he was thrown back upon his own resources to impress his convictions upon the world. So the establishment of his printing-press at Kelmscott Manor, coincides with his withdrawal from active Socialism.

Again, his power of quick absorption and assimilation made him a past master of the craft, in which he was also aided by his previous hand-illumination of favorite poems, and his studies in wood-engraving. The Kelmscott Press created printing as a fine art in England and America, popularized good design in book-covers, and produced a series of beautiful books, the finest of which, the great folio edition of Chaucer, was a tribute of Morris to the literary guide and master of his youth.

In the full activity of his labor as printer and publisher, death overtook him; but not before he had drawn the portrait of the ideal handicraftsman, in whom we recognize his own likeness.

"The true workman," he says, "must put his own individual intelligence and enthusiasm into the goods which he fashions. He must have a natural aptitude for his work so strong that no education can force him away from his special bent. He must be allowed to think of what he is doing, and to vary his work as the circumstances of it vary, and his own moods. He must be forever stirring to make the piece at which he is at work better than the last. He must refuse at anybody's bidding to turn out,—I won't say a bad,—but even an indifferent piece of work, whatever the public wants, or thinks it wants. He must have a voice, and a voice worth listening to, in the whole affair."

The production of this skilled handicraftsman was, in Morris's belief, an ideal not beyond realization. His system was that of setting the nearest person to do whatever work needed to be done. He preferred general intelligence to innate manual dexterity. He inveighed against that excessive division of labor which cramps and sterilizes the modern artificer. He demanded a knowledge of drawing as the basis of all manual arts and as an essential element of a general education which should be worthy of the name. In a word, he sought to unite the artist and the workman in one person, and thus to prevent the making of designs which the designer can not produce with his own hands.

Although the artistic principles of Morris have been questioned, it is acknowledged that personally he made them successful. In his own case, he did not divorce practice and theory; since to his immense production of designs,—which in textile fabrics alone numbered more than six hundred,—he added the experience of a thorough craftsman. Furthermore, he did not allow his own interests and occupations, absorbing and exacting though they were, to blind him to the larger questions of the hour, in which he could be of service to his country, his century and the world; as is evidenced by his action and prominence in the Society for the Preservation of Ancient Buildings, and by the fearless enthusiasm with which he disseminated Socialistic propaganda. He laid down no empty formulas, and like his master Chaucer's "Poure Parson," first he wrought, and afterward he taught. As we have before said, his art and his Socialism were one and inseparable; for he entered upon his political course blankly ignorant of economics and in the effort to make possible for the workman "a life to which the perception and creation of beauty,—the enjoyment of real pleasure that is,—shall be felt to be as necessary as daily bread." Like Karl Marx, he seemed to believe that the relations of man to man have formed an ascending evolutionary series, developed through the successive organic periods of history, and that they are now undergoing a last crisis, at whose end, these relations having been those of master and slave in the ancient republics, lord and serf in the Middle Ages, capitalist and laborer in the nineteenth century, shall ultimately, under the happy reign of Socialism, become those of brother and brother.

THE SEVEN LAMPS

THE singular and non-committal titles given by Ruskin to his lectures and books are still a frequent subject of comment among well-informed persons. For although they are always pertinent, yet their relations to the subject-matter are not such as would be readily perceived even by the careful and the imaginative. They are elaborately prepared, and the work of a scholar, who drew them from ancient, or mediaeval sources of history, philosophy or language. Among the most attractive and appropriate of these titles is that of "The Seven Lamps of Architecture." To explain it, we must go back to the great Jewish symbol of Light and Law: the Menorah, or seven-branched candlestick, which is so sacred and significant in the history of the Hebrews, and which acquired a new value when it was associated by the historic Church with the rite of baptism; coming then to signify the acceptance of the illumination and of the seven gifts of the Holy Spirit.

This figure, as was most natural, attracted Ruskin, for whom art was ever a faith and a religion. He adapted and extended its meaning until it stood in his mind for the perfect expression of the builder's art, wherein lay, as in the solar spectrum, seven distinct but harmonious elements.

These elements, lamps, or spirits, as he variously names them, are familiar principles treated in Ruskin's own superlative way.

The Lamp of Sacrifice would seem, if reduced to its lowest terms, to be that spirit of self-denial and self-forgetfulness which is felt by the true artist or craftsman, who sinks his personality into his work, and works not for gain, or even fame, but solely to express in visible form what his brain has conceived.

The Lamp of Truth is that spirit of honesty in building which resists falsity of assertion in the nature of the material used, and the quantity of labor exercised.

The Lamps of Power and Beauty represent the constructive and decorative elements in architecture: the first showing the power of the human mind to gather, co-ordinate and govern principles discovered at large; the second imitating and reflecting the loveliness found in Nature: as for example, the Gothic system of ornament which is based upon plant-forms.

The Lamp of Life is the expression of vital energy: the impress of the mind of the master left upon his work.

The Lamp of Memory is the

creative spirit of all truly great architecture: that is, the monumental, which conquers the forgetfulness of men by perpetuating the story of some great cause, leader, or victory.

Finally, the Lamp of Obedience is a wise observance of fixed principles which results in enduring work; it is the opposite of that license which builds but for a day, and is the slave of its own vagaries.

❧ ❧

The title of the "Fors Charigera" has proven itself a crux to many. And this not without reason, since the work is numbered among the later writings of Ruskin, and is much less easy of access than the "Lamps" or the "Stones." It is a series of letters addressed to workingmen, and first published periodically; the series beginning in 1871. The imaginative title was suggested to the master from an old print, and is ingeniously explained by him at the outset. "Fors Charigera is the Fate who bears the club, key or nail:" the instrument representing strength, as the club, or nail, and wisdom as the key; the whole device symbolising the guiding or compelling forces of human life.

The "Aratra Pentelici" is a treatise on the principles of sculpture: the title attracting the lover of ancient art by its suggestions of the soil of Greece, teeming with the splendid remains of antique beauty, and with the marble which hides within itself lovely conceptions denied to all save the creative artist. "Aratra Pentelici," the plough of Pentelicus, is a title of which the imaginative power sustains the interest of the reader as he turns the pages of a somewhat technical and quite dogmatic argument.

An equal power lies in the choice of the descriptive title: "The Laws of Fesule," which points to the mountain suburb of Florence as to the generating-point and focus of the Italian renascence of art.

❧ ❧

"The Queen of the Air" is an exposition of the Greek myths of cloud and storm; while "The Ethics of the Dust are a series of lectures upon crytallization. Other semi-scientific writings bear the titles of "Proserpina," which is a study of wayside flowers; "Deucalion," the name of the Greek representative of the biblical Noah, applied by Ruskin to his own observations upon the lapse of the waves and the life of the stars; "Frondes Agrestes," boughs from the fields,

are extracts selected from "Modern Painters" by the author himself. And so it would be possible for us to pass on through a literary product of three hundred works, everywhere met by suggestions of that fertile chaos of ideas and impulses which represent for us the most unique personality of Victorian England.

UTILITY--SIMPLICITY--BEAUTY

THE owner of a new house often hesitates before the task of providing it with furnishings. He must, he believes, make sacrifices in one of two directions. Either he must allow the claims of beauty to usurp those of utility, and so detract from the essential qualities of his home; or he must content himself with surroundings less attractive than those of his neighbors. If he chooses the objects which he regards as beautiful, he fills his rooms with slender tables, chairs and seats, delicately constructed, perhaps charged with marquetry, and almost invariably covered with easily perishable fabrics. If, on the contrary, he decides to purchase serviceable things for everyday use, he too often acquires a collection of articles ugly in form, crude and impure in color, and the very sight of which induces depression and melancholy.

To avoid these results he has first to learn the wholesome lesson of simplicity. The home, assuming, of course, that it represents the station of its occupants, should never be encumbered with things of doubtful use, or questionable aesthetic value. The few articles necessary for the maintenance of comfort, habitual occupation and the healthful enjoyment of the senses, are the only ones to be admitted into living, bed, or dining rooms. Further, old things are best, since they have been tried and proven and not found wanting. That is: objects not such as satisfied customs and fashions which are now obsolete; but such as represent primitive ideas and therefore essentials; such as frankly state their purpose and honestly meet the needs which they were intended to supply; doing this without affectation of crudeness, and with regard to modern consideration for comfort and sanitation.

If we take, for example, the bed as often now modeled with a view to decorative effect, we shall find it raised on a dais and surrounded by heavy draperies; both of which features are relics of a past time, serving no useful end, and contrary to modern ideas of cleanliness and health. The dais and the draperies formerly protected the bed from cold and dampness, and it is most interesting to note the development of this idea of isolation, from the cupboard beds of the Brittany peasants up to the great couch of the French sovereigns. The model of the bed best suited to the present time, when the value of pure air and the curative power of sunlight are fully recognized, is no derivative model. It must simply show solidity, simplicity, and a due regard for sanitary principles.

And so we might pass on through the list of household furnishings; condemning with justice those that copy and imitate; those that are wanting in honesty and originality; as when, for instance, a chair intended for constant use, shows the slender proportions of the style Louis Seize; or again, when decoration simulates constructive principle, as in the introduction of false mortices that fasten nothing; or when a certain combination of curves or angles appears throughout the work of a designer, until it loses all meaning, and becomes for the eye, what the refrain of a nursery rhyme is to the ear.

If then these essentials of utility, that is: adaptability to purpose, and simplicity be assured, beauty will not be slow to

follow. The necessities of construction demand a sufficient variety of line to satisfy the aesthetic cravings of the eye for pure form; while the delights of color wait upon the use of our native and scarcely appreciated woods. It would seem that the American craftsman might receive, as addressed to himself, the words of our patriot poet, when he wrote:

> *"That is best which lieth nearest,*
> *Shape from that thy course in art."*

THE ECONOMIC FOUNDATION OF ART

EVERY organism, whether it be social or biological, if it is to survive, must seek pleasure and avoid pain. Without accepting any particular theory of ethics, it is safe at least to say that the things which give pleasure are better than those which give pain. The best social relations are those securing the greatest amount of happiness to those who maintain them.

Pleasure consists in the satisfaction of impulses and desires. Hitherto the struggle for existence has been so hard that the great majority of mankind have found all their energies exhausted in the effort simply to avoid hunger and cold, and the idea of a society that would secure even these primal necessities to all its members has been looked upon as Utopian.

Our analysis of man's wants, instincts and impulses has usually been very imperfect; excluding some of the motive forces, which from the point of view of the social student are fundamental. Prof. Jacques Loeb of the University of Chicago, in his work on the comparative physiology of the brain, has expressed this fact as follows:

"Human happiness is based upon the possibility of a natural and harmonious satisfaction of the instincts. One of the most important instincts is usually not even recognized as such, namely: the instinct of workmanship. Lawyers, criminologists, and philosophers frequently imagine that only want makes man work. This is an erroneous view. We are forced to be active in the same way as ants or bees. The instinct of workmanship would be the greatest source of happiness, if it were not for the fact that our present social and economic organization allows only a few to gratify this instinct."

The present social organization has divided the functions of the social body, and then failed to correlate them in such a manner as to obtain that unity and completeness which is essential to either human happiness or artistic beauty. Turn in whatever direction we will, only disfigured fragments appear. Every human function fails of any adequate healthful, natural gratification. None of them succeeds in giving any large, full measure of pleasure, while nearly all give rise to great pain and suffering.

The importance of this fact cannot be overestimated. The words artist and artistic have

come to be so much the playthings of certain coteries that it is only when a Ruskin or a Morris uses them, and in some way correlates them with the whole of life that they interest any save the dilettanti. But if it be true that that thing is artistic which gives the greatest pleasure to the minds most fitted to understand it, and if the chief end of life is to seek pleasure, the conclusion follows that the chief aim of social workers should be to make society artistic. Viewed in this way, the word artistic obtains a much deeper meaning than when spoken at an afternoon tea concerning some elaborate piece of bric-a-brac.

Artistic, in the sense in which I wish to use it, (and I believe that it will be generally admitted that this is the true and best sense of the word), means possessing such a unity, and correlation of parts to the whole, as to give the greatest amount of pleasure possible. Incidentally this implies a similar artistic wholeness and power of appreciation on the part of the persons who come in contact with the object. It implies, that, if the greatest possible pleasure is to be derived, both man and environment should possess this quality of symmetrical completion and correlation.

Using the word artistic in this broad and true sense, let us glance for a moment to see wherein our present society fails of being artistic. In the first place, the word art has been stolen from this very sense and applied to something which is perhaps more isolated and detached from the essential portions of life than almost any other one feature. The word is to-day ordinarily used only in speaking of painted canvases or highly specialized tone combinations, which are not only utterly unrelated to the remainder of society, but which demand that both those who produce this "art," and those who enjoy it, shall be isolated from all connection with the vital essential social processes. What the result has been upon both "art" and the "artistic public" has been told often enough by those much more fitted than I to tell the story, and need not detain us here. Very few of these "artists" have ever dreamed that they should seek to make all of life artistic, rather than to produce something whose beauty is appreciable only because of contrast with the hideous ugliness of the life by which it is surrounded. Isolated art is never truly pleasurable.

Other phases of society present this same inartistic isolation with its painful accompaniments. It is a fact of frequent observation by social students that the modern person does not know how to "play." Play, if it is to have any essential meaning, should signify the pleasurable exercise of human faculties. But it is true that the majority of mankind at the pres-

ent time, even if they had the opportunity, would not know how to obtain any intense pleasure from such an exercise.

The classical example of this ignorance is the London cabman, whose idea of a holiday is to rent a friend's cab and ride on the inside over the same route that he follows, seated on the box, every other day in the year. But how much wiser are the remainder of the population? Great buildings with expensive apparatus are constructed simply for the purpose of giving an opportunity to move different muscles of the body in a healthful manner. Even then, the gymnasium soon becomes a "bore," and the daily "exercise" a "task." So, various games are invented, and the more completely these can be isolated from all vital social relations, the more highly they are valued, until golf, polo, steam-yachting, and automobile racing become the ideal of social recreation. But in every one of these fields, it soon becomes evident that the main element of enjoyment is the utterly unsocial one of snobbishness. These games are principally enjoyed because their practice conveys a certain badge of respectability. This is proven by the fact that those who can do these things best: the "professionals," the pugilists, wrestlers, jockeys, chauffeurs, etc., not only do not find any enjoyment in their "work," but are despised by those who claim to be aiming at the very goal which the others have attained.

But it is when we come to study the "amusements" of the great mass of the people that the painfulness of their pleasures becomes fully apparent. Their idea of enjoyment is generally based upon some form of eating or drinking: a most significant commentary in itself on the nature of the daily life of the great toiling masses of mankind. The principal pleasurable thought connected with Thanksgiving and Christmas, in the minds of millions of people, is the possibility of eating and drinking to a condition of stupid satiety. The very idea of marking off one day from the remainder of the year to indicate the time when the sense of hunger and taste is fully satisfied, is enough to answer those who would call the critics of our present society "pig philosophers." Incidentally it might be worth while to notice another sign that commercialism has influenced nearly all so-called amusements by the introduction of a financial consideration in the form of gambling. This shows once more the absolute impossibility of completely isolating any phase of life from the industrial basis of society.

Let us examine another social function and observe how near it comes to meeting the test which we have set up as artistic. Education, as well

as "play" and "art," has been isolated from all social relations. The result has been painful to the child, as well as ineffectual in reaching the end of instruction. The "cramming" process, especially when it deals with dry facts isolated from all relation to the social whole, is now recognized to be a painful, and hence an injurious process to those who are subjected to it.

We have thus seen that owing to their isolation from vital social relations, neither art, education, nor even amusement, as now understood, gives pleasure, and this just because all these interests are defective in those relations toward society as a whole, which would make them truly artistic.

If we turn now to the actual social basis, the productive process, the creation of "goods," what do we see? Is there any pleasure for the great producing masses in their work? To ask the question is to answer it. On every hand, performance of the essential labor of society is looked upon as an evil to be avoided, and few indeed who are actually concerned with it, ever think of looking there for something pleasurable, artistic, enjoyable. The production of "goods" has become an evil. Here we find the fundamental cause of the whole "inartistic," and hence painful, character of our present society. This is one more witness to the truth of the philosophy of economic determinism. Unless the production of the necessities of life can be made beautiful, pleasurable and instructive, our whole society must remain disorganized, disintegrated, productive of pain, and inartistic. A school, a factory, a studio, or a gymnasium, as a thing by itself, is an anomaly and must fail of its purpose. What is needed at the present time is a process of synthesis and correlation. Tolstoi has seen a portion of this truth, but he becomes ridiculous in proposing his remedy. He can only rail at division of labor and specialization of function. He demands that we go back to the period of cumbersome individualistic labor, with its imperfect production, but better correlation, rather than that we push on to the possibilities of a higher, grander and more artistic correlation of the marvelously more perfect processes of to-day.

This truth has been partially seen by workers in many fields and, in consequence, many partial attempts at correlation have been made. One of the most interesting of these attempts is found in the field of education. In the kindergarten movement an effort is made to unite play and instruction, and in the manual training work to unite creative processes with instruction. But perhaps the most significant of the attempts as yet made is the new handicrafts movement. There are two

reasons why this movement is more significant than the others. In the first place, it aims at a somewhat wider correlation than any of the other movements, since it includes in its synthesis three factors, instead of two. It aims at the correlation of productive work, beautiful forms, and to some extent, pleasurable exertion. Its representatives would unite workshop, studio and playroom. More important still, they have realized in an indefinite and as yet often very imperfect way, that the basis of any social movement must be the fundamental productive process. Therefore they have begun their work in connection with that process. Nevertheless, this movement, also, in many ways, is fundamentally defective. One of its defects is that among the social factors which we have enumerated, (and our classification makes no pretense of being exhaustive), the handicrafts movement neglects the educational factor. Save through occasional lectures, publications, exhibitions, and a few apprentices, it does little educational work. It bears little effective relation to the great formative forces that are really determining the minds of future generations.

The problem before him who would make modern society "artistic," is so to synthesize its activities as to make the work of those who perform the great productive processes at once pleasant and educative. This sounds simple, but when once the people of any society shall find their highest pleasure and fullest education in creating the necessities of that society, we shall have come as close to a perfect system as the mind of man has yet been able to conceive.

At the same time, any adequate examination of our present social organization should convince anyone that such an ideal is utterly impossible of even approximate realization, without a complete revolution. All attempts to realize any portion of this ideal within that society must be recognized as largely Utopian. Moreover unless these facts are fully comprehended, such attempts are liable to become ludicrous. It is necessary only to study the movements already mentioned to show how they deteriorate in present society. A kindergarten established as an "institution" apart from the home becomes a place where tired, over-worked mothers "get rid" of their children, and where maiden ladies deprived of normal family relationship, play at motherhood. The very philosophy itself degenerates into a dilettante, parrot-like repetition of phrases, and the whole thing becomes to a great degree farcical. Manual training and "domestic science," kept apart from the productive sources of society and directed by a parasitic class, become either "fads," and burlesques upon the thing originally conceived, or, worse,

they reverse the philosophy upon which they rest, and become training schools for servants and subordinates. Industrial handicraft shops cut off from all connection with the actual creative productive social processes, become the playthings of dilettanti, and the generators of "aesthetic crazes."

All such efforts are imperfect, unsymmetrical and "inartistic," because they lack that wholeness and unity which artistic goodness and beauty demand. They only deal with a small portion of society, and, most important of all, not with the *essential portion.* The only real, vital portion of present society, as indeed of every other society, is the portion which supplies wants, produces goods, and maintains life. All the movements enumerated leave this portion of society untouched.

Finding themselves shut out from the actual productive processes, too many of these would-be craftsmen play at production in private workshops. Seeing no way to correlate the gigantic industrial forces of to-day, and to use them for their purposes, they look backward to a simpler and inferior social stage, and become reactionary. Even Morris was not wholly free from this defect. But one thing William Morris never did, (and in this he was unlike too many of his imitators), and that was to cut himself off from all the forces that were working to make his ideals possible. He was able to see that the difficulties confronting him were inherent in the society within which he was working, and that the only hope of realizing his ideals lay in overthrowing that society, or rather in hastening its growth through the capitalist stage into the co-operative stage, the next step in social evolution. Let me emphasize this point, since it is the most vital one in this whole discussion. From a hundred points, Capitalism presents a hostile attitude toward all efforts to restore the conditions of healthful, pleasurable, beautiful workmanship. Competition denies the product entrance to the actual social market, and compels it to circulate within a limited, unnatural, subsidized market. Wage-slavery deprives the producer of all desire to improve his product, or of the possibility of individual initiative did he desire it. Exploitation deprives the overwhelming majority of the hope of ever possessing anything of actual beauty or artistic merit. An environment of greed develops the coarseness of the parvenu among the bourgeoisie and the coarseness of a debased animality among the proletariat. Under these conditions any movement toward the revival of the beautiful, the pleasant, and the good,—in short of the artistic,—which does not connect itself with the great revolutionary movement of the proletariat, has cut itself off from the only hope of realiz-

ing its own ideal. It has condemned itself to a narrow, incomplete, and unsymmetrical synthesis, to a most inartistic and uncraftsmanlike attitude, to a stultification in in fact of everything for which it claims to stand. Its followers can have no vital connection with society, no broad outlook, unless they can connect themselves with the actual productive forces of society. But they cannot do this in the privately-owned competitive factories of to-day. The only place in which they can come in contact with the real producers of goods is in the political socialist movement. Here they can join hands with those who constitute the essential productive factor of the present society, and who must be the dominant factor in the coming society, and can work with them for a common end. In this way, they can really make their force felt upon the coming generation and strengthen their influence with the present.

The founders of the movement recognized this, and William Morris is known fully as well for his activity in the political socialist movement, as for his efforts in the revival of artistic work. But his followers to-day have very generally forgotten the most essential portion of his teachings, and know absolutely nothing of the actual laborers and the labor movement. It would be an easy but ungracious task to point out specific instances of the degradation of the movement brought about by this isolation from what should be its foundation. Suffice to say that separated from all fundamental connection with social life, it has lapsed into vagaries, and has often strayed so far from its original paths as to be well-nigh lost in dilettantism and eccentricity. I am glad to see that there are, at present, signs of a true revival of craftsmanship which, by virtue of the fact that it will embrace a wider, fuller synthesis than any previous movement, shall be fully entitled to call itself "artistic."

BEAUTIFUL BOOKS

"FOR him was lever have at his beddes heed
Twenty bokes clad in blak or reed,
Of Aristotle and his philosophye
Than robes riche, or fithele or gay sautrye."

Thus Chaucer, our first great master of English letters, describes the passion of a bibliophile. And, as always at his master's touch, he conjures up a picture. We can see the gaunt, ill-favored "clerke of Oxenford," in his narrow cell sparsely furnished with bed, desk and chair, the property of his college, while a crucifix and a score of books constitute his only personal possessions. These books, the source of mediaeval scholarly delight, were not only clad, but as well written, in black and red. They were issued from places which, were it not for history, and for the careful preservation of numbers of the books themselves, would be inconceivable to those who exercise their arts and crafts in the printeries and binderies of to-day. These precious volumes, at the time when Chaucer wrote his Canterbury Tales, were transcribed and multiplied in the abbeys of England and the continent by monks who literally spent their lives in the *scriptoria*, or writing-rooms, of their conventual dwellings.

Oftentimes, it was to a single book that they devoted the best efforts of their genius and manhood. And thus the book came to represent for the scribe all that hearth and home, secular enterprise, wife and child stood for in the eyes of the man of action. The *scriptoria* not seldom opened upon a court, as we find exemplified in notable specimens of monastic architecture; they were then called "carols:" a corruption of the word square, applied to them because of their shape. And there, in favoring light and quiet, the work of transcribing progressed. When we examine the hour-books, the Gospels, and the Psalters thus produced, we receive a strong impression, not only from the exquisite art of the old illuminators, but also from the spirit of self-consecration which animated the lonely men who wrought with such loving care, and which still breathes from every page of these beautiful books. At such moments, it seems sure that Fra Angelico was not the only mediaeval artist who prayed between the strokes of his brush; rather that he was but the type of a period when art and religion were united, and when both were allied to labor. From the eighth to the fourteenth century, we find this art of illumination flowering in different countries: in Ireland, at the first named point of time, when the splendid "Book of Kells" and its similars came into existence; in France, advancing slowly to perfection, until in Dante's time, as we know by his allusions in the Divine Comedy, it was regarded as an art peculiar to the French; in Italy, reaching the climax of a splendid maturity just before the invention of movable type. The artists of each of these countries had, as was inevitable, their distinctive style derived from conditions of race and environment. The great Irish manuscripts are characterized by their interlaced ornament, as intricate as the geometrical designs of the Moors, and far more interesting historically, since much of Celtic mythology and legend is therein involved. In the "Book of Kells," the borders and initial letters show long systems of curiously interwoven strands, like the threads of a rope, or the fibres of basketry. In both design and color, they have a decorative value which gives an extreme pleasure to the most inexperienced eye. Beside and beyond this, there is a religious idea running through the maze of scroll-work and twisted knots. These beautiful convolutions are artistic *motifs* derived from the dragons and writhing serpents which play so prominent a part in the tales of the Gods of the North. And the same *motifs* which make distinctive the illuminated manuscripts of the Celts recur again and again in the carvings of Runic crosses, and the chiseled ornaments of churches, throughout Ireland and Scotland and in the Isle of Man. Oftentimes, even the beasts and reptiles which symbolized

the powers of evil and darkness, form an integral part of the design: the bodies winding through the strands, and the heads making terminal ornaments. Occasionally, too, the human figure is frankly apparent in the design, as is the case in the Gospel of Mac Regol at Oxford; or else, in singular modification, it may be traced by the initiated eye, as on the shaft of a noted wayside cross near Ashbourne, England. Here, by the repetition of the units of an interlaced geometrical design, a human trunk is simulated; the head is suggested by an elongated oval terminal loop; the legs by separated strands pendent from the interlaced pattern; and the feet by the frayed ends of the strands turned at right angles to their length. These and other equally fanciful conceits originated in a very remote past, and arose from the desire of man to put himself in relation with the forces of nature, and to express that desire in visible form. Then, slowly, as the aesthetic faculty was developed in these Northern peoples by advancing civilization, the symbolism was lost, leaving behind it that element of the grotesque which carries their restricted art to so high a place in the history of ornament. Indeed, to examine in a critical sense these Irish illuminated manuscripts is to agree with the saying of William Morris, that the only work of art which surpasses a complete mediaeval book is a complete mediaeval building.

If now, as we have seen, symbolism, strength and originality are the characteristics of the early book-designs of Northern Europe, we find later, in those of the French, compensating qualities. Delicacy and grace, a certain subtle inventiveness, and accuracy of execution distinguish the missals and Psalters which are known in the annals of art by the names of the sovereigns and princes who first possessed them. In these are found exquisite miniatures, imitations of nature, and conventionalized ornament, rendered with a light touch and in a gaiety of mood that belong alone to the Gallic race. These manuscripts bear a sign manual as unmistakable as those of their Northern predecessors. To replace the interest excited by the legend of the man fighting the dragon, told in scroll, twist, and knot, one finds a new pleasure in discovering, one by one, the details of the design. The large capital letters often form frames for little genre pictures which are not unworthy of the predecessors of Meissonnier; or, again, they are garlands of heavy foliage from the depths of which show the soft wing, or the bright eye of a bird, or the brush of a squirrel, or fox. Between the time when the monks of Ireland produced their wonderful books, and the moment when Dante made his famous allusion to the *French art of illuminating*, the universe had lost its terrors for man: the world had become a pleasant dwelling-place, and the teeming, multiform life of nature cried out to be admired and enjoyed. And here again, decorative art, more plainly than words can do, indicates the exact stage of the then existing social development. The French in the thirteenth century had the same restless sense of perfection which characterizes their most modern efforts. A page of the latest French prose, considered from the point of view of style, and by reason of the pleasure that it gives the ear, through harmony of sound and beauty of rhythm, is matched by the French illuminated written book in its appeal to the sense of sight.

The Italian manuscripts offer other beauties; certain examples of the fourteenth century being perhaps more frequently employed as models and for suggestions than those of any other country and period. Their ornamentation is less intricate and symbolic than those of the peoples beyond the Alps; since the Italians inherited by right the traditions of classic art: rejecting the occult and the grotesque, and presenting everywhere slightly conventionalized natural forms. Among the most beautiful features of these manuscripts are the floriated borders which surround the text, often giving the appearance of a shower of brilliant petals arranged symmetrically by chance, and which the next breath of

air might disperse and carry away: so delicately are they placed upon the page. The colors too are beautifully blended in both support and contrast: the ones most usually employed being the blue now known as Gobelin, containing a grayish cast and somehow suggesting transparency; a red perfectly corresponding with the blue, bearing upon the crimson overcast with white of the raspberry; a violet chording with the blue, as a lower note chords with a higher musical tone; an emerald green more vivid than the other colors; and finally, traceries in gold and points of black which co-ordinate the design, after the manner of a scheme of punctuation.

Thus we may faintly describe the art of illumination as practised by three differing peoples in the Middle Ages; the first school touching the times of barbarism, and reflecting the sense of mystery and terror which then overhung the world; the second reaching its perfection simultaneously and in the same country with the Gothic cathedral, and, therefore, again recalling William Morris' comparison of the book with the church; the third fermenting with the ideas of the Renascence, discarding symbolism, and simplifying its forms as if in preparation for the age of printing.

With the invention of this new art began, as was inevitable, the decay of the beautiful book of the Middle Ages. The rich materials which had made it a precious possession of sovereigns and princes were successively discarded, in order that the word of wisdom might reach the people. The jewel coffers of palaces, the great libraries with their locks and chains confining the heavy volumes to strict places, were no longer to be the sole guardians of human thought registered in visible form. The hour was already foretold in which the very peasant should clasp his book to his breast with that satisfaction which comes with the words: "A poor thing, but mine own!"

The vellum book of the Middle Ages was a very great advance in luxury upon the papyrus roll of classic antiquity, since the value of the latter resided largely in the labor expended upon it, and not in the material itself. The roll used by public officers, orators and teachers had needed no costly cover for protection or ornament. But the vellum book was at first the prerogative of royalty, since in early times none but clerks and kings could read and the latter hardly. So, not seldom, the cover was of gold, silver, or ivory, heavily set with jewels: rubies, emeralds, amethysts and pearls; as we may find by visiting the sacristies of certain great continental cathedrals, or museums like those of Paris and Vienna. But as time passed, the nobles became milder in manners

and customs, and literacy extended. Then too, the industries dependent upon the silkworm were established with brilliant results. These conditions therefore changed the character of the book as to its outer covering, until in the fifteenth and sixteenth centuries we find the Tudor princesses delighting in book covers and casings fashioned from rich Italian stuffs, such as velvets and damasks; these materials being embroidered with pearls, and studded with gems. Leather bindings, the most satisfactory ever devised and the oldest now in active service, were used as early as the twelfth century. They gradually superseded all other forms of preserving and adorning the book, until under the French craftsmen of the sixteenth and seventeenth centuries they attained a perfection which offers the standard and guide to the present workers in the same branch of art-artisanship. This perfection is so well recognized that many connoisseurs have accepted the statement made by a French writer: "Book-binding is altogether a French art;" although a so emphatic expression can be excused only by reason of the patriotism of the one who uttered it. Still it remains true that no master of this fascinating craft, be he Teuton or Saxon, can ignore the work of the binders of the courts of the Valois and Bourbon kings. The artistic processes—especially the decoration technically known as "tooling,"—were first practised in Italy, but once known in France, they advanced to a point of excellence never attained in the first named country.

In common with all the arts, that of book-binding received its first great impetus from the pleasure and luxury-loving monarch, Francis First, of whom it was well said in sonorous Latin that he was no less famous in letters than in arms. He not only built the splendid castles which line the banks of the Loire, and are so fitted to their surroundings that they seem part and parcel of Nature herself; he also opened for his people a wide path toward intellectual supremacy and material wealth by founding the galleries of the Louvre; he was further a most notable book collector, and transmitted his exquisite taste to his immediate descendants, and by so doing assured for them a redeeming trait amid their frivolous or their noxious characteristics.

The daughter-in-law of Francis First, Catherine de' Medici, brought from her cultured native city the love of literature for itself, as well as the desire for the acquisition of beautiful books. This was most natural, since throughout the fifteenth century, Florence had been the refuge of the Greek scholars, who, driven from Constantinople by the Turks, had fled with their treasures of rare manuscripts into Italy, to beg hos-

pitality of the citizen-sovereigns of the most famous town of the Peninsula. The Medici were not less patrons of literature than bibliophiles, as we now understand the term; that is: experts in judging the beauty, the workmanship, and the money value of any given book. From 1465 until well into the sixteenth century, the books printed in Italy were the finest in the world: a fact which was due to the existence in that country of the last great school of illumination, and also to the great Venetian publisher, Aldus Manutius, of whom we shall speak later. It was natural then that Catherine de' Medici, as the heir of both the tastes and the commercial sense of her ancestors, should seek to acquire an enviable library. She is known to have possessed at least four thousand volumes of great value as to the design and execution of their bindings. But the artists and craftsmen who brought them into existence are unknown, and the books themselves are, in large proportions, lost. Many of them exist under newer exteriors in the great national libraries of France; a number of them are found in the British Museum; still others, after long wanderings, have become the treasures of private collections. For the Queen was deeply in debt, and at her death, her books became the property of the Crown, and were rebound, in order to remove from their covers the arms and devices of their first owner. This fact is to be deeply regretted, as it would be of great interest to examine in its entirety a library now impossible to obtain or collect, at any price, or in any country.

Another woman bibliophile near the throne, at this time, was Diana de Poitiers, the mistress of Catherine's husband, Henry Second. This noble lady had also her special binders and decorators, and, as the book-cover then, in addition to its other functions, served those of the modern book-plate, the crescent of the goddess Diana, combined with the initial of the king's name, shone upon every volume in the royal favorite's collection.

The sons of Catherine de' Medici shared more or less in the cultured tastes, as well as in the passions and vices of their mother. Under their patronage, the celebrated bookbinders and booksellers, Nicholas and Clovis Eve, rose to a reputation which still lives through their exquisite work. These two brothers represented the first of a number of families of noted French binders; the art passing from father to son, extending into collateral branches, sometimes lasting through three, four, or five generations, and distinguishing a large number of individuals.

It will be thus seen how wide-

spread was the demand for beautiful books and how honorable and lucrative was the calling of the craftsmen connected with their production. And then, as now, amateur book-binding was a favorite occupation of the leisure classes, ranking princes among its devotees, and even one king: Henry Third, the last of the sons of Catherine de' Medici to occupy the throne of France.

Beaten leather book bound in white calf
By Miss Nordhoff

But the critical taste for beautiful books was best advanced in France, and, owing to the influence of that country, throughout Europe, by a noble, Jean Grolier, whose public diplomatic career is now forgotten, while his services to the arts of book-binding and printing are constantly gaining wider recognition, as his name is chosen to designate societies of bibliophiles in countries distant from the place of his birth. He was in his day statesman, financier. scholar, and, for the qualities distinguishing each of these phases of his intellect, he was praised by his friend, Erasmus, who represented him as learned, modest, courteous, a model of integrity and the ornament of France. Grolier, whose biography is ignored by many for whom his name as a bibliophile is a household word, was born in Lyons toward the end of the fifteenth century, and bore the title of Vicomte d' Aguesy. At that time, the relations between France and Northern Italy were close and uninterrupted, owing to marriages between princes, treaties and commercial enterprises, and Grolier received the appointment of treasurer of the duchy of Milan: an office which he occupied for nearly twenty years. During his residence in Italy, he made the acquaintance of Aldus Manutius, the "scholar printer" of Venice, assisting him and his successors financially in the production of beautiful volumes, several of which were dedicated to Grolier and bound in the Aldine workshops. Once during his tenure of office at Milan, he was sent by Francis First on a political mission to Pope Clement VII., and, while in Rome, became familiar with the treasures of the Vatican library. On his return to France, he was made treasurer-general of the kingdom, and established himself in Paris; carrying into the court and literary circles of that capital the refining influences which he had derived from the mother-country of the modern arts. He died in 1565, at his sumptuous residence, where he had gathered his library, the result of infinite pains and the highest development of taste. These priceless books reached the number of three thousand, of which all but a small fraction have been either totally destroyed, or are lurking under the disguises of newer bindings in libraries, or the shops of antiquarians; three hundred and fifty volumes only being recognized as the authentic possessions of this greatest of historic bibliophiles. The marks of Grolier's ownership so eagerly welcomed by the seeker after value, whether aesthetic or commercial, are the inscription printed in a single line across the lower part of the front cover, JO. GROLERII ET AMICORUM (the property of Jean Grolier and his friends), and also the Bible quotation adopted by him as a personal motto, or legend: PORTIO MEA, DOMINE, SIT TERRA

VIVENTRUM (O Lord, let my portion be in the land of the living!) But though every leaf of his most cherished possessions should perish, the inspiration and patronage which Grolier gave to book-printers and book-binders could never be forgotten, since the assistance lent by him was one of the most potent factors in the advancement of art and learning, active in sixteenth century France. And further, the passion for beautiful books, which formed so strong an element of his life, was with him, as it will be found in every case to be, the accomplishment, the counterpart, and the contrast of hard labor in the most serious and prosaic fields.

As the arts of printing and of book-binding are too closely allied to be considered separately, a few notes upon the life of Aldus Manutius and upon the publishing house of which he was the founder, will not be amiss in this place. Aldus (to use the name by which he is best known) was first a scholar, and afterward a craftsman. His early studies, pursued at Rome and Ferrara, were for the most part in the Latin language and literature. He became the instructor of an Italian prince, and brilliantly fulfilled the duties of his office. But it was not until he reached mature age that he began the study of Greek, through which he was destined to gain his greatest fame. In turning toward the language of philosophy, he yielded to the influence of the "New Learning," whose tide swept over Europe in the latter half of the fifteenth century, awakening terror in the minds of the long-established intellectual and spiritual authorities, and giving rise to the warning: "Beware of the Greeks, lest ye be made heretics." With the acumen, thoroughness and singular diligence that distinguished him, Aldus mastered the great difficulties of his latest study, and became so well versed in Greek literature that his judgments upon the authenticity and purity of the texts which he afterward edited, came to be accepted by the learned world. To him are due twenty-eight *first editions* of the Greek classics, as well as a much greater number of works in Latin. But sincere as were his efforts in furthering the cause of classic learning, his services to the art of typography were infinitely greater. He reformed and remodeled the type which he found in use, on the establishment of his press at Venice, in 1488. In place of the Gothic characters which practically reproduced those of the latest illuminated manuscripts, he substituted the Roman alphabet in type of his own design. His toil was unremitted, for he felt as few have done, the shortness of human life. And to the end that he might accomplish all that he knew to be latent within him, he had placed over his desk, in his work-cabinet, a tablet warning away all

intruders and idlers. The Medici gave him high tokens of their regard, and the Pope, Leo X., favored him with numerous privileges. But at last jealousy wrought its work and he died at the hands of Venetian assassins.

The books issued from the Aldine press during the life of its founder were the finest in the world, and, until 1560, Italian bindings were marked by graceful, free designs, which even the technical skill already gained by the French could not outbalance. A younger son of Aldus, known as Paul Manutius, continued the work begun by his father, but publishing the Latin somewhat in preference to the Greek classics. He was led to this choice partly by his perfect knowledge of the former, which enabled him to write with the purity and elegance of the Augustan age, and partly by the commission of the Holy See, which directed him to publish the writings af the Church Fathers, and attached him to the Library of the Vatican. Paul was a worthy successor of his father, and his to-day priceless edition of Cicero can be compared with any of the earlier masterpieces of his house.

Again the press was continued by the son of a great scholar and craftsman, but this time disastrously. The Aldus third in succession had not the practical gifts of his predecessors, and, furthermore, competitors in his art had arisen, both at home and abroad. He provided scantily for himself and his family by teaching languages in Venice, Bologna, Pisa and finally in Rome, where he died at the end of the sixteenth century, in abject distress, after being forced to see the great enter-

prise by which his name had become famous, pass into the ownership of strangers.

The arts relative to the printing and binding of books flourished in Italy with the Aldine press for less than a century. But in proportion as they rapidly declined in Italy they rose in Northern Europe.

Among these distinguished publishers, three families claim especial attention: the Elzevirs, the Estiennes, and the Plantins. The members of the first group were Hollanders, who, establishing their press in 1583, continued for a century to send out from Leyden and Amsterdam an uninterrupted course of fine editions of the classics. They distinguished themselves, as is generally known, by the elegance of their duodecimo and even smaller volumes. Their editions of Virgil, Terence, the New Testament, and the Psalter—all adorned with illuminated initial letters—became and have remained models, by reason of great correctness of text and rare typographical beauty. They were less learned than the Estiennes of Paris, who were somewhat earlier than they, and their works in Hebrew and Greek will not bear comparison with those of the French house. Criticism has been made recently also by the best English typographers upon their compressed and somewhat wiry characters which have served largely as models for the modern Roman type, to the neglect of the more legible and logical designs of the fifteenth century Venetian printers, Aldus, and more especially Nicholas Jenson, the master and guide of William Morris. Still, the fame of the Elzevirs is so justly great that it can not be materially lessened, and their beautiful productions are among the principal treasures of public and private libraries throughout the world.

The Estiennes are known today to a much more limited circle of bibliophiles. They were descendants of an old and noble family of Provence, the first printer and publisher of which braved disinheritance to enter the exercise of his chosen craft at the beginning of the sixteenth century. Five generations of Estiennes, working principally in Paris and in Geneva, rendered great services to the cause of learning. Like all the celebrated early printers, they were scholars of continental reputation. The most noted of them, the first bearing the name of Robert, added to his intellectual powers artistic ability of a high order, and the alphabet which he invented is yet greatly admired. To ensure correctness of text, he posted his proofs publicly, and offered rewards to those who should discover errors in his readings. In religion he was a protestant, which fact was the occasion to him and to his accomplished son Henry

of many financial losses and of exile from France. The most permanently valuable productions of the Estiennes were dictionaries in the Latin and Greek languages, which have served as bases for standard modern works. The history of the Estienne house runs parallel to that of the Alduses and the Elzevirs, in that the enterprise lasted a century, and the fortune acquired by the elder members of the family wasted away in the hands of the later generations.

The Plantin press was made famous through the agency of a single man, French by birth, although his work was accomplished at Antwerp. His life was a short one, but within its limits he founded a publishing house which ranked first among the establishments of its kind, active in the latter half of the sixteenth century. He differed from the Alduses, the Elzevirs and the Estiennes in possessing a wide acquaintance with the modern languages and in recognizing their function in education. He frequently gave employment to twenty presses, and his collection of type was the richest then known; so that he was able to print works in all the languages of Europe. His books are magnificent specimens of printing, correct in matter, and elegant in execution, although his type falls under the criticism already quoted as having been made upon the alphabet of the Elzevirs: that it is compressed laterally, that it has too many joined or compound letters, and that it loses character and legibility by being too slender or "wiry."

To examine the extant masterpieces of these early printers and binders is to experience a pleasure approaching in degree that which is felt in the presence of a picture by an old master. As a brilliant example, we may take the Elzevir Virgil, published in 1676, and called the greatest book ever issued from the press of those perfect craftsmen; a work which called forth in its time the quaint description: "The tiny letters rival pitch in blackness. The paper is equally white as snow." Or, as a thing of beauty, we may prefer the exquisite religious volume sent out by the same house, entitled, "L'aimable mere de Jesus." It is in shape a narrow rectangle, a few inches in length. Its back is rounded in that swelling curve which is the ideal of binders; the five divisions of the back being sharply marked by horizontal projections. Its cover, of the leather known as "crushed levant," has a superb deep green tone, and shows the grain of the skin to the exact point desired by experts. Finally, the middle of the front cover is ornamented by a long, straight lily branch, which emphasizes and echoes the form of the book, at the same time that it symbolizes the purity of the Blessed Virgin, the graces of whom are celebrated in the contents of the book.

The masterpieces of historic book-making, printing apart, and considered only as to binding, are most often found in France, where the art was persistently practised; twenty individuals of the same family sometimes obtaining a well-earned reputation, either for general excellence in the exercise of their craft, or yet for the skilful manipulation of a single tool. To the latter class of workmen belonged Le Gascon, who lived in the latter half of the seventeenth century, and whose influence extended to England, Holland, Germany, and Italy. It is estimated that it would to-day require skilled labor to the amount of one hundred pounds in time-value to copy the "tooling" upon a certain beautiful book bound in his workshop. His instruments have been accurately copied in the hope to equal his effects, but the delicate hand of the master is wanting, and thus far attempts at reproduction have failed. This elaborate gilding, first learned from Italy, was separated in France into a number of divisions, or methods. It was applied in intricate arabesques, in small repeated isolated designs, in continuous patterns appropriately named "dentelles," or laces, in unbroken line, or in stipple. Each of these methods had its master, and each, when examined alone, seems the height and perfection of art. Another beautiful method of ornamentation (to-day brilliantly illustrated by Marius Michel, the modern French binder) was the so-called leather mosaic-work, in which several colors with gold were combined on the book-cover, sometimes into a continuous arabesque, or a repeated "all-over" design, but most often into a geometrical figure occupying the middle of the cover.

In French book-binding, as time went on, the designs changed, according to the influences dominant for the moment at court. Under Louis XIV. they were symmetrical and sober; under Louis Fifteenth, in the work of Pasdeloup, the favorite binder of Madame de Pompadour, they were delicate and exquisite, as is evidenced by the beautiful book: "The Loves of Daphnis and Chloe," which was sold a few years since for the equivalent of three thousand five hundred dollars.

For a period, the religious movement of the Jansenists was reflected in the art of which we are treating, for its promoters were scholars and educators, and the classics took on a sombre dress. But for three centuries and more, far down into the reign of Napoleon First, collectors and craftsmen fostered in France the art of book-binding; being materially aided in their efforts by the Gild of St. John, which was founded in 1401, which included scribes, illuminators, printers, bookbinders, and booksellers, and which continued active until suppressed by the Revolution. To-day, the art is repre-

sented in France by a group of art-artisans of exquisite and patient skill, chief among whom ranks M. Marius Michel, who is both craftsman and writer.

As to printing, pure and simple, the primacy was gained late in the nineteenth century for England by William Morris, whose influence, extending throughout the United Kingdom and America, wrought the most radical improvements in typography.

The Kelmscott Press, as one of the most worthy and practical enterprises of the great craftsman, deserves the attention of all to whom printing appeals, either as a fine art, or merely as a medium for the transmission of knowledge, thought, or sentiment; since the eye is largely responsible for the impression made upon the brain, and since the ease, comfort, pleasure, or pain, attendant upon the act of reading results largely from the design, color, and composition of the printed page.

By competent critics it is said that the books issued from the Kelmscott Press are, consideration being made for their aims and intentions, the finest and most harmonious ever produced. They were the result of ceaseless experiment and the highest intelligence. They brought fame to England in an art in which she did not early excel—owing to political and social causes. The Hundred Years' War with France and the Wars of the Roses destroyed the native school of illumination, so that when printing was introduced there were no trained illuminators or scribes to further the production of beautiful books, as was the case in Italy, France and

Germany. The books printed by Caxton at his Westminster press were not comparable with those of his continental contemporaries, and these beginnings, of necessity inartistic, retarded the development of printing as a fine art. Another unfavorable condition resided in the fact that Richard Third excluded the book-trade from the protection which he granted to other commercial and industrial enterprises. The first advance gained by the printers of the continent was only with difficulty overcome by the English, whom it continued to affect for centuries. It was, therefore, an accomplishment for England not easily estimated when Morris produced his Kelmscott Chaucer, which has been called by enthusiastic admirers, "the noblest book ever printed," "the finest book ever issued," "the greatest triumph of English typography," and which, even if these opinions shall be modified, will always remain an epoch-making work.

It is interesting to study the steps by which Morris attained his happy results as a printer. He has related his experience in a "note," written in his direct, simple style, in which, at the very beginning, he sums up, as if unconsciously, the qualities of good printing:

"I began," he writes, "with the hope of producing books which should have a definite claim to beauty, while, at the same time, they should be easy to read, and should not dazzle the eye, or trouble the intellect by eccentricity of form in the letters. I have always been a great admirer of the calligraphy of the Middle Ages, and of the earlier printing which took its place. As to the fifteenth century books, I had noticed that they were always beautiful by force of the mere typography, even without the added ornament, with which many of them are so lavishly supplied. And it was the essence of my undertaking to produce books which it would be a pleasure to look upon as pieces of printing and arrangement of type. Looking at my adventure from this point of view then, I found I had to consider chiefly the following things: the paper, the form of the type, the relative spacing of the letters, the words, and the lines; and lastly the position of the printed matter upon the page."

For raw materials and for workmen to fashion them ready for his use, Morris sought long and patiently; taking his models of paper and type from the early books which he so admired, and adapting them to modern needs and requirements.

His experiments in alphabets are particularly interesting, as he relates them. By instinct, he first turned toward the Roman letter, pure in form; severe, without needless excrescences; solid, with-

out here and there an arbitrary thickening or thinning of the line, which is the essential fault of the ordinary modern letter. He afterward set himself to produce a fount of Gothic type which should not be open to the charge of illegibility so often, and with reason, preferred against it. He expressed himself to the effect that "letters should be designed by artists and not by engineers," and with the principles of clearness and beauty as his ideals, he perfected three founts named from the books in which they were destined to be used.

The first, based upon Roman characters, became known as the Golden, from the twelfth century story of saints and martyrs, called "The Golden Legend," which it was Morris' purpose to edit and publish.

The second, the Troy type, which its designer preferred to either of the others, shows the influence of the beautiful alphabets of the early printers of Mainz, Augsburg and Nuremberg. At the same time it has a strong individuality, and could never be mistaken for any of the mediaeval founts. It has been pirated on the continent, and remodeled in America, where, in various modifications, it is known as "Venetian," "Italian," or "Jenson." It received its name from the French cycle of heroic romances which William Morris translated, and issued under the name of "The Recuyell of the Historyes of Troye."

The third type used at the Kelmscott press, called the Chaucer, differs from the Troy only in size,—the first being Pica, and the second Great Primer. It is seen in the book which is, by far, the most important achievement of the Kelmscott Press.

These studies and experiments in type occasioned heavy expenditures in time, energy, and money,—such as the purchase of rare *incunabula* (specimens of early printing: the word derived from the Latin, cradle); the destruction of castings which proved unsuccessful or inartistic; and photography upon an extensive scale, by which the enlarged forms of the letters might be studied, not only individually, but also as to the causes of their share in the effect of the general composition of the page.

The Kelmscott Press, set in operation in 1891, produced its masterpiece, the works of Chaucer, in the spring of 1896, a year and nine months after the great book had been begun. This is in form a folio, the pages containing double columns of text, and each surrounded by floriated borders, of which there are fourteen variations. It is further ornamented by eighty-seven illustrations by Sir Edward Burne-Jones, in that

artist's most characteristic Pre-Raphaelite style. As the crowning perfection of the Chaucer, Morris was to have designed special bindings, but owing to his failing health, the only scheme that he was able to complete was for a full white pigskin covering, which has been executed at the Doves Bindery upon forty-eight copies of the work, including two printed upon vellum.

To afford a worthy comparison to the Kelmscott Chaucer, it was Mr. Morris' intention to issue Froissart's chronicles, in Lord Berner's translation. This was to have been in two volumes folio, with beautiful initials and heraldic ornaments throughout, and a large frontispiece drawn by Sir Edward Burne-Jones. A few pages had been put in type, but no sheet had been printed, when the death of William Morris occurred in the autumn of 1896. The Kelmscott Press was closed in 1898, after an existence of less than seven years, and the completion of a comparatively small number of books. But its influence is to-day universal, and is constantly increasing in strength. Through the clearness and beauty of the printed page, it was a vital power toward making knowledge " amiable and lovely to all mankind."

THE turn of the year has a meaning which antedates its religious significance and has its source in Nature itself. The phenomena of light as among the chief necessities of life, health and pleasure, received the close attention of even primitive peoples. Thus it was natural to mark the period at which the sun appears to begin the recovery of its lost strength by rejoicings and feastings. Hence the Yule-tide festival, with its name derived from the wheel which is pictured in the Gothic and Saxon calendars. The turn of the year with its suggestions of coming verdure was marked also by the December Saturnalia in ancient Rome, a festival which filled the houses of the citizens with green boughs, and promoted good will between master and servants to the point that for a week the rich supplied their own wants and the poor were attended with loving forethought. Furthermore, on the day corresponding to the twenty-fourth December of the Christian calendar, occurs the Feast of Lights among the Hebrews, when they do honor to the symbol of their faith, the great Menorah, or Seven-Branched Candlestick. And once again the Principle of Light was glorified in the Festival of the Unconquered Sun, which the first Christian Roman Emperors clothed with a new significance when they associated it with the natal day of the Christ. And thus it is that old and forgotten meanings and a world of traditions lie hidden in the salutation which is now sounding in many tongues throughout the civilized world "Merry Christmas."

A Visit to the Workshops of The United Crafts at Eastwood, New York

HE lives and the work of many foreign leaders of artistic, economic and social movements have been somewhat extensively treated in the pages of The Craftsman. Through these articles it was hoped to combat the spirit of commercialism which is the worst peril of our prosperous new century. But in the first anniversary number of the periodical founded in the interests of art allied to labor, and designed to be the organ of a body of sincere and forthright workmen, known under the name of The United Crafts, it is well, nay, necessary, to acquaint those who shall be interested, with the work, the aims and the principles of the company which has newly been formed in a village of Central New York.

The workshops of the United Crafts are situated among the green hills of Onondaga, three miles from Syracuse, in a country which is beautiful, refreshing, varying in every direction, yet always restful. Surely, if there be anything in the claim that a beautiful environment adds a tonic to the worker and is a stimulant to his ideals and ambitions, this band of workers has all that nature can supply. The shops are modern, accessible by both electric and steam railways, and we paused a moment to contrast them with that half ruined group of buildings selected by William Morris at Merton Abbey, where the River Wandel often caused appalling disaster by frequently driving the laborers out of house and home. But no floods can reach the workshops of the United Crafts.

From the drafting office in New York to the workshops in Eastwood is a great step. Here surely is the place to handle the problems before us. No genuine artist can visit this hive of workers without being impressed with its healthy condition. Here is the co-operative force of the old guilds with less of the speculations with which most of our commercial offices are crowded. It would be foolish to claim for any colony of workers in this country the inherent ability displayed by the great craftsmen in the Normandy, Tuscany, or Bavaria of the Middle Ages, or in the colonies established by William Morris and his followers in England, which in our own day have flourished to so wonderful an extent. The claim of the United Crafts to serious consideration at our hands is established because they have made so signal a start in the right direction. Their work is excellent. It has been tested. There is something bold, clear and distinguished about these chairs, tables and interiors. The workers have a knack of giving flash-

light pictures with a few bold strokes. There is evidence of no little thought. There is freedom about the shapes, a breezy independence, a sturdy human democracy. This furniture is made to withstand daily use. It is the product of a quaint, moving, strong personality. These craftsmen are no mere copyists.

Mr. Gustave Stickley, of Syracuse, will succeed; he is the leader of the United Crafts, controlling their destinies. If he has done but one thing in the world, and nothing more, he has prompted many of us to review the simple lives of a great people. This man rose, as it were, out of the forests, in answer to the cry: "Who shall deliver us from the expensive living, the thralldom of extravagance, the hereditament of conventions?" This man helps us because he is a student of life in all its phases and aspects.

The severe furniture made by the United Crafts has done something to foster rugged independence and masterful resolution, and to exhibit a resourcefulness greatly needed in these times. Because the problem of living a simple life is the easier for simple surroundings which tend to bring people closer together, and because the press of this country is so often clamoring against the over-indulgence of the rich as a national calamity, it is refreshing to find a member of the intellectual minority bold enough to raise the banner in favor of a grave, sober, simple environment, pregnant with underlying sense of brotherhood and community of interests. It has been said that a man must first make himself before he can make others.

The control of the United Crafts is secure in the hands of so sagacious and resourceful a leader. In these days we are compelled to seek distinction in the field of commerce as well as in that of art. These enthusiasts exhibit consummate tact; using material which they understand, which is in itself a protest against the false appearance of the modern world in its insatiable love of novelty and glitter. It is significant of the material used by the United Crafts that it is as old as the everlasting hills. These workers have no secret compounds, no manipulations or trade secrets to divert attention from the essence of their work. The materials are frankly handled.

The general character and tone of their furniture is wonderfully healthy, soothing and refreshing. It is very difficult to estimate the permanent value of work such as this which captivates at the first glance. The work of the United Crafts produced dismay among the furniture dealers, when it was shown at their annual exposition two years ago, and the first temptation was to copy. This led to exaggeration and crudities wholly out of keeping with the original. There is a frankness of construction everywhere evident. Pins, wedges, mortise and tenon frankly appear, not unlike the method

Rush Seat Workers

Joiners

adopted in Mediaeval days and again reminding us of Spanish work. There is a ring and rhythm in this work when at its best. Wood, metal and leather unite in melodious chorus; the whole treatment showing great skill, strength and delicacy.

Few things have been more interesting than a summary of the search for the oak: the seasoned timber with which so much of this furniture is made. Its excellence calls for special mention. It is delightfully subtile in appearance; while a closer examination leads to the discovery of other qualities. In the first place, it is curious to note how regularly it cuts. It might be alive, it is so willing to be shaped, as if endowed with life, that one is greatly tempted to carve it, or to test the addition of some quaint inlays of metal, ivory or bone, as used by the early guilds. This oak accepts color, is strangely sensitive to the chemical action of spirits, is vigorous, beautifully marked, yet delicate to a degree. The hunt for this oak was well worth the trouble, because of the bitter clamor against the ordinary material doing duty for that name. American oak has been unjustly maligned, in spite of the coarseness and rankness of the wood offered in the open market.

Among the productions of the Eastwood craftwork, metal and leather play almost as important a part as that filled by oak. The utmost care has been taken to secure metal workers who can shape handles, door knobs, hinges, metal bands, nail heads, and a thousand and one enrichments invited and required in this work. Iron and copper seem on the whole to have suffered less by the change of fashion and to be more workable than any of our commoner materials. Difficult of course it is, but not impossible, to secure a man who will hammer out of the simplest materials shapes that are delightful, free, vigorous, and which do not involve complicated conditions at every turn.

As to the tanning of leather, I greatly regret not being able to write intelligently about this. Not that I feel ignorant of the result, but despairingly so of the cause. An examination of the leather used by the United Crafts discloses a material of singular charm. The leather is not only yielding to the touch, beautiful to handle, but elastic and distinctly *leathery,* if I may coin the last word.

The leather workers have undoubtedly discovered some process by which the hides of sheep and cattle can be tanned; preserving, at the same time, the grain, the fibre, and the softness, yet retaining the strength, durability and wearing properties of a live hide. Again, this leather seems susceptible to the influence of any color and resembles oak in this respect. Ornament is scarcely welcome as a proposed enrichment. The leather is good enough to leave alone. At the same time, experiments are making with such ornaments as lacing and rough modeling of the surface and back in a

crude fashion, resembling the quaint markings of the Mexican Indians on their green hides.

There is certainly a strange fascination in seeing rushes, reeds, and other tenants of our swamps run through a small hand press to extract the water and air, and in watching them as they are twisted in various plaits and deftly woven into a solid surface for the seats of chairs and panels for screens.

The designing and making of furniture and metal work, the tanning of leather and weaving of fabrics are by no means the main contribution to the furnishing of the home. The main strength of the United Crafts, in the future, will lie in preparing the house itself. It is intended that staircases, partitions, panels, door and window trimmings, floorings, and in fact everything that contributes to the interior of the house, shall be made at these shops. This the craftsmen have been forced to do, in order that their furniture may be acceptable, and because of the poverty and singularly misleading background of the average home. It is not enough to preach simplicity or to illustrate charming and skilfully contrived interiors; to discourse learnedly or otherwise about "the atmosphere," and, at the same time, be blind to the knowledge that much of the furniture made here will ultimately be found crowded into some modern interior, very expensive possibly, and very beautifully made, but often inconsistent and singularly out of harmony with the cult of simplicity of which we all have just now so much to say.

The United Crafts believe in the brotherhood of man. In the hope that to an extent their workmen may be inspired with the same feeling, it is intended to hold weekly meetings for them in the new establishment in Syracuse, where friendly debate, brief addresses, and genial discussion will be used as methods to secure harmony and unity of effort. Meanwhile, an irresistible enthusiasm is evident to all who visit their workshops.

Much will be done during the coming winter to make the lives of the workmen pleasant. There will be music, brief lectures illustrating subjects of current interest, and some intelligent attention will be paid to the social and personal requirements of the men and women workers.

This is one way of solving the problems of the workshop. It is luminous and thorough. It charms with rude sturdiness of character, with directness of things, and exhibits a freedom of spirit. This wholesome, happy company curiously assorted, breathes mountain air which does much to break the passion of discontent. To leave the United Crafts at Eastwood and to return to the city is like relinquishing so much power and inspiration.

The United Crafts in their efforts to preserve the character of their work, think of it as a whole, in that it should harmoniously express

an idea and an emotion. Whatever may be the ultimate policy of the public in employing workers to assist them in the construction of their houses, the claim of the workshop should certainly always have the preference. Workmen may not always succeed in the clever manufacture of sketches—pictorial art is not their strong point,— but their ability to grapple with the practical needs of the moment, their close touch with the requirements of the occasion, their intrinsic and inherent knowledge of the cost, nature and character of the work itself, is an evidence of their fitness to do it. Their work is vital.

THE NECESSITY FOR USING OUR EYES, IF WE ARE TO BE ARTISTS, HAVING BEEN ADMITTED, THE QUESTION COMES: HOW ARE WE TO GET PEOPLE TO USE THEIR EYES, ALWAYS KEEPING IN MIND THE FACT THAT FOR SOME TIME AFTER THEY HAVE BEGUN TO DO SO THEY WILL BE A TORMENT TO THEMSELVES AND THEIR NEIGHBORS, AS I AM.

WILLIAM MORRIS
ARCHITECTURE AND HISTORY
AND WESTMINSTER ABBEY

I HAVE met but one or two persons in the course of my life who understood the art of Walking—that is, of taking walks,—who had a genius, so to speak, for sauntering, *which word is beautifully derived "from idle people who roved about the country, in the Middle Ages, and asked charity, under pretense of going* à la Sainte Terre,"*—to the Holy Land,—'till the children exclaimed: "There goes a* Sainte Terrer,"*—a Saunterer, a Holy Lander. They who never go to the Holy Land in their walks, as they pretend, are indeed vagabonds, but they who do go there are saunterers in the good sense such as I mean.*

Henry D. Thoreau

Dining-room, Mr. Stickley's House

A Visit to the House of Mr. Stickley

Samuel Howe

I PURPOSE this month to extend somewhat farther the series of considerations with which, in the October number of this magazine, I opened my plea for a rehearing of the imminent and now all important question of securing appropriate and simple decorative elements for the modern house.

In the former article I dealt mainly with the making of furniture in the workshops of The United Crafts at Eastwood, giving a glimpse of the daily life among the workers, briefly outlining the frank handling of well-prepared material, and in a general way citing those conditions of industry which have given such flavor to one of the most vital subjects of the present day.

Now I write of the house itself, and I have selected the house of Mr. Stickley as an illustration, because it is so singularly free from pretension. It contains evidence of serious thought and honest intent, with abundant freshness and wholesomeness, which are innovations in these days of machine carving and jelly mold enrichments.

Unlike modern literature, in which, if we are wise, we say all we can, the matter of house building needs some of the outward barriers of repression against the false enthusiasm that promotes tinsel at the cost of sterling gold, and modern shams in place of sound principles. And a curious fact remains, that in spite of all our modern ease of communication, men still remain individual. In-

terchange is powerless to subdue it and man can still, by giving thought, stamp his individuality on his house, so that when you look at the house, you view the man. Ideals are as portable as bonds, and individuality alone, despite the value of coöperation, frequently shapes the destiny of man and house. This is brought home to us in viewing the house of Mr. Stickley. I purpose to confine my remarks to the interior of the house, remembering certain limitations which had to be accepted because they were imposed by the general plan.

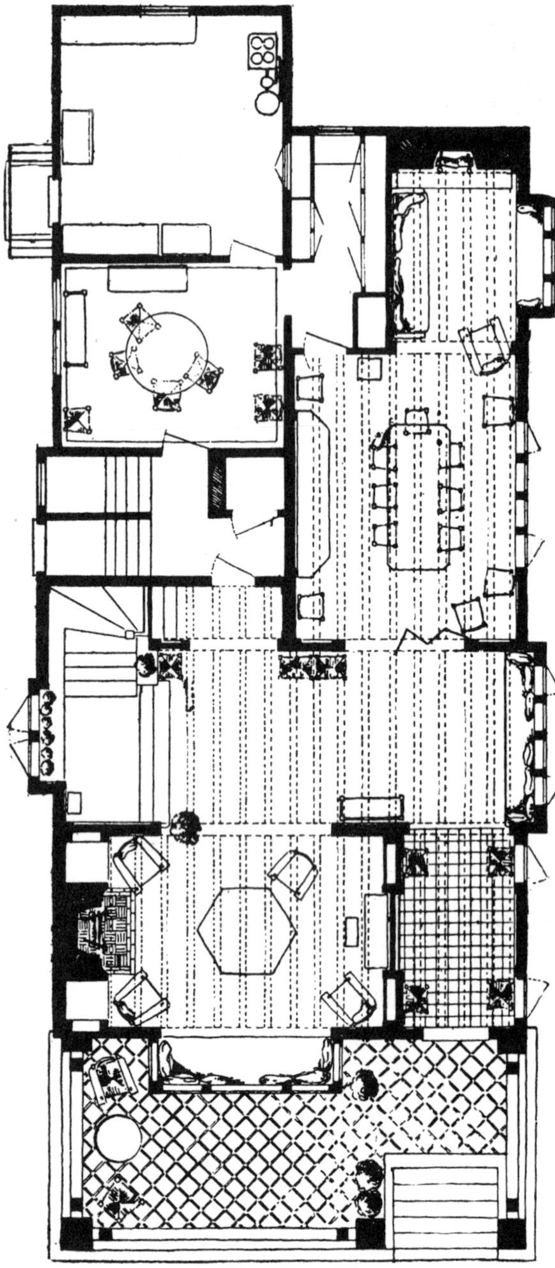

First Floor Plan

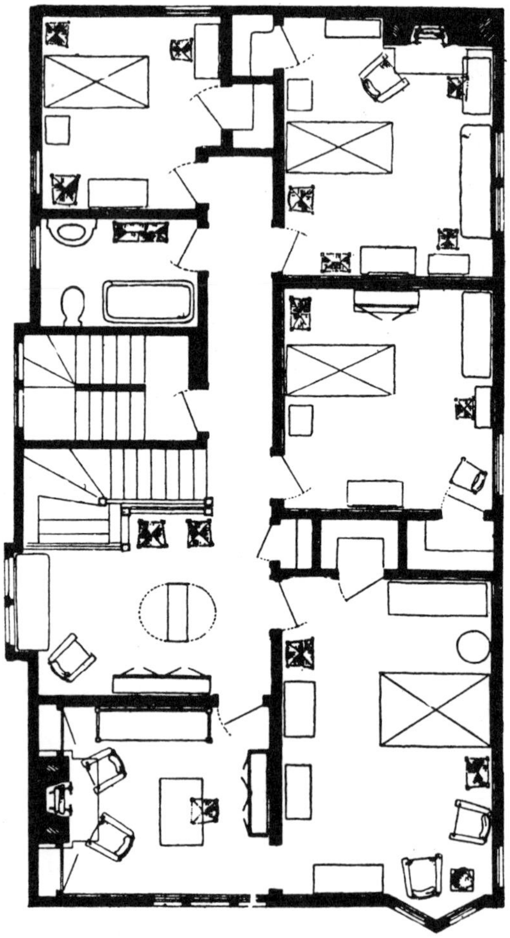

Second Floor Plan

HEN I enter I note a rich grandeur in the passion for size, scale and sense of bigness. How soothing—wistful—simple, is this house. The quiet sense of humanity pervades it. The soul of the workman is manifest in his work. We hear his rugged laugh, half defiant of criticism. There is daring, and I might say almost arrogance, in some of the detail. It has been said that the reign of the fireside is over and that with it, the sense of home has perished from among us. Surely a glance at these liberal hearths shows that this statement is not yet true.

The square impost which marks the entrance to dining room and library, denotes a very much plainer, franker use of structural features than is usual. It looks really able to support the house. The scale is big—it thrills. It has neither base nor cap, even that would be a mistake. The composition is stronger as it is.

Let us look at the casement windows for a moment. They are well proportioned, long and low, with mullions of severely simple outline, cutting the window into four equal openings. As we pass from one window to another, we note how well adapted they are for plants; how happy they would look then, with the sun streaming in, and what great secrets can the children tell as they hide behind the cushions in the long deep seat beside them. This hall is large for a comparatively small house and impresses one with a sense of grandness by its well-considered contrast. When it is said that the most clearly and typically expressive of modern homes do not hold us in awe with their linear dimensions, but rather cheer by the welcome they extend to us, surely, this house should be included in the category. We do not often get vaulted interiors in these days. The Anglo-Saxon has always been a lover of beamed ceilings. Here beams, row after row, mark and intensify the perspective, leaving long panels of plaster between them. Tastes differ as to the color the surfaces should show. White or shades of ivory is the tone generally in favor with the professional mind. In this instance the surfaces are white. This gives a variation of texture, a play of light and shade, which reminds us of the monastic buildings and cloistered courts of Spain and Italy. One point of unlikeness to the conventional house is in the floors, which instead of being laid with narrow

View head of Staircase

boards, have broad chestnut of varying widths and lengths, frankly showing nails; the wood being darkened by aqua-ammonia and rubbed and polished with a mixture of beeswax and turpentine. The fireplaces are of common red brick, built solidly into the house, not added on as a mere lining to conceal a poorly constructed frame. When we look at the drawings of interiors here presented, we must remember how difficult it is for sketches to retain their freshness when added to the frigid zone of a page of type. They are intended to be "strong," not "pretty," and to illustrate facts rather than enthusiasm.

It is like hoisting a danger signal to speak out loud to Mr. Stickley of ornament, yet all people do not know this. "It is very grand," said one visitor, "but have you no ornament, carving or draperies in your house, Mr. Stickley?"

"No draperies, thank you, and as for ornament,—have we not our friends?"

"Ah! a courtier, I declare! In a measure you are right. The truest ornament to a house is the family—the wife and children, then, as you say, the friends."

No fiercer architectural battle has been fought than that in which the question of ornament supplies the field. Some ornament resents leadership. It affects to govern and not with a small voice, but with a shout. Not content to be seen, it must be heard. It

eschews moderation. Assuming that collective ignorance represents dominant wisdom, it justifies its intolerance by its popularity. The lovers of accessive and aggressive beauty clamor for more ornament, which grows as it goes, a snowball on a muddy road. Not alone is this house remarkable because of its conspicuous absence of carving, molding, and inlay by way of ornament, but because of the singularly frank manner in which they have been omitted. No false construction is allowed to take the place of these popular idols by presenting rudely wrought, primitive forms as an architectural expedient.

View in Hall, showing Stairs

So I salute the man who, refusing the many dangers which confront him in the search for an acceptable solution of the housebuilding problem, rescues from the dust of ages enough of the fundamental characteristics of the past to present so valuable an illustration of the true understanding of the problem. This severe treatment is truly a welcome understanding, disciplined, chastened, yet always wholesome, modest and noble. I like Mr. Stickley's house because it is strong, robust, wholesome, free from affectation, vagaries; yet it might be, and I trust it will be, softened with the addition of furnishing details. Nature would help with her flowers, plants and potted shrubs, never more welcome than when they show against a background of polished oak.

All human interests combining human endeavors and social growths in this world have, at a certain stage of their development, required organization; and Work, the grandest of human interests, does now require it : : : :

Thomas Carlyle

Truly a boundless significance lies in work, whereby the humblest craftsman comes to attain much which is of indispensable use, but which he who is of no craft, were he never so high, runs the risk of missing

Thomas Carlyle

He that can work is a born king of something : : : : : :

Thomas Carlyle

We stand for an education that is of the deed and not of the word, a training in practicality at every turn : : : : : : :

Thomas Carlyle

Laborare est Orare: to work is to pray

Maxim of the Monks of the Middle Ages

The wealth of nations, as of men, consists in substance not in ciphers

John Ruskin

Intelligence is perfected not in one, in another, or in many, but in all : : : : :

Giordano Bruno

Only mankind together is the true man. The individual can be joyous and happy only when he has the courage to feel himself not the whole : : : : : :

Goethe

That man is richest who, having perfected his functions to the utmost, has also the widest helpful influence, both personal and by means of his possessions over the lives of others : :

William Morris

The New Industrialism *Oscar Lovell Triggs*

I

I KNOW what you are thinking: you are saying to yourselves: "What right has a student and teacher of literature, who belongs, therefore, to a non-pecuniary profession, who is at the farthest remove from the work-a-day conditions of field and factory, what right has such a person, who is not even a sociologist, to discourse on the subject of Industrialism?" You conceive that you might learn something worth while from a "labor leader," or from a "captain of industry," or from a professional "sociologist," but you are at a loss to understand what merit of instruction may attach to the words of a "man of letters."

But perhaps it will appear that my treatment of the subject is justified for the very reason that I am not a president of a labor union, not the manager of a great business, and not a scientific sociologist. You will observe that my subject is *The New Industrialism.* It is quite possible that the new industrialism is something about which labor leaders and industrial captains and scientific sociologists know very little: these men will tell you of things as they are, of production and consumption, of competition, of the conflict between capital and labor, of strikes, of all the phenomena, in short, of the old industrialism. But who among them have dreamed dreams or seen visions? Who have insight into the obscure tendencies of the times? Who indulge in the hope of industrial betterment? Who believe in the doctrine of human perfectibility? Who have sufficient faith in humanity to believe that a social order will appear to be controlled by principles of good-will? When the need of prophecy arises, the exponents of the old order keep silence, must keep silence from lack of vision. Literature on the other hand is visionary, speculative. Imagination is the test of capacity with respect to what is hidden or far removed. The truest analysis of the industrial conditions of the present time has been made by Tolstoi, a novelist; the truest synthesis of the new tendencies in industry has been made by Zola, another novelist. John Ruskin the artist, not John Mill the logician, perfected the most complete system of political economy yet devised for the upbuilding of a true social state. William Morris, a mere poet, inaugurated the most significant movement in the industrial world in recent history. It is clear, then, I think, that the new industrialism is a subject which need not be avoided by any poet, essayist, novelist, artist or educator. Indeed, and this is the whole point of my discourse, the new industrialism is coming into the world just because artists and educators are aban-

doning their own specialized pursuits and are undertaking to be constructive in the field of industry. In short, the new industrialism is a form of labor which aims to be artistic on the one hand and educative on the other. Art, education, labor: these are the three elements destined to coalesce that they may form a new industrial order.

II

In separation the activities represented by the three terms, art education, and labor, are highly specialized. Art and education are quite closely akin in their cultural significance; labor standing apart as distinctly non-cultural. But again these differ in respect to motive. The specialized artist has commonly a highly sensitized nature; he is sensitive emotionally and sensationally. Living the intensive life, absorbed in impressions, wrapped up in his visions, the artist tends to develop a strong individuality. He lives within and for self, and being thus non-social in his nature, he inclines toward unconventionality, and is frequently erratic. He asks from education a certain discipline and some few ideas, and from labor a modicum of physical energy. He asks from the world for himself only the barest necessities. Working apart in a room which he calls his studio, the artist is the purest type of free self-centered and non-social activity. The teacher leaves the studio for the school-room. At once he is brought into contact with other personalities to which he stands in the relation of master. His problem is, in part, like the artist's: one of expression; but lest he fail as a teacher, he must develop also the social qualities. The secret of teaching lies in sympathy. Knowledge he may have, force of character he may possess, but without the ability to understand others and to live according to social standards, he is wanting in the supreme quality which makes for his success. The educator, then, is the purest type of social activity.

The artist works from personal motives, the teacher from social motives. If other motives intrude, if either is ambitious for fame, or position, or money, if he seek rewards outside of that satisfaction which inheres in self-expression with the one and in the consciousness of social service with the other, to that degree he loses the rewards pertaining to his own specialized activity. The true artist or the true teacher is never interested in money payment for his work, beyond, of course, what is needed for a decent living. The best work in art and education is never paid for in current coin. How often one reads of an author or artist what I saw stated recently of Maeterlinck: "Material success in life, fame, wealth: these things he passes indifferently by." This is as it must be. The intrusion of the motive of extraneous gain is always

detrimental to success in these specialized fields. I must insist upon the recognition of this fact, because it furnishes the main distinction between artistic and educational motives and those which operate to-day in industry.

I have analyzed the artist and the teacher. Let us now turn to the workman. What are the springs of his activity? The workman has so long been regarded and employed as a mere agent in production that he is now reduced to accept the one reward which a mechanicalized system can give him: a money wage. He can not, like the artist, take pleasure in his work, which is, indeed, as to its processes, almost intolerable. He cannot, like the teacher, take pleasure in observing the results of his labor. The social motive probably never enters his consciousness. By reason of the division of labor he is not even aware of the completed product. At no time can he say: "I am the maker of this thing. I made it after an image in my mind. I dedicate it to the service of mankind." The design was not his to start with; the product is not his to end with. He knows himself to be but one of innumerable agents coöperating in a result which he does not understand. Lacking, then, the rewards that pertain to art and education, he accepts a money wage. Hating his work, he seeks to reduce the length of the working day. Loving his wages or the things his wages procure, he strives to increase the amount of his hire. His weapon is the strike, he strikes for less work and more pay. Behind his strife is perhaps the vague thought that he, too, if he had the will, would serve his own ends, or those of the social order.

Here then the three men stand to-day in the form in which history has shaped them. Not one of them is really perfect; not one is fully integral; not one but is unhappy and discontented. The specialization of faculty has been carried in each one to an extreme. Peculiar dangers, therefore, attach to each class. The artist, living alone in his studio, grows unsocial and ceases to respond to the demands made upon him by life itself. The teacher is so subject to social control that he loses individuality and tends to become mechanicalized and conventional. The workman is so sunken in his wage-slavery that he is dehumanized altogether. What is needed at this juncture in history is a new synthesis of life, a bringing together: the correction of specialization by the cultivation of the numberless faculties possessed by man.

III

Let us try to think of a place which is studio, school-room and workshop in one. Let us conceive a person who is at once artist, student and workman. The place may be called a workshop, the person a craftsman. This synthetic workshop is like the studio, since its work is conducted in freedom. It is unlike the studio in

so far as its productions are made for real uses and at social demand. The workshop is like the school in that it affords opportunity for community life. It is unlike the school in that it is more than instructional and seeks to be productive.

The workshop is like the factory, inasmuch as it is devoted to real production. It is unlike the factory in that the nexus between the members is a natural one and is not dependent upon an extraneous wage. The craftsman is an artist because he works to the ends of self-expression; he is the designer and, so far as practicable, the maker of the form designed. The craftsman is an educator because his work, being free and pleasurable, is itself educative, to both the master and his apprentices. The craftsman is a workman because he directs machinery and applies physical energy to material things.

IV

The workshop I have described is not imaginary, nor is the craftsman referred to a fiction. Within my own lifetime I have observed these changes; I have seen many artists' studios transformed into workshops. I have seen many school-rooms set with work-benches and equipped with tools for manual training. I have seen more than one factory conducted for artistic and educational motives. And I have noted the conversion of one of the greatest of English poets into the finest craftsman in Europe.

The place I select for special description is the Rookwood Pottery at Cincinnati. The building itself first attracts one's attention. In an old English dress, it faces the city at the edge of a bluff and is distinguished for its picturesqueness. It is clear that the site was chosen for other than "business" reasons. Sanitary, aesthetic, and probably social considerations were taken into account in the selection of the site. This of itself marks the place apart, since in most factories such considerations are commonly ignored; economy of work, not convenience of life, being their object. It is soon discovered that the pottery was established for ends other than private profit making. The motive of the founder, a high-minded and philanthropic woman, was to experiment with American clays in the hope of creating and perfecting a given artistic product. For over twenty years the motive, which may be termed both artistic and educational, has been in effect determining the output of the factory. While the business as such is a paying one, the business motive has been subordinated to higher cultural considerations. The sincerity and integrity which characterize Rookwood ware are an evidence of an ideal unity first achieved in the factory itself. Without further inquiry, one knows that as the business is not conducted strictly for money profit, so the work is not done solely for a money wage. Here,

then, in a single institution, artistic, social and industrial principles coalesce to form the purest type of the ideal workshop known to me.

For the ideal craftsman I turn back to William Morris, the "poet-upholsterer," as he was called in derision by an English lord, who probably had some admiration for poets, but none for upholsterers. Here was an upholsterer of a new type, an artistic type, and it is not surprising that English lords found it difficult to perceive the connection between art and craft. The significance of this man in the world's history continually increases. His was a strange career, quite unparalleled in the completeness of its evolution. Only Tolstoi among his contemporaries shows contrasts as violent. Only Ruskin among his associates had a history as varied and spiritual. The significance of Morris lies just at this point: he combines aristocracy and democracy, conservatism and liberalism; he unites capital and labor; he associates the arts and the crafts; he is individualistic, but also as strongly socialistic. You will pardon me if I tell again a well-known story and trace the thread of his personal history. He was born in 1834 of Welsh ancestry on his father's side. His boyhood was spent at Walthamstow and Marlborough, villages near London, where he attended school and began to take interest in art and archæology. In 1852 he matriculated at Exeter college, Oxford, being intended by his mother for the church. At this time, Oxford was subject to a revival of mediævalism which took the form of a High Church movement in religion and of Preraphaelitism in art. Under these influences, Morris became a student of the past and sought to create for himself an ideal world of romance. Up to this time, his tastes were wholly aristocratic. He was an author of recognized merit; writing verses and stories of exquisite but remote beauty. Rumors of social disturbance descending from the Great Black Country left him unmoved. He had formed, however, an acquaintance with Ruskin and, though he did not then feel the social implications of "Modern Painters" and "The Stones of Venice," he was impelled instinctively to follow his great leader. Through the influence of Burne-Jones, his college friend, he abandoned his plans for Holy Orders and resolved to devote his life to the service of art. On leaving Oxford, he entered the office of a London architect and learned the art of building and decoration. Thenceforth, his life developed along practical lines. In 1860, he built near London a home, the famous "Red House;" designing and executing for it the decoration and furniture. The next year, with a group of other artists, he established at Merton Abbey the first genuine workshop of the new industrialism. Again we note the artistic and social motives involved in this workshop. These

artist-craftsmen were resolved to join art and labor. They were to make objects of common use, but these objects were to be so made that pleasure would accrue to both the maker and the user. In all the arts of the hand, Morris himself worked with utmost patience and devotion. He learned the crafts of carving, weaving, dyeing, cloth-printing, embroidery, glass-staining or painting, tile-making, engraving, printing, and manuscript-illumination. He was skilled in all the work of the factory beyond the skill of the best of his fellow craftsmen, and beside being the master craftsman, he was also the firm's poet. In 1878, appeared one of the world's great epics, the Story of Sigurd. This, however, was the last of his important books on literary themes. From 1870 he was a militant social reformer, devoting his talents to a cause: a cause which may be defined as the socialization of art and the moralization of industry. Here, then, is the first great craftsman of the new industrial order. This craftsman was poet, artist, and socialist. He was impelled by cultural and human motives. The political economists had declared that love of money was the spring of human action. Here was a man who refuted in all his conduct everything the political economists had stated as true of mankind. It will be well at this time to examine the principles of the economy which accords with the practice of the new industrialism.

V

Our guide in this rather obscure field is John Ruskin. The beginning and end of economic activity, let us agree, is human life. It is necessary to inquire always at the presentation of any problems what is best for man, not what is best for the raw materials, or for the machine, or for the completed product. The new social science is then, as Professor J. A. Hobson states it, "a science of the relation of efforts and satisfactions in a society": in other words, a science of human life in its social phases. The error of economists in the past has lain in their assumption that mercantile economy is identical with political economy. Wealth means well-being, and social well-being may or may not have anything to do with the accumulation and exchange of material products. "He is a rich man," declares Ruskin, "who, having perfected the func-

tions of his own life to the utmost, has also the widest and most helpful influence, both personal and by means of his possessions, over the lives of others." Wealth is spiritual as well as material. To secure wealth in the material sense may be the ambition of many, but quite as many are moved to action by motives of human affection. The "economic man," assumed to exist by the old economists, never has existed and never can exist. All men are conscious, rational and emotional, and possess what is called soul. As I have shown in the earlier part of this paper, the artist and the teacher are not mercantile in their instincts, or covetous in their desires. They possess wealth, but wealth of a non-marketable kind. They have rewards, but rewards not measurable in terms of a wage. The assumption that what is fundamental in man is hatred of work on the negative side and greed of gold on the positive side, is disproved by these two classes, at least, in every community. The organized system of industry is of course largely mercantile. Men are regarded as so many factors in production, implying so much salary for superintendence, or so much wage for labor. But now the query arises: Is it not possible for rational beings to organize a system of industry in which rewards shall be cultural, rather than mercantile? Instead of mechanicalizing society by applying industrial principles, is it not possible to humanize society by socializing industry? Are not honesty, friendship, temperance, intellectual taste, social culture, desirable for workmen? Is not a world of free men something we should seek to attain? I can imagine nothing more frightful than a world conducted on the principle of greed, nothing more beautiful than the world at work, if the motive to work be pleasure in the work itself. The problem of carrying over into industrialism the motives which operate in art and education, the problem of making life integral: this is the problem that modern political economy is called upon to solve. The charge that sentimental elements are introduced into the question is of course well taken. The subject is, in truth, complicated, but it is believed that after all is said, the world is moved by sentiment, and not by the motives the political economists allege. Some of the maxims of the new philosophy may next be considered.

VI

The first is the well known saying of Ruskin: "Life without labor is guilt, labor without art is brutality." This statement contains practically all the issues at hazard. It involves first a principle of morality. He who lives without work, who subsists, that is, by the labor of others, whose splendid idleness is made possible by the painful overstrain of others' lives, this one is guilty of social

theft. The worker, on his part, who is deprived of the natural solace of the work itself, whose toil is always painful and undesired, lives a life that is less than human. If society is ever to be moralized, two things must happen. There must be equality of obligation on the one hand, and, on the other, an equal opportunity to share in the results of civilization. A political economy that is not grounded in justice, that is not concerned with the common weal, is not worthy its name. "If there is any one point," wrote Ruskin in one of his famous prefaces, "which in six thousand years of thinking about right and wrong, wise and good men have agreed upon, or successively by experiment discovered, it is that God dislikes idle or cruel people more than others; that His first order is: 'Work while you have light,' and His second: 'Be merciful while you have mercy.'"

The second tenet of our philosophy is the saying of Morris: "One day we shall win back art to our daily labor; win back art, that is to say, the pleasure of life, to the people." Ruskin's maxim is moral, involving the sense of justice. Morris's maxim is social, implying a certain common condition of living. This second statement passes beyond the first in defining that most difficult word which is employed in both, the word art. Art: the pleasure of life. You have thought that art must be defined in terms of music or painting. How can it be a phase of common life? Does Morris mean that when life becomes pleasurable the world will be made up of poets, painters and musicians? Or does he mean that when the conditions of freedom and independence, which now pertain to an artist here and there, the special favorites of fortune, become universal, life will be pleasurable? Perhaps, again, you have thought that pleasure was something rare and unusual, pertaining to education, or art, or athletics, or the stage. How can it be a pleasure to live and work? Certainly, at the present time, pleasure does not attach to industry. It is doubtful if it even attaches to what we call "our pleasures." True happiness is rarely possible to-day, because of the social disintegration incident to classes and institutions. Life is at no time truly integral: it is divided, isolated, and, therefore, artificial and forced and painful. Pleasure, someone defines, consists in the satisfaction of impulses and desires. Perhaps our most insistent desire is to be active, to be doing something. We are, indeed, forced to be active in the same way as ants and bees and the wild animals of the wood. And associated with this desire is an instinct which has been termed "the instinct of workmanship." This is really the activity and impulse which we call art. At the present time, the free play of the instinct of workmanship is given to but few persons; hence art lives a poor, thin life among rare exceptional men who

for the most part scorn the common laborers below them, wholly unaware that their very existence as a class hangs upon the right solution of a social problem. The future happiness of the human race is dependent upon the emancipation of labor. The problem of art is, therefore, primarily a social problem.

Another very important principle of our system is formulated by Hobson: "It is to improved quality and character of consumption that we can alone look for a guarantee of social progress." These are the words of a professional economist; they seem more formal and accurate than those employed by Ruskin and Morris. But when their significance is perceived, their bearing is seen to be cultural and social. This principle involves the substitution of qualitative for quantitative methods of estimating the results of civilization. In explaining the maxim it will be well to turn at once to that field where its effects would be first noted: the field of machine-production. Perhaps you have wondered why Ruskin and Morris antagonized the machine so harshly. In part, of course, their criticism was directed not to the machine, but to the uses of the machine required in competitive commerce. This is the way Morris regarded the matter: "And all that mastery over the powers of nature which the last hundred years or less has given us: what has it done for us under this system? In the opinion of John Stuart Mill, it was doubtful if all the mechanicalized inventions of modern times have done anything to lighten the toil of labour: be sure there is no doubt that they were not made for that end, but to 'make a profit.' Those almost miraculous machines, which, if orderly forethought had dealt with them, might even now be speedily extinguishing all irksome and unintelligent labor, *leaving us free* to raise the standard of skill of hand and energy of mind in our workmen, and to produce afresh that loveliness and order which only the hand of man guided by his soul can produce,—what have they done for us now? Those machines of which the civilized world is so proud, has it any right to be proud of the use they have been put to by commercial war and waste?" The explanation of this attitude toward the machine is that Morris was interested in the kind, the quality, the character of civilization. The moment you adopt a human standard for economy, you no longer measure industrial agents or products by quantitative or statistical rules, but ask instead: "What is the relation of the machine to culture?"

I think I know the main truths respecting the machine. The machines are not of course to be destroyed. Being an extension of the human frame, representing more and swifter hands and feet, they have the same justification as hands and feet, providing they are controlled by rational will. Instead of destroying the

machine, the secret of industrial progress is to improve the machine to such a degree that its action becomes completely automatic. The genius of the machine is routine. When once perfected, it will accomplish one monotonous task endlessly. As in biological and psychological evolution human progress consists in reducing from conscious to automatic action all those bodily processes which become so well established as to work harmoniously by themselves, whereby the mind is left free to range the true world of consciousness with free play and spontaneity, so social progress consists in consigning to machinery all those duties which relate to primitive and common needs: needs of food, clothing and shelter, but reserving for conscious and self-directive arts and crafts those interests which from very nature are individual. "Order," remarks Hobson on this point, "order, exactitude, persistence, conformity to unbending law, these are the lessons which must emanate from the machine. Machinery can exactly reproduce; it can, therefore, teach the lesson of exact reproduction, an education of quantitative measurements. The defect of machinery, from the educative point of view, is its absolute conservatism. The law of machinery is a law of statical order: that everything conforms to a pattern, that present actions precisely resemble past and future actions. Now the law of human life is dynamic; requiring order, not as valuable in itself, but as the condition of progress. The law of human life is that no experience, no thought or feeling is an exact copy of any other. Therefore, if you confine a man to expending his energy in trying to conform exactly to the movements of a machine, you teach him to abrogate the very principle of life." Now that is well and correctly said. Imagine the human world made up of automatic beings: suppose the offices of desire and thought and love were fulfilled with the same unthinking regularity as the winking of the eye-lids, what meaning would life possess? Try now to imagine the whole world mechanicalized: a world in which there is no room for individualized conduct, a world reduced to mathematical routine, a world necessarily without arts, without crafts, without culture. Are you willing even to conceive the kind of world that would be? We want machinery. We want more and ever more of it. But when machinery has done its work, when all our common and primitive needs are satisfied by quantitative production, when everything that is really mechanical in conduct is mechanicalized, then we escape into a transcendental sphere where the will is free, where conduct is vital every moment. Turn back to the last quotation from Morris. Read till you come to the words: "leaving us free." There is, then, a region where the machine is not calculated to operate. Yes! and the larger the mechanicalized world,

the larger in circumference must be the purely human sphere outside of it. In the mechanical sphere all estimates are quantitative; in the human sphere they are all qualitative. It is true: all social progress comes by way of increase of character. Character in the man requires character in the things we use. In so far as industry is personalized, its field of endeavor will be that which I have described as the new industrialism. The quality of our spiritual resources is, in truth, as Hobson implies, "the guarantee of social progress."

One final thought I approach with a certain quiet joy, for I perceive that in the new industrialism none of the evils of the old order inhere. The substitution of character for materials changes the whole aspect of life. The severity of competition, the reason of competition indeed, is due to the limitation of material things. In the lower order of industries there are more workers than places, more consumers than objects. There is a limit to quantities. And what one gets another must lose. Quantitative consumption is always selfish. But no limitation applies to qualities. See the painter's few crude materials; then consider the value of the completed painting. I was reading recently in Thoreau's "Walden" the story of the farmer and the poet. The farmer supposed the poet had taken a few wild apples; in reality he had got the most valuable part of the farm. He had "fairly impounded it, milked it, skimmed it, and got all the cream, and left the farmer only the skimmed milk." Yet the poet had taken nothing measurable away. Thus variable are judgments in respect to material and spiritual properties. In a cultural society, generous emulation takes the place of fierce competition. The gain of one is the wealth of all. It is inevitable that those who enter the field of the higher industrialism develop the more sympathetic social motives. A worker who exercises his own individuality in work learns to respect the individuality of other workers. If he enjoys his work, at once his desire rises to bring others under the same conditions of enjoyment. This is the real explanation of the "socialism" of Ruskin, Morris, and Walter Crane. I am inclined to believe that the development of a fraternal commonwealth is dependent upon the dissemination of the principles of industrial art.

I will not now pursue the quest of maxims of political economy. This much is learned: the political economy of the future will be concerned not merely with questions of mercantile production and exchange, but also with problems of essential justice and of the common wealth.

Our own duty under the conditions is clear. When all is said, the control of industry is in the hands of consumers. At the pres-

ent time, consumption is absolutely universal, while production is partial and confined to classes. By the exercise of choice in purchasing, by discrimination and compelling respect for one's own individuality and humor, it is possible for buyers ultimately to condition production. When culture and taste are observed among buyers, they will appear among workers. The people are responsible for the machine and the department store. Let us see about the making of a better system.

CONCERNING CLASSICAL KNOWLEDGE

I DO NOT THINK THAT I AM SAYING TOO MUCH WHEN I ASSERT THAT HE WHO HAS NOT KNOWN THE WORKS OF THE ANCIENTS HAS LIVED WITHOUT KNOWING WHAT BEAUTY IS.

HEGEL
MISCELLANIES

A Craftsman House

A Craftsman House Design

HARVEY ELLIS

IT is purposed in this design to erect a house for an average family, on a city or suburban lot of fifty feet front and not less than one hundred twenty-five feet deep. It is further assumed that the amount available for this purpose is four thousand dollars, a sum sufficient, with ordinary economy, to build a structure that will be in the best sense of the word "homely." A house which shall be convenient, harmonious, and related in all its parts. A structure fit and, therefore, a work of art; for nowhere is the axiom of "fitness is beauty" so obvious as in a domestic structure. With the amount named, visions of stone baronial homes, miniature Elizabethan and other architectural bric-a-brac, are, of course, out of the question, and as a house of wood has always a look of temporary existence, even if it be substantial, it is deemed best to build a solid wooden frame, covered in the ordinary manner with sheathing paper and wooden sheathing, over which is placed metal lathe. This, in turn, is given a coat of cement, "rough cast," which is unimpaired by the extremes of temperature or weather, rain or frost, and which has an interesting texture and a color varying from a dead white up to a faint creamy yellow. This, together with a shingled roof stained a Venetian red, with the exterior woodwork also stained (not painted) a rich, full yellow olive green, and the interior of the house exactly expressed in constructive terms, will reasonably result in a good design. For, to quote an old saw of the Ecole des Beaux-Arts—"A good plan makes a good elevation—," and this is true, if the designer is honest and frank with himself and with his material.

Varying with local conditions, the foundations of the proposed house may be of brick or stone; care, of course, being taken in any event, that they are so constructed that anything like a damp cellar is an impossibility. This, with a competent builder and a proper overseer, is a matter of little difficulty.

The framing of the house depends also on local conditions, and may be of either spruce or hemlock, and, in order to obviate shrinkage and consequent settling and cracking of plaster, preferably what is known as balloon framed.

It seems desirable from motives economic and aesthetic to make the interior finish of selected chestnut, the floors of hard pine and to leave the plaster with a sand finish. The material being chosen, the plan may be taken up. At the outset, let us abandon precedent as much as may be, and try, if possible, to think of no house as ever having been designed before. This, of course, brings us back to first principles: What is a house for and how may its various functions best be accommodated to the all-important consideration—the price?

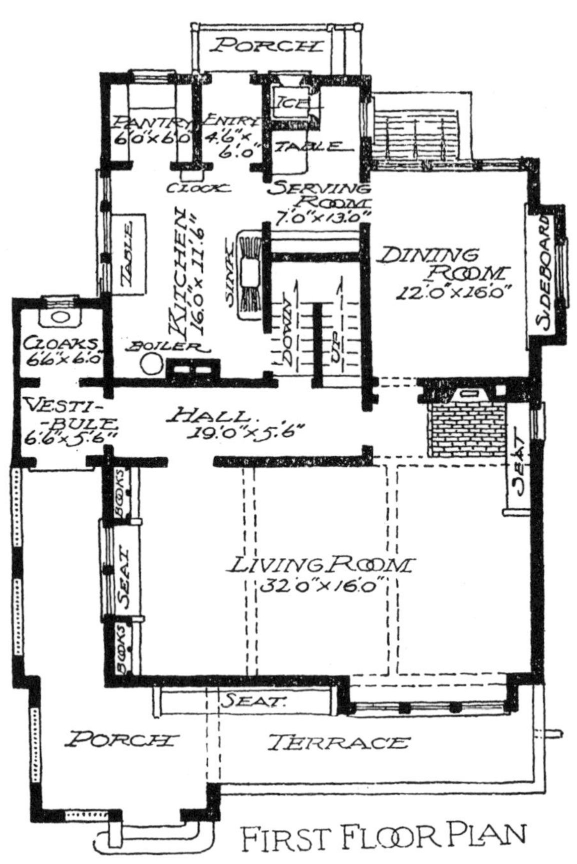

FIRST FLOOR PLAN

The width of the house makes it desirable that little, if any light shall be taken into the house on either side, such provision resulting from the desire for privacy. This would seem to indicate that the long sides of the house should face respectively to the front and the rear. Let us then lay out a big, generous room, which shall be the gathering place for the family. This will be the great room of the house and, for the reasons just stated, should be placed with its long axis parallel to the street. Allowing for a means of communication with the front and the rear of the lot, we find that we are able to give to it the extreme length of thirty-two feet, and this determining, to a certain extent, the width of the room, gives a hall thirty-two by sixteen, which are generous proportions for a house of this class. It is natural that the dining room, which is second in importance in the house, shall be of easy access from the living room, and that the dining room, in turn, shall communicate rapidly with the kitchen; also, that the kitchen shall communicate directly and privately with the front door; that the service from the kitchen to the dining room shall be through a serving room; that all odors from the kitchen shall be cut off from the living room by means of double doors; and that these last shall be easy of

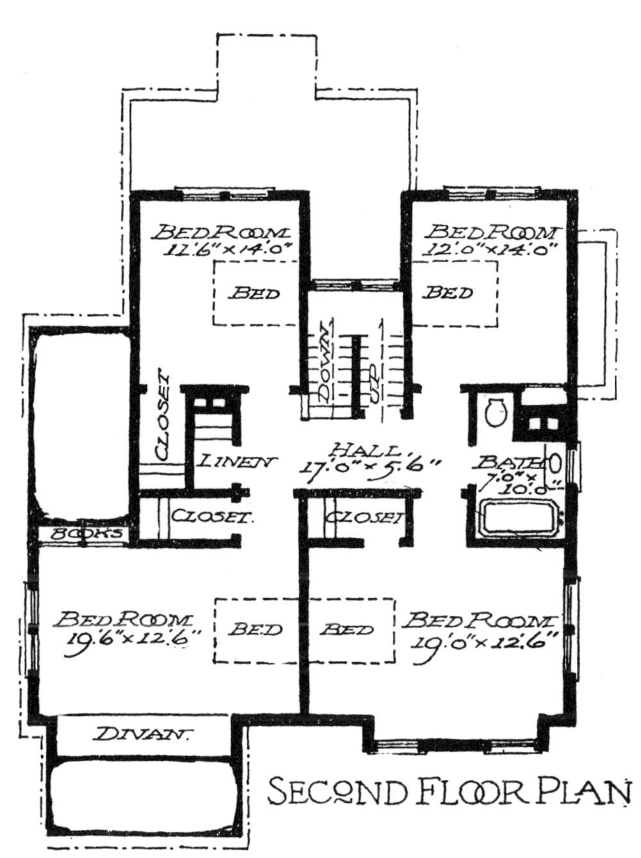

SECOND FLOOR PLAN

access to the second story with little loss of room, and if possible, by means of one flight of stairs, leading from the cellar bottom to the attic floor.

In connection with all this, a chimney must be provided which shall relieve not only the furnace in the cellar, but the grate and range from the first floor, and aid the ventilation of the second story.

The conditions demanded for the stair case would seem to indicate a close departure from the living room, thus bringing it to the center of the house. This in turn, naturally involves the placing of the dining room and kitchen on either sides of the staircase; leaving in the rear of the same the serving room required. It now becomes necessary to find an avenue from the staircase to the front door, and also, communication with the kitchen: which is done by a fairly spacious hall leading to a vestibule, the latter communicating with the coat-room and lavatory. The vestibules are insisted upon, because in the average climate of the United States we find extremes of temperature, which almost demand that all outside openings in the house should have double doors; although they are often omitted and the deficiency is supplied by the exasperating storm doors, that serve no useful function except to call attention

to the lack of forethought in the building of the house to which they are attached.

The landing of the staircase on the second floor arranges it so that no other disposition of the bedrooms, closets and bath rooms, is possible. The advantage of the center staircase is now obvious, as the maximum of bedrooms is obtained with the minimum of hall: all the doors in the second story being practically at equal distance from the head of the staircase, and the bathroom convenient equally to all. Therefore, without the sacrifice of too much space in the bed rooms, closet room is obtained of sufficient quantity to satisfy the most exacting housewife. In the attic, if it be desired, an extra room may be "finished off," leaving ample room for storage, trunks, etc., a provision which seems to be indispensable in the average American house.

The interior walls are all rough plaster and have color applied to them with a large flat brush while they are still wet: a process which incorporates the color in the plaster and gives it an agreeable texture, by reason of the markings make by the brush; the result being a beautiful tint of the color employed, free from the painty look so often seen in colored walls, and making the observer question the material. This method is identical with the old Italian *buon fresco,* used by Michelangelo in the Sistine Chapel, a fact which is a sufficient guarantee as to its practicability and permanence. It may be said in passing that an artistic descendant of the great master is not needed to apply it, as no greater talent is required than that possessed by the average plasterer.

The skeleton of the house now being obtained and the necessities of the house provided, it is time to turn our attention to the finish, conveniences, and the many little arrangements which make for comfort, and which, if properly restrained, produce what is described by that much abused phrase, "an artistic interior."

As has been noted, the living room is of unusual size for a house of this class, and it is laid out in such a manner as further to enhance this quality. It will be seen by the accompanying illustrations that the fireplace is treated in a large, open way; faced with large square tiles of uneven surface and of colors running from dark green blue through blue green to the normal green, indiscriminately. In the center of this facing is set a plaster cast after one of the Della Robbia terra cottas, tinted in faint tones and finished in wax. This, together with the dark red brick hearth, forms a strong color note for this end of the room. The woodwork throughout the room is "fumed" to a rich brown; and the walls are tinted a pale, sappy green; while the leather seats in the fire place and book case are of a pale golden yellow. The floors are of yellow brown and the ceiling of the gray of the plaster. This somewhat quiet scheme of color is enlivened by the placing of an arras hang-

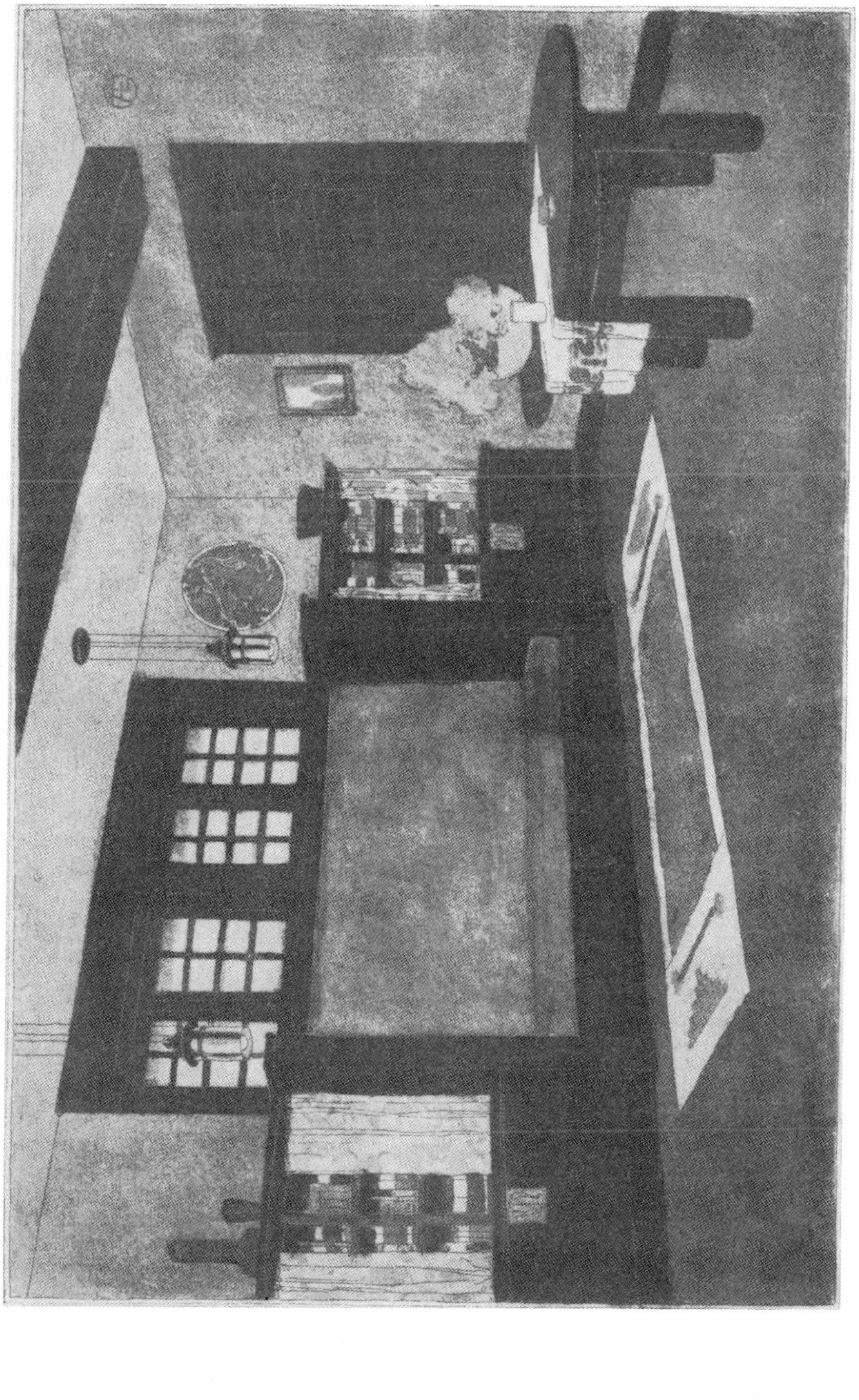

Bookcase and Seat in Living Room

ing on the wall, opposite the bookcase. This hanging is designed expressly for this particular place and is intended as a manifestation of a return to the more straight-forward decorations on honest wall hangings of the time prior to the Renascence and the establishment of state tapestry factories: events which have left no choice between the hangings of palaces and the stupid machine made wall paper, following the prevailing mode, without regard to what the surroundings may be. The hanging in question is of tan "open mesh linen," with the designs in heavy outline, and some of the more important spaces filled in with pale greens, blues and faded rose; the whole making a most pleasing and quiet piece of decoration, which really decorates, and which has the additional advantage of being within the means at our command; the expense lying almost entirely in the design, expressly made and never to be duplicated.

The opposite end of the room has an attractive arrangement for a generous seat, flanked by bookcases and cabinets on either side, and with a high, wide window over the center of the composition. The seat is upholstered with a warm, golden yellow leather, and the curtains of the bookcase are in tints of white, gold and blue. The varying hues and tints of the room are brought together by a large Donegal rug, the color of which is largely made up of grass green, with a border of blues, greens, pale reds and white; the white predominating.

The windows in this room, as indeed are all the windows in the house, save the window in the sideboard alcove in the dining room, are casement windows, cut up into small panes, as shown by the illustration, and glazed with ordinary double thick American glass, without any suspicion in the house of "plate;" for while plate glass has no doubt, uses which excuse its existence, it would absolutely nullify the homely quality desired in this structure.

Pictures, as pictures, have been avoided in the design and furnishing of this room, as being superfluous and discordant. A small mirror, however, is placed at the proper eye-height by the side of the door leading into the hall.

The dining room, being used at special periods, rather than continuously, admits of a trifle stronger and more brilliant treatment. Here, the walls are a strong golden yellow, the ceiling the gray of the plaster, and the woodwork a rich olive green; the visible wall in the alcove for the sideboard is a dark, dull Indian red, and the floor a golden yellow, with a large moss-green rug in the center. Extending about the room is a small pseudo-frieze, which has for its color a bright Venetian red. The windows are hung with a fabric akin to India silk, whose color is, largely, a creamy white, old rose and gold. The leaded window over the

Dining Room, showing Sideboard

sideboard is framed with broad bands of blackened copper; while the martins in the designs are of a dark gray blue, with circles or halos about their heads of a bright yellow, and all against a background of cloudy, milk-colored opaque glass, which has faint streaks of dull turquoise blue running through it.

The hall of communication between the front door, the living room and the staircase being the first apartment entered by the visitor, naturally calls for a cheerful treatment that shall give a presage of the hospitality to be found beyond. In view of this, the general tone of the hall is golden, running from a full dark orange to a pale lemon yellow, which should be contrasted at the extreme end of the hall by some object of pottery, or a fabric of a dull violet. In this hall, if the owner is fortunate enough to possess, or can obtain two or three Japanese prints of a good period and by approved masters, such as Hokusai, Hiroshige, Toyokuni or Utarmaro, he would do well to have them framed in parchment mats about five inches wide, enclosed in dull ebony frames not to exceed one-half

Fireplace in Living Room

inch in width, and hung at irregular intervals and heights, with two supports to each frame. What little furniture is to be found in the hall should preferably be of the finish known as Flemish oak, and any rug or rugs used ought, if harmonized with the scheme, to carry a large quantity of dull red and purplish brown, with some white, and with accents of dark turquoise blue. The kitchen,—that too often neglected room,—has had volume after volume written upon its practical side, but seldom, if ever, has a voice been lifted up for its aesthetic aspects; and, as a formula for a practical, successful working kitchen is so well known, it is not necessary to study this branch, save with the plumber and range maker. But for those who think that the chemistry of cooking is somewhat influenced, and possibly elevated, by proper surroundings, the color treatment of the kitchen generally is a matter of some moment.

If the owner desires to do something verging on the extravagant, there is no better covering for a kitchen floor that what is known as rubber interlocked tile, which is agreeable to the eye, easy for the feet, and absolutely noiseless beneath the step; three conditions particularly appropriate for a room of this kind. This tile, it is suggested, should be farther carried up the side walls, so as to form a wainscoting of reasonable height all around the room, and increased at the sink, range and kitchen table, to a height of about five feet, except where interrupted by windows. Above this, a French glazed paper is recommended which may be readily cleaned with a damp sponge, and which can now be obtained in patterns most agreeable and attractive.

The kitchen under ordinary circumstances, being one of the warmest rooms in the house, it would seem appropriate that the color scheme of the room be something suggestive of coolness. For this reason let the rubber tiles be of blues and greens, and the paper, above the wainscoting, of a greenish gray, with pale lemon yellow ceiling, which will satisfy the eye, and remove from the kitchen its usual ugly and neglected appearance.

The treatment of the hall on the first floor may with advantage be continued up the staircase and in the second story. The bedrooms varying, as they are exposed to the various points of the compass, should be treated with schemes of warm or cool colors. The northwest room of the house, for instance, being from its location the coldest room on this floor, would seem to demand a coloration of yellows and orange, or reds and orange, and those on the southwest equally schemes of greens and blues, with the understanding that in any of the rooms, whatever the prevailing tone of the room may be, it is dead and uninteresting without some small object which presents, by way of foil, its own complementary color.

In this design it is especially desired that the frigid white and blue decorations of the ordinary bathroom be avoided. If there is

any one place in the house that should look, as well as be comfortable, it is the bathroom, and it is for this reason that a warm scheme of yellow or red is recommended for this room.

The résumé of the color and decorative suggestions for these various rooms shows that no item of expense has been added to the cost of the house merely for the sake of decoration, but that infinite care has been exercised in the judicious and proper selection of the colors to be employed and in the combination of the material necessary for the living and constructive purposes. Therefore, if no error be made in the selections, the result should be: a house that is a home; that is comfortable, economical, good to look at, good to be in; a house that is hospitable and homely.

Hiroshigi

L'ART NOUVEAU*

S. BING

Translated from the French by IRENE SARGENT

THE CRAFTSMAN having decided to open its columns to a discussion of "L'Art Nouveau: its Significance and Value," the initial article appeared in December, 1902, over the signature of Professor A. D. F. Hamlin of Columbia University. This article actuated a reply from M. Jean Schopfer of Paris, which was published in the June issue, 1903. And now it would seem fitting, before closing the debate, to hear the argument of the one who, eight years since, had the good fortune of aiding the latent aspirations of the period to assume a visible existence, and of serving as sponsor to the new life.

The article of Professor Hamlin is without doubt one of the most conscientious and impartial studies of the question that have yet appeared. I am, however, far from sharing all the ideas of the writer, and, although some points have already found an eloquent opponent in M. Schopfer, I willingly again revert to them.

To begin: I fully support Professor Hamlin, when he opens the discussion with the following statement:

" '*L'Art Nouveau*' is the name of a movement, not of a style; it has come into use to designate a great variety in forms and development of design, which have in common little, except an underlying character against the commonplace. . . ."

I interrupt the quotation at this point because I do not agree with the end of the sentence, which declares that the followers of the movement concur only in "their common hatred of the historical style."

Before presenting my objections, I must say that it appears to me illogical to apply the same scale of criticism to two sides of the question which can not be included within the same field of vision. A separate judgment must be granted to the initial principle of the movement and the infinite multiplicity of its applications, which are all individual and a forced combination of the good, the indifferent and the bad.

I. THE PRINCIPLE OF L'ART NOUVEAU

IS it accurate to say that no definite aim has been generated by *L'Art Nouveau*, and that its disciples are united only by a negation? The truth is this: that no definite style was prescribed, since the work to be done was a work of liberation. The title of *L'Art Nouveau* designated a field lying outside the narrow boundaries within which, beneath the pressure of a time-honored slavery, a class of degenerate products was approaching extinction. It designated a free soil upon which any one could build according to his own desires. Therefore, there was no pre-conceived idea, no restraint as to the form of expression. But there was, nevertheless, a common idea: differing from the one ascribed to the followers of *L'Art Nouveau* by Professor Hamlin. The true bond between the innovators resided in the hatred of stagnation. If, therefore, Professor Hamlin is right in speaking of a negation as the point of departure of the new movement, this negation

*In the year 1895, the writer of these pages founded in the rue de Provence, Paris, a center open to all the forces of artistic innovation. In order to designate the tendencies of this enterprise, he devised the title of *L'Art Nouveau,* without suspecting then that this combination of words would gain the doubtful honor of serving as a label for miscellaneous creations, some of which were to reach the limits of license and folly.

consisted solely in an energetic protest against the hiatus which, for an entire century, had suspended animation in that branch of art. Far from proceeding as Nihilists, the initiators of *L'Art Nouveau* sought beneath the accumulated ashes of

Teapot: silver; designed by Colonna

old systems the spark of that former life which had developed the arts of the people, slowly, generation after generation, from the distant cradle of human civilization down to the sudden paralysis caused by the brutal shock of the French Revolution.

Here, therefore, side by side with the departure "from a fixed point" there is a first step "toward one:" an initial agreement established in view of an "affirmative purpose," consisting in the determination not to despise the work of our predecessors, but to do what they would have done in our place: they who would never have debased themselves to counterfeit the genius of their ancestors; who would never have wished to sterilize the genius of their own generation.

But our minds being heavily burdened with old memories, how was it possible to resume the march of progress so long interrupted? Where seek a trustworthy guide? What rules were to be observed? A reversion to free Nature could alone restore and rejuvenate our spirits. From this infallible code of all the laws of beauty we were forced to ask the secret of a new advance, capable of enriching the old formulas with a new power of development. And this development it was necessary to urge forward in a manner conformable to all other branches of contemporaneous aesthetics, in a manner adequate to our form of society and our actual needs. In a word, we were forced to subordinate the general character of our environment to all the conditions of modern life. It was necessary, at the same time, to restore certain essential principles which had long previously fallen into neglect. These necessities were: to subject each object to a strict system of logic relative to the use

Brooch: gold enamel and ivory, by Marcel Bing

for which it is destined and to the material from which it is formed; to emphasize purely organic structure, especially in cabinet-making; to show clearly the part played by every detail in the architecture of an object; to avoid, as one would flee from leprosy, the falsehood of a fictitious luxury consisting in falsifying every material and in carrying ornament to extremes.

Such, in essence, are the principles which formed the basis of agreement for the initiators of the movement, whose effects, dur-

ing its active period, we are now to observe.

THE PRODUCTIONS OF L'ART NOUVEAU

IT has seemed to me judicious not to confuse the doctrines which gave birth to *L'Art Nouveau* with the applications which have been made of it. I shall protest much more strenuously against the custom of subjecting all these productions indiscriminately to a sole and summary judgment. I do not direct my protest against Professor Hamlin, nor solely against the very limited number of other writers who have treated the question: I accuse the whole body of art critics of having, in this instance, seriously failed in professional duty. In the presence of a sudden and disconcerting growth, in the face of the daily mounting flood of productions contrasting not only by reason of their novelty with familiar forms, but often also differing among themselves, the critics have left the public absolutely without guidance. The special publications devoted to applied art, which arose in great number, had no object other than to make pass in review before the eyes of the reader (it were better to say the spectator), after the manner of a kaleidoscope, in a chance order of appearance, the assemblage of all new efforts, whether more or less successful. But among those who assumed the somewhat grave responsibility of instructing the public regarding the artistic phenomena of each day, among those even who declared with emphasis that there should no longer be an aristocratic art, and that all artistic manifestations: painting, sculpture or the products of the industrial arts, had equal rank, no one assumed the duty of making a serious study of this subject,—that is, no one in position to speak with authority. *L'Art Nouveau*, it is true, if it be considered as a whole, has no cohesive principle.* It could not have such, when employing its activity upon a virgin soil, in a field where every one was bound to display his individual temperament. But in the midst of the myriad attempts whose tangled skein can not be straightened by the layman, we, the critics, point out certain efforts, each one of which in the respect that concerns it, converges toward a definite ideal, an aim clearly perceived. We say: Reject the mass of worthless efforts, eliminate all abortive work, imitations, and commercial products, but save from irreparable destruction anything that can contribute, though it were only as a very germ, to future fertility, if you do not intend to pronounce death sentence

Electric Lamp: "Porcelaine Leuconoé;" designed by Colonna

*Professor Hamlin rightfully says: "Its tendencies are for the present divergent and separative."

upon all those of our faculties whose exercise beautifies our dwellings!

It is not to be expected that I should produce in these pages an extended critical work. Not only would my militant attitude in the question prevent me from such audacity, but such an endeavor would considerably exceed the limits of the present plan. I shall content myself with making here a rapid examination of the path followed by *L'Art Nouveau:* beginning with its first general manifestation, which, as I have previously stated, occurred in 1895, in the galleries of the *Rue de Provence,* Paris.

It would be difficult to say which, for the moment, triumphed in this fateful struggle —the chorus of approval, or the cries of indignation. The fact remains that the impression then made was powerful enough to create a large following of recruits, impatient to enroll themselves beneath the banner displayed by the vanguard. Unhappily, it is much easier to submit a new order of productions to public examination than to make the public understand the reasons which governed the creation of such objects and prescribed to them their forms. The adepts of the second hour were divided into different classes. There were artists, sculptors or painters whose somewhat vagabond imagination was more familiar with dreams and poetry than with practical ideas. They designed tables supported by nymphs with soft, sinuous bodies, or by strange figures savage in their symbolism, with muscles swollen and writhing under efforts which had no sign of humanity. There were also young middle class women who abandoned the needle, the crochet-hook and the piano, that they might pyrograve leather, or hammer copper into works which were almost touching in their artistic poverty: all these being, of course, more or less sedative and too restricted in their reach to compromise seriously the good cause and prevent its progress. The dangerous evil: that which could strike at the vital part of the idea, and possibly occasion its utter failure, was to arise elsewhere.

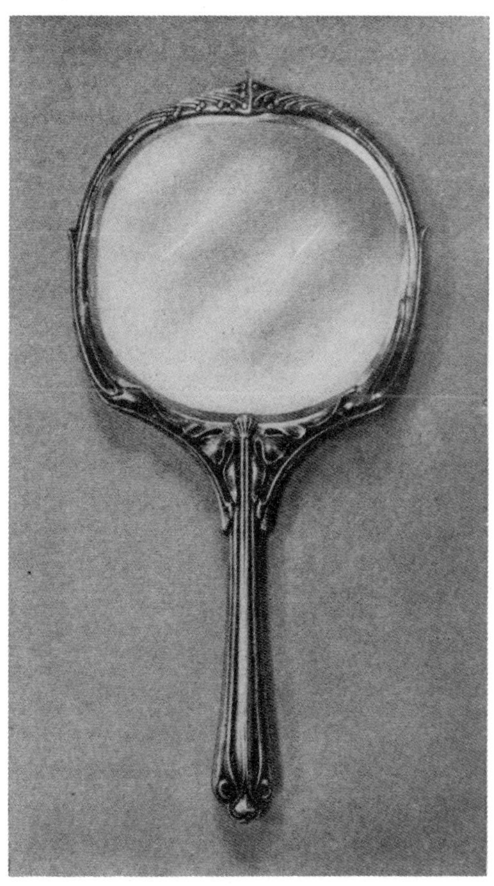

Hand-mirror: silver bronze; designed by Marcel Bing

Throughout the course of history no epoch-making idea of idealistic tendencies has ever arisen, which has not been quickly counterfeited by the army of profit-seekers who have enrolled themselves beneath its banner to protect their purely mercantile schemes. But never, perhaps, has this phenomenon been so strikingly instanced as in the case in point. Owing to the feeble state of certain industries, as, for example, that of cabinet-making, an opportunity was afforded to profit by the effect produced by the rise of *L'Art Nouveau.* But

it must not be believed that, spurred by this impulse, the leaders of industry set themselves without loss of time to a deep study of the necessary principles. Far from that! Nothing, in their minds, was more easy than to produce *L'Art Nouveau*, since that, according to their point of view, must be simply the art of improvising something else than the works of yesterday. They therefore gave the pencil into the hands of their designers with orders to trace upon the paper outlines interlacing in all directions, writhing into fantastic expansions, meeting in snail-spirals, framing asymmetrical panels within which bloomed the reproduction of some natural growth, exact to the point of photography. In fact, it was not difficult to produce *L'Art Nouveau* of this species. Nor was it costly, since it required neither preliminary studies, nor the use of valuable material, nor great care in execution. The product was abundant, too abundant, and the public, accepting the name for the thing in itself, did not hesitate to accept this product under the official title which assured its success. It need not be explained that the more eccentric it was, the more quickly it was received as *L'Art Nouveau*. I might—but I refrain—cite the instance of a museum, the most famous of its class, whose representative selected for his collections a coffer overburdened with fantastic floriated ornament, preferably to a wardrobe full of symmetrical grace; explaining meanwhile that the character of the latter piece was not sufficiently accentuated to deserve the name of *L'Art Nouveau*.

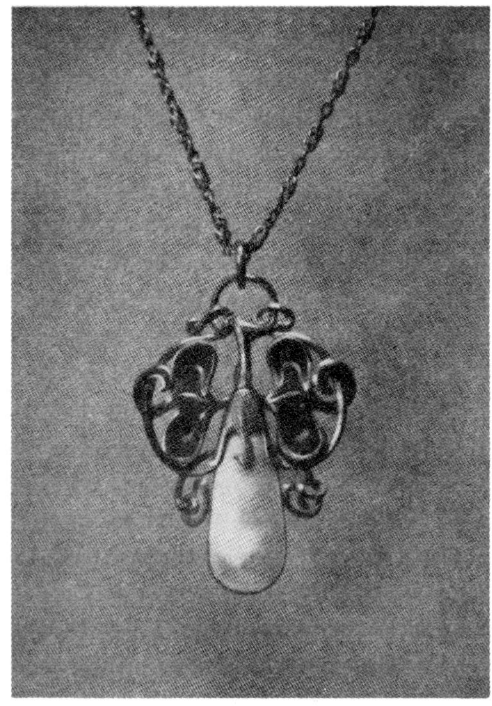

Pendant: gold enamel and pearl; designed by Colonna

But slowly, vision having grown more experienced and critical, begins to distinguish the true from the false. In the midst of the obscuring chaos, there are discernible clear ideals of art tending toward a definite purpose. The work of elimination being complete, each one will choose the species of production that shall best adapt itself to his taste, while waiting for future generations—the supreme judges of men and things—to make final classification, according to degrees of merit. Future judges will all acknowledge the indelible mark of our epoch, without it being necessary, as Professor Hamlin would desire, for all our artists to concur in an absolute identity of style, as once they did. Such freedom will leave a wider field open to the imagination of those who create, and will permit each individual to impress his personality upon the places in which he passes his life. Far from regretting this variety in the forms of expression, let us enjoy the proffered riches, and let us now seek to acquaint ourselves with the origin and the nature of these divergences as well as to compare their merit.

Two principal and parallel currents can be discerned in the direction of the movement: the system of purely ornamental lines already indicated by Professor Ham-

Pendant: gold enamel and pearl, by Marcel Bing

lin, and the system of floral elements; each of the two systems having fervent champions and active detractors. In every new cause it is well that uncompromising elements arise, exaggerating partial virtues, which later, wisely proportioned, unite in a definitive, well-balanced whole. The divergence in the first phases of *L'Art Nouveau* are attributable less to questions of individual temperament than to questions of race. In these first phases, the principal part was not played by the country which had long occupied the first place in European decorative art. France remained attached with what might almost be termed patriotic tenderness to traditions whose roots struck into the lowest depths of the soil of the fatherland.

The initial movement, as Professor Hamlin himself observes, began in England, under the influence of the Pre-Raphaelites and the ideas of Ruskin, and was carried into practical affairs by the admirable genius of William Morris. But if insurrection arose then against the frightful ugliness of contemporary productions, it did not declare the imperative need of a renewal of youth conformable to the modern spirit. Highly aristocratic natures, who would willingly have witnessed the destruction of railways guilty of killing the beauty of the landscape—such as these necessarily produced works echoing the art of primitive times dominated by the poetry of an abstract dream. They projected over the world a soft light, full of charm indeed, but which, as a distant reflection of extinct suns, could not have a prolonged existence, nor even a warmth sufficient to light new centers. This episode will remain in the history of art as an attractive chapter too rapidly closed. Latterly, England has taken a new direction under the guidance of numerous artists, the most noted of whom are mentioned by Professor Hamlin. Among them only a fraction are faithful to the Morris traditions.

To Belgium belongs in all justice the honor of having first devised truly modern formulas for the interior decoration of European dwellings.*

In the year 1894 there was founded at Brussels, under the guidance of M. Octave Maus, a society of artists designated as *La libre Esthétique*, having as its object to assemble in an annual exhibition all works of essentially modern character. This was the first occasion when the aristocratic arts of painting and sculpture admitted without blushing to their companionship the commonalty of industrial productions. Already there appeared manifestations of a

*In order not to extend unduly the length of this article, I must set aside architecture, which, it must be said, has not sufficiently acknowledged the progress of other branches of art which it should have assisted, since it had not, as leader and chief, been able to guide them by a bold initiative.

real value, the outcome of reflective minds steadily pursuing individual aims. I have always retained a most favorable memory of certain model tenements exhibited at *La libre Esthétique* by Serrurier-Bovy of Liège, who had succeeded in uniting with a low net cost all desirable requisites of beauty, hygiene and comfort. But the man sufficiently gifted to engender really bold ideas and to realize them in all the perfection permitted by their species, was Henri van de Velde, professor of aesthetics at one of the free institutions at Brussels. He executed in 1895 for the establishment of *L'Art Nouveau*, Paris, a series of interiors, which he followed by other works exhibited at Dresden in 1897, and which not only constituted in Europe the first important examples (*ensembles*) of modern decorative art, but have since remained the most perfect types of the species. This species was the development of the line—the decorative line shown in its full and single power.

The cradle of this species of art was, therefore, Belgium, the country belonging to the Flemish race, whose tranquil and positive mind demanded an art of austere character adapted to patriarchal customs: hostile to the principles of the light fancy which willingly takes inspiration from the slender grace of the flower. If, through an apparent failure in logic, France served as the stage for the first appearance of an art so little French in its essence, it was because at that time, only eight years since, there was as yet nothing beside it; no conception sufficiently mature to serve the projected uprisal which had as its first aim to sound the awakening call, while waiting to give later an impetus and aim more conformable to the national spirit.

In Germany, the situation, for several reasons, was altogether different. First, a close relationship unites the German with the Flemish character. Further, it must be recognized that Germany, long wanting in intuition, has always shown a great receptivity toward all external influences. Now, the novelty shown in the exhibits of *L'Art Nouveau*, Paris, at the Dresden Exposition of 1897, produced an impression strong enough to be echoed throughout Germany: this was the real point of de-

Pendant: gold enamel, by Marcel Bing

parture for the German *Art Nouveau*, to the development of which, van de Velde, afterward called into the country, himself contributed. Austria, who, in previous years, had madly abandoned herself to a sort of art for exportation devised by England for the use of the unthinking masses of the continent, followed, in her turn, the same path. By a kind of fatal law all imitators seem condemned to an impulse of exaggeration, which changes

Toilet Box: porcelain; designed by de Feure

into shocking defects all doubtful portions and details of the model. It was thus that in Germany and especially in Austria the insistent scourge of tortured, swollen and tentacular lines grew more and more aggravated, thus causing an abuse most harmful to the reputation of *L'Art Nouveau.* Artists of solid worth have, nevertheless, arisen in the Teutonic countries, but they have need of casting off the foreign *impedimenta* which weights their inspiration and occasions the cruel errors by which the taste of Professor Hamlin is so justly offended in presence of the works of the Darmstadt colony: a body now dispersed.

To sum up, we may say that combinations purely linear permit the designer to obtain, particularly in cabinet-making, broad and robust effects, a clear and logical structural arrangement. The reverse of these qualities, if they are formulated into intangible and exclusive rules, gives rise to a monotony which does not delay its appearance. Quickly the artist reaches the limits of his possibilities, inspiration ceases, and astonishment arises at the fact that all power was expended in the initial effort.

At such a moment it is evident that a return to Divine Nature, always fresh and new in her counsels, can solely and incessantly restore failing inspiration. In reviewing the history of the decorative arts in France, one will remark that always the artists of this country, with the exception of those of the sixteenth and a part of the seventeenth century, have had an acute sense of this truth. By receiving inspiration from these lovers of nature, the artists of our own time will accomplish each day more happily a difficult task which they alone, perhaps, are capable of fulfilling. The work before them consists in fusing into a harmonious whole the two apparently hostile principles of robustness and grace: the solid and crude art asserted by the Northern countries, and the delicate refinement peculiar to the Latin races; it consists in giving prominence to the strongest structural laws with a constant regard for practical results; but, at the same time, in banishing all heaviness of effect, all sterility of line, and, if the limits of value permit, in adding a flavor of fine elegance; it consists, in a word, in satisfying the demands of strict logic, in providing pleasure for the eye, and even in inviting the caress of the touch. Thus will France prove that, during her long sleep, she has not allowed the qualities with which Nature so generously endowed her to fall into decline.

But the influence of France will never again dominate the world so completely as

in former times. As communication between the different nations becomes easy and constant, as frontiers grow nearer, and the exchange of ideas multiplies, one may imagine each separate people as fearing lest the formidable leveling wind that is now passing over the world, seize and carry away the last traces of independence. As one retires from the great central fires of humanity, lesser flames start upward with fuller impetus and force.

We have seen Belgium set up within her narrow limits an art possessing a distinct savor of the soil, but still an art of somewhat broad characteristics. Beyond her frontier, Holland, on the contrary, engendered, a decade since, a local style extremely accentuated, revealing at times beauties too striking not to deserve mention in every study of the present movement and development. It is the more necessary to speak of these works for the reason that they are little known to the outside world. Not only does their strictly national character, strongly marked with ancestral Javanese influence, predestine them to local adaptations within the frontier limits, but it must be added that the greater number of Dutch artists show a mysterious and singular disdain for cosmopolitan reputation. There is now in Holland a large constellation of talents which deserves the honor of a monograph. But let it suffice here to cite as especially worthy of mention the names of Dysselhof, Toorup, Thorn-Prikker and Huytema.

Boudoir Chair: designed by de Feure

Mounting higher toward the North, we

find Denmark, who, beside her celebrated porcelains, has developed in all branches of her art, under the wise direction of Pietro Krohn, the affable curator of the Museum of Decorative Arts, Copenhagen, a national growth: a style extremely pure in its robustness. Still farther Northward, Sweden and Norway have participated no less ardently in the universal impulse toward a renewal of the ancient Scandinavian art, revived without essential weakening of its original character.

Cabinet: designed by de Feure

Finally, it would be wanting in strict duty to pass over in silence a similar movement of the highest interest which has been observed for several years on the extreme limits of Northern Europe: that is to say, in Russia. There, in the midst of a peasant population of primitive manners and customs, great colonies of art-workers—weavers, embroiderers, sculptors, potters, iron-workers and cabinet-makers—have been founded under the patronage of the highest personalities of the Empire. Artists of reputation—such as Monsieur S. Malioutine and Mademoiselle Davydoff—indicate the paths and the models to be followed. The enterprise is directed with unflinching activity by ladies of the high aristocracy, among whom it is impossible not to mention the Princess Marie Ténicheff, the generous founder of the remarkable people's workshops at Talachkino, and also Madame Jakounchikoff, founder of the workshops at Smolenka, in the Government of Tamboff, a lady who, with unwearying devotion, consecrates her life to an admirable task. The productions of these colonies are not repeated and unvarying copies of old Russian models, nor are they, what one could fear still more, pretentious imitations of objects more recently created in Western Europe. There truly exists something resembling a species of Russian *Art Nouveau;* for it is very new and, at the same time, thoroughly Russian. It is possible for these noble institutions to pass onward to a future of extraordinary possibilities, if no social catastrophe occur to destroy them.

I have waited until the end to acknowledge that America has already furnished a contribution to the universal efforts of our times, which is now sufficiently noteworthy and valuable to merit for her the esteem of all friends of art. To limit myself to my personal knowledge, I shall mention men like the deceased archeologist Moore, like John La Farge and Louis Tiffany, whom the old continent would have been proud to possess, and I shall point to industries like the American manufactures of colored glass, the Rookwood and Grueby potteries, which have taken equal rank with the European establishments of similar character. But the branch in which the Americans have passed to immediate mastership is in the conception and execution of objects destined for practical use in household interiors. No designers have more clearly understood that the first impression of beauty, of the most essential beauty, emanates from every object which assumes the exact character of its use and purpose.

Jardinière: pottery mounted in silver; designed by Colonna

I express the conviction that America, more than any other country of the world, is the soil predestined to the most brilliant bloom of a future art which shall be vigorous and prolific. When she shall have acquired, in the province of ideal aims, a consciousness of her own possibilities, as precise and clear as the confidence already gained in other domains of intellectual force, she will quickly cast off the tutelage of the Old World, under which she put forth her first steps upon the sunlit path of art. America, as I have already said elsewhere, has a marked advantage over us, in that her brain is not haunted by the phantoms of memory; her young imagination can allow itself a free career, and, in fashioning objects, it does not restrict the hand to a limited number of similar and conventional movements. America, taken all in all, is indeed only a ramification of our ancient sources, and consequently the heir of our traditions. But again, she has a special destiny, occasioned by the fact that she does not possess, like us, the *cult*, the *religion* of these same traditions. Her rare privilege is to profit by our old maturity and, mingling therein the impulse of her vigorous youth, to gain advantage from all technical secrets, all devices and processes taught by the experience of centuries,

and to place all this practical and proven knowledge at the service of a fresh mind which knows no other guide than the intuitions of taste and the natural laws of logic.

EDITOR'S NOTE.—The editors of THE CRAFTSMAN regard themselves as most fortunate to have been able to present in the pages of their magazine an extended and just appreciation of a great art movement, concerning which there is so little definite information among the people.

In the issue of December, 1902, Professor A. D. F. Hamlin of Columbia University offered a judgment of *L'Art Nouveau,* bearing principally upon its manifestations in architecture.

This paper excited the interest of several distinguished French critics, who, while awakened to admiration by the knowledge and justice displayed by the American writer, found yet occasion to differ with his opinion that *L'Art Nouveau* was based upon a negation and tended toward no definite aim.

This opinion was opposed in the issue of July, 1903, by M. Jean Schopfer, a Parisian authority known in the United States by his writings, as well as by his repeated appearance in the lecture-rooms of the Eastern universities.

M. Schopfer's article was a criticism of the *Art Nouveau* movement, judged from the historical point of view. It was calm, broad, logical and masterly: in every way calculated to remove the prejudice created in America by the vagaries of those whose position in regard to the movement may be compared to that of the lawless camp-followers of a well-disciplined army marching to the conquest of liberty. This second article was comprehensive in its treatment and included in its survey the decorative and "lesser arts." It was, therefore, of wide general interest, and it obtained the appreciation and comment which it deserved.

The third division of the discussion just now presented bears the signature of the highly distinguished critic and patron of art, M. S. Bing of Paris. He it was who gave the name to the latest phase of modern art: watching its development from germ to bloom; seeing abortive growths fall away from the parent source of life, and other fairer types poisoned by hostile and noxious influences; but permitted at last to witness the definite success of a persistent and healthy organism, whose infancy he had wisely fostered. M. Bing's article appeals not alone to artists and those interested in æsthetic subjects: through it throbs the pulse of that modern life which is supremely creative, and capable of reducing the ideal to the real, the definite and the practical. M. Bing has proven that *L'Art Nouveau* is neither based upon a negation, nor destructive in its aims. He gives account of his sponsorship over a young cause which, a decade since, agitated within the narrow boundaries of an old Parisian street, has since spread over the world. He makes also a prophecy for the future of art in which there is no racial exclusiveness. He shows that nothing that is artistic is foreign to him.

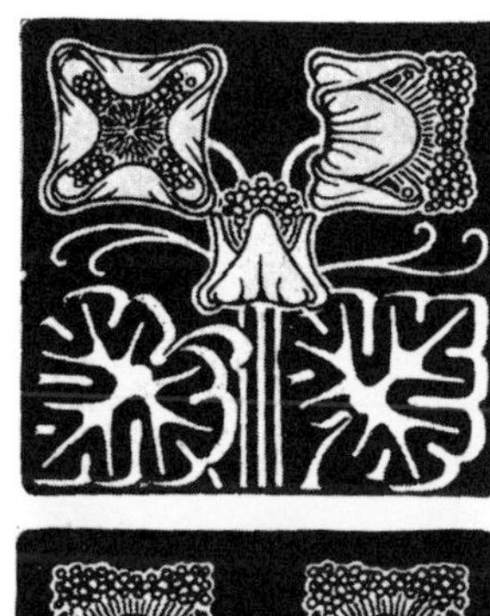

Designs by M. Verneuil

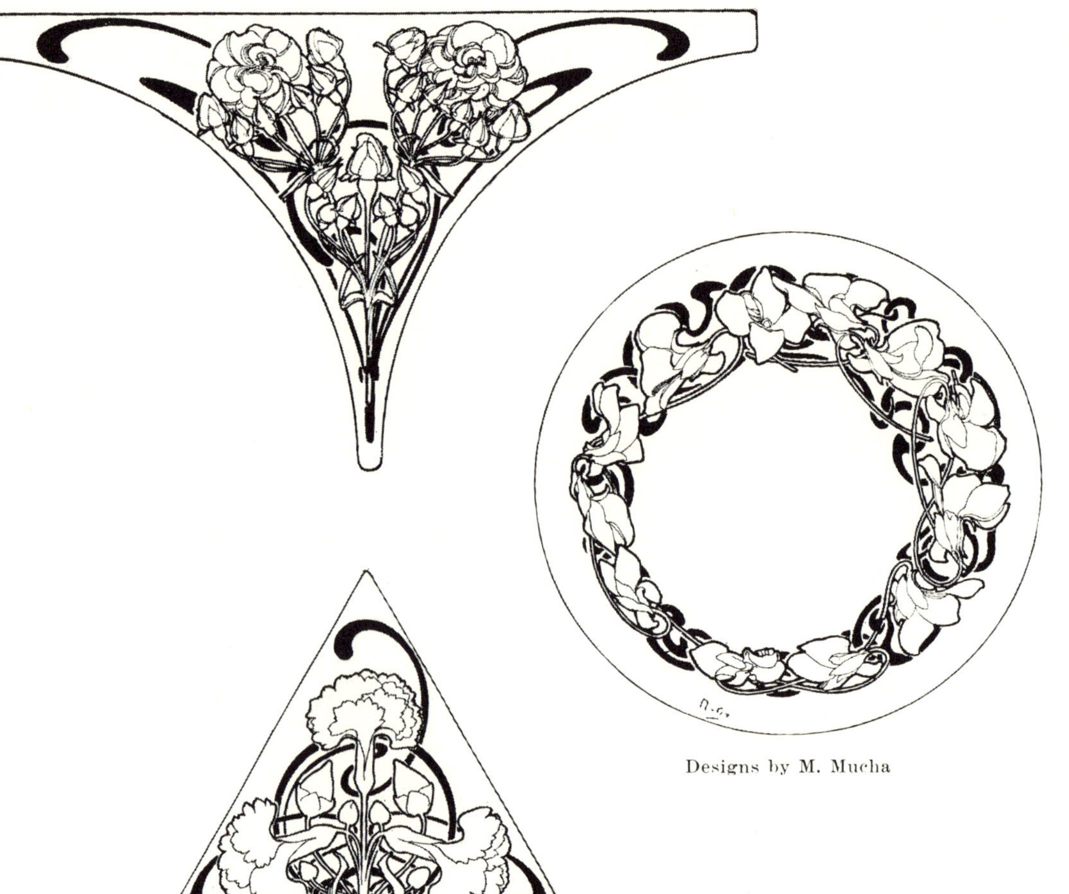

Designs by M. Mucha

Designs by M. Mucha

Design by M. Grasset

Designs by M Grasset

Designs by M. Auriol

Rooks: inlay by Voysey

ART AND THE BEAUTY OF EARTH: WILLIAM MORRIS

SURELY there is no square mile of earth's inhabitable surface that is not beautiful in its own way, if we men will only abstain from wilfully destroying that beauty of the earth that I claim as the right of every man who will earn it by due labor; a decent house with decent surroundings for every honest and industrious family; that is the claim which I make of you in the name of art. Is it such an exorbitant claim to make of a civilization that is too apt to boast in after-dinner speeches; too apt to thrust her blessings on far-off peoples at the cannon's mouth before she has improved the quality of those blessings so far that they are worth having at any price, even the smallest?

Well, I am afraid that claim is exorbitant. Both you as representatives of the manufacturing districts, and I as representing the metropolis, seem hitherto to have assumed that, at any rate; nor is there one family in a thousand that has established its claim to the right aforesaid.

Look you, as I sit at work at home, which is at Hammersmith, close to the river, I often hear go past the window some of that ruffianism of which a good deal has been said before at recurring intervals. As I hear the yells and shrieks and all the degradations cast on the glorious tongue of Shakspere and Milton, as I see the brutal, reckless faces and figures go past me, it rouses the recklessness and brutality in me also, and fierce wrath takes possession of me till I remember, as I hope I mostly do, that it was my good luck only of being born respectable and rich that has put me on this side of the window among delightful books and lovely works of art, and not on the other side, in the empty street, the foul and degraded lodgings. What words can say what all that means? Do not think, I beg of you, that I am speaking rhetorically or saying that, when I think of all this, I feel that the one great thing I desire is that this great country should shake off from her all foreign and colonial entaglements, and turn that mighty force of her respectable people to giving the children of the poor the pleasures and the hopes of men. Is that really impossible? Is there no hope of it? If so, I can only say that civilization is a delusion and a lie; there is no such thing and no hope of such a thing.

But since I wish to live, and even to be happy, I can not believe it impossible. I know by my own feelings and desires what

these men want, what would have saved them from this lowest depth of savagery: employment which would foster their self-respect and win the praise and sympathy of their fellows, and dwellings which they could come to with pleasure, surroundings which would soothe and elevate them, reasonable labor, reasonable rest. There is only one thing that can give them this, and that thing art.

Drawn by Seitei Watanabe

Wind: inlay by Voysey

Drawn by Seitei Watanabe

BROWNING'S MESSAGE TO ARTISTS AND CRAFTSMEN OF TO-DAY

BY GEORGE WHARTON JAMES

THE poet, the prophet, the seer. How often he writes in one age, far in advance of his time, the peculiar message needed for the next. Browning is gone, but his message lives. It had power and force when he wrote it. It has greater potency to-day. It is needed more to-day than then. He was no trifler with life and its duties. He was no unthinking optimist. He believed in directing natural impulses, making the most of them, getting the best out of them. In effect, he said, "We are going along well only if we get well out of our going. We need not worry about the future if we are doing our best now. But let us be sure that we are doing our best."

In "Andrea del Sarto," his great poem on the faultless painter, he preaches his powerful sermon to the Artists and Craftsmen of to-day.

Hear ye then and heed!

No one questioned the work of Andrea. Even in his own day his technique was regarded as perfect, "faultless." Pigments, canvas, brushes, lent themselves to him and obeyed his every behest. He thought and desired, and immediately his thoughts and desires were made manifest upon the brilliant and striking canvas upon his easel.

The world came and worshipped at his shrine; bowed at his feet, flattered, fêted, praised him. Money flowed into his coffers. His fellow painters envied him, congratulated him upon his godlike and perfect gifts, hated him for his supremacy over them. Yet his good will, his courtesy, his high breeding, his gentleness, in a measure won them and softened the fury of their envy, and assuaged somewhat the pangs of their jealousy. Yet, poor fellow, he felt as none of them dreamed he felt. He had a personal skeleton in his own closet, he, the happy, to-be-envied, the elect. Sadness and sorrow were his constant companions. Every new achievement in the eyes of the world was a new sorrow to himself. Every new triumph was a new failure to him.

For he felt that he did not possess that heaven-born aspiration,—desire, longing, passion,—that alone makes work worthy. With consummate art and skill Browning, the most conscientious poet of all time, reveals the painter's inner soul,—shows his secret sorrow.

"I often am much wearier than you think,
This evening more than usual."

Yes! who knows, who can know, the sorrow of the soul looking upon its own glaring imperfections, incompletenesses. And the keenness of such sorrow is the fact that it is for what the world never dreams to exist. The cry of weakness of the man who leads, like Savonarola, or Cromwell. The cry of uncertainty of the dogmatist, like Calvin. The cry for wisdom in him whom the world counts wise. The cry of inability in whom the world counts its most able.

Del Sarto knew his ability from the world's standpoint. He had seen even the critical world pass sentence on the vulgar mass called his "work."

"Things done, that took the eye and had the price;
O'er which, from level stand,
The low world laid its hand,
Found straightway to its mind, could value in a
trice."

He was no fool. He could truthfully exclaim:

"I am bold to say,
I can do with my pencil what I know,
What I see, what at bottom of my heart
I wish for, if I ever wish so deep—
Do easily, too,—when I say, perfectly,
I do not boast, perhaps."

He could compare his own work with that of his compeers. He knew well enough that when the critics praised their work they were praising his. And there was no boasting in recognizing acknowledged facts.

And he knew, too, how easily such masterly work flowed from his fingers. It was easy—there was no effort. It seemed as if everything lent itself to his moods when work was to be done. Pigments mixed easily; the subtlest colors came without thought; brushes obeyed his lightest touch. Other men struggled for years to find the right pigments, and when they thought they had succeeded, weary hours were spent in trying to compel certain color combinations which would not come, yet to Andrea these things came without thought, without struggle.

"I do what many dream of, all their lives,
Dream?—Strive to do, and agonize to do,
And fail in doing. I could count twenty such
On twice your fingers, and not leave this town,
Who strive—You don't know how the others strive
To paint a little thing like that."

Conscious power! "I do what many dream of." Dream! nay, they strive and agonize to do. "You don't know how the others strive." It is impossible to conceive the effort, the anguish, the heart-rending struggle of some souls to accomplish what to them is ideal, and yet what to others, to the Andrea del Sartos, comes so easily. And in that fact the truly humble masters exclaim with him:

"I am judged.
There burns a truer light of God in them,
In their vexed beating stuffed and stopped-up brain,
Heart, or whate'er else, than goes on to prompt
This low-pulsed forthright craftsman's hand of mine."

Yes! he knew that it was aspiration, longing, soul's desire that counted. A quarter-farthing rushlight kept as fully aflame as possible was more worthy in the great master artist's eyes than a two-penny candle guttered and flaring with charred wick. His hand was that of a "forthright craftsman," but its pulse was low. It is the high pulse that counts, the throbbing brain, the anxious, reaching-out heart, the straining nerves.

How goes it, brother craftsman of to-day? Are you a "low-pulsed forthright craftsman," content with your own achievements; self contented in the admiring gratulations of those who do not know what you feel they ought to know? Are you resting upon something found made, instead of reaching out, even though it be through "acts uncouth," to something higher and better? Rest assured if you are of the self-contented class you will never know the joy of soaring heavenward.

Poor Andrea could see that:

"Their works drop groundward, but themselves, I know,
Reach many a time a heaven that's shut to me.
Enter and take their place there sure enough,
Though they come back and cannot tell the world."

Ah, yes! The striving soul enters heaven, even though its achievement be small. God measures by effort, not accomplishment. For:

"What is our failure here but a triumph's evidence
For the fullness of the days?"

"What I aspired to be,
And was not, comforts me."

Andrea knew that though his "works were nearer heaven," he "sat here."

And where was the joy of having his works approach heaven if he himself were tied down to earth? The artist is greater and of more importance than the art. It is *he* that should be in heaven, or going thitherwards, through his art, and not his art

soaring higher than himself.

Then that cry of passionate admiration for the "sudden blood" of the striving artists:

"The sudden blood of these men! at a word—
Praise them, it boils, or blame them, it boils too."

They live intensely, fiercely, furiously. A word of either praise or blame stirs the blood to frenzy. That is life! That is to abound in life! Oh, for the quick, living, pulsing blood, the pouring stream that flows, flows swift, fast, strong.

Andrea knew the difference between them and himself:

"I, painting from myself and to myself,
Know what I do, am unmoved by men's blame
Or their praise either."

But he lacked the fire, the life, the all-abounding vigor and aspiration that stir the soul to its deepest depths and make its highest flights possible. He could do what he desired, what he willed, but was that enough?

"Ah! but a man's reach should exceed his grasp,
Or what's a heaven for?"

Then read his mournful criticism of his fellow painter's work. In technique imperfect, in detail faulty, it yet possessed the greatest quality of all. As Andrea could see, this imperfect draughtsman "poured his soul out that heaven might so replenish him." An arm here is wrongly put, the body is wrongly drawn, but,—and here is the important point,—*the soul is right.*

"He means right—that, a child may understand."

Andrea could alter the arm and make the body's lines perfect, but "all the play, the insight and the stretch," the passion and the creative power were not in him. Poor Andrea! And that power comes alone of love. Love, love, love, love is the moving, the creative, the godlike power.

To the Artist and Craftsman, Browning should ever be an inspiration. His three poems, Andrea del Sarto, Abt Vogler and Rabbi Ben Ezra should be, by them, learned by heart and recited daily. Like a cold bath to the body they tone up the nerves of the soul, quicken the inner pulses and stimulate them to higher endeavors, and more god-like achievements.

Design by M. Simas

Rodin The Waves

Rodin . The Metamorphosis

A PLEA FOR THE DECORATIVE BOOK-PLATE. BY FRANK CHOUTEAU BROWN

A distinct change in the artistic quality of book-plate designs is very evident in those which have been produced within the last few years. Even in more conservative and older countries, the designed book-plate has been given more and more attention by modern artists of repute. The result is that to-day no more beautiful designs are executed in any branch of artistic endeavor than some of those made to decorate the books in private libraries.

When starting out to secure a book-plate design, many people make the mistake of overburdening it with all their family history, or of trying to express through it the manifestations of a widely varied life. Either their ideas are too fully, if somewhat vaguely, formed—when it is practically impossible for another individual to make a satisfactory interpretation of them in pen and ink, or, having no ideas at all, they are

unable to make even the few appropriate suggestions that will allow the artist to incorporate something individual into the design.

It is best to strike a mean between these two extremes. Then, the designer will learn more or less about his client's individual fads or fancies, something of his personality and family, as well as the kind of books and the things in which he is interested, possibly his business or occupation; while, at the same time, the designer, for the best result, should not be too closely restricted.

The book-plate need not express anything of the bookish quality;—it is not absolutely necessary that it should show a book, or books, a library, or anything of the sort. This is an error that seems, however, to have acquired a very wide acceptance, and is undoubtedly a survival, even

though an unacknowledged one, of old-country conservatism. The plate itself need not be "bookish" in subject, but it must have somewhat of this quality in its treatment, in order to fit it for its place and purpose. The label should express individuality, if only by differing in some essential from the conventional design, and the desire for a "bookish plate" tends to restrict the problem to too narrow and ordinary a field.

Again, and finally, the only excuse and reason for being that we can give to the modern book-plate is its decorative quality. It must be so designed that it will become an appropriate part of any book. It is rarely indeed that any drawn design is seen so frequently as the book-plate must be, by the person possessing it, and it must be so carefully considered that it will meet the test of constant use and never become tiresome. So, at the end, we discover that the book-

plate is, after all, but the outcome of the desire of the individual to possess an attractive symbol,—something that is personal to

him in its meaning; and that the revival of interest in the "Ex Libris" is but another instance of the awakening consideration

given by the people of the present day to good printing, to the decoration of houses, the designing of furniture,—the general

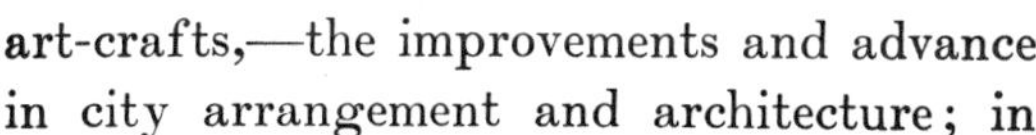

art-crafts,—the improvements and advance in city arrangement and architecture; in short, that broad movement in the arts that has distinguished the beginning of this

century, and which may be regarded as the first evidences of an artistic renascence too long delayed.

Sun's Disc: Guatemala

A BIT OF AMERICAN FOLK-MUSIC ❧ TWO PUEBLO INDIAN GRINDING SONGS. ❧ BY NATALIE CURTIS

I STOOD beneath the dazzling blue sky of New Mexico. Around me rose the white walls of the Indian pueblo, Laguna. The Indian women were returning from the railroad, whither they had gone to sell their pottery to the passengers of the Santa Fé. I watched them as they trod the rocky trail in single file. It seemed impossible to believe that this bright bit of picturesque life was American. The brilliancy, and indeed the whole suggestiveness of the scene was oriental. The women carried earthen jars upon their heads and trays of smaller ware in their hands. Their skirts were short above the knee, and their legs were heavily swathed in buckskin: a time-honored protection against reptile and cactus. Over the head was thrown a bright shawl which hung to the bottom of the short skirt like a mantle.

The people of Laguna came early under Spanish influence and have been nominally Christian for three hundred years. But the Indian has woven into the Roman Catholic faith the bright strands of native custom and belief. For the old rain-dances are still held on the plaza, even before the square church. But what the Spaniard failed to do, the American is now accomplishing, the stamping out of "all things Indian": the deliberate crushing of every spark of native pride, the killing of a people's aspiration toward the good, the true and the beautiful in any direction other than the Anglo-Saxon.

I knew and loved the Indians of the Hopi pueblos in Arizona: a refined and gentle folk, as full of instinctive courtesy as the Japanese. I found their music and poetry to be of a high order of development. I had come to Laguna to observe how far the music of the Mexican pueblos was tinged with Spanish influence. I had hoped that these people, like the Hopis, would sing as they left their village in wagons to load wood, or as they returned from a day's work in the fields. But alas, the spirit of this pueblo seemed crushed. The poet is a day-laborer on the railroad, the potter makes cheap cups to sell to the tourist. Art, the expression of man's joy in his work, as William Morris has it, is fast fading away, and the natural utterance of a healthy people, the unconscious burst of song, is almost stilled. More and more do the lives of these Indians become silent and colorless.

The sun was bright, but my thoughts were shadowed. Was there, then, no spontaneous bit of music to be heard among these people?

Suddenly a voice rose high and clear, and at the same time I caught the rhythmic scraping sound of the grinding-stone. Some woman near at hand was grinding corn and singing at her work. It

is the custom of the pueblo Indians to grind the corn between two great stones. One is a slab which is set into the grinding-trough at a slight angle. The other, cube-like, is rubbed by the grinder up and down over the corn upon the understone, with much the same motion that we use in rubbing clothes upon a washboard. The grinding-troughs, two, and sometimes three in number, are set into the floor of the house. They are simply square frames to hold the understone, with gutters on each side of the stone and at the base, for the scooping up of the corn, and as a receptacle for the ground particles.

As the women grind, with rhythmic swing, they sing. And the sweet, unusual melodies with the high scraping accompaniment of the grinding, make a music as phantom-strange to unaccustomed ears as are, to the eye, the lilac mountain-peaks and tinted desert wastes of New Mexico.

The voice sang on and I turned to seek it. I made my way through the little street with its terraces of roofs. The song seemed to come from the upper section of a square white house. Led by the sound I climbed a ladder to the roof of the first story, which was at once the floor and balcony of the second. At my coming the song ceased, and instead I heard a rapid whisper: "Aico! Aico!" (American, American). I paused at the open door of this upper chamber that led upon the roof. Outside all was blue sky. Within were coolness, emptiness, bare whitewashed walls. Two pueblo women knelt at the grinding troughs; the younger grinding the corn to finest powder, the elder sifting the ground meal through a sieve. They laughed shyly as I entered and sat down with them.

Who was the singer? At the question the elder pointed to the girl at the grinding-trough. The maiden flashed a smile as I asked her to repeat the song. Silently she bent over her work. A few swift sweeps of the grinding-stone and then, as though born of the rhythm, the clear voice rose once more.

As the girl swayed over her work, her glossy black hair hung straight before her face, shielding her sweet shyness from the stranger. These women part the hair across the middle of the head, tying it behind with a woven band, and allowing the front part to grow so long that, unless swept to one side and twisted behind the ear, as is the custom, it would fall over the face to the chin.

The girl paused at the end of her song, and laughed softly behind her loosened locks.

"Tell me what the song means," I said, turning to the elder woman, who had been to school and spoke English.

The two conferred together in their own tongue, then sought to tell me of their song.

"It is about the water in the rocks," said the elder. "After rain the water stands in the rocks, and it is good fresh water—medicine

water. And in the song we say: 'Look to the southwest, look to the southeast! The clouds are coming toward the spring; the clouds will bring the water.' You see, we usually get our rains from the southwest and the southeast. That is the meaning of the song; but it is hard to tell in English," she faltered.

Then again the maiden sang.

"And this song is about the butterflies, blue and red and yellow and white, telling them to fly to the flowers. At the end of the song we say to the butterflies: 'Go, butterfly, now go, for that is all!' "

Then said I: "I shall write these songs on paper, just as you have seen songs written in books in the schools. Then people will know that Indian songs are beautiful, and the songs will never wholly be lost, or forgotten."

The girl's eyes grew large. But the elder woman said slowly: "Many songs are forgotten. Our people do not sing as they used. I do not hear the songs I heard before I went to school."

"And these songs you have sung for me, are they new?" I asked.

"No, they are old," she answered. "The words are old words, words we do not use in talking now. I heard these songs when I was little. I think they must be very old."

"Do not forget them," I said, "and teach them to your children!"

But the woman only gazed before her, dull and sad.

What use, indeed, in the face of the crushing present to preserve anything of the past for a lustreless and alien future?

But my heart held the hope that these songs, reverently recorded, might one day be given back to their original creators by Americans who will find some beauty in the true life of a people whom we strive to educate, but never seek to know.

The Craftsman Building

THOUGHTS OCCASIONED BY AN ANNIVERSARY: A PLEA FOR A DEMOCRATIC ART BY GUSTAV STICKLEY

AS ONE earnestly devoted to a movement in which I have the utmost faith, and to which I have given the best of my life and energies, I am emboldened to advance certain arguments which I believe to be sane and tenable. This I have chosen to do at a milestone of my efforts: that is, on the anniversary of the birth of The Craftsman, in which, for three years, I have endeavored to express my personal, specific views—often laboring under the difficulty of fitting a first conception to a tangible, practical reality.

The plea which I am about to make is one for simplicity in all that pertains to the environment of material life under a democracy, where practically all work with either hand or brain; the leisure class being reduced to a minimum.

I was led to my present position of thought by my observations and experiences as a cabinetmaker, arriving at many of the conclusions of William Morris, but reaching them from a direction opposite to the one taken by that great benefactor of society, who was first a thinker and afterward a craftsman. For while I advanced slowly from the fact to the principle underlying the fact, he reasoned broadly from the cause to the effect.

At first, in obedience to the public demand, I produced in my workshops adaptations of the historic styles, but always under silent protest: my opposition developing, as I believe, out of a course of reading, largely from Ruskin and Emerson, which I followed in my early youth. More and more did I resent these imitations which, multiplied to infinity, could not preserve a spark of the spirit, the vivacity, the grace of their originals. Yet even this lack of life was not for me their gravest defect. As I saw them growing beneath the hands of my workmen and afterward displayed in the shops, they did not appear to me more out of place in these, their temporary surroundings, than they did in their final destination, the homes of the people. Everything was there against them. They fitted into no scheme of life, or of decorative art capable of being realized by the persons who had acquired them. Sometimes, indeed, a pretentious, scenic background was prepared for them, but in such cases with what seemed to me a pitiable result of unreality. They had the air of being placed upon a stage, and of awaiting the use and occupancy of persons who, in rented costumes and under assumed names, should recite studied parts.

My impression deepened into a conviction after a European jour-

ney which I made in the interests of my craft. Then, for the first time, I saw the French styles in their proper surroundings, acting as integral parts of palace architecture, as at Versailles; as well as these and all other historical types arranged in their proper sequence at South Kensington, precisely as specimens once having had organic life, are classified in a Museum of Natural History.

In presence of these visible objects, the course which I had long wished to follow, shaped itself clearly before me. I returned home strong in my new faith. I reasoned that as each period is marked by some definite accomplishment or characteristic, so each period must also have its peculiar art; since it is art that holds the mirror up to life and catches its perfect reflection.

In France I had seen a republic attempting to patch with a workman's blouse the old rents made in the web of society by monarchies and empires. In England I had witnessed everywhere the power of the middle classes, in comparison with which the effete nobility appeared as a relic of the past, a pageant as antiquated as the Lord Mayor's Show. In America, as I looked about me with a clearer, keener vision than ever before, I recognized that the salvation of the country lay also with the workers, rather than with the possessors of hereditary culture, or of immense wealth and the power attendant upon it. I realized that the twentieth century, then a few years distant, was to be, like the thirteenth, distinctively an Age of the People. Then the judgment—justified by facts—of a certain critic, upon the work of William Morris, rose in my mind with the compelling force of a battle cry: "He changed the look of half the houses in London, and substituted beauty for ugliness all over the kingdom."

This statement assumed for me the character of a revelation in which the socialism of the reformer clothed itself in a mild, beneficent aspect, expressing the true meaning of the word; becoming a work pursued peacefully for the good of his fellows: a socialism of art—art made homely and brought within the reach of all.

I resolved to make a radical change in the productions of my own workshops, and not to be deflected from my adopted purpose by either obstacle or disappointment.

In making preparations for my new departure, I found others setting out with objects similar to my own. This was to be expected, since the germs of revolution never concentrate in a single locality or a single brain. Reform was in the air, seeking soils favorable to its development.

I resolved to join no factional band, however companionable it might be, in whose members the cause had generated that heat of enthusiasm which is all too liable to produce abortive efforts. I further resolved that I would never again be an imitator, and I set my face toward absolute radicalism. At that time, the revulsion toward simplicity created in America the so-called Dutch, Tyrolean peasant,

and Mission styles; while from the other side of the Atlantic ripples of influence reached us: from France, Belgium, and from Japan as misunderstood by the Europeans. The shop windows of our large cities began to display ill-assorted collections of cabinet-making, ranging from the heavy to the fragile; in many cases showing no understanding on the part of their designer of the physical qualities of the material used; since bamboo was translated into wood, and attempts were made to render the delicate pliableness of plant-stems in a hard, resisting medium.

In these collections I saw plain evidences of anarchy, instead of an impulse toward reform. If such examples showed the marks of their release from the rule of the historic styles, they had effected but an exchange of tyrants. They had bartered the tyranny of order for the tyranny of chaos. The modern movement, lacking concentration, squandering its energies upon new imitations, was in danger of defeat and annihilation.

I began to seek remedial measures for adoption in my own workshops. As I thought more closely upon this subject, most important to me; as I studied from both practical and historical points of view, I became convinced that the designers of cabinet-making used their eyes and their memories too freely and their reasoning powers too little. Studying their methods closely, I saw their hands mechanically tracing upon drawing paper familiar lines which recurred to them when they formed the mental picture of a chair or table. For the most part, they too indolently accepted tradition. They did not question or think.

By this means of observation, I was led to the only course of action in which I saw development for myself and future good for my workmen. I cast aside my traditions, forgot the formulas which I had learned years previously, and began to study structural principles; finding them, as I proceeded, the same in architecture, as in the lesser building art of cabinet-making. From the careful examination of the Gothic cathedral I first learned thoroughly the relations between construction and decoration: finding the best examples of the great mediaeval style adequately ornamented by features, which, like the flying buttress, gave them strength and support; finding also the decadence of the art in later specimens wherein these same features were allowed to exceed their functions, and decoration, like a parasitic plant, spread over the fabric to sap and undermine its foundations.

I thus clearly recognized the dangers of applied ornament and advanced a step from which I have never retrograded. I endeavored to turn such structural devices as the mortise and tenon to ornamental use; to employ them in such a way as to force them to give accent and variety to the outlines of the objects in which they occurred.

This lesson of constructive *versus* applied ornament, derived from the Gothic, was supplemented by one of another and yet allied nature,

which I found awaiting me in classic architecture. The Greek temples revealed themselves to me as the plainest examples of the structural style. Their plan is a concept of the primitive man, and, even in their most advanced stage of development, the timber construction, so to speak, is never obscured. The columns, with their fluted shafts, recall more vividly than words can do, the boles of forest trees with their grooved bark. The frieze, with its alternate ornamental markings of vertical lines and circles, is but an allusion to the first type of temple, when planks, set on edge, and tree-trunks were hastily assembled to form a sheltering roof over the god, the treasure and the worshipers. In these edifices, however late the period of their erection, the structural quality is never lost, never even greatly obscured to the eye. The principle of construction involved is a question of weight and mass, and from its skilful treatment results a whole, simple enough to be included in a single glance and conveying an impression of harmony and repose. To sum up, one may say that these buildings, accepted as types of beauty by many centuries and civilizations, were primitive—almost crude in plan; that in them the structural idea persisted to the end, clear and dominant; that they were developed and embellished by subtile modifications of line, by the use of beautiful color and diversified material, by ornament arising from necessities of construction and appearing therefore spontaneous and fitting.

Fortified by this second object lesson, I determined to adhere strictly to simplicity of plan; to express construction frankly; above all, to be modern: a resolution which here requires a word of explanation. In order to illustrate my meaning, I will take the example of a bed. This object, when modeled for decorative effect, I often saw raised on a daïs and surrounded by heavy draperies; both of which features are relics of a past time serving no useful end, and being opposed to advanced ideas of cleanliness and health. They formerly protected the bed from cold and dampness; isolating it from its surroundings and creating a focal point of comfort and warmth. Historically, it is interesting to trace the development of this idea of isolation from the cupboard beds of the Brittany peasants up to the great couches of the French monarchs. But the idea has lost its practical value and the devices have no longer a reason for being. The modern bed, on the contrary, should be constructed with a recognition of the necessity of pure air and of the curative power of sunlight.

The principle of this extreme example I found paralleled in the greater part of objects modeled after old types. For this reason I came to regard with distrust any design which suggested historical development. I sought structural qualities only; choosing rather to be reproached—although justly—for crudity, rather than to set out upon a path which could lead nowhere but to the old commonplaces, even though the way should be long and circuitous. But this crudity, as in the case of the temple construction, I regarded as a mere point

CABINET MAKING IN FUMED OAK, BUILT UPON THE SIMPLEST STRUCTURAL LINES, AND DEPENDENT FOR DECORATIVE EFFECT UPON THE COLOR AND SURFACE TREATMENT OF THE MATERIALS EMPLOYED

of departure from which to develop in certain legitimate directions.

Having now thoroughly assimilated my two lessons: the one relating to plan, the other bearing upon the relations of structure to ornament, I recognized that I had made real progress in my efforts, while I also realized the seriousness of the difficulties which yet lay before me. But I did not falter or waver. The very crudity of my structural plan, as I apprehended it, was to me a proof of its vital power, as well as of a promise of progress, because *formlessness* never follows hard upon crudeness; because also decadence is the natural sequence of over-refinement.

The greatest of the problems next demanding my attention was how I might afford gratification to the eye, while remaining faithful to my newly adopted structural principles. I felt that the solution of this question lay largely in the proper use of color, but the means to attain this end were not ready to my hand. They awaited development, which was tentative and slow, owing to reasons which I shall explain.

As a cabinet-maker, I was bound to obtain my color-effects largely from wood, aided in some instances by leather and textiles: all of which materials had yet to be adjusted to my structural scheme and thereupon dependent ideas of decoration.

As an American by birth, I chose to work with native growths. I felt the possibilities of our forest products to be great, and I wished to experiment with them; following a desire as spontaneous as that obeyed by the East Indian who carves into designs like wrought iron his heavy, close-grained teak-wood. To speak with all modesty, I determined to treat my chief material by an educative process: in other words, to draw out in it all the potential qualities which I knew it to possess.

One thing I had greatly in my favor. My structural lines made no demands upon the wood which it was not able to meet. They emphasized growth and grain, instead of thwarting them at every turn. They showed that the material was cut and suggested no idea of molding, which should be left to the metal worker. But in order fully to accomplish my object, a long series of experiments confronted me, which now, at the end of several years, I count as only fairly begun. Still, within a comparatively short time, I gained results which more than encouraged me. Through the careful preservation of grain and the development of surface qualities, there resulted beauties which softened the asperities of my outlines: arresting the eye and thereby preventing it from a too rapid seizure of the structural scheme of small objects; by the same means, also, prolonging the interest of the observer and the gratification of his sense of sight. The woods, so treated, invited upon their surface a constant play of light and shade, infinite and never repeated, in studying which I experienced a previously unknown delight, made up of reminiscences of the forest and of

pictures of masters. Encouraged, or rather inspired by this success, I resolved to limit myself to the use of such woods as lay nearest to my use, and to devote much of my energy to expand their qualities and heighten their value. At the same time, my antipathy increased toward the glazes which conceal and obliterate the exquisite work of Nature; actually violating the substances created by the Divine Intelligence and perfected by cycles of years. I realized that the cabinet-maker should receive his material reverently and touch it but to reveal and continue the mysterious and beautiful operations begun in secret, when the wood was yet a living tree.

Having arrived at this point of my labors, I saw attractive glimpses of a path far beyond. My thoughts rose from the lesser to the greater of the building arts. I realized that, in our country, new materials await use and new thoughts development. A youthful enthusiasm for my expanded scheme possessed me, and I reasoned as a moment of exaltation might permit:

"Since the genius of the American is structural, as is proven by his government, his control of natural resources, his mastery of finance, let the building art—the lesser as well as the greater—provide him with surroundings in which he shall see his own powers reflected. In the appointments of his dwelling, let the structural idea be dominant, and the materials employed be, as far as is possible, native products, in order that the scheme may be unified and typical—above all, democratic."

My enthusiasm remained with me, lapsing into a steady courage which tided me over all disappointments. I felt that I was serving the people, in company with many others in various walks of life whom I saw preaching, teaching and practising what I venture to call the gospel of simplicity. In speaking thus strongly, I trust that I shall not be censured as one who over-estimates his own ability, or yet as narrow-minded and wishing to establish one standard of life and art for all sorts and conditions of men. I recognize individuality, the direction given to thought and taste by specific education, the influences exerted by high culture: I admit all these to be beneficial to society. I furthermore acknowledge that luxury and simplicity are comparative, rather than absolute terms, and that they must be judged with the care and seriousness demanded by a question of law. I desire to make clear that I am not constituting myself a critic, or arbiter; that I do not question the conduct or the aestheticism of those whose training, accompanied by wealth, permits them to choose and acquire beautiful objects which, rich in suggestiveness—both artistic and historic—increase for their possessors the pleasures of life. Such persons as these, it is unnecessary to say, are outside the circle of my observation and beyond the need of service other than their own. They constitute a favored minority. They are cosmopolites in the

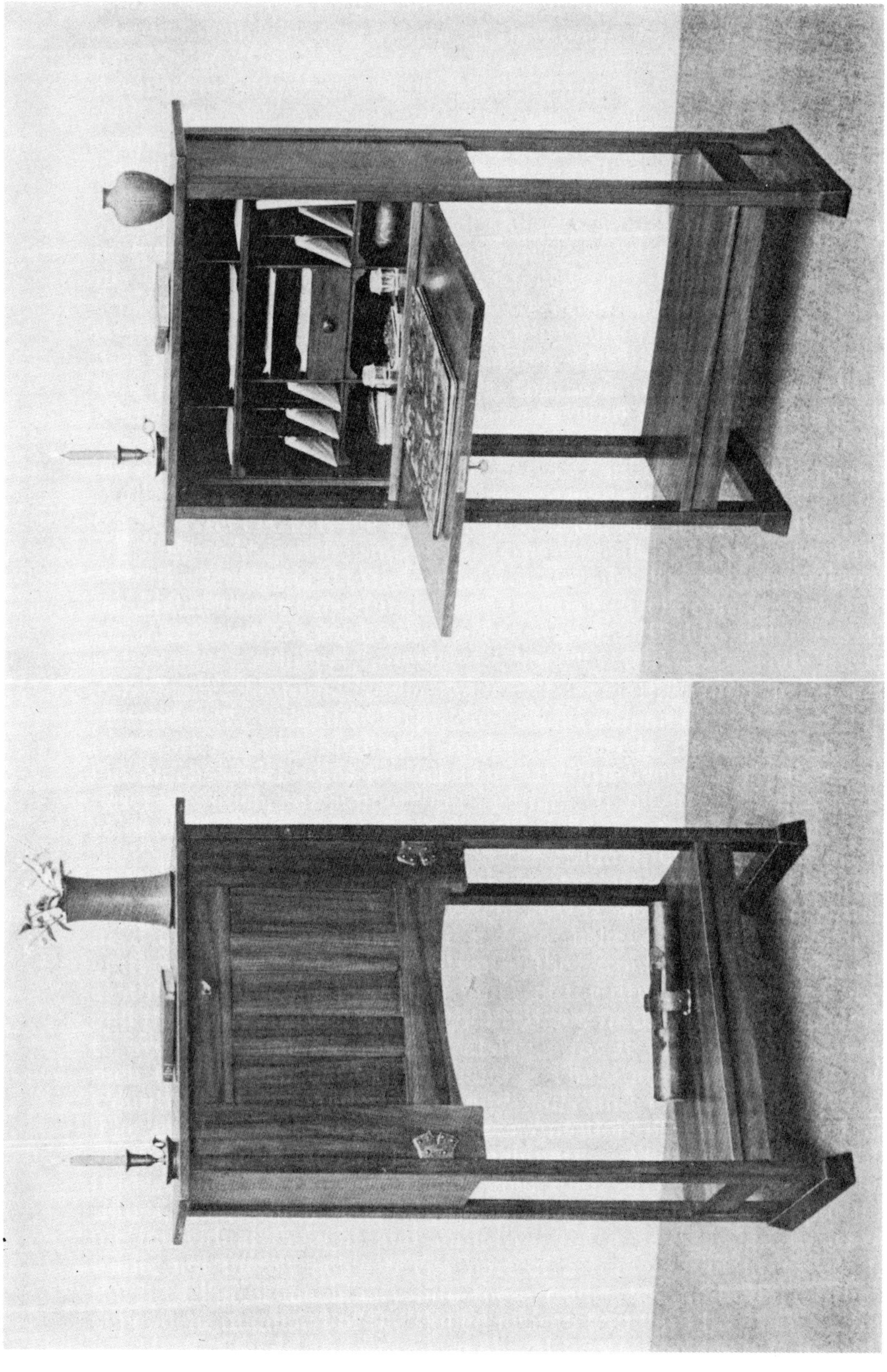

HAZELWOOD DESK (OPEN AND CLOSED), IN WHICH THE SLENDER PROPORTIONS AND SHARP PROFILE ARE CAREFULLY ADAPTED TO THE DELICATE COLOR EFFECTS OF THE WOOD

true sense—citizens of the world—and entitled from their experience to hold broad views of art and life.

But they in whose interest I make my plea for a democratic household art, constitute the majority of our American people. They are the busy workers, "troubled about many things:" professional people; men and women of business; toilers who reach out after objects of beauty and refinement, as if they were the flowers of a "Paradise Lost." They are the real Americans, deserving the dignity of this name, since they must always provide the brawn and sinew of the nation. They are the great middle classes, possessed of moderate culture and moderate material resources, modest in schemes and action, average in all but in virtues. Called upon to meet stern issues, they have remaining little leisure in which to study problems of other and milder nature. But as offering such great and constant service, these same middle classes should be the objects of solicitude in all that makes for their comfort, their pleasure and mental development. For them art should not be allowed to remain as a subject of consideration for critics. It should be brought to their homes and become for them a part and parcel of their daily lives. A simple, democratic art should provide them with material surroundings conducive to plain living and high thinking, to the development of the sense of order, symmetry and proportion.

This plea is certainly inspired by a practical idea, for aesthetic influences are daily gaining wider recognition as factors of usefulness. It is acknowledged that form and color appeal to the senses with imperious force, which is the more compelling because of its very silence. Words are forgotten in their rapid succession; the impression of personal contact wears away; but a significance exists in the individuality of material things which is comparable with human character. We are brought into daily relations with people whom we feel to be honest, inspiring, depressing, or dangerous. Their influences upon us are inexplicable and subtile, but yet they direct and compel us toward good or evil. They give us pleasure or pain. It is the same with material things. To illustrate the influence of structural form, we have but to revert to the two great examples which I have already used: the Gothic architecture, with its pyramidal effects, uplifts us and sweeps us away, as it were with a flame of enthusiasm; the Greek, on the contrary, settles us in our surroundings with a feeling of reliance and ease, as we note the harmony, the delicate balance, created by its verticals and horizontals. It matters not whether these principles are shown in large or in small, in open-air, or in interior architecture. Indeed, the small things are always with us, they are our constant companions, not too good for "human nature's daily food," and, therefore, we are subject to them. Non-structural objects, those whose forms present a chaos of lines which the eye can follow only lazily or hopelessly, should be swept out from the dwell-

ings of the people, since, in the mental world, they are the same as volcanoes and earthquakes in the world of matter. They are creators of disorder and destruction. The shapes of things surrounding the working members of society should carry ideas of stability and symmetry in order to induce a correspondence of thought in those to whose eyes they present themselves. They should not picture the world in a state of flux.

The tranquil environment demanded by work and thought, and supplied by art is admirably exemplified in the mural painting of Puvis de Chavannes, in the amphitheatre of the Sorbonne, where the figure of the lecturer, projected against the straight, slender boles of the trees of the Sacred Wood assumes the charm of mystery and thus makes willing listeners of the students.

In taking leave of this branch of my subject I can not too strongly insist upon the influence of material form over mental mood, as inspiring hope, courage, good humor and their attendants, or, on the contrary, as generating the opposites of these lubricators of the wheels of life. I insist that the people and, above all, the children of the people, should be afforded the advantages of a democratic art: one that should insure the comfort and the beauty of their homes and by this means decrease the resistance which they unconsciously make against their surroundings. To accomplish this much-to-be-desired end, the school and the workshop must unite their forces. The public schools must teach art practically: analyzing form and structure, treating them for their own sakes, and not as matters of historical development. The workshop must give the practical demonstration of these principles in the products which they send out, and thus an educative process will be furthered which, in the end, can not fail to create a public as sound in judgment, as just in criticism, as were the Greeks, the Florentines, the French, German and Flemish burghers of the Middle Ages: a result inevitable in any country or period in which art is truly democratic.

But I must not omit to add an earnest plea for the education of the color-sense, as yet undeveloped to a regrettable degree among the people. This sense it is which makes the poor man rich to abundance; for riches, rightly understood, are but the possession of the faculty for enjoyment. The eye to be soothed, or to be excited to pleasure, has but to turn to the outside world. It is thence that the art which seeks to be educative, must draw its lesson, rather than from the secondary sources provided by the sciences of physics and chemistry. And once again for a precedent we must turn to Puvis de Chavannes, whose retina was said to be developed beyond that of any other known individual of the nineteenth century. For that reason his color-combinations appeal less strongly to the eye of the peasant than those of the other modern French masters of decoration. But in his selections the teachings of Nature may be read as in an open book. His dark verdure-tones, so prominent wherever he laid his hand to a wall,

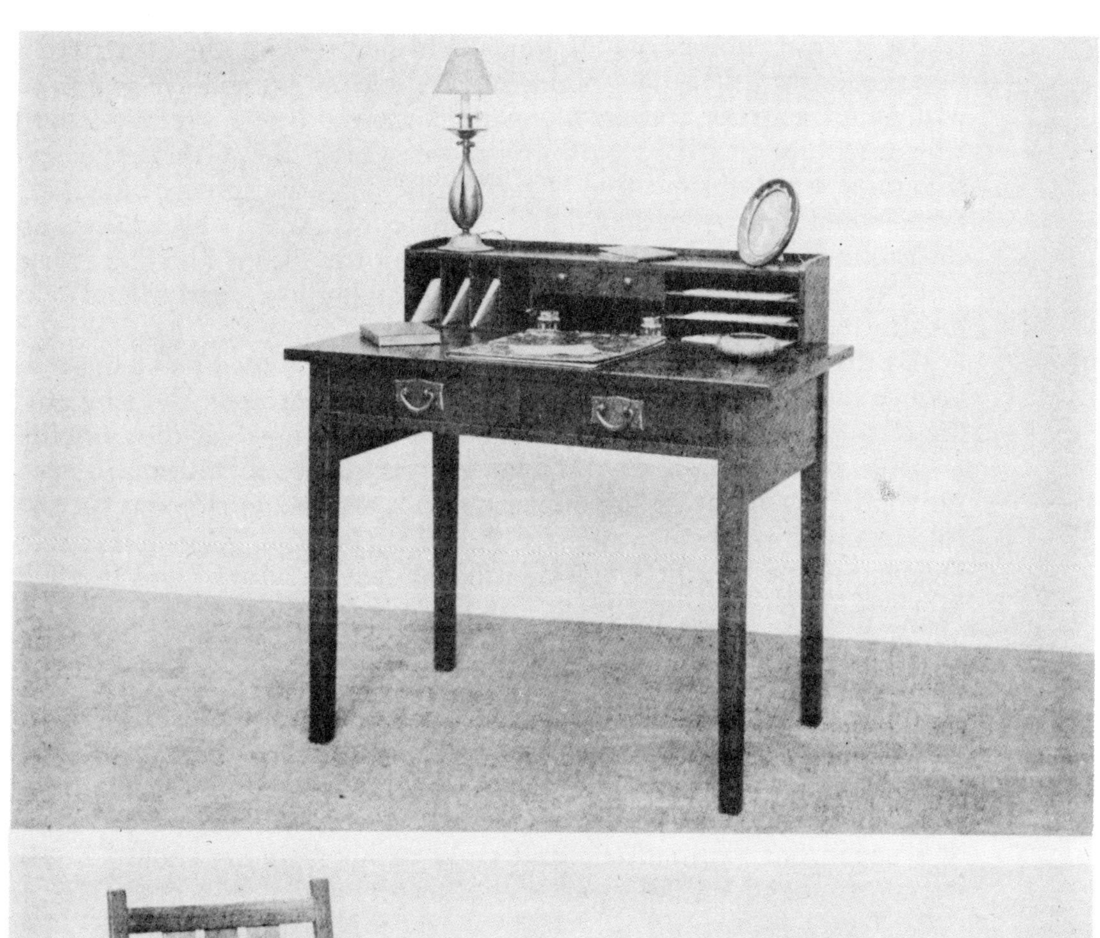

CABINET MAKING IN FUMED OAK, BUILT UPON THE SIMPLEST STRUCTURAL LINES, AND DEPENDENT FOR DECORATIVE EFFECT UPON THE COLOR AND SURFACE TREATMENT OF THE MATERIALS EMPLOYED

repeat the intention of the Universal Mother, who clothed the trees in that same color, that they might soothe the tired human eye and brain with what a great Italian has named their "divine green silence." The air-blues of M. Puvis are those which the Greeks did not recognize as color, since they regarded them as atmospheric effects due to mass and density, rather than to inherent quality. His violets are such tones as pass absolutely unnoticed by the infant and the savage who, at the sight of reds, are provoked to laughter and seized with the desire of possession.

By this illustration I have sought to explain to how great a degree I believe the success of democratic art is dependent upon the educative use of color. And further, as a proof of the sound basis of my belief, I will point once more to William Morris, whose revolution in decorative art, regenerating not only England, but the world, was successful largely through his refined use of the gamut of color-notes. Refinement in the specific sense, like that shown by Morris and Puvis, is urgently demanded among us for the advancement of art, and the more complex refinement of the English craftsman will be, perhaps, the better guide, until we shall have simplified our vision sufficiently to enjoy the primitive refinement of the French painter. But let the work be hastened! Vulgarity in color cries out with strident voice from public and private interiors, from the workshop, and the window of the merchant. To substitute for this harshness the clear, pure note of a beneficent, sympathetic and truly democratic art should be the strenuous purpose alike of artists, educators and producers.

IT may appear that I have abandoned the plain tale of my experiences to wander widely in the field of speculation. But in so doing I have sought only to indicate the benefit which personally I have derived from my self-appointed lessons, and to express my belief that were the principles underlying them diffused among the people, they would accomplish much moral and aesthetic good. I may further acknowledge that this very desire led me to found The Craftsman, in October, 1901, when my experiments in my own craft had reached a stage of development which permitted me a degree of leisure. As I set myself to prepare the initial number, it seemed most fitting to me that this should be devoted to William Morris, whose example of courage in radical and lonely experiment had sustained me through the trials of my modest undertaking. Therefore, this number appeared as practically a monograph dealing with the patron saint of "integral education" from the different points of view of art, socialism, business affairs and friendship. By this publication I sought to honor an abstract principle in which I was interested to the limit of my energies and resources, as well as to pay homage to one of the strongest Anglo-Saxon heroes of the nineteenth century.

In the succeeding number it remained for me to satisfy the claims

of a more personal and intimate gratitude. I therefore devoted the second issue to an appreciation of John Ruskin, the writer whose exaltation, or rather, divine madness, awakened within me, in the days of my early youth, ambitions to which I have never proved recreant.

Having liquidated these moral debts, I felt myself free to proceed to develop the magazine from a monograph to a periodical composed of writings which, while diversified in both subject and treatment, should yet offer a consistent, unified whole; which should teach the lessons, in my judgment so desirable to propagate, without trace of fatiguing pedantry. This scheme I found difficult to realize, and my new enterprise, although one of my most cherished undertakings, weighed heavily upon me. For while, in my craft-experiments, my work and myself were the only factors with which I had to deal, I had here to struggle with the unknown quantity of the public. But indications quickly proved to me that my premises were correct ones, and that I was again advancing, although with necessary slowness, to the solution of another self-set problem. Worthy exponents of modern thought and of the new art acknowledged the sincerity of my efforts by offering to lend their names and pens to the columns of The Craftsman; while the press and the public were quick to apprehend the trend of my labor as an aspiration toward a democratic art. Especially may this be said of numerous eminent educators who have aided me with their wise counsel, as well as of artists in general, and of the officers of public and private cultural societies, one of whom, as a labor inspired by enthusiasm and friendliness, prepared the scheme for the articles upon certain phases of municipal art, begun in the issue of January, 1904, and to be continued until the end of the year.

A discussion of the wilful and somewhat dangerous tendencies shown by the modern decorative art of the continent, opened early in the life of the magazine by Professor Hamlin of the architectural department of Columbia University, attracted much attention abroad; the very sponsor of the term "L'Art Nouveau," M. S. Bing of Paris, deeming the arguments published of sufficient weight to demand his own explanation of the origin and significance of the movement.

Upon occasion, liberal space has been devoted to illustrations and descriptions of the smaller and finer objects of industrial art; as, for example, the jewelry of M. René Lalique, who by force of his genius, has placed himself among the first artists of France, and whose productions are honored in the Gallery of the Luxembourg side by side with the most celebrated modern canvases.

Thus, while gradually increasing the number of the classes of subjects treated in the magazine, I have sought to do this strictly in accordance with my first idea of the enterprise: for, at the beginning, my purpose was to publish any writing which might increase public respect for honest, intelligent labor; advance the cause of civic improvement; diffuse a critical knowledge of modern art, as shown in

its most characteristic examples chosen from the fine, decorative, or industrial divisions; advocate the "integral education," or in other words, the simultaneous training of hand and brain; and thus help to make the workshop an adjunct of the school.

Throughout the existence of The Craftsman I have sought with great zeal, unflinching purpose and perfect modesty, to benefit the people. In the future I shall not relax my efforts.

I DO not want art for a few, any more than education for a few, or freedom for a few. No, rather than art should live this poor, thin life among a few exceptional men, despising those beneath them for an ignorance for which they themselves are responsible, for a brutality that they will not struggle with rather than this, I would that the world should indeed sweep away all art for awhile, as I said before I thought it possible she might do; rather than the wheat should rot in the miser's granary, I would that the earth had it, that it might yet have a chance to quicken in the dark.

WILLIAM MORRIS IN
"THE LESSER ARTS."

THE BEAUTY OF UGLINESS, BY ERNEST CROSBY

IN my former papers I have shown that the nineteenth century was the century of ugliness, and that the labor-saving machinery which it gave us in exchange for the beauty of life degraded the workman without really adding materially to the happiness of the consumer. Some of my readers and critics have called this pessimistic, and so it would be, if I had intended to stop there. But pessimism is the root of optimism and you have to be thoroughly persuaded that things are in a bad way before you are willing to set to work to improve them.

And if I have said that the nineteenth century was ugly, I have not said that ugliness was an unmixed evil, for it is not. There is a beauty in ugliness; in fact, the greatest of all beauties, for ugliness usually tells the truth, while beauty is often a liar. The worst sin is hypocrisy and ugliness knows nothing of this. Anything which is ugly at heart ought to look ugly on the surface and has no business to look otherwise. All that we have a right to ask of a face is that it should honestly represent the soul behind it. It is a mistake to whiten sepulchres or battleships. It is their duty to look grim and forbidding. Corruption should be inscribed on the front of the one, and hatred on the other. A slaughter house should have a crude and cruel architecture, recalling the iron age, and when I saw last week the plans of a beautiful building (erected to the memory of an innocent baby, too!), devoted to the torture of animals in the name of science—falsely so-called—it was clear enough to me that here artists and architects had been prostituting beauty to evil uses.

The nineteenth century was guilty of no such subterfuge. It felt the ugliness at its core, and it did the best thing that it could under the circumstances: it let it come to the surface. If it had tried to conceal it, keep it in, and to look pretty notwithstanding, it would have died the death. It is better to break out in ulcers than to let the poison ferment within. Outside and inside should match, and the outside of the nineteenth century, its devastated forests, its black and bleak mining

regions, its slums and factories and polluted streams, were merely the outward and visible signs of inward and spiritual disease. The real trouble was that men were harboring a false ideal of life, and it broke out in eruption all over the surface of things. And now with the surface of things ugly, it is harder than ever to cultivate beautiful, sane and healthy ideals again, for ugliness begets ugliness. I have seen villages in the South which were clearly designed as the background of lynchings, and it is a labor of Hercules to be and to act more beautiful than your environment.

And yet this is the one obvious thing to do. We have never suffered from lack of energy, and the preaching of strenuousness was never more out of place than in America, but we have had low ideals, and the preachers of strenuousness have nothing better to offer us. Our ideal has been to get something for nothing: to reap the forbidden fruit of the tree of others' labor; to rise (or rather to sink) from earnings to income; to seek an "independence" in absolute dependence upon the toil of others; and to shave a profit from the hire of the laborer. Our northern woods have fallen, not for the house-builder, but for the timber-speculator. Coal mines are worked, with an eye, not to the hearthstone, but to the dividend. Railways serve the stockholder and not the traveler. The nineteenth century slaved and slaved, not because things were useful or beautiful, but because they paid. It never cared at all what it was doing, but only for the reflex action upon the doer. Its God was the market, and it built its cities not to live in, but to rent. It is easy to see that such a false motive must be disastrous to all beauty and to all art. Once admit that you are making a thing merely to sell, and you open the door to every commercial villainy. Make it to use, and, at once, all the muses hover about you. The peddler who cried: "razors to sell," and when told by a customer that his razors did not shave, answered that they were "to sell" and not "to shave"—is a good symbol of the nineteenth century. If the twentieth is to be any better, we must go to the root of the matter and set up a new ideal. Profit-mongering, which is nothing but gambling with our workmen as counters, must cease, before the world can begin to be beautiful truthfully, and before art can be anything but a hollow, mincing lie.

"THERE are two books from which I collect my Divinity; besides that written one of God, another of His servant Nature, that universal and publick Manuscript, that lies expans'd unto the Eyes of all: those that never saw Him in the one, have discovered Him in the other."

SIR THOMAS BROWNE.

THE BORDER ANALYZED AS A DECORATIVE AGENT. FROM THE FRENCH OF A. GRASSET, TRANSLATED BY IRENE SARGENT

A THEORETICAL study of ornament can be very useful to the decorator; at the same time, it may interest the lay lover of art, by disclosing to him the laws of composition. It will further reveal all the difficulties which must be conquered by the designer.

With the intention of fulfilling the valuable ends just mentioned, a selection of notes is here offered, drawn from an exhaustive preface written by M. Grasset for a volume of decorative borders recently published, which is destined to render the most important services to the public.

GENERALITIES

Every border serves to bound a plain or a wrought surface, in order to emphasize its general form. When, as upon a vertical wall —for instance, that of an apartment—the border runs only above, near the ceiling, and below, directly over the baseboard, the decorative feature serves as a modulation leading to the ceiling, at one extremity, and to the moldings at the other. But when a border completely surrounds a surface, as, for instance, that of a dish, it emphasizes not only the edges of this object, but it may further constitute its only ornament; becoming then a true frame.

The elaboration of the border is made proportionate to that of the ground; the former part always exceeding the latter in richness, and often projecting itself upon a perfectly plain surface.

Generally speaking, the border consists of three parts: first, the field destined to receive the ornament and occupying the greater part of the space; second, the listels, which are rectilinear bands, simple or multiple, limiting the field on either hand, in the direction of its length. The listels placed at the exterior boundary of the field are

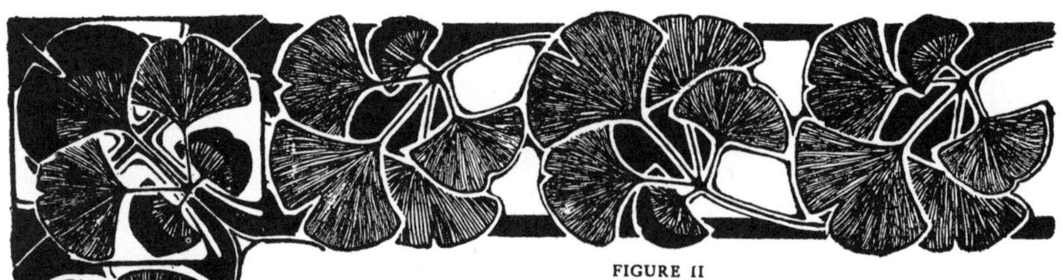

FIGURE II

more numerous, or more important, than those which define it against the ground, and take the name of *talons*. The *talons* are also called *galons* when they themselves receive decoration.

But borders are not always enclosed between listels, and, quite often, especially when they are executed in painting, their inner portion, contiguous to the ground, need not be limited by these bands of enclosure. In this case, the principal field upon which the ornaments are displayed, is the background itself. Only, if this solution were accepted, the border would show a disagreeable thinness, unless the ornaments were thickly distributed. Therefore, a background is carefully prepared in a tone approaching that of the ornament, which gives the required effect of solidity. For it must not be forgotten that the principal essential of a border is to bound and to limit sharply. Now, experience has shown that when the background is light, the field of the border should be dark, and that when the ground is dark, the field of the border should be light. This is a truth more often misunderstood than one would suppose possible, and not seldom a superb border fails to produce an adequate effect, because this principle has been ignored in its composition.

FRIEZES AND VERTICALS

An important question lies in the sharp distinction which must be made between borders and friezes. The latter, in general, possess horizontal elements only, and can not be turned about. In a frieze, the artist is at liberty to use his imagination; but, if the reproduction of the frieze is to be executed by mechanical means, the adjustment of the parts must be kept in mind, and the subject chosen must not be so striking that its frequent repetition becomes fatiguing. On the contrary, it is preferable to adopt a certain similarity of surface, color, and effect, which scarcely reveals the recurrence of the *motif* at the point of juncture.

Again, a distinction must be made between borders and verticals. As their name indicates, the latter can not be used except in a single vertical situation. Their composition precludes them from being set horizontally, or turned upside down. Their use, like that of friezes,

is limited, and they can not be repeated in a great number of mechanical reproductions, except in the case of the walls of a room which, having a plain surface, may be decorated at fixed distances. These perpendiculars should be accompanied, at top and bottom, by one or two special borders with a defining listel or a joining *motif* determining, in this instance, the width of the intervening spaces.

FIGURE III

INDETERMINATE BORDERS

If friezes and perpendiculars are subject to no other conditions than those which have just been indicated, it is otherwise with the border. The latter, playing a more modest and more usual part, fulfils its best use when it may be placed equally well, above or below, at the right or the left; having these characteristics, it may be called an indeterminate border.

The composition of borders of this class is restricted in possibilities, although it can be effected in several ways: first of all, by the simple repetition of the same, or similar *motifs,* having no direction; but a very definite balance may be obtained by the alternation of equal *motifs,* if their axes are perpendicular to the two edges of the border, and if the *motifs* are symmetrical upon these axes. However, the *motifs* are not necessarily attached to the listels which limit the field, and it is possible to employ systems of juxtaposed and alternate curves having no connection with the listels. Further, use can be made of a waved line, in the concaves of which may be placed *motifs* having no top or bottom; or an all-over pattern may be employed, set in an order which is exactly repeated, as is shown in Figure VII. It is seen that the axes must always be perpendicular to the length of the border; then, the *motifs* placed upon the line B. C. (the axis) will be cut into two equal parts; the whole design being contained in the triangle A. B. C. A good example of reversible border occurs in Figure I., in which the floral design is equally effective, if it be turned top downward.

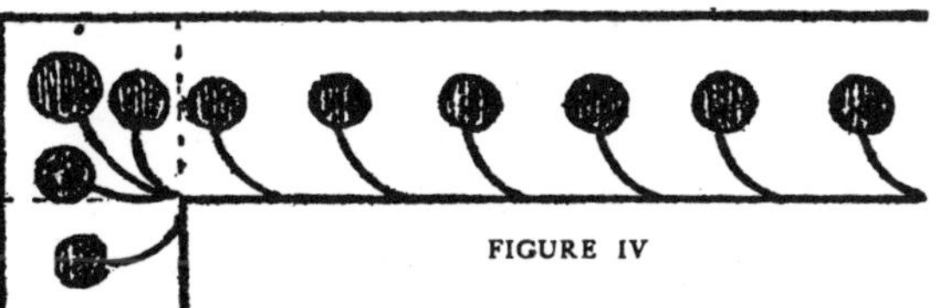

FIGURE IV

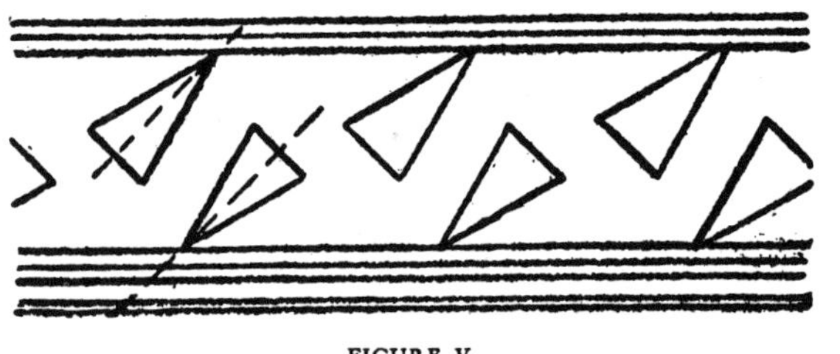

FIGURE V

CONTINUOUS ALTERNATING BORDERS

Next to the borders which we have just noted, alternating designs are the most practical, for the exact alternation of the *motifs* gives them a perfect equilibrium in a direction in which they appear to proceed, or rather, to run.

If we consider regular and equal *motifs* placed upon oblique axes parallel to each other, their alternation will be perfectly balanced. These *motifs* would produce a reversible border, if the inclination of the axes did not occur in an opposite direction for the vertical and for the horizontal border; and, further, if account being taken of the exterior of the surface so bordered, the *motifs* were not ascending on the right, and descending on the left, or vice versa, as is often the case.

FIGURE VI

Contrasted oblique axes will give the same result, whether the lines are straight or curved. (As an example of the first condition, see Figure XI.) In the balance of a subsequent figure, there is noticeable a line or movement, of which the festoon is a type. (Figure IX.) This line can be materially absent, and yet make its presence felt beneath very thick ornaments, composed simply of alternate *motifs.*

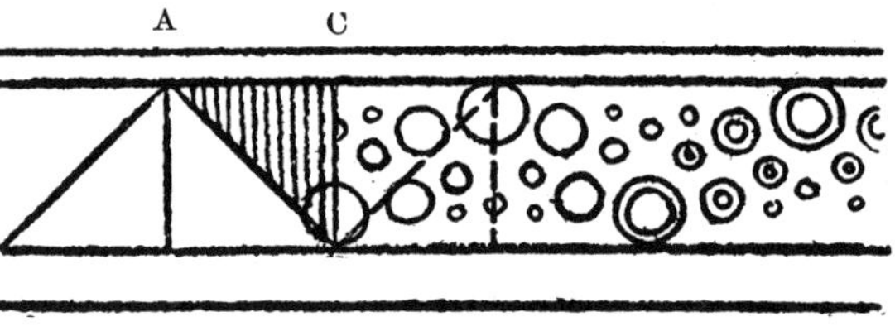

FIGURE VII

In borders of this kind, if the listels are equal and there is no *talon,* it will be possible to place them at the right and the left of the space to be framed, under the form of ascending *motifs* having the same direction. The two horizontal directions may then be the same, or they may be opposite, as is indicated in Figure XIV.

FIGURE VIII

To a certain degree, these alternating borders may be made similar to those of the reversible class, if care be taken to balance the principal elements upward and downward; the attachment only of the *mo-*

tifs will then proceed in a non-reversible direction, and the less visible the attachment, the more available will be the border. Thus, if in Figure III., the upper border is a good example of alternation, we must not forget that it demands a symmetrical opposing *motif,* because of a black ground filled above and exteriorly to the left. But nothing would be easier than to treat the other side similarly, so as to be able to place the design horizontally or vertically, without having recourse to its symmetrical correspondent. In the case of a border upon paper hangings, it would be easy to turn it upside down, upon its axis or axes, in the middle of the panel to be bordered, and thus to obtain a perfectly balanced effect.

FIGURE IX

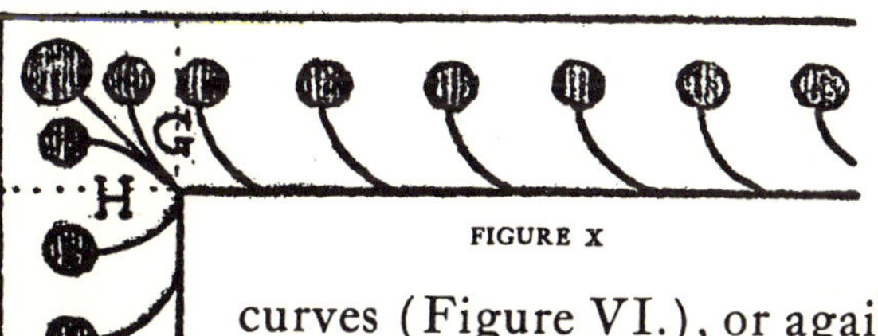

FIGURE X

Alternating borders can therefore have their *motifs,* either grafted upon the two listels, as in Figure XII., or formed of juxtaposed curves (Figure VI.), or again, of modulated curves (Figure VIII.). But it is preferable to dissimilate as much as possible the course of the movement, in order that the design may be easily reversible. (Figure XIII.)

UNILATERAL BORDERS

Beside alternating borders, there are unilateral designs which in themselves form a characteristic division. Of the latter two principal classes may be distinguished: those which, composed like the alternating borders, vary the alternated *motif,* and offer balance sufficient to make them easy to use; and those in which the two borders differ greatly in importance and composition. The latter are reversed to the right, if they run to the left; but the effect may be corrected by the addition of opposing *motifs.*

A large proportion of unilateral borders may be reversed without injury to the design, upon condition that the side destined to edge the ground be always turned toward the latter. But, as borders are not always applied to vertical walls, there are cases in which a unilateral design is not only permissible, but rather required, as is true of borders upon plates, tables, table-cloths, and the like.

If the unilateral border becomes such that it can be placed only in a single position, it is then a frieze properly speaking, and re-enters the class first treated in the present article.

DIAGONAL BORDERS

True diagonal borders are less frequently used than others, and are designed especially for execution in painting (Figure XV.). In such rendering, the stencil pattern can be reversed for a diagonal border having an opposite direction. But the inclination must be the same, for if there is a vertical *motif,* as in Figure XV., this condition becomes necessary; but if, on the contrary, the *motif* is composed of a single pattern, the inclination, as well as the inversion, is ineffective. But all alternating borders may be used as diagonal patterns: the latter being specialized only by the presence of vertical *motifs.*

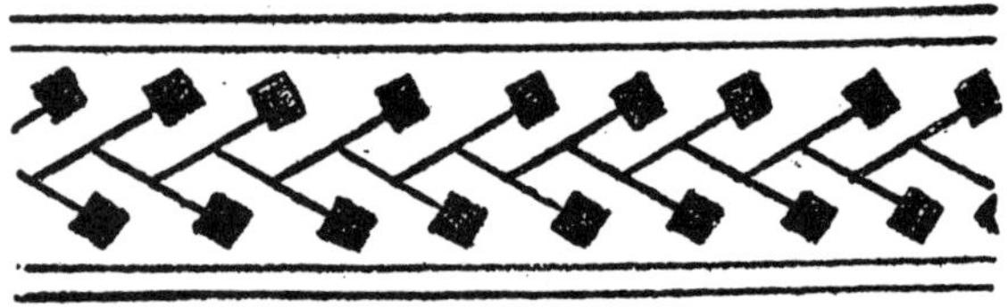

FIGURE XI

FIGURE XII

CIRCULAR BORDERS

Any straight border can be easily adapted to a circle by a change which slightly contracts its inner side. A necessary precaution is to establish the whole number of divisions within which each *motif* or unit will be contained, and if there are alternating borders, there must be an even number of divisions; so that the adjustment may be normal, unless the two alternating *motifs* are contained in a single division. This observation has its usefulness, when both sides of a stencil plate are used. It must be noted also that each circular surface to be bordered, requires a stencil-plate adapted to its radius.

ANGLES

The question of the angle is one of the most difficult existing in the entire subject of borders. The problem varies, according as the border is composed of two separate designs, symmetrical one with the other, or again if it be simple, and run in a single direction. The first problem is very easy to solve; the second is much more difficult, but, at the same time, of much greater commercial importance.

A principle resulting from experience, requires that the angle *motif* of a border be more important than that of the running portion, and that the angle be accentuated exteriorly: a precaution without which the border would have no character.

In commercial designs which demand economy

FIGURE XIII

of drawing, the problem becomes somewhat difficult. If we construct a regular *motif* upon an oblique axis, in an alternating or a unilateral border, there will be a difference in the breadth of the backgrounds which separate the *motifs* of the border from the ornament of the angle, as is shown in Figure X., in which the void H is noted as larger than the void G, and the angle *motif* no longer appears to belong to its border. The best means to employ is to incline the movement of the supports of the angle *motif* in the same direction as those of the running border, attempting to provide the angle with *motifs* proportionately stronger and more numerous (Figure IV.).

It is useless to formulate any rules concerning borders without fixed direction, since they can be cut at any point between two units of design; the only essential condition being that similarity of form shall exist between the angle-*motif* and the units of the sides. An observation applicable to all borders, concerns especially those showing an ornamented background, the which must adjust itself also to the background of the angle, without leaving the juncture visible.

FIGURE XIV

In designs subjected to mechanical reproduction, sometimes a special case occurs. This is when the ground and the border are woven separately to be adapted to each other in different lengths and widths. In this case, if the border is very ornate and quite broad, it will be composed of two principal and different *motifs,* repeated at short and regular intervals, and arranged so as to adjust themselves together at an angle of forty-five degrees; thus forming a new *motif* composed of the two halves of the other two. The place of the *motifs* is regulated by the width of the breadths of the background material, which can include one or several, and the adjustment of the angle is thus always exact. These two *motifs* can be designed with the greatest freedom, on condition that a line at an inclination of forty-five degrees, in a direction symmetrical for each of them and bisecting them, allows a perfect adjustment. The background will be occupied by running ornament subjected to the same rule. Here, the limited space at our disposal forbids us to establish an exact formula regulating the distance between the two *motifs;* but the beautiful antique oriental borders, composed of large animal *motifs,* are the best models from which modern art can seek its inspiration, although it must express

itself in new formulas. Further, in antique art, which has produced so many marvels, we find splendid examples of borders in which all the principles which we have barely indicated, attain full development. For this reason, any designer wishing to create something comparable with the old work, must have studied the latter thoroughly and patiently sought the beauty contained therein, the like of which can not spring full-grown from the brain of the greatest genius. Thus in oriental borders, always very simple in principle, and, for the most part, belonging to the alternating system, we note the use of a festoon rather simple in detail with somewhat wide *motifs* which cross at the curves and prevent a too easy reading of the plan. When these *motifs* are derived from animal forms, viewed from the long side of their silhouette, the directions of their lines are put in opposition, in order to produce a satisfying balance.

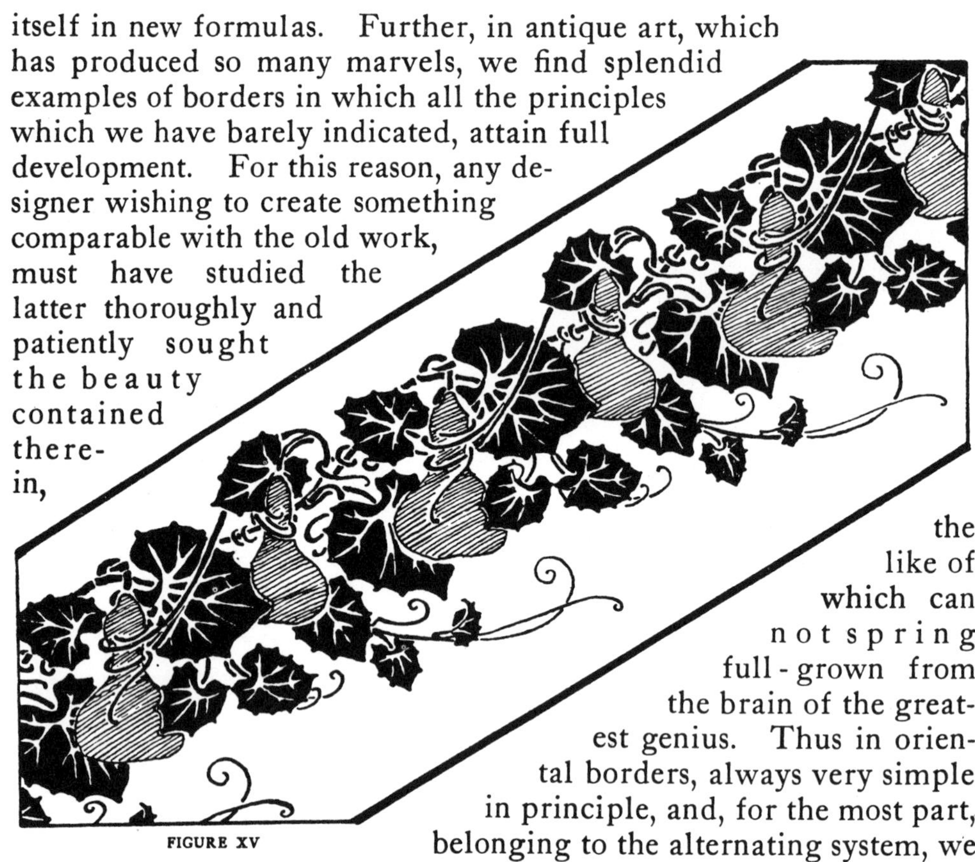

FIGURE XV

Beyond this richness, there remains a more modest field to be cultivated. This is that of pure ornament, too much abandoned to-day for exact natural forms, which quickly weary us, because they permit no play of fancy. These considerations appear very ambitious for simple borders, but they apply to all departments of decorative art.

Finally, a fact plain to all decorators must here be noted: namely, that a design must be accurately adapted to the material in which it is executed. For example, decorative glass, incrustation, *repoussé,* require numerous "simplifications"; while sculpture and painting demand enrichment; stamping and weaving require strict conditions of execution and economy for a repetition of the same *motifs;* while the sculpture of frames and tapestry-weaving allow a variety limited only by the proper balance of lines and of *motifs.*

The tapestries of the Renascence period and of the seventeenth century have bequeathed us the finest borders ever designed, and it would be difficult to surpass their sumptuous effects. These borders

are often composed of great garlands of flowers, mingled with the most pleasing ornament; at other times, the flowers are mingled with figures, which form *motifs* at the angles. But always there is observable a regular repetition of the same masses in which all the details are different, while the centers, above and below, are occupied by special *motifs* designed to receive inscriptions. It is evident that, if such borders can serve as models for painted decoration, they are not adaptable to industrial purposes.

The subject which we have here treated is susceptible of ample development, but in the present article we have taken but a succinct glance at the laws governing the composition of borders; limiting ourselves to the most essential conditions.

—From Art et Décoration, for November, 1904.

A MONOGRAPH ON MONOGRAMS

The monogram should be carefully made, of a striking pattern, a mark which one can feel is a credit to his taste, and that can be taken as a decorative *motif* in the ornamentation of all sorts of things. It was the decorative value and common use of heraldic devices which makes us regret so keenly the decadence of armorial art.

HOME TRAINING IN CABINET WORK. PRACTICAL TALKS ON STRUCTURAL WOOD WORKING. FOURTH OF THE SERIES

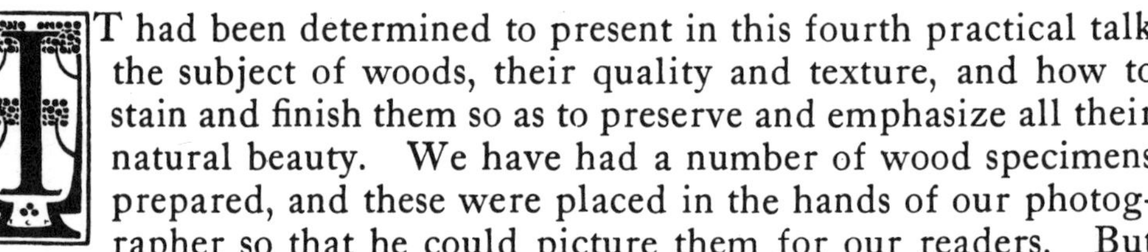

IT had been determined to present in this fourth practical talk the subject of woods, their quality and texture, and how to stain and finish them so as to preserve and emphasize all their natural beauty. We have had a number of wood specimens prepared, and these were placed in the hands of our photographer so that he could picture them for our readers. But he has found the task rather more difficult than he supposed, owing to our insistence that the grain and texture of the wood shall be clearly shown. He promises success in later endeavors, hence we are compelled to defer our "wood talk" until the next issue.

While these are to be practical lessons in actual wood-working I deem it of the highest practical importance, even thus early in the series, to give a few suggestions on "Individualism in Design." It is well for the beginner to work from good models designed for him, and to do his work thoroughly and well. But it is equally good for him—and far more important in the end — that he begin to look around at the source of all inspiration, Nature, and think for himself to the end that he create his own designs. A copyist can never be a real artist, no matter what the field in which he works. He may have the greatest ability in the world to alter and change and combine, but if he seeks for his inspiration solely from what some one else has done, he is a copyist and not an artist. It is what we do ourselves, of our own impelling, that is of value to us.

In cabinet making I would suggest the fullest exercise of this free spirit. Think for yourself. Design to meet your own demands. Work out problems of your own. Don't do things in a certain way because other people do them, but because you have decided that that is the best possible way. If you can see a better way go ahead and try it.

Yet here it is essential that one most important principle be not overlooked. Remember this. Never do a thing unless something definite justifies it. Don't follow your own whims, any more than you follow those of other people. Do things because they need to be done. Let your design grow out of necessity. Many of the most strikingly artistic and beautiful things that have come down to us out of the past were made simply because the creators met each difficulty in a masterly way as it arose. In other words, they did nothing without a reason. So should you discipline yourself, that everything you do has a clear reason therefor in your own mind.

It must also be distinctly understood that the proper preparation for this freedom, both of the mind and in design and work, can only come to full fruition by compelling your hands to obey you in doing whatever you have undertaken. Do not think for one moment that you can do good individualistic work, until you have demonstrated that you can copy so that the sternest critic must commend what you have done. Bliss Carman never wrote a truer thing than when he said: "I have an idea that evil came on earth when the first man or woman said, 'That isn't the best I can do, but it is well enough.' In that sentence the primitive curse was pronounced, and until we banish it from the world again we shall be doomed to inefficiency, sickness and unhappiness. Thoroughness is an elemental virtue. In nature nothing is slighted, but the least and the greatest of tasks are performed with equal care, and diligence, and patience, and love, and intelligence. We are ineffectual because we are slovenly and lazy and content to have things half done; we are willing to sit down and give up before the thing is finished. Whereas we should never stop short of an utmost effort toward perfection, so long as there is a breath in our body."

Now that is something worth writing out and hanging over one's work-bench. It is on a line with St. Paul's: "I have fought a good fight," or Robert Browning's emphatic words, where in the preface to his poems he says: "Having hitherto done my utmost in the art to which my life is a devotion, I cannot undertake to increase the effort."

And in spite of its commercialism, its hurry, its apparent disregard of true art, this individualism in art is what the world is looking for to-day. It needs the man who knows what is good, and who boldly declares it, and then stands by his declaration. This is *my* thought, *my* design, *my* work. As one writer has well said:

"A blacksmith whistling at his forge may fashion a horseshoe after some fancy of his own and watch with delight the soft red iron take shape beneath his blows; when cold he finds that in some manner he has impressed his individuality upon his work, so that he could pick the shoe out of a thousand, even as he would know his own child among a million."

LIBRARY TABLE

THIS useful piece is of good size, having a top thirty-two by fifty-four inches. Instead of having a shelf underneath, a series of slats, placed at a slight distance apart, is introduced. In building it, put the ends together first. The sides of the drawers are dovetailed, and each drawer has a stop underneath it to keep it from going in too far. This stop should hold the face of the drawer one-sixteenth of an inch back of the front rail. The practical reason for this is that, should the piece shrink in any degree, the unevenness is less likely to show when the drawer is thus slightly recessed. Bevel off the lower edges of the legs to prevent tearing the carpet, and carefully sandpaper the edges of the top to remove the sharpness. Oak is the best material of which to construct this table, as it is needed to be substantial, strong and firm. The pulls are of copper or iron, hammered preferably, yet any good pulls will serve admirably.

MILL BILL FOR LIBRARY TABLE

		Rough			Finish	
Pieces	No.	Long	Wide	Thick	Wide	Thick
Top	1	55 in.	33 in.	1¼ in.	32 in.	1⅛ in.
Legs	4	30 in.	2⅞ in.	2⅞ in.	2¾ in.	2¾ in.
End stretcher	2	28 in.	3¾ in.	1⅜-in.	3½ in.	1¼ in.
End uprights	18	15 in.	1¼ in.	1 in.	1 in.	¾ in.
Shelf slats	9	45 in.	1¼ in.	1 in.	1 in.	¾ in.
End rail	2	28 in.	5¼ in.	1⅜ in.	5 in.	1¼ in.
Back rail	1	45 in.	5¼ in.	1 in.	5 in.	⅞ in.
Front rail	1	45 in.	2¾ in.	1 in.	2½ in.	⅞ in.
Division rails	3	7 in.	1½ in.	1 in.	1¼ in.	⅞ in.
Ledger rails	4	28 in.	1½ in.	1 in.	1¼ in.	⅞ in.
Drawer fronts	2	19 in.	5¼ in.	1 in.	5 in.	⅞ in.
Drawer Backs	2	19 in.	5¼ in.	¾ in.	5 in.	½ in.
Drawer sides	4	27 in.	5¼ in.	¾ in.	5 in.	½ in.
Drawer bottoms	2	19 in.	27½ in.	¾ in.	27 in.	½ in.

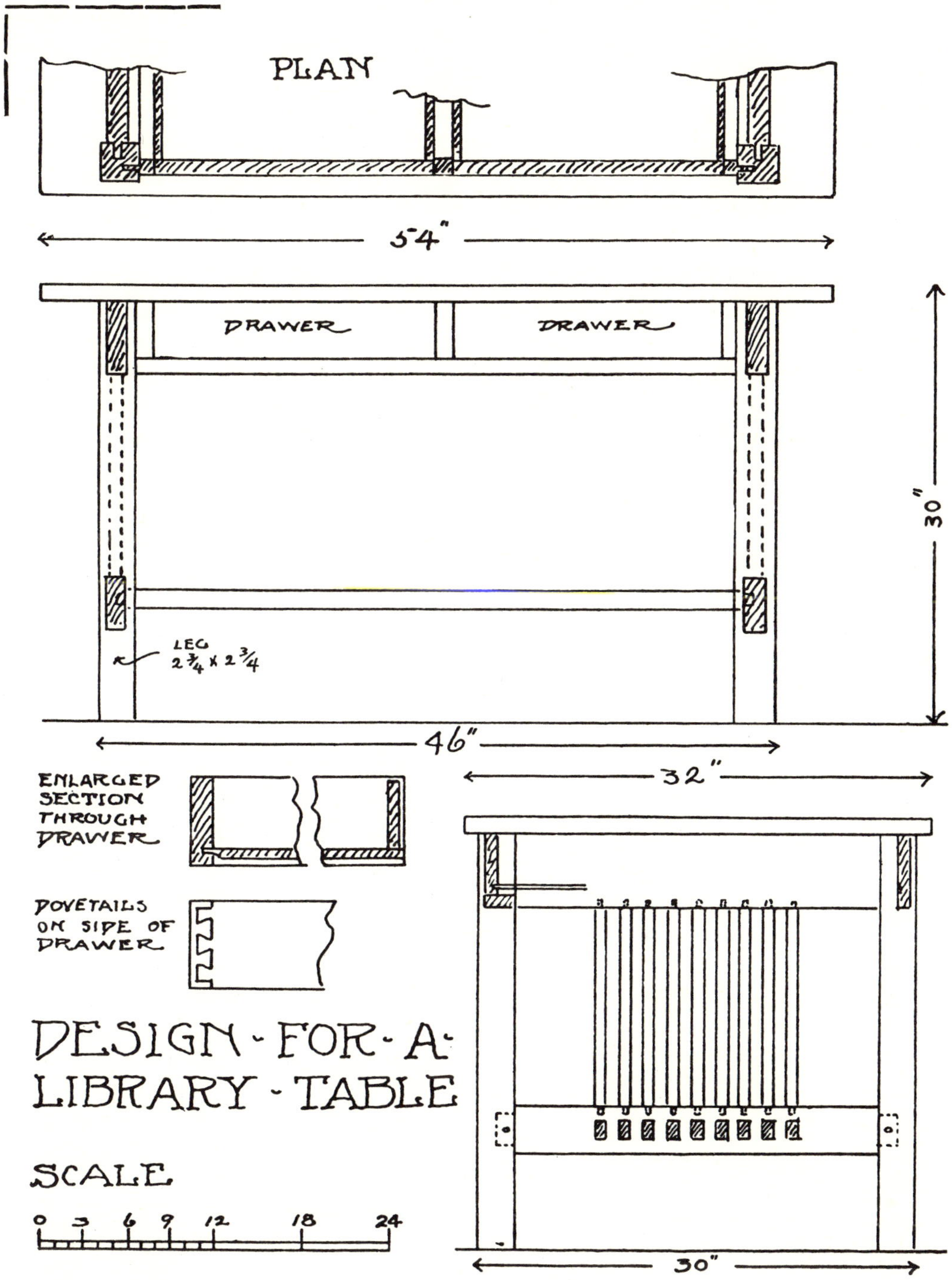

PLAN

DRAWER

DRAWER

LEG 2 3/4 x 2 3/4

ENLARGED SECTION THROUGH DRAWER

DOVETAILS ON SIDE OF DRAWER

DESIGN · FOR · A · LIBRARY · TABLE

SCALE

RITERS innumerable have expatiated, and justly too, upon the beauty of the trees—the trunk, the branches, the leaves, the shadows they cast and the shelter the branches and leaves afford to the birds. The mystery of the vast forests; even the cutting down of trees, the rafting of them down the streams to the mill, and,

eventually, the singing of the saws that divide them into lumber, have been subjects for writings and poems that move and stir the soul.

And, in addition, there exists in wood a quality so satisfying that the proper use of it in the structural features of a house produces an effect of completeness which does away with the need of elaborate furnishings or decoration. I believe that one reason why so many people pile unnecessary furniture, pictures and bric-a-brac into their houses is because the *necessary* furniture, the woodwork (or other treatment) of the walls, and the color scheme as a whole are not interesting enough. This is a point that can hardly be too strongly emphasized in its bearing upon the creation of beautiful and restful surroundings in the home.

If the woodwork of your house is finished so that the natural beauty of the woods is enhanced; if the same thing were done in the furniture; and you then see that the color scheme of woodwork, furniture and hangings harmonize, you cannot fail to secure in each room a charm and beauty that is a great step accomplished towards the simplicity and restfulness that it is so desirable to gain. For let it never be forgotten that if a room is pleasing and restful, one of the highest and best of results has been attained.

LET us now consider the color treatment of woods with a view to their practical uses, which will be commented upon as we proceed. In the treatment of woods that contain tannic acid, such as oak and chestnut, ammonia is the agent for chemical coloring, either by fuming or direct application. The tannic acid and ammonia combine and produce a chemical change which permanently and beautifully tones the wood without in any way injuring its texture or durability. In the case of woods that contain lime—and I speak now not as a chemist, but using the terms of the practical cabinet-maker, who, in such matters, speaks generally rather than with scientific accuracy,—the coloring agent to be used is chloride of potash.

There is a decided difference between the ordinary method of treating quarter sawn oak and the one I have so long followed. The aim has generally been to emphasize the ray flake, and where it was not prominent enough, or present in large enough quantity, to create it by means of added pigment,—in other words to paint it in. When this painted-in-flake is enameled,—varnished over—it is difficult to detect it from the real thing. In my experiments, however, I decided that a far more pleasing and beautiful result would be obtained by softening rather than heightening the distinctiveness of the flake. So for months I persisted in my endeavor to discover a way by which I could "bring together," harmonize, as it were, these two markedly contrasting features in the same piece of wood. This was finally effected by the use of ammonia, either by direct application or by

fumes. The ammonia combines with the tannic acid in the oak to produce a chemical change, and thus "tone down" and color the flake to the desired shade. As far as I know this is the only practically successful method yet discovered to cope with the difficulties offered by the ray flake. Pigment applied to the surface of the flake has no appreciable result, as it is almost as hard and impenetrable as glass. In what I have written above I would not have it thought, because of this somewhat lengthy description of my own experiments, that I make any claim to the discovery of the use of ammonia. Many others have used it, and still do so, and others may have produced the same results on oak, but in my case it was the outcome of personal experimentation.

The subject of wood finishing in general is much too long to be adequately treated within the limits of the space available in a single number of THE CRAFTSMAN, but the division of woods into classes, each of which is susceptible to certain methods of finishing which apply with nearly equal advantage to all the woods in the class designated, makes it a simple matter to take up in detail these sections one by one, until methods and formulae have been given for the treatment of all woods in general use.

Among the easily obtained native woods used for cabinet making and interior house trim, white oak, chestnut, ash and elm come into one class as regards treatment. All of these woods have a strong, well-defined grain, and are so alike in nature that they are all affected in much the same way by the same process or method of finishing. This class of woods has been selected as the subject of the present article, and we will endeavor to make clear to our readers such of our methods of finishing them as may be of practical use to the inexperienced worker. It must be stated, however, that the formulae and instructions given here are not those which would be practicable in a large factory, where great quantities of furniture are to be turned out at low cost, but are addressed to those who take up cabinet making on a smaller scale, or who wish to learn how to obtain a desirable effect in the finish of interior trim. The best effects are to be obtained only by a comparatively expensive and laborious process, which necessarily demands a personal interest and energy on the part of the worker. And also it should be understood that our methods of finishing are for the purpose of getting the best possible results from the wood itself as well as the most pleasing effect in completing the color scheme of a room, and never for the purpose of imitating a more costly wood in the finish of a cheaper one. The beauty of each wood is peculiarly its own, and the sole aim of our finishing is to show that beauty to the best advantage.

Of the woods in the class we are discussing now, oak and chestnut are the only ones affected by the fumes of ammonia. As was discovered some years ago by the use of oaken beams and panelling in the woodwork of fine stables, the effect of ammonia on this wood is to produce quickly the mellow darkness of hue that formerly was supposed to come from age

alone. Careful experiment showed that this effect resulted from a certain affinity between the tannic acid in the wood and the ammonia with which the air was heavily charged, and that the same result could be artificially produced by subjecting to the fumes of strong ammonia any wood which contained a sufficient percentage of tannin. This process is the only one known that acts upon the glassy pith rays as well as the softer parts of the wood, coloring all together in an even tone so that the figure is marked only by its difference in texture. This result can not be accomplished by stains, and for this reason we always subject these woods to more or less fuming before applying a stain.

In fuming woods the best results are obtained by shutting the piece into an air-tight box or closet, on the floor of which has been placed a shallow dish containing liquor ammonia (26 per cent). The length of time required to fume to a good color depends largely upon the tightness of the compartment, but as a rule forty-eight hours is enough. Where fuming is not practicable, as in the case of a piece too large for any available compartment, or of the trim of a room, a satisfactory result can be obtained by applying liquor ammonia (26 per cent) direct to the wood with a sponge or brush. In either case, the wood must be in its natural condition when treated, as any previous application of oil or stain would prevent the ammonia from taking effect.

After the wood is thoroughly dry from the first application, sandpaper it carefully with fine sandpaper, then apply another coat of ammonia and sandpaper as before.

Some pieces fume much darker than others, according to the amount of tannin left free to attract the ammonia after the wood has been kiln-dried. Where any sapwood has been left on, that part will be found unaffected by the fumes. To meet these conditions, it is necessary to make a "touch-up" to even up the color. This is done by mixing Vandyke brown, ground in japan, with German lacquer, commonly known as "banana liquid," and adding a very little lampblack, also ground in japan. The mixture may be thinned with wood alcohol to the right consistency for use, and the color of the piece to be touched up will decide the proportion of black to be added to the brown. In touching up the lighter portions of the wood, the stain may be smoothly blended with the dark tint of the perfectly fumed parts by rubbing along the line where they join with a piece of soft, dry cheesecloth, closely following the brush. If the stain should dry too fast and the color is left uneven, dampen the cloth slightly with alcohol.

After fuming, sandpapering and touching up a piece of furniture, apply a coat of lacquer made of one-third white shellac and two-thirds German lacquer. If the fuming process has resulted in a shade dark enough to be satisfactory, this lacquer may be applied clear, if not, it may be darkened by the addition of a small quantity of the stain used in touching up. Care must be taken, however, not to add enough color to show laps and brushmarks. The danger of this makes it often more advisable to apply two coats of lacquer, each containing a very little color. If this is done, sandpaper each coat with very fine sandpaper after it is thoroughly dry, and then apply one or more coats of prepared floor wax. These directions, if carefully followed, should give the same effects that characterize the Craftsman furniture.

A DAUGHTER OF EVE

PHOTOGRAPH BY FRANCES ALLEN, DEERFIELD, MASSACHUSETTS

TWO LEADERS OF "YOUNG RUSSIA": MAXIM GORKY (PIESHKOV) AND LEONIDE ANDREYEV

These two men, with their colleagues Shalyapin, Bunin, Jelyeshev and Chirikov, and the priest George Gapon, are the thinkers and the writers who most insistently demand liberty, citizenship, and the means of progress for the masses of the Russian people. Andreyev, represented with his zither, offers a significant figure. We can imagine that he has just been playing upon this favorite instrument of the peasant some of the folk-melodies which the western world knows through the composers Balakirev and Runsky Kortchakoff: a music, melancholy, passionate, wild almost to savagery, in short, "a voice from the deep," crying out for the dawn of a new era.

I have come from below, from the nethermost ground of life, where is naught but sludge and murk. I am the truthful voice of life, the harsh cry of those who still abide down there and who have let me come up to witness their suffering. They also long to rise to self-respect, to light and freedom.

—MAXIM GORKY

THE ARCHITECTURAL DISCUSSION: FORM AND FUNCTION ARTISTICALLY CONSIDERED. BY LOUIS H. SULLIVAN

HE sincere purpose of THE CRAFTSMAN in opening its pages to a frank expression of opinion and comment on the subject of modern architectural needs and tendencies, was to stimulate thought and discussion in the profession.

The limits of time and space restrict the discussion in the present issue to a further presentation of an interesting and lucid point of view by Louis H. Sullivan of Chicago. In a letter to the Editor, Mr. Sullivan writes:

"I like the spirit you are infusing into THE CRAFTSMAN. It comes at a critical time,—a time of ferment, a time of epoch-making changes. I hope you have the courage to see and grasp the opportunity to draw out opinion and define an issue, believing that you realize how noble a system of design (architectural thinking) might be founded upon the superb underlying qualities of the American people,—a people in whom I have a profound faith, in spite of our temporary era of insanity. America has long owed the world a new and sane philosophy, in gratitude for that liberty of mind which centuries of struggle have prepared for it."

As a timely and pertinent addition to the present phase of the discussion, THE CRAFTSMAN reproduces from an article by Mr. Sullivan in the *Lippincott Magazine* of 1896, entitled, "The Tall Office Building Artistically Considered," the following extracts, regretting that space will not permit giving the entire article, the keynote of which is that *"Form ever follows function. This is the law."* [EDITOR.]

THE architects of this land and generation are now brought face to face with something new under the sun,—namely, that evolution and integration of social conditions, that special grouping of them, which results in a demand for the erection of tall office buildings. It is not my purpose to discuss the social conditions; I accept them as the fact, and say at once that the design of the tall office building must be recognized and confronted at the outset as a problem to be solved,—a vital problem, pressing for a true solution. . . . How shall we impart to this sterile pile, this crude, harsh, brutal agglomeration, this stark, staring exclamation of eternal strife, the gracious-

ness of those higher forms of sensibility and culture that rest on the lower and fiercer passions? How shall we proclaim from the dizzy height of this strange, weird, modern housetop the peaceful evangel of sentiment, of beauty, the cult of a higher life?

This is the problem; and we must seek the solution of it in a process analogous to its own evolution,—indeed, a continuation of it,—namely, by proceeding step by step from general to special aspects, from coarser to finer considerations. It is my belief that it is of the very essence of every problem that it contains and suggests its own solution. This I believe to be natural law. . . . As I am here seeking not for an individual or special solution, but for a true normal type, the attention must be confined to those conditions that, in the main, are constant in tall office buildings, and every mere incidental and accidental variation eliminated from the consideration, as harmful to the clearness of the main inquiry.

The practical horizontal and vertical division or office unit is naturally based on a room of comfortable area and height, and the size of this standard office room as naturally predetermines the standard structural unit, and, approximately, the size of window-openings. In turn, these purely arbitrary units of structure form in an equally natural way the true basis of the artistic development of the exterior. Of course the structural spacings and openings in the first or mercantile story are required to be the largest of all; those in the second or quasi-mercantile story are of a somewhat similar nature. The spacings and openings in the attic are of no importance whatsoever (the windows have no actual value), for light may be taken from the top, and no recognition of a cellular division is necessary in the structural spacing. Hence it follows inevitably, and in the simplest possible way, that if we follow our natural instincts without thought of books, rules, precedents, or any such educational impedimenta to a spontaneous and "sensible" result, we will in the following manner design the exterior of our tall office building,—to wit:

Beginning with the first story, we give this a main entrance that attracts the eye to its location, and the remainder of the story we treat in a more or less liberal, expansive, sumptuous way,—a way based exactly on the practical necessities, but expressed with a sentiment of largeness and freedom. The second story we treat in a similar way, but usually with milder pretension. Above this, throughout the indefinite number of typical office-tiers, we take our cue from the individual cell, which requires a window with its separating pier, its sill and lintel, and we, without more ado, make them *look* all alike because they *are* all alike. This brings us to the attic, which, having no division into office-cells, and no special requirement for lighting, gives us the power to show by means of its broad expanse of wall, and its dominating weight and character, that which is the fact,—namely, that the series of office-tiers has come definitely to an end.

This may perhaps seem a bald result and a heartless, pessimistic way of stating it, but even so we certainly have advanced a most characteristic stage beyond the imagined sinister building of the speculator-engineer-builder combination. For the hand of the architect is now definitely felt in the decisive position at once taken, and the suggestion of a thoroughly sound, logical, coherent expression of the conditions is becoming apparent. When I say the hand of the architect, I do not mean necessarily the accomplished and trained architect. I mean only a man with a strong natural liking for buildings, and a disposition to shape them in what seems to his unaffected nature a direct and simple way. He will probably tread an innocent path from his problem to its solution, and therein he will show an enviable gift of logic. If he have some gift for form in detail, some feeling for form purely and simply as form, some love for that, his result, in addition to its simple straightforward naturalness and completeness in general statement, will have something of the charm of sentiment.

However, thus far the results are only partial and tentative at best; relatively true, they are but superficial. We are doubtless right in our instinct, but we must seek a fuller justification, a finer sanction, for it. . . . What is the chief characteristic of the tall office building? And at once we answer, it is lofty. This loftiness is to the artist-nature its thrilling aspect. It is the very open organ-tone in its appeal. It must be in turn the dominant chord in his expression of it, the true excitant of his imagination. It must be tall, every inch of it tall. The force and power of altitude must be in it, the glory and pride of exaltation must be in it. It must be every inch a proud and soaring thing, rising in sheer exultation that from bottom to top it is a unit without a single dissenting line,—that it is the new, the unexpected, the eloquent peroration of most bald, most sinister, most forbidding conditions.

THE man who designs in this spirit and with this sense of responsibility to the generation he lives in must be no coward, no denier, no bookworm, no dilettante. He must live of his life and for his life in the fullest, most consummate sense. He must realize at once and with the grasp of inspiration that the problem of the tall office building is one of the most stupendous, one of the most magnificent opportunities that the Lord of Nature in His beneficence has ever offered to the proud spirit of man.

That this has not been perceived—indeed, has been flatly denied—is an exhibition of human perversity that must give us pause. . . . As to the former and serious views held by discerning and thoughtful critics, I shall, with however much of regret, dissent from them for the purposes of this demonstration, for I regard them as secondary only, non-essential, and as touching not at all upon the vital spot, upon

the quick of the entire matter, upon the true, the immovable philosophy of the architectural art.

This view let me now state, for it brings to the solution of the problem a final, comprehensive formula: All things in nature have a shape, that is to say, a form, an outward semblance, that tells us what they are, that distinguishes them from ourselves and from each other. Unfailingly in nature these shapes express the inner life, the native quality, of the animal, tree, bird, fish, that they present to us; they are so characteristic, so recognizable, that we say, simply, it is "natural" it should be so. Yet the moment we peer beneath this surface of things, the moment we look through the tranquil reflection of ourselves and the clouds above us, down into the clear, fluent, unfathomable depths of nature, how startling is the silence of it, how amazing the flow of life, how absorbing the mystery! Unceasingly the essence of things is taking shape in the matter of things, and this unspeakable process we call birth and growth. Awhile the spirit and the matter fade away together, and it is this that we call decadence, death. These two happenings seem joined and interdependent, blended into one like a bubble and its iridescence and they seem borne along upon a slowly moving air. This air is wonderful past all understanding.

Yet to the steadfast eye of one standing upon the shore of things, looking chiefly and most lovingly upon that side on which the sun shines and that we feel joyously to be life, the heart is ever gladdened by the beauty, the exquisite spontaneity, with which life seeks and takes on its forms in an accord perfectly responsive to its needs. It seems ever as though the life and the form were absolutely one and inseparable, so adequate is the sense of fufillment. . . . It is the pervading law of all things organic and inorganic, of all things physical and metaphysical, of all things human and all things superhuman, of all true manifestations of the head, of the heart, of the soul, that the life is recognizable in its expression, that *form ever follows function. This is the law.*

Shall we, then, daily violate this law in our art? Are we so decadent, so imbecile, so utterly weak of eyesight, that we cannot perceive this truth so simple, so very simple? Is it indeed a truth so transparent that we see through it but do not see it? Is it really then a very marvelous thing, or is it rather so commonplace, so everyday, so near a thing to us, that we cannot perceive that the shape, form, outward expression, design, or whatever we may choose, of the tall office building should in the very nature of things follow the functions of the building, and that where the function does not change, the form is not to change?

DOES not this readily, clearly, and conclusively show that the lower one or two stories will take on a special character suited to the special needs, that the tiers of typical offices, having the

same unchanging function, shall continue in the same unchanging form, and that as to the attic, specific and conclusive as it is in its very nature, its function shall equally be so in force, in significance, in continuity, in conclusiveness of outward expression? From this results, naturally, spontaneously, unwittingly, a three-part division,—not from any theory, symbol, or fancied logic.

And thus the design of the tall office building takes its place with all other architectural types made when architecture, as has happened once in many years, was a living art. Witness the Greek temple, the Gothic cathedral, the mediaeval fortress.

And thus, when native instinct and sensibility shall govern the exercise of our beloved art; when the known law, the respected law, shall be that form ever follows function; when our architects shall cease strutting and prattling handcuffed and vainglorious in the asylum of a foreign school; when it is truly felt, cheerfully accepted, that this law opens up the airy sunshine of green fields, and gives to us a freedom that the very beauty and sumptuousness of the outworking of the law itself as exhibited in nature will deter any sane, any sensitive man from changing into license; when it becomes evident that we are merely speaking a foreign language with a noticeable American accent, whereas each and every architect in the land might, under the benign influence of this very law, express in the simplest, most modest, most natural way that which it is in him to say; that he might really and would surely develop his own characteristic individuality, and that the architectural art with him would certainly become a living form of speech, a natural form of utterance, giving surcease to him and adding treasures small and great to the growing art of his land; when we know and feel that Nature is our friend, not our implacable enemy,—that an afternoon in the country, an hour by the sea, a full open view of one single day, through dawn, high noon, and twilight, will suggest to us so much that is rhythmical, deep, and eternal in the vast art of architecture, something so deep, so true, that all the narrow formalities, hard-and-fast rules, and strangling bonds of the schools cannot stifle it in us,—then it may be proclaimed that we are on the highroad to a natural and satisfying art, an architecture that will soon become a fine art in the true, the best sense of the word, an art that will live because it will be of the people, for the people, and by the people.

OUR HOME DEPARTMENT

SINCE the publication of our article on stenciling fabrics, in the Home Department of THE CRAFTSMAN for May, 1905, we have received a number of requests for a like article on designs and methods of wall stenciling.

While they are always to be made interesting in color, division of wall-spaces and structural features, applied ornamentation of any sort should be but sparingly used if the effect of restfulness so necessary to a home atmosphere is to be preserved. The

STENCIL OF CONVENTIONALIZED TREES

The method of stenciling is much the same as that applied to fabrics, but there are certain limitations governing the designs that go to make a successful wall decoration. The first principle, and one that should be kept in mind first, last and all the time, is the careful avoidance of over-decoration. Any form of ornamentation that obtrudes itself, either in color or design, is dangerous for the walls, which are essentially the background of the room.

danger of richly colored and mechanically-produced patterns which repeat themselves all over the walls, as in the case of most figured wall-papers and friezes, is that they seem constantly to be clamoring for notice, so that the whole effect becomes fussy and restless. This applies as well to painted or stenciled walls, unless great care is exercised in the choice of color and design, so that the decoration does not assert itself unduly in the room considered as a whole,

STENCIL SHOWING CONNECTED SPOT PATTERN—WILD ROSE MOTIF

but rather serves simply to relieve a plain space which might otherwise look bare.

To quote from a well-known English decorator whose utterances upon this subject are authoritative: "Any ornament you notice when you do not look for it, or perhaps I might better say, when you do not wish to think of it, is necessarily in bad taste....... Now no flat mechanical ornament, designed to cover a large space, should ever be so designed that you are able easily to trace the pattern at the other side of the room. Please do not understand from this that it should be *small* in design; far from it; things small in design are almost necessarily finikin and therefore unreposeful; but being quiet and retiring in color and contrast of tones, whether large or small, let it reveal, when you come to have leisure to examine it, vigorous, broad and direct treatment, good, loving, thoughtful drawing, real artistic conception, and perception of beauty in form and line."

This is a good foundation upon which to base all designs and color effects in wall stenciling. The color, of course, must be chosen to furnish just the requisite amount of contrast to the wall covering to afford the needed decorative touch that relieves the plainness of frieze or panel without attracting to itself an undue amount of attention in the general scheme of the room, and these colors depend in every case upon the wall and surroundings. As to the designs, those illustrated here are fair examples of Craftsman ideas in either continuous or "spot" patterns.

As to the method of making the stencils and applying the colors, it is necessary only to repeat the directions that have been given before with reference to stenciling on fabrics. A stencil in itself is no more than a sheet of metal or heavy paper so cut that the pattern is formed by the open spaces. Metal is frequently used by professional decorators, to whose interest it is to make a stencil as durable as possible, but for home use the paper stencil is by far the best. A heavy paper or cardboard, prepared for use, is obtainable, but where it is not convenient to procure this stencil paper, an excellent substitute will be found in the ordinary manila paper.

STENCIL SHOWING WILD CARROT MOTIF.

When this latter is used, the paper should be treated with a preparation of linseed oil, to which turpentine and japan dryer have been added in the following proportions: one-half as much turpentine as oil, and after these two have been well mixed, one-third as much japan as turpentine.

When this preparation has somewhat dried out, the stencil is ready for cutting. This is best accomplished by using a knife with the point slightly rounded and sharpened at both edges, using great care to leave the edges of the pattern clean and crisp, and not to sever any of the lines which hold the pattern together, and which are technically known as "ties." The best results in cutting may be obtained by tacking a piece of thick paper over a smooth board, and laying upon it the pattern to be cut out. A sheet of glass is often placed under the pattern instead of the board, but this is apt to dull the knife too quickly; the board is better, especially when covered so that the grain is not felt. When cut, the stencil is ready for use, except for a finishing coat of thin white shellac, which toughens the paper and makes it impervious to moisture of any kind.

SPOT PATTERN FOR WALL PANEL

In applying the pattern to the wall it is best to use a round bristle brush and only the smallest possible quantity of dye or paint. The best effect is obtained, not with the ordinary brush strokes, but by stippling on the pigment with quick repeated taps of the end of the brush.

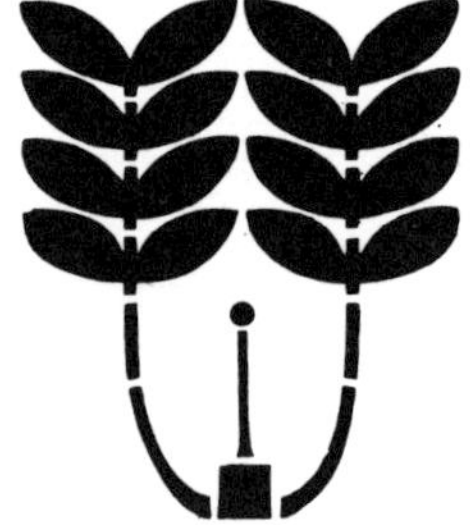

STENCIL SHOWING SPOT PATTERN FOR PANEL BELOW FRIEZE

OUR HOME DEPARTMENT

OF all rooms in the house, the one where the skill of the woman wise in color and deft with her needle is most evident is the bedroom. Unless the room is situated on the shady side of the house, where warm color effects are needed to make up for the absence of sunshine, the color scheme of a bedroom is usually carried out in cool and delicate tints, giving the best possible chance for subtle accents here and there in the way of color and form, such as only needlework can give.

So many applications have been made to THE CRAFTSMAN for additional needlework designs especially suited to

bedroom accessories, that this month the Home Department is devoted to the illustration and explanation of three new designs here published for the first time. In addition to scarfs and bed-covers, the same design and material appears in portières for closet doors, and sometimes in window curtains, if THE CRAFTSMAN idea as presented here is to be carried out. The conventionalized flower and leaf *motifs* are so simple that no sense of wearisome repetition is felt in their appearance on hangings as well as scarfs and bed-cover, but rather a pleasant realization of the recurrence of a needed color accent in the general effect.

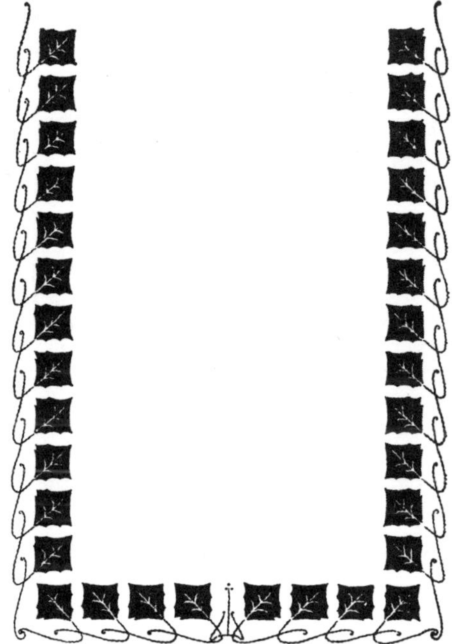

IVY DESIGN FOR BED COVER

In a room where the walls are gray-green and the woodwork stained so that a suggestion of moss green appeared in its gray-brown tones,—as is frequently the case with cypress wood trim when finished in gray,—the ivy *motif* first illustrated here would be charmingly in keeping. In such surroundings it would be best if developed on linen that is almost white, but shows a very slight suggestion of green,—just the merest tinge. The leaves in appliqué would be in a darker tone of linen, possibly somewhat gray in color, and the stems and couching in a brighter green. The line of couching that masks the edge of the hem is made of five or six strands of linen floss caught down with a coarse buttonhole stitch. In this case it would be best to use a thread of the same rather than another tone. As in all appliqué, the linen leaves are carefully cut out, leaving edge enough to turn under, and are first basted into position and then buttonholed down with the floss. The stems and veinings are of floss and in simple outline stitch. The bed-cover shows a design that outlines the top of the bed like a border running across the foot and up the sides to the pillows. This sort of spread is to

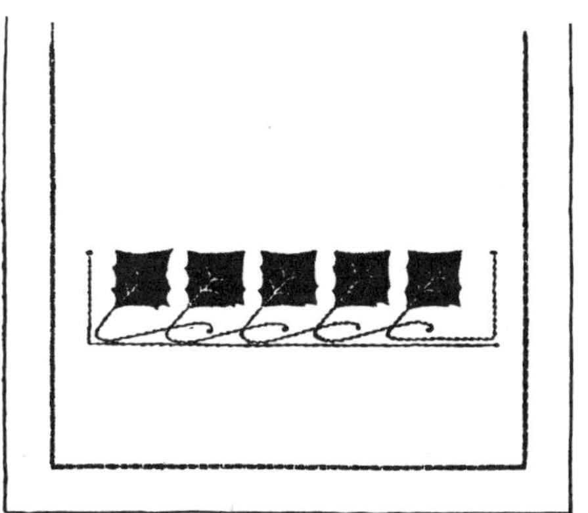

IVY BORDER FOR SCARF

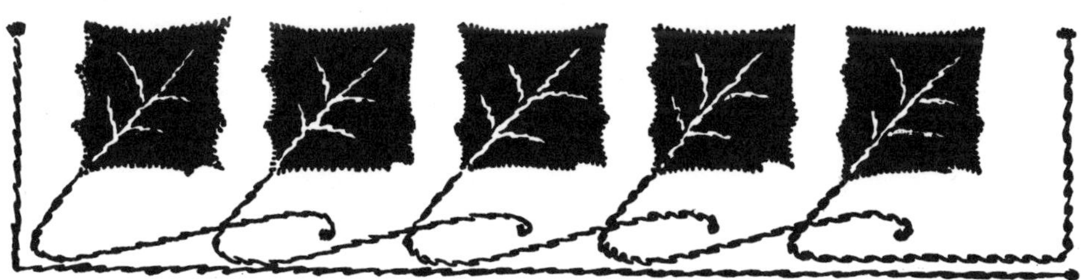

DETAIL OF IVY MOTIF

be tucked in all around, though, of course, the same design might easily be used on a spread made to hang to the floor at foot and sides. Again, the design is so arranged as to be very easily adjusted according to individual fancy. It might run around the edge of the bed on top, or be set far enough in to leave a border of the material at the edge,—or it could even be made into a central ornament in the shape of a parallelogram. It is merely a matter of the repetition of the single leaf pattern a greater or less number of times.

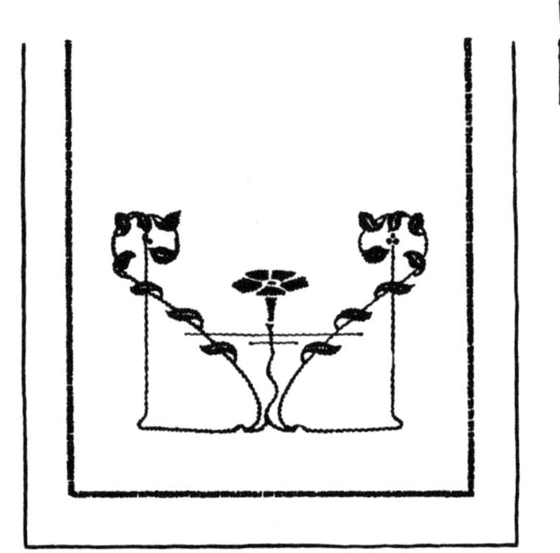

PERIWINKLE DESIGN FOR SCARF

Another design suitable for a room in cool tones is the periwinkle or myrtle *motif*. No appliqué is used in this design, which is carried out entirely in needlework, the outline and "over-and-over" stitches being used, as well as the lines of couching and occasional French knots. If carried out as suggested here, the material would be the cool gray homespun.

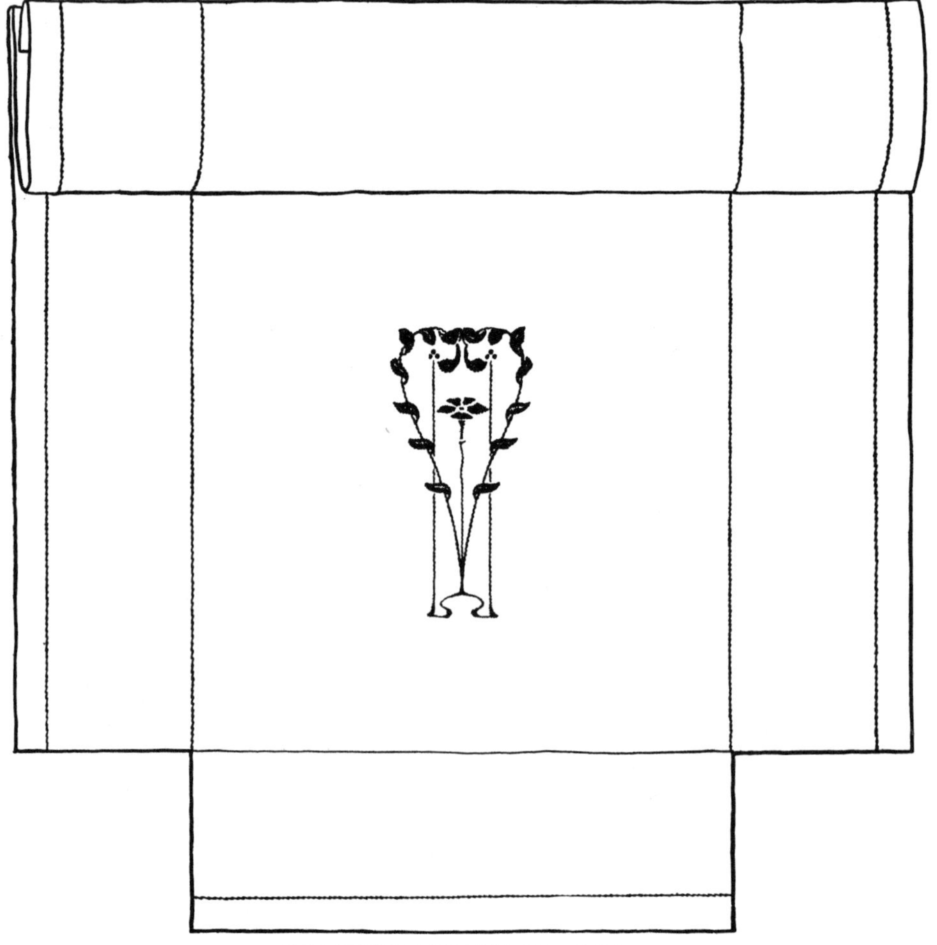

PERIWINKLE DESIGN FOR BED COVER

The needlework would be done in linen floss,—the flower part of the design in the dull soft blue of the flower itself, the leaves and stems in a very grayish green, and the small dots in a washed-out rose-color. The couched lines would be of the same green as the stems. The working out of this *motif* is not so simple as the one preceding, for different applications of it appear in the different pieces.

POPPY DESIGN FOR SCARF

Especially appropriate for a bedroom is the poppy *motif* with its suggestion of sleep. The material upon which this design is developed may be either inexpensive unbleached muslin, or any cream-colored fabric as fine and costly as may be desired. The shade needed to carry out the color scheme in the model suggested here is exactly the warm creamy tint of unbleached muslin. The poppy itself is

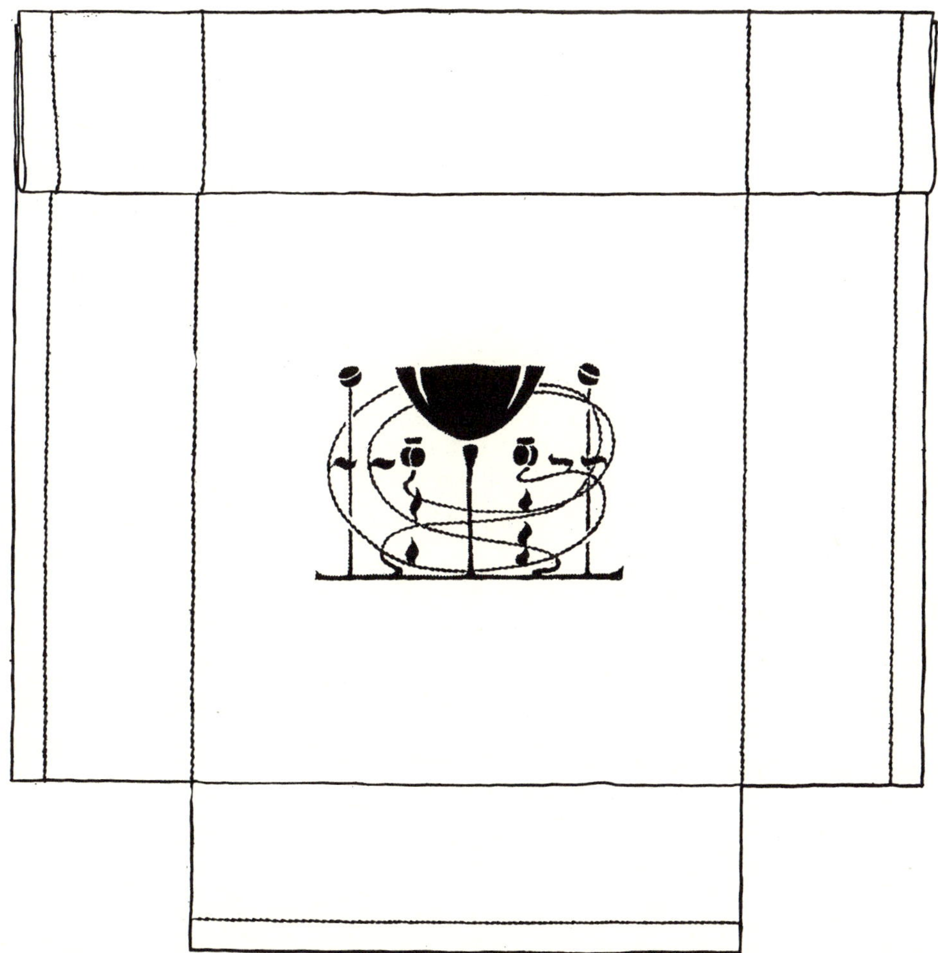

POPPY DESIGN FOR BED COVER

appliquéd, and on the creamy ground suggested would be of linen in a soft old rose or pomegranate tone. The leaves and stems, done in needlework, would be of linen floss in pale moss green, and the outlined hems,—used here in place of the couched lines shown in the other two designs,—would be in a little lighter shade of the same green.

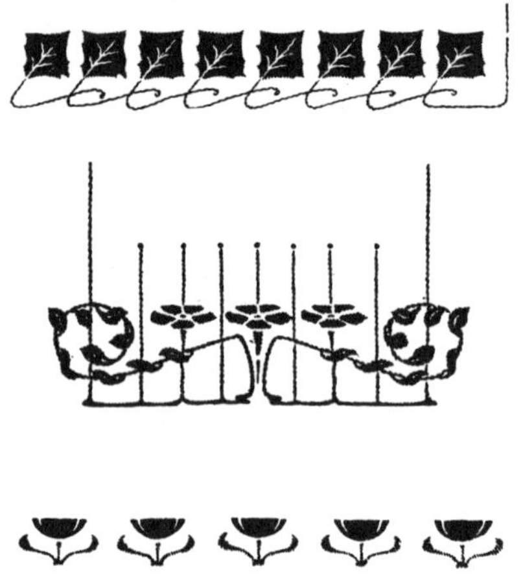

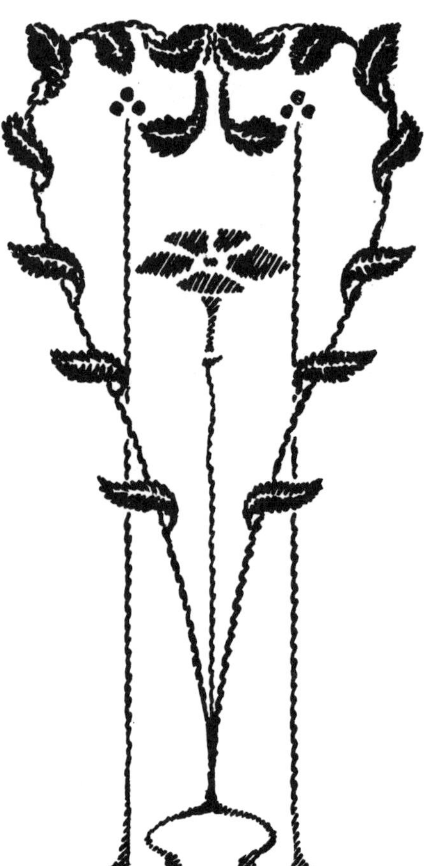

DETAIL OF PERIWINKLE MOTIF

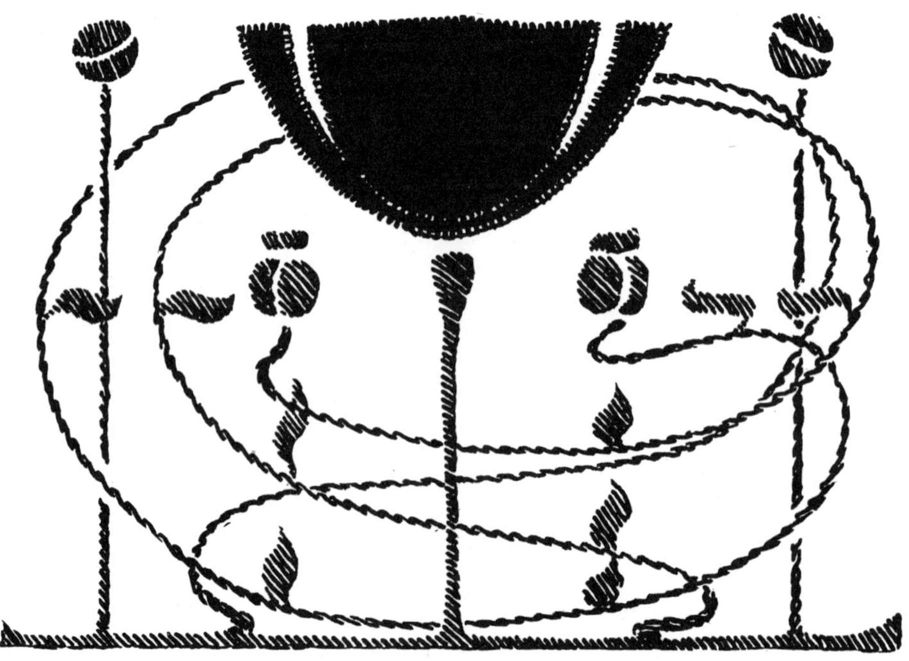

DETAIL OF POPPY MOTIF

TELLING HISTORY BY PHOTOGRAPHS. RECORDS OF OUR NORTH AMERICAN INDIANS BEING PRESERVED BY PICTURES

WE are just waking up here in America to appreciating the big interests of our own country and to a sense of cherishing our original greatness. We are painting our plains, protecting our forests, creating game preserves, and at last—not saving the existence of the North American Indian, the most picturesque roving people on earth, but making and preserving records of them from an historical, scientific and artistic point of view.

We as a nation are not doing this. Just one man, an American, an explorer, an artist with the camera, has conceived and is carrying into execution the gigantic idea of making complete photographic and text records of the North American Indians so far as they exist in a primitive condition to-day.

Mr. Edward S. Curtis has been already working for six years on this project. The Smithsonian Institution at Washington has known about his purpose, President Roosevelt has kept in close touch with his work, ethnologists and photographers have followed his progress with interest; but until the recent exhibitions of Indian photographs and the stereopticon lectures at the Waldorf, New York, the general public has had very little idea of the scope and beauty of Mr. Curtis' intention and achievement. It has already been said in print of this work that "if Mr. Curtis lives and keeps his health for ten years he will have accumulated material for the greatest artistic and historical work in American ethnology that has ever been conceived of." Toward this end, Mr. Curtis has already fifteen hundred characteristic Indian photographs.

In the recent exhibit in New York, about two hundred prints of the thousand already made, were on the walls. But something of the purpose in making the collection is quickly felt even in this limited display. Each primitive tribe—as far as captured by Mr. Curtis' camera—is presented in its own group, with every variation of type, young and old, with home structures, environment, handicrafts, games and ceremonies presented intimately and sympathetically. These pictures tell the history, the legends, the myths, the manners and customs of a vanishing tribe as no printed page, however vivid, could set forth.

AND the photographs themselves, quite apart from their historic and scientific value, show a fresh, far step in the progress of photography into the realm of fine arts. Mr. Curtis has so far improved on old methods of printing and finishing as to have practically invented processes in photographic presentation. His

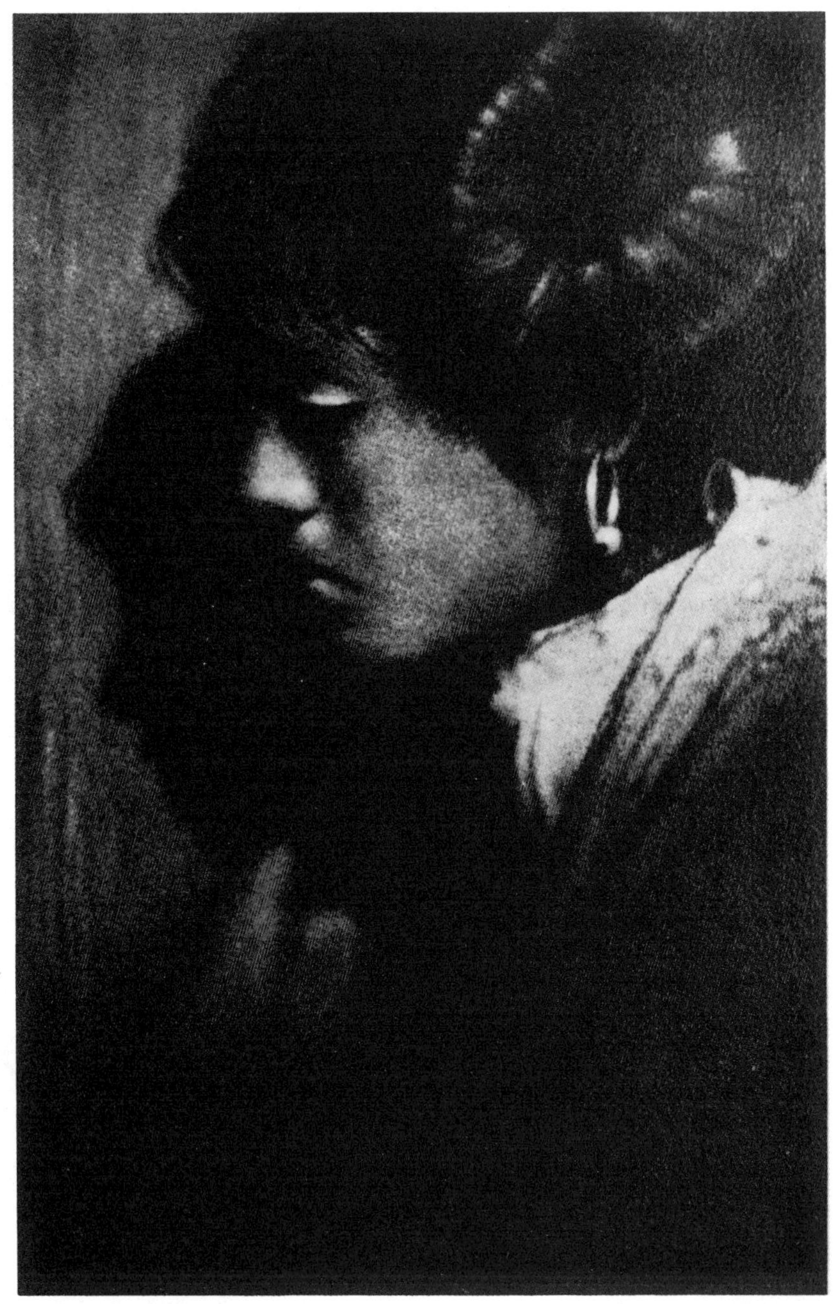

Copyrighted 1905 by Edward S. Curtis

"A HOPI INDIAN MATRON"
PHOTOGRAPH BY E. S. CURTIS

tones, his rough surfaced papers, his color combinations are a new art, or a new science, as one classes camera work. And to those who know nothing of methods and improvements these photographs of picturesque people, employed in primitive ways, their homes and their country, are beautiful pictures, as paintings are beautiful, because of the marvelous way in which nature is reproduced. There are most luminous atmospheric effects, a glimmer of sunlight, a deep still night, desolate plains seen through dust clouds and astonishing contrasts of light and shade as sunbeams gleam down gorges through narrow crevices.

There is apparently nothing in the way of difficulties that he cannot overcome, from the shyness of the Indian nature to illusive quality of air and sunlight. And all by tenacious labor, following insight. For a picture of three Sioux Chiefs he visited Montana three times, and cultivated his models at intervals for three years.

Mr. Curtis is first of all a craftsman, and after that equally a historian, a scientist, an artist and an understanding human being; if he collects facts, they are accurate; if he traces the civilization of Indian tribes, he is consistent; if he makes a picture, it is with the latest improvement in methods; if he wants the confidence of a tribe of people, he visits them and wins their liking and trust—so that each phase of his endeavor can stand alone; his pictures by themselves are perfect, his ethnological researches are of themselves also complete.

When his records are finished Mr. Curtis expects to have from fifteen to twenty volumes, illustrated with from one thousand to fifteen hundred of his own photographs, the text to be gathered by himself, accurate and interesting, and subject to final editing by ethnological authorities. President Roosevelt, in a letter regarding Mr. Curtis' project wrote, "I esteem it a matter of great moment that for our good fortune Mr. Curtis should have had the will and the power to preserve as he has in his pictures this strange and beautiful, and now vanishing life."

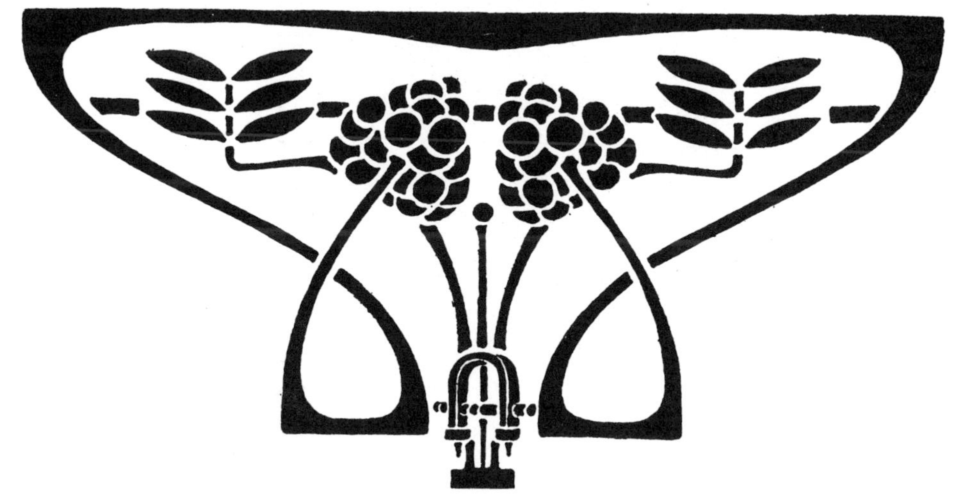

Courtesy of Miss Jane Addams, Chicago

RECENT PICTURE OF TOLSTOY IN PEASANT DRESS

A GREAT INIQUITY: EXTRACTS FROM THE FAMOUS LETTER ON LAND OWNERSHIP IN RUSSIA: BY LEO TOLSTOY

IN connection with the present troubles in Russia and the world-wide interest in the probable outcome of the situation, it seems most timely to give the clear-cut views of Tolstoy on the subject, as expressed in his famous letter to the *London Times,* written in July, 1905, at his home in Yasnaia Poliana. According to Tolstoy's wishes, the letter was made free of copyright, and portions of it were reproduced at the time. It never appeared in full in this country, however, until its recent publication, in pamphlet form, by The Public Publishing Company of Chicago. When THE CRAFTSMAN received it for review, it was immediately apparent that the interest of the subject was sufficient to warrant copious extracts, sufficient to give, in Tolstoy's own words, a clear idea of his position with regard to this question so vital to the future of his country. It is significant, also, that he gives unqualified approval and endorsement to the single-tax theory of Henry George. The portrait of Tolstoy here reproduced is from the same pamphlet, and is believed to be otherwise unknown in this country. The original is the property of Miss Jane Addams, of Hull-House, Chicago, and is regarded by its owner as an exceptionally faithful portrait of the great Russian in his home surroundings. It is said that the circulation of this portrait is interdicted in Russia, presumably because the minds of the peasantry might be inflamed by the simple peasant dress and pose, giving to their friend the appearance of a prophet. [Editor's Note]

USSIA is living through an important time destined to have enormous results. The proximity and inevitableness of the approaching change, is, as indeed is always the case, especially keenly felt by those classes of society who by their position are free from the necessity of physical labor absorbing all their time and power, and therefore have the possibility of occupying themselves with political questions. These men—the nobles, merchants, Government officials, doctors, engineers, professors, teachers, artists, students, advocates, chiefly townspeople, the so-called "Intellectuals"—are now in Russia directing the movement which is taking place, and they devote all their powers to the alteration of the existing political order, and to replacing it by another regarded by this or that party as the most expedient and likely to insure the liberty and welfare of the Russian people. These men, continually suffering from every kind of restriction and coercion on the part of the Government, from arbitrary exile, incarcerations, prohibition of meetings, prohibition of books, newspapers, strikes, unions—from the limitation of the rights of various nationalities, and at the same time living a life completely estranged from the majority of the Russian agricultural people, naturally see in these restrictions the chief evil, and in the liberation of it the chief welfare, of the Russian people.

Thus think the Liberals. So, also, think the Social Democrats, who hope, through popular representation, by the aid of the State

power, to realize a new social order in accordance with their theory. So also think the revolutionaries, hoping by substituting a new Government for the existing one, to establish laws insuring the greatest freedom and welfare of the whole people.

And yet one need only for a time free oneself from the idea which has taken root amongst "Intellectuals," to see that the work now before Russia is the introduction into our country of those same forms of political life which have been introduced into Europe and America, and are supposed to insure the liberty and welfare of all the citizens—and to simply think of what is morally wrong in our life, in order to see quite clearly that the chief evil from which the whole of the Russian people are unceasingly and cruelly suffering—an evil of which they are keenly conscious and to which they are continually pointing—cannot be removed by any political reforms, just as it is not up to the present time removed by any of the political reforms of Europe and America. This evil—the fundamental evil from which the Russian people, as well as the peoples of Europe and America, are suffering—is the fact that the majority of the people are deprived of the indisputable natural right of every man to use a portion of the land on which he was born. It is sufficient to understand all the criminality, the sinfulness of the situation in this respect, in order to understand that until this atrocity, continually being committed by the owners of the land, shall cease, no political reforms will give freedom and welfare to the people, but that, on the contrary, only the emancipation of the majority of the people from that land-slavery in which they are now held, can render political reforms, not a plaything and a tool for personal aims in the hands of politicians, but the real expression of the will of the people.

It is this thought which I wish to communicate in this article to to those who, at the present important moment for Russia, desire to serve not their personal aims, but the true welfare of the Russian people.

THE other day I was walking along the high road to Tula. It was on the Saturday of Holy Week; the people were driving in lines of carts, with calves, hens, horses, cows (some of the cows were being conveyed in the carts, so starved were they). A wrinkled old woman was leading a lean, sickly cow. I knew the old woman and asked her why she was leading the cow. "She's without milk," said the woman. "I ought to sell her and buy one with milk. Likely I'll have to add ten roubles, but I have only five. Where shall I take it? During the winter we have to spend eighteen roubles on flour, and we've only got one bread-winner. I live alone with my daughter-in-law and four grandchildren; my son is houseporter in town."

"Why doesn't your son live at home?" I asked. "He's nothing

to work on," was her reply. "What's our land? Just enough for Kvas."

A woman passed driving along with a boy wearing a little cap. She knew me, clambered out, and offered me her boy for service. The boy is quite a tiny fellow with quick, intelligent eyes. "He looks small, but he can do everything," she says. "But why do you hire out such a little one?' "Well, sir, at least it'll be one mouth less to feed. I have four besides myself, and only one allotment. God knows, we've nothing to eat. They ask for bread and I've none to give them." With whomsoever one talks, all complain of their want and all similarly from one side or another come back to the sole reason. There is insufficient bread, and bread is insufficient because there is no land.

These may be mere casual meetings on the road; but cross all Russia, all its peasant world, and one may observe all the dreadful calamities and sufferings which proceed from the obvious cause that the agricultural masses are deprived of land. Half of the Russian peasantry live so that for them the question is not how to improve their position, but only how not to die of hunger, they and their families, and this only because they have no land. Traverse all Russia and ask all the working people why their life is hard, what they want; and all of them with one voice will say one and the same thing, that which they unceasingly desire and expect, and for which they unceasingly hope, of which they unceasingly think.

And they cannot help thinking and feeling this, for, apart from the chief thing, the insufficiency of land for the maintenance of most of them, they cannot but feel themselves the slaves of the landed gentry, and merchants, and landowners whose estates have surrounded their small insufficient allotments; and they cannot but think and feel this, for every minute, for a bag of grass, for a handful of fuel without which they cannot live, for a horse gone astray from their land on to the landlord's, they perpetually suffer fines, blows, humiliation.

THE evil and injustice of private property in land have been pointed out a thousand years ago by the prophets and sages of old. Later progressive thinkers of Europe have been oftener and oftener pointing it out. With special clearness did the workers of the French Revolution do so. In latter days, owing to the increase of the population and the siezing by the rich of a great quantity of previously free land, also owing to general enlightenment and the spread of humanitarianism this injustice has become so obvious that not only the progressive, but even the most average people cannot help seeing and feeling it. But men, especially those who profit by the advantages of landed property—the owners themselves, as well as those whose interests are connected with this institution—are so accustomed to this order of things, they have for so long profited by it,

have so much depended upon it, that often they themselves do not see its injustice, and they use all possible means to conceal from themselves and others the truth which is disclosing itself more and more clearly, and to crush, extinguish, and distort it, or, if these do not succeed, to hush it up.

Continuing, Tolstoy gives a comprehensive resumé of the teachings of Henry George on the land question, and the reasons why they are not more widely known. He say: Thanks to the collective efforts of all those interested in defending the institution of landed property, the teaching of George, irresistibly convincing in its simplicity and clearness, remains almost unknown, and of late years has attracted less and less attention...... People do not argue with the teaching of George, they simply do not know it. And it is impossible to do otherwise with his teaching, for he who becomes acquainted with it cannot but agree.

However strange this temporary blindness of the political workers of Europe and America, it can be explained by the fact that in Europe and America people have already gone so far along a wrong road that the majority of their population is already torn from the land (in America it has never lived on the land), and lives either in factories or by hired agricultural labor, and desires and demands only one thing—the improvement of its position as hired laborers. It is therefore comprehensible that to the political workers of Europe and America—listening to the demands of the majority—it may seem that the chief means for the improvement of the position of the people consists in tariffs, trusts and colonies, but to the Russian people in Russia, where the agricultural population composes eighty per cent. of the whole nation, where all this people request only one thing—that opportunity be given them to remain in this state—it would seem, it should be clear, that for the improvement of the position of the people something else is necessary.

THE people of Europe and America are in the position of a man who has gone so far along a road which at first appeared the right one, but which the further he goes the more it removes him from his object, that he is afraid of confessing his mistake. But the Russians are yet standing before the turning of the path and can, according to the wise saying, "ask their way while yet on the road."

And what are those Russian people doing, who desire, or, at all events, say they desire, to organize a good life for the people? In everything they slavishly imitate whatever is being done in Europe and America.

For the arrangement of a good life for the people they are concerned with the freedom of the press, religious tolerance, liberty of union, tariffs, conditional punishment, the separation of the Church from the State, coöperative associations, future communalization of the implements of work, and, above all, with representative govern-

ment—that same representative government which has long existed in European and American states, but whose existence has not in the slightest contributed, nor does now contribute, not only to the solution, but even to the raising of that one land problem which involves all difficulties. If Russian political workers do speak about land abuse, which they for some reason call the "agrarian" question—probably thinking that this silly word will conceal the substance of the matter—they speak of it not in the sense that private landed property is an evil which should be abolished, but in the sense that it is necessary in some way or other, by various patchings and palliatives, to plaster up, hush up, and pass over this essential, ancient, and cruel, this obvious and crying injustice, which is awaiting its turn for abolition not only in Russia, but in the whole world. In Russia where a hundred million of the masses unceasingly suffer from the seizure of the land by private owners, and unceasingly cry out about it, the position of those people who are vainly searching everywhere but where it really is for the means of improving the condition of the people, reminds one exactly of that which takes place on the stage when all the spectators see perfectly well the man who has hidden himself, and the actors themselves ought to see him, but pretend they do not, intentionally distracting each other's attention and seeing everything except that which it is necessary for them to see, but which they do not wish to see.

PEOPLE have driven a herd of cows, on the milk products of which they are fed, into an enclosure. The cows have eaten up and trampled the forage in the enclosure, they are hungry, they have chewed each other's tails, they low and moan, imploring to be released from the enclosure and set free in the pastures. But the very men who feed themselves on the milk of these cows have set around the enclosure plantations of mint, or plants for dyeing purposes, and of tobacco; they have cultivated flowers, laid out a race-course, a park, and a lawn tennis ground, and they do not let out the cows lest they spoil these arrangements. But the cows bellow, get thin, and the men begin to be afraid that the cows may cease to yield milk, and they invent various means of improving the condition of these cows. They erect sheds over them, they introduce wet brushes for rubbing the cows, they gild their horns, alter the hour of milking, concern themselves with the housing and treating of invalid and old cows, they invent new and improved methods of milking, they expect that some kind of wonderfully nutritious grass they have sown in the enclosure will grow up, they argue about these and many other varied matters, but they do not, cannot—without disturbing all they have arranged around the enclosure—do the only simple thing necessary for themselves as well as for the cows—to wit, the taking down of the fence and granting the cows their natural freedom of using in plenty the pastures surrounding them.

Acting thus, men act unreasonably, but there is an explanation of their action; they are sorry for the fate of all they have arranged around the enclosure. But what shall we call those people who have set nothing around the fence, but who, out of imitation of those who do not set their cows free, owing to what they had arranged around the enclosure, also keep their cows inside the fence, and assert that they do so for the welfare of the cows themselves?

Precisely thus act those Russians, both Governmental and anti-Governmental, who arrange for the Russian people, unceasingly suffering from the want of land, for every kind of European institution, forgetting and denying the chief thing: that which alone the Russian people requires—the liberation of the land from private property, the establishment of equal rights on the land for all men.

The true bread-supporters of these European parasites are the laborers they do not see in India, Africa, Australia, and partly in Russia. But it is not so for us Russians; we have no colonies where slaves invisible to ourselves feed us for manufacturing produce. Our bread-winners, suffering, hungry, are always before our eyes, and we cannot transfer the burden of our iniquitous life to distant colonies, that slaves invisible to us should feed us.

OUR sins are always before us. And behold, instead of entering into the needs of those who support us, instead of hearing their cries and endeavoring to satisfy them, we, under pretext of serving them, also prepare, according to the European sample, Socialistic organizations for the future, and in the present occupy ourselves with what amuses and distracts us, and appears to be directed to the welfare of the people out of whom we are squeezing their last strength in order to support us, their parasites.

For the welfare of the people, we endeavor to abolish the censorship of books, arbitrary banishments, and to organize everywhere schools, common and agricultural, to increase the numbers of hospitals, to cancel passports and monopolies, to institute strict inspection in the factories, to reward maimed workers, to mark boundaries between properties, to contribute through banks to the purchase of land by peasants, and much else.

One need only enter into the unceasing sufferings of millions of the people; the dying out from want of the aged women, and children, and of the workers from excessive work and insufficient food—one need only enter into the servitude, the humiliations, all the useless expenditures of strength, into the deprivations, into all the horror of the needless calamaties of the Russian people and rural population which all proceed from insufficiency of land—in order that it should become quite clear that all such measures as the abolition of censorship, of arbitrary banishment, etc., which are being striven after by the pseudo-defenders of the people, even were they to be realized,

would form only the most insignificant drop in the ocean of that want from which the people are suffering.

But not only do those concerned with the welfare of the people, while inventing alterations, trifling, unimportant, both in quantity and quality, leave a hundred millions of people in unceasing slavery owing to the seizure of the land—more than this, many of these people, of the most progressive amongst them, desire that the suffering of this people should by its continual increase, drive them to the necessity—after leaving on their way millions of victims, perished from want and depravity—of exchanging their customary and happy, favorite and reasonable agricultural life for that improved factory life which they have invented, for them.

The Russian people—owing to their agricultural environment, their love for this form of life, their Christian trend of character, owing to the circumstances that they, almost alone of all European nations, continue to be an agricultural nation and desire to remain such—are, as it were, providentially placed by historic conditions for the solution of what is called the labor question, in such a position as to stand in the front of the true progressive movement of all mankind. Yet it is this Russian people who is invited by its fancied representatives and leaders to follow in the wake of the dying out and entangled European and American nations, to become depraved, and to relinquish its own calling as quickly as possible in order to become like Europeans in general.

THE question will be solved, not by those who will endeavor to mitigate the evil or to invent alleviations for the people or to postpone the task of the future, but by those who will understand, that, however one may mitigate a wrong, it remains a wrong, and that it is senseless to invent alleviations for a man we are torturing, and that one cannot postpone when people are suffering, but should immediately take the best way of solving the difficulty and immediately apply it in practice. The method of solving the land problem has been elaborated by Henry George to such a degree of perfection that, *under the existing State organization and compulsory taxation* it is impossible to invent any other better, more just, practical and peaceful solution.

"To beat down and cover up the truth that I have tried to-night to make clear to you (said Henry George). Selfishness will call on ignorance. But it has in it the germinative force of truth, and the times are ripe for it. The ground is plowed; the seed is set; the good tree will grow. So little now; only the eye of faith can see it."

And I think that Henry George is right, that the removal of the sin of landed property is near, that the movement called forth by Henry George was the last birth-throe, and that the birth is on the point of taking place; the liberation of men from the sufferings they have so long borne must now be realized. Besides this, I think (and

I would like to contribute to this, in however small a measure) that the removal of this great universal sin—a removal which will form an epoch in the history of mankind—is to be effected precisely by the Russian Slavonian people, who are, by their spiritual and economic character, predestined for this great universal task—that the Russian people should not become proletarians in imitation of the peoples of Europe and America, but, on the contrary, that they should solve the land question at home by the abolition of landed property, and show other nations the way to a rational, free and happy life, outside industrial, factory, or capitalistic coercion and slavery—that in this lies their great historic calling.

I would like to think that we Russian parasites, reared by and having received leisure for mental work through the people's labor, will understand our sin, and, independently of our personal advantage, in the name of the truth that condemns us, will endeavor to undo it.

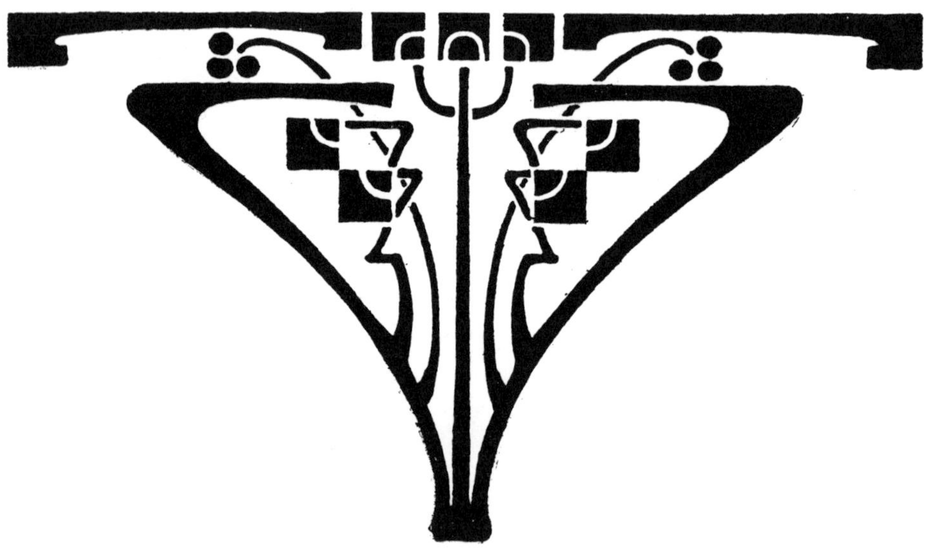

HOPI INDIANS—GENTLE FOLK: A PEOPLE WITHOUT NEED OF COURTS, JAILS OR ASYLUMS: BY LOUIS AKIN

N the vague North of Arizona, beyond that clean-cut horizon of keenest blue, and yet two days' travel through the Painted Desert—a spot that has felt less of the White Man's influence than any inhabited place in America—lies the land where the Hopi and his ancestors have dwelt in contented independence for unknown centuries; where ruin upon ruin, older than Egypt, verifies the oral traditions of archaic times, and where to-day these good people live, love and labor in ways but little changed from the utmost simplicity of prehistoric ages.

To those few in the outer world who ever heard of them at all they are mostly known as Moquis—this through the publicity gained by their annual Snake Dance. But *Moqui* or *Moki* is a misnomer. Hopi is how they would have us know them—because it is right, and because it means something to them and is justly symbolic of their racial characteristics. Peaceful—gentle is its significance—and the worst word they know to apply to an offender is ka-hopi—the negative of Hopi—or pas-ka-hopi, the superlative of this; and any one as bad as this is hopeless. Moki in their language means dead, and the accepted theory of its first application to them as a tribal name is that the Navajo, their long-time enemy, in a spirit of derision so called them on account of their distaste for warfare, and love of a quiet-stay-at-home life. According to the Navajo code they were "dead ones." From the Navajo, whose country entirely surrounds the Hopi, the early traders and settlers acquired the word Moki before ever seeing the Hopi; and from the trader it easily passed without question to the Government representatives, so it now stands as the official appellation in the Indian Department. But ask a Hopi if he is a Moqui—his quick resentment will be convincing enough.

The Hopi Reservation, about fifty miles square, is entirely within the boundaries of the great Navajo Reservation, but under separate administration. There are seven villages through which two thousand Indians are scattered. The first faint view of Oraibi, the largest village, is gained five or six miles down the trail, where by close attention the block-like houses can be picked out and distinguished above the like-formed rock of the mesa which they crown.

In following the horse trail directly, the view grows plainer and then is lost, as the way winds closer, up through scrubby peach orchards and melon patches, past a deep, Oriental-looking spring, then squarely up a narrow, precipitous passage where your pony climbs like the goat he has to be, and out on the summit full into the village street. At once everybody in town knows there are strangers within the walls. It isn't wireless—it's dogs.

HOPI MEN IN THE STREETS OF ORAIBI

A HOPI MATRON PREPARING CORN FOR THE MILL STONE

A BAHANA (White Man) has no reason to complain of his reception, for the Hopi has a strong, fine sense of hospitality. Appear at his door, and a courteous form of welcome awaits you. He bids you enter, expresses "thanks that you have come," shows you to a seat and then adds a phrase to the effect that "you are welcome to remain forever." The mother or daughter brings food and you eat whether it looks inviting or not, if you'd retain their utmost goodwill and respect. But it's all good, take my word for it, and don't wait for knives and forks; it's good form to dip or gouge into anything with your own original tools. And then, when you go, you are asked most cordially to "come again very soon."

My first visit was on a flat hunting expedition, accompanied by youthful Mah-si′-wa, who could speak a little English, and the first place I entered was the one I wanted and finally secured. It was the upper floor of a two-story house, occupied then by the family, but Nav-ah-hong-a-ni-ma was willing to rent it out and move downstairs, as it was nearing autumn when they all move into the lower stories for more warmth. So, upon my quickly agreeing to pay her seventy-five cents a week for two or three weeks—all she asked and which astonished her, for she had expected me to offer her twenty-five cents, and have an hour's joyous haggling before coming to an agreement at fifty—she moved her few chattels out and swept the floor. The room was about eighteen by thirty-five feet, a door at each end and a couple of small windows of one pane of glass set directly into adobe. The front ten feet of the floor was some two feet above the rest, with stone steps to reach it, and that higher part half partitioned off by a low wall part way, giving it a gallery effect. In three corners were tiny, quaint fireplaces, one a sunken oven, and in the other corner the mealing stones, set in a shallow trough in the adobe floor with a wee, unglazed window beside them. A broad, low banquette on one side offered a cozy couching place with another half partition at one end, giving it semi-privacy. Then there were sundry cubby holes in the walls and a couple of storage bins which furnished seating space. The stone walls were smoothly plastered with adobe by hand, in a way that leaves no square corners or hard, straight lines, and all but the floor was neatly whitewashed with pure, white clay.

Hung to pegs near the ceiling, and forming almost a frieze around the room, were bunches of dried herbs, red peppers, dried muskmelon, dried boiled sweet-corn-on-the-cob, neat packages of corn-husks cured for various uses, and ears of choicest corn of many colors for next year's seeding. All this I asked her to leave, for I liked it, and also I kindly permitted her to leave a large pile of cool, ripe watermelons in one corner. Then she brought water in a wikurra, I bought a load of scrubby fagots that Sah-koy′-um-na had just brought in, unpacked my few food supplies from the traders, and my blankets and painting duffle, and was at home. "At home"

is correct. That first day was my reception day though no cards were sent out. Nearly all the men in the village, some of the women and a few of the bolder or more curious children came. All were interested to know what object I could have in coming there and settling in such an apparently permanent way in the midst of them.

These gentle folk are very susceptible to gentle treatment and it wasn't long till I began to feel highly gratified to see that I was winning their confidence to an unexpected degree, even in the conservative faction. Yes, even the children, playing about the streets in their little bronze pelts, soon reached a point of confidence where they wouldn't run screaming for home or the nearest shelter when I appeared, and eventually the time came when they'd run joyously to me, calling me by name—my Hopi name—instead of scattering; then, indeed, was my pride unspeakable. The ambitions of a few recent school teachers to augment their roster had led them to drag their nets very closely for kindergartners, and the unnecessarily brutal means they employed were quite truly enough to justify all mothers and weaned infants in their terror of a Bahana.

MY two or three weeks lengthened into months, and yet into nearly a year, before I finally jogged down the trail for the last time toward the outer world, with a very small roll of canvases, but a great wealth of happy memories; for I didn't do much actual work, the conditions were against it. There was too much of living interest in this new world that I found myself a part of. How could I paint when Ke-wan-i-um′-ti-wa came to spend an afternoon in my education, making me get up and "act out" things to be sure I had my lessons right? How could I paint when an old grandmother wanted me to see by every detail how much better than modern methods was the good old way of building up the clay for a piece of pottery? Or, when Pu-hu′-nim-ka, with a tiny yucca-fiber brush in her deft, tapering fingers, permitted me to watch her penciling the old, intricate design on one of her gracefully modeled bowls? Or, when Ku-ku-ti′-ti-wa, the lame boy, came to borrow tools and get advice in fashioning a finger-ring of lead, set with a rough, blue stone, the model for one he planned to make in silver and turquoise when he had acquired the necessary tools and knowledge for that advanced work? How could I paint when there was a rabbit drive to join, or the spinning "bee" for the bridal robes of some good friend's daughter, or a ceremonial foot-race, or when our Katcinas were going to Shungopavi to dance, to show "those Shungopavis" how easy it is to make the rain come when a people have superior knowledge and stand high with the Cloud Spirits, or when there was a nine days' ceremony on at home and never a minute of it, day or night, that hadn't some real interest in it.

So I didn't paint and there are no regrets. When old Ho-ve′-i-

ma, the crier,—he of the great voice—stood on the highest house-top and announced that on the third day all were invited to come to the fields of one who was too old and feeble to get his planting done alone, and help him to finish it, it was worth more to me to join the groups that trailed down into the plains before sunrise and see two weeks' work done in a few hours by people who live very near to the Golden Rule. And the charm of it is that such communal work is done with the utmost cheerfulness; song and laughter are everywhere, and when the task is done there's always a big dinner ready at the home of the one benefited, in which also the woman of the house has had the co-operation of her friends. Such occasions come often, as when a man wishes to start a new blanket. If he were to spin all the yarn alone he'd spend weeks at it; but let him invite his friends to come to a kiva on a certain day to help him, and presto! all the yarn is spun in no time, everybody has a good, social time and a dinner, and he is ready to set up his loom next day. An odd feature of Hopi life is this, that the men do all the spinning, weaving, embroidering of ceremonial robes, knitting of leggins and the sewing of the garments made popular by the advent of calicoes and velvets. This, too, in addition to cultivating the fields, herding the flocks, gathering the fire-wood and taking their part in the many ceremonies.

Every man is an artist unto himself, in a way, in Hopi-land, for every man has his part in religious rites some time each year, which requires of him the painting of various symbolic designs; so every man is able to go out and gather from Mother Earth his own necessary colors, grind and prepare them, make his brushes of yucca-fiber, and finish his work neatly and artistically.

Then, too, they make for one festal occasion many Katcina dolls, carved from cottonwood in very simple forms that have come down to them as correct from the days when stone and bone tools superinduced simplicity of treatment, then painted in the detail of costume of some particular variety of Katcina. There are about two hundred and fifty separate and distinct Katcina personages, each of whom has some special influence with some of the various Elemental Spirits. In the Katcina ceremonies, which last all through the planting and growing season, these mythical beings are impersonated by variously masked and costumed groups of dancers who, for the time, lose their own identity and are consecrated to the rites of the occasion and spend days in song and prayer for the successful growth and maturity of the crops. These dolls are given to the little girls, with decorated bows and arrows for the boys, on the last morning of the Powamu ceremony which marks the opening of the Katcina season in February. More than mere gift, they symbolize the good-will of the Katcina represented and are more highly prized as blessings than as toys.

OFFERING SACRED CORN MEAL TO THE RISING SUN IN GRAND CAÑON

It would seem as though there is hardly an act in the day's work or play that hasn't some religious association, and it is all sincere to the very utmost, not thoughtless form. When a man smokes a cigarette or pipe, each puff of smoke is a cloud symbol and implies a prayer for rain—and he means it. When a man brings home from the hunt a rabbit or two, his wife or mother takes them at the door, lays them on the floor, gets a pinch of sacred meal and breathes a prayer of gratitude while scattering it over the game—and she means

it. It is distinctly a religion of environment. As life and happiness depend upon the success of the agricultural crops, each of the elements that has any part in their germination, growth and maturity is represented by a spirit to whom supplication is made to that end in many ways, all with the utmost fervor and sincerity. They do not recognize one Great Spirit, but there is the "Sun Spirit," the "Moon Spirit," "Cloud," "Thunder," "Lightning," "Wind," and "Fire" spirits, "Spirit of Germination," of the "Underworld" who keeps the springs running, and yet a few more. At any rate they *live* it day by day, and it has been effective enough to keep them a gentle, peaceful, honest, industrious people, with a pure blood and no necessity for courts of justice, jails or orphan asylums for untold ages.

In all my time there I never saw the remotest sign of a quarrel between men, women, or children, and though my house was open most of the time and littered over with things that every visitor coveted, I never had a theft but through one man. There must be exceptions to even the Golden Rule. He got away with a pipe and some silver buttons once when posing for me, and though I forbade him coming to my house and denounced him in well-defined terms, he came cheerfully along just the same, bearing no malice for my harsh words.

THE Paradise or Spirit House of the Hopi is in Grand Cañon, and there is sent, during certain important ceremonies, a messenger priest who makes a votive deposit in the shrine erected there, tenders a prayer offering of sacred corn meal to the rising sun and carries back with him certain waters and herbs for use in further rites. Shrines are everywhere in the vicinity of Hopi towns. Some are shrines to distant mountains, rivers, the ocean, some to prehistoric or traditional homes of ancestors or clans, and in nearly every field is some manner of shrine in which to deposit especial prayer offerings prepared by the priests for the purpose, which the fortunate ones proudly carry to the fields with perfect confidence in their efficacy. The indoor religious ceremonies are held in underground chambers known as kivas, of which there are fourteen in Oraibi. Each man belongs to some one of the fraternities occupying these kivas.

There are songs for every work-a-day act or occupation, for any mood, for any weather. It may be Nah-si'-kwap-ti-wa, off before sunrise on his old burro after a load of scrubby wood, from six or eight miles back on the higher mesas, whose vocal expression of the joy of living comes drifting back to you in the gray dawn, or it may be a shepherd on his early way to the corrals, or two or three young gods in breech-clouts, astride one burro, "pegging it" toward the fields. It may be a group of little animate bronzes playing in the sand, or Mrs. Masho'-hong-wa crooning over her youngest, or perhaps an ardent youth who stands alone and stately out on the rocks towards the sunset, yet within good hearing of "Her" who is of a

bevy of maidens taking the twilight hour away from the corn-grinding.

But always there is someone, somewhere, singing.

FRUIT BOWL DESIGNED BY ALBERT A. SOUTHWICK.
EXECUTED BY LOUIS TIFFANY & CO.

THE·ENTRANCE·AND·VINE·COVERED·WALL: ABOUT·THE·GARDEN

SWEDENBORGIAN CHURCH · NEAR THE·GOLDEN·GATE SANFRANCISCO·CAL:

AN·IDEAL·COUNTRY·CHURCH·SET·DOWN·IN·HER·OWN·GARDEN

THE·TOWER & GARDEN

A DEPARTURE IN CHURCH BUILDING—THE SECOND NEW JERUSALEM CHURCH IN CALIFORNIA: BY A STRANGER

"IF thou shouldst ever come by chance or choice to Modena,
Stop at a palace near the Reggio gate"—

are the opening words of a poem by an English poet that tells in succeeding lines of a picture of a beautiful bride and of her joy and jest and tragic death. Now, I would change these words to read: If thou shouldst ever come by choice or chance to San Francisco, stop at a Church out near the Golden Gate, and in a few succeeding prose lines tell of a joy entirely free from jest, and of life instead of death.

A strong, simple-minded man, one who appreciates and loves the simplicity of nature, conceived the idea of giving to his people of the city a simple country meeting-house. Others of his kind joined hands with him, and to-day on the sunny side of one of San Francisco's barren hills, in the heart of one of the best residence sections, you will find an ideal village church, set down in its own garden. And that garden is not filled with rows of little green mounds and their attending headstones, but is a grassy slope extending to the concrete wall, whose severe lines are hidden by the caressing touch of numerous and varied vines. This grassy slope is spotted o'er with trees, so naturally grouped that one feels God's hand had dropped the olive, thorn-apple and pine cone from which these trees have grown. The dark red of the Japanese plum tree and rich green of the stately English yew and Italian cypress give variety. As our eyes were filled with their beauty, our hearts were likewise filled with thankfulness to these distant lands for their contribution to this garden symphony.

Amid the shrubbery one will find a simple iron cross rising from an ivy-covered stone base, which was taken from one of the old Spanish Missions before the days of preservation and restoration began. There is also a Japanese cypress that tells the story of its centuries by its knots and gnarls.

We enter through an iron gate and tiled portico, by a long box of ferns, that hold their leafy fronds aloft exultingly, and all unconsciously are thrown into bold relief by the dark red wall behind them. Before we realize it we are right in the garden, and in the inclosure comes the feeling of "A world of strife shut out and a world of love shut in."

DURING these autumnal days the simple tower surmounted by its small iron cross is truly beautifully attired in its dress of Ampelopsis leaves; while close by a single white rose is trying to tell its tale of June days with a few belated blossoms; and at her feet we found red, ripe, wild strawberries doing their best to

AN · OLD · FASHIONED · FIRE · PLACE IN · THE · SWEDENBORGIAN · CHURCH

A · SIMPLE · ALTAR · AND · TIMBERED · CEILING

emphasize her story of the spring-time. Close by the walk that leads to the entrance is a round, shallow basin—partially shown in the picture of the tower—which the gardener always leaves full of water for the birds. "Whosoever shall give to drink unto one of these little ones, shall in no wise lose his reward."

Over the entrance, supported by a bamboo trellis, is a grape-vine, and as we stepped under its shadows the strings of our hearts were vibrant with the memory of the Master's words: "I am the vine, ye are the branches." The sweet silence of this simple garden had pervaded our spirits, and we were content to remain within its spell, when the lines of the poem reverberated through our minds like a long lost voice, saying:—

"But ere thou go, enter the house
—— prithee, forget it not—
And look awhile upon some pictures there."

The atmosphere of reverence which one perceives with his first breath is a strong rebuke to the simply curious person who would enter. Instantly we feel that it is no place for the being who does not care to hear his Maker's voice. Before one is seated there is the consciousness of a friendly feeling extended by the warmth that comes from a generous supply of pine knots ablaze upon an ample hearth in an old-fashioned fireplace near the door. The piney odor, unhewn timbers and profusion of pine boughs, both green and brown, make one feel that the forest is near.

The room is longest from east to west, and the walls of the gable ends are finished in rough gray plaster, while the ceiling is wooden, the arch of which is supported by Madrono timbers with the bark on, selected for that purpose, while they were yet a part of the forest in the Santa Cruz mountains. On the north side there are no windows, but instead, four pictures. These pictures have no frames except the plain, dark stained panels of the wall set between the uncut timbers that support the roof. Consequently one can easily imagine one is looking through a window away off into the meadow or the hills.

I AM informed that these pictures depict the four California seasons, and if they needed names, could be aptly described by passages of Scripture. The first,—Winter—where large, old trees lift their giant branches aloft, forming nave and chancel with their leafy arches, against a cold, dark sky, might be called "The Groves were God's first Temples." The second,—Spring—with its stream of water running through a fresh, green meadow under a sky filled with departing rain clouds, "For lo, the winter is past, the rain is over and gone, the flowers appear on the earth, the time of the singing of birds is come." The third,—Summer—with its burdened field made more yellow by the summer glow that comes with waning light, suggests that "The harvest truly is plenteous, but the labourers are few," and likewise the command, "Thrust in thy sickle and reap, for the harvest of the earth is ripe." The fourth,—Autumn—is just a plain country road ascending an ordinary hill, through sere, brown fields, awaiting the awakening the rain will bring. But the sight of that *ascending* road fills one's soul with an Excelsior feeling, and to the listening ear comes the words: "And an highway shall be there, and a way, and it shall be called, The way of Holiness."

"When the twilight veils the sky," and there is no longer any sun to make this beautiful place light, numerous candles, held in place by wrought-iron candelabra, shed forth their soft light. The picture of the altar shows how the pine, with bough and cone, is used for decoration. But beyond its simple beauty it is to us a symbol of the ideal Christian. "For he shall be as a tree planted by the waters." "His countenance is as Lebanon, excellent as the cedars." Over the altar is a small, round window. We know not the artist's thought when he made this expression of it in glass, but flower and bird at once suggest, "Consider the lilies" and "Are not two sparrows sold for a farthing? and one of them shall not fall on the ground without your Father."

THREE BEGGARS AT THE DOOR
OF A HOUSE—DATE 1648

These reproductions of Rembrandt's etchings are taken from the collection in the Boston Museum of Fine Arts, through the courtesy of Mr. Emil H. Richter, Curator of the Department of Prints.

LANDSCAPE WITH RUINED TOWER—ETCHED ABOUT 1649

VIEW OF OMVAL, NEAR AMSTERDAM—DATED 1645

THE USE AND ABUSE OF MACHINERY, AND ITS RELATION TO THE ARTS AND CRAFTS

SHORT time ago I received a circular issued by the management of a prominent Arts and Crafts Society of which I am a member, in which the announcement was made that an exhibition of representative handicraft work would be held early in the coming year for the purpose of showing the "great strides" recently made in America in the development of artistic craftsmanship. According to the announcement, the exhibits are to be limited strictly to "handiwork of original design, as the exhibition is organized for the one purpose of showing the supremacy of the hand over the machine, in craft work making claim to artistic quality."

This circular seems to me to express so exactly the prevailing idea of what is meant by the word "craftsmanship," that I am impelled to make at least the effort to show how serious are the limitations of this idea, and how far it is from going to the root of the matter and revealing the one essential element of craftsmanship, which is not the mere idea of doing things by hand, but the putting of thought, care and individuality into the task of making honestly and well something that satisfies a real need. In the revolt against the utter lack of vitality or of artistic quality in the great mass of machine-made products that owe their existence solely to the artificial demand created by commercialism, enthusiasts for the revival of the handicrafts have not only allowed themselves to be carried to an extreme in the opposite direction, but have fallen into the selfsame sin against true craftsmanship by encouraging the making of things for which there is no manner of need, and which, not being the outgrowth of a fundamental necessity, have in them no element of living art.

The time is ripe for the birth in this country of a national art—an art that shall express the strongly individual characteristics of the American people, but, like all art, it must spring in the first place from the common needs of the common people. All new growth must start from a return to root needs, or root principles, and unless there is a going back to these to gain a fresh point of departure, all that is done expresses merely the restlessness of a constant search after novelty, not the natural growth of a new and vital form of art. Merely to make things by hand implies no advance in the development of an art that shall live and make its own place in world-history as a true record of the thought and life of this age, any more than the making of them after "original designs" implies that these designs are the outgrowth of thought based upon that need which is the root of inspiration to the true craftsman, as well as upon his personal desire for self-expression.

THERE is no question that the Arts and Crafts movement is a step in the right direction. It is one phase of the world-wide desire to get rid of the cumbersome artificialities that clog so much of modern life. But is it making "great strides" in the development of artistic craftsmanship in America? It is interesting, and it sounds well, to speak of "showing the supremacy of the hand over the machine," but can it be put to the test of a generally practical application and can an exhibition held for this sole purpose mark any distinct advance? In England, the original home of the Arts and Crafts movement and where it has attained its greatest development, there is no sign that a new school of art is growing up, for the great majority of the exhibitions are merely exhibitions of individual cleverness at playing with new toys that mean no more than the old. On the continent, the followers of L'Art Nouveau are for the most part committing fantastic extravagances that simply emphasize their desire to revolt from the conventional, without giving the world anything better in its place. There is evidently an honest desire to produce something that shall be simple and strong and beautiful, but only in isolated instances is that desire fulfilled. For the most part, all that is achieved is a jumble of so-called decorative forms that are founded neither upon need nor reason, and so are worse than the forms they seek to replace, and do nothing beyond adding to the world's stock of useless things.

It seems to me that the trouble with it all is the placing of the cart before the horse. The work of the old craftsman, being the outgrowth of direct need, not only was an honest expression of himself, but typified the life and thought of the age. It was founded upon sound principles of construction, because his sole thought was to make something that should serve fully the purpose for which it was intended. If it was ornamented, the decoration was a secondary thing that grew naturally out of the structure of the piece because the worker felt the need of expression for his own idea of beauty. Now, the decorative form is the first consideration, and the structure is made to conform to it, an evidence on the face of it that the piece exists to express a decorative idea, not because there is any real need for it. It is play instead of work and it embodies no element sufficiently vital to carry it beyond the realm of the studio. Because of this it evokes no real response from the great body of the people, and so is no true expression of the collective thought of the age.

It is a sense of the vitality that distinguishes the handiwork of former days that has produced the present reaction to handiwork as infinitely superior to any product of the machine. As a matter of fact, given the real need for production and the fundamental desire for honest self-expression, the machine can be put to all its legitimate uses as an aid to, and a preparation for, the work of the hand, and the

result be quite as vital and satisfying as the best work of the hand alone. The mere question of hand work as opposed to machine work is largely superficial. The prime object of the industrial arts is to produce articles which satisfy some material or mechanical requirement, and any method of working is allowable which really effects that object in the simplest and most straightforward manner. The modern trouble lies not with the use of machinery, but with the abuse of it, and the hope of reform would seem to be in the direction of a return to the spirit which animated the workers of a more primitive age, and not merely to an imitation of their method of working.

THE invention of modern machinery is in itself a notable achievement of the true spirit of craftsmanship. In ninety-nine cases out of a hundred, the inventor of a machine that is meant to do any particular work, is himself a master of that work and has turned all his ability toward the finding of some means by which it may be more perfectly, as well as more easily, done. When rightly used, that machine is simply a tool in the hands of the skilled worker, and in no way detracts from the quality of his work. Almost anything that can legitimately be done by machinery can be done much more swiftly, accurately and economically than by hand. Also, to use a good machine that runs well and does its work as if by magic affords fully as much pleasure to the worker as the most interesting hand work. It is simply the best means to attain a desired end, and his interest is in the work itself and the result he is trying to produce —not in the way he is doing it. Naturally, in making this statement I refer only to purely mechanical labor, where the quickest and most economical way of doing the thing required is just so much gained in time and strength. For instance, to use an illustration that is surely on my own ground, an expert carpenter or cabinet-maker will save much time that can be used to better advantage, and will lose nothing of the artistic quality of his work, if he makes use of the adequate modern machines for sawing, planing, boring, mortising, scraping, sandpapering and otherwise preparing his material for use, instead of insisting that all these things be done by hand. It should be the privilege of every worker to take advantage of all the improved methods of working that relieve him from the tedium and fatigue of purely mechanical toil, for by this means he gains leisure for the thought necessary to working out his designs, and for the finer touches that the hand alone can give. So long as he remains master of his machinery it will serve him well, and his power of artistic expression will be freed rather than stifled by turning over to it work it is meant to do.

The trouble is that we have allowed the machine to master us. The possibility of quick, easy and cheap production has so intoxicated us that we have gone on producing in a sort of insane prolificness, and

our imaginary needs have grown with it. Originally intended to make simpler and easier the doing of necessary things, the introduction of machinery with its train of attendant evils has so complicated and befuddled our standards of living that we have less and less time for enjoyment and for growth, and nervous prostration is the characteristic disease of the age. The old simile of the sewing machine exactly expresses the state of affairs. Its introduction was to be a boon to overworked woman by relieving her of the tedious hours of stitchery and so giving her more leisure for other things or for rest, but to her the means of doing ten times as much work in an hour as she could do by hand meant simply an opportunity to put ten tucks into a garment instead of one. Instead of adding something to her life, the machine took away more than it brought, for it encouraged the desire for senseless and needless elaboration and so made her work harder and more confining than before. When she ornamented a garment made by hand, the ornamentation was the expression of her own thought of beauty, but with the mechanical ornamentation made possible by the machine there grew up in her mind a false idea of mere elaboration for its own sake, and so the machine mastered instead of serving her.

AND one of the chief dangers of machinery lies in this very matter of mechanical ornamentation. True ornament is always the spontaneous expression of the individuality of the worker. The construction of the thing he makes may be more or less arbitrarily determined by the use to which that thing is to be put, but when it comes to decorating it he is his own master and it is his own idea that he must express if his work is to have in it the element of art. If a man makes a chair that is in itself everything a chair should be, he has first of all satisfied a real need for a strong and comfortable seat, and if he chooses to carve it after his own thought of what it needs to make it beautiful, his work, be it fine or crude, is art. But if he makes a chair that is first of all shaped by the mere desire to produce a novelty, and then proceeds to overlay it with a mass of machine-made carving or embossing that is utterly meaningless and has no other purpose than to appeal to false standards of the desirability of elaboration, in order that the chair may find more ready sale, he has merely added to the heterogeneous mass of superfluous and bad stuff with which our homes are too much cumbered as it is. This is a danger of machinery, for it is most easily done in that way, but the same thing applies to meaningless ornamentation done by hand. Handiwork is no better than machinery if the thing produced be needless and without meaning, and the principle to be established appears to me to be, not the supremacy of the hand over the machine, but the supremacy of the thing that is needed over that which is made more or less as a pastime.

The much-talked-of return to simpler and better things and the revival of the old spirit of craftsmanship can come about only through a process of drastic elimination, followed by a return to primitive principles of construction based on primitive needs. It is not a piling-up of new things that is needed, but a new point of departure from which can be developed a genuine national art. When a thing is made because it is needed, that need creates its own limitations of form and decoration, and with that in mind one can not go very far wrong. In spite of all the talk about the revival of handiwork as the one essential to the development of "artistic craftsmanship," it is impossible to reverse the conditions that have obtained since the introduction of machinery and to return to making everything by hand. Machinery can not be abolished, nor should it be, but it can be mastered by the growth of truer standards and made to keep in its place and to do its own work. If people would reject all machine-made ornamentation as false to the fundamental principles of decoration and therefore inherently bad, they would go far toward limiting the machine to its legitimate uses, and the best and most vital forms of handicraft would spring up spontaneously and flourish under modern conditions as lustily as they did of old. Also, if the needless things were relentlessly thrown out of the house, there would be a just appreciation of what remained, and the making of the really necessary belongings would once more be a matter sufficiently important to warrant individual care and thought. This once established, there would be no danger in the use of machinery, and no need to give exhibitions for the one purpose of showing the supremacy of hand work, for the real friendliness of machinery to the handicrafts would be shown in the growth of an industrial art as vital and lasting as that of the mediaeval craftsmen toward whose methods of work it is now the fashion to cast such longing eyes.

SALOMÉ AND HEROD
Drawn by Frances Lea

"WILL YOU INDEED GIVE ME WHATSOEVER I SHALL ASK?"

FOUR GARGOYLES AMONG THE SIX HUNDRED USED TO DECORATE THE BUILDINGS OF THE COLLEGE OF THE CITY OF NEW YORK

ALS IK KAN

TO CRYSTALLIZE into a public and official utterance from the highest source in the nation a protest which, in one form or another, has become the prevailing thought of the people, is to give it a significance and a driving force that brings it home with a shock to the conservative, and startles, even while it delights, the radical who advocates sweeping reforms. Considered in this light, it is no wonder that the much-discussed President's message has been a veritable bombshell, and that the echoes of the explosion are still rolling far and wide. Yet, in its bearing upon questions of social, industrial, and political reform, it is only an expression of the change which has taken place during the past few years in the public attitude toward our great problems of special priv-

ileges, political and corporate corruption, and the social and industrial inequality which accords so ill with the fundamental principles of the Republic. The most hopeful sign of these strenuous and progressive times is the widely-manifested disposition to investigate and protest against evil conditions that heretofore have been accepted, however unwillingly, as a part of the established order of things, and President Roosevelt has only given utterance to the prevailing thought of the great mass of the people.

Naturally, the excitement centers about those clauses of the message which deal with the curbing of corporate greed, and with the taking of measures to restrain the accumulation of enormous fortunes by private individuals through the exploitation of public properties and utilities for private gain.

It is admitted that the prosperity of a country depends upon the industry and activity of its producing class, and it is also an unquestioned fact that hard times are brought about by the congestion of the market through the manipulation of the speculative or gambling class that exists upon the exploitation of the products of others. When the cry of "over-production" is raised, it does not mean over-production, but under-consumption, brought about by the diminution of the purchasing power among the great mass of the people. This diminution of purchasing power is the direct result of the methods of monopolists, and is the obverse of the richly gilded shield of American commercialism; and measures taken to restrict the inordinate power of the monopolies, especially of monopolies in commodities that are common necessities, can hardly be held responsible for precipitating a reaction in our prosperity.

The world progresses, even though at times the course of its onward movement seems eccentric, and the fact is significant that the stones of social theory which the builders rejected yesterday become to-day the corner-stones of social statesmanship. As Emerson says: "Every revolution was first a thought in one man's mind, and when the same thought occurs to another man it is the key to that era." After the publication of the President's message, Mr. Carnegie, with special reference to the clause which advocates a tax upon inheritances, sent to Mr. Roosevelt a copy of his book, "The Gospel of Wealth," in which, sixteen years ago, he had advocated the same measure. In January 1848, the famous *Communist Manifesto* of Marx and Engels advocated the graduated taxation of incomes and inheritances, not as a solution of the social problem, but as a means to that end. It is less than sixty years since the proposition of this measure terrified half the civilized world, and now it comes as an official utterance from the President of the United States, and only here and there is heard the cry of "Socialism!" It is a new era. The old individualism of American politics, which was the reflex of the economic conditions of the ante-bellum period, is replaced in our day by an ever growing sense of collective responsibility, itself the product of changed economic conditions. A comparison of the messages of any of the Presidents before Lincoln with the recent message of President Roosevelt would afford a basis for a most suggestive and illuminating study of sociology. We have reached a point in our development where we are no longer frightened by scare-words. Here and there, critics of the President's courageously stated protest against the accumulation of immense private fortunes, and the creation of plutocratic dynasties, have raised the cry that it is dangerous and revolutionary, but it is safe to say that the great majority of the American people accustomed to serious thought upon social conditions are in hearty sympathy with the President's point of view.

That the immense fortunes to which in recent years we have become accustomed are a menace to the safety and

stability of the republican form of government is not seriously questioned. Two or three years ago a list was published of the names of twenty-four men who, between them, directly or indirectly, represented and in a measure controlled one-twelfth of the total national wealth, and all these men were on the directorate of a single industrial concern—the so-called Steel Trust. It requires no argument to show that in the creation of such powerful dynasties of finance and industrial rule lies a great danger to the institutions of a free and democratic people.

It is no hardship for the heirs of a multimillionaire to have the State resume a part of the fortune which it helped him to make. The grandson of Marshall Field, for instance, the fourteen-year-old boy—a British subject by the way—who inherited one hundred and fifty millions, might even forfeit half to the commonweal and struggle along on seventy-five millions without suffering from actual privation. These enormous fortunes can not be regarded as the product solely of the genius or industry of their owners, or of the men by whom they were accumulated. It is true that in most cases both genius and industry are required for the accumulation, but, as Mr. Carnegie demonstrated with notable clearness in the address which he delivered recently at the convention of the National Civic Federation, the individual is largely an accident, the community on one hand and great natural resources on the other hand being in almost every case the main sources of wealth, which can not with justice or wisdom be regarded wholly as private property.

Not very long ago, a small plot of land in New York City sold for seven hundred thousand dollars, which seventy-five years ago had brought only eighteen thousand dollars. Every dollar of that vast increase was due to the communal energy and growth, and in nowise due to the activities of the profiting individual owning it. Such cases as this, and hundreds might be cited, explain the automatic growth of John Jacob Astor's modest fortune of two hundred and fifty thousand dollars, made in the fur trade, into the immense Astor estates of to-day, which aggregate in value more than four hundred million dollars.

The as yet little exploited land thefts, by which millions of acres of our best timber and mineral lands have been stolen from the public domain, have been and are sources of prodigious and far-reaching corruption; and another has been the reckless granting of more than two hundred millions of acres of our best land to railroad corporations, an area almost equal to the combined territory of Great Britain and Ireland, with France added, these supporting a population of seventy-five millions of people.

These are only a few instances, but they would seem sufficient to refute the accusation that Mr. Roosevelt's recommendation of drastic remedial measures is likely to bring about hard times, or to arouse the discontent of the great mass of the people by its unnecessary zeal. Surely it does not take a fanatic or a Socialist to realize that if, for instance, a corporation succeed in so controlling the supply of any commodity that the consumers of that commodity are dependent upon the corporation, the only assurance of public safety lies in the federal control of that commodity, and that, if the enormous inflation of private fortunes be checked by the imposition of an inheritance tax that shall compel the return to the State of a portion to be used for the benefit of the commonwealth that helped to make it, the result would not be likely to bring about an uprising of the discontented masses. The impossibility of a wise and socially safe use of these great fortunes by their owners becomes increasingly evident. When, as in the case of Mr. Carnegie, an attempt is made to use any considerable proportion in public benefactions, such as the building of libraries, art galleries, and museums,

and the creation of pension funds, the whole nation suffers irreparable loss of self-respect and responsibility. It is not well for any nation to develop the instinct of looking to individuals to do what society as a whole ought to do.

That sooner or later a way must, and will, be found to stop the exploitation of public resources and needs for private gain and display is certain. The taxation of inheritances, progressively to the expropriation of the fruits of privilege, and all unequal advantages in the human struggle, must sooner or later pass from the domain of theory to that of accomplished fact. Taxation of inheritances is not a panacea for all the ills of society, but it is a long step toward the goal of social justice. That it should be so vigorously proposed by the President of the greatest republic in history, and so well considered by such men as discussed the matter before the Civic Federation, is a sign of progress that is epoch-making in its significance.

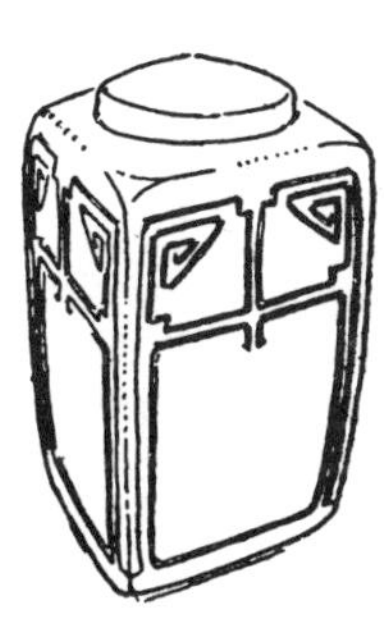

From a Print by Hiroshige.

"TENDERNESS AND CHARM IN THE GROUP OF HOME SWALLOWS DARTING TOWARD A *Nanten* BUSH IN THE ROSY EVENING LIGHT."

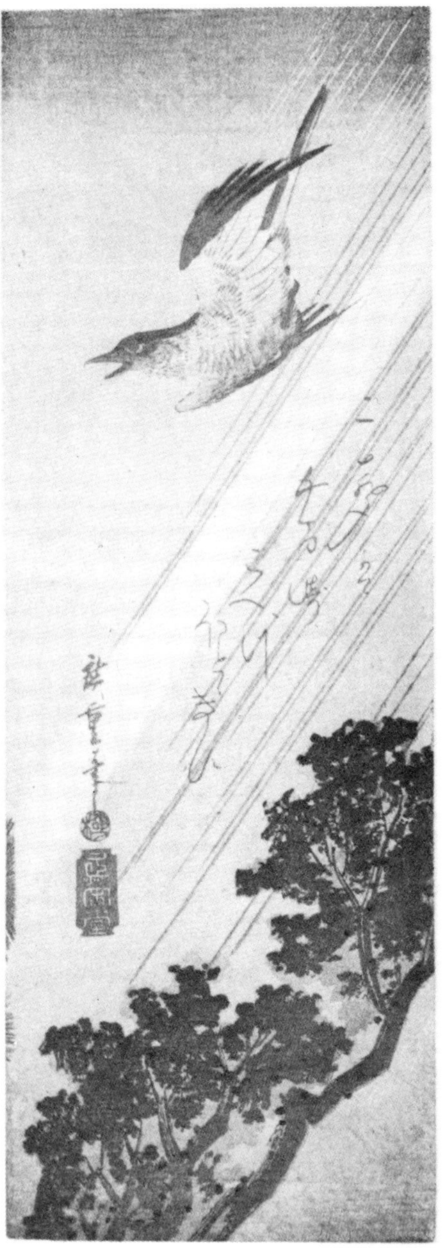

From a Print by Hiroshige.

"ALMOST WE CAN HEAR THE EXULTANT CRY OF THE WILD HAWK DASHING THROUGH THE BLAST OF A STORM * * * THE TIPS OF THE PINE TREES BELOW."

DESIGN IN THEORY AND PRACTICE: A SERIES OF LESSONS: BY ERNEST A. BATCHELDER: NUMBER III

"Understand this clearly: you can teach a man to draw a straight line and to cut one; to strike a curved line and to carve it; and to copy and carve any number of given lines or forms with admirable speed and precision: . . . but if you ask him to think about any of those forms, to consider if he cannot find any better in his own head, he stops; his execution becomes hesitating; he thinks, and ten to one he thinks wrong; ten to one he makes a mistake in the first touch he gives to his work as a thinking being."

JOHN RUSKIN.

THE construction of good curves is quite akin to the planning of good proportions. A few general hints may be offered, and their observance should enable one to venture beyond the commonplace without becoming entangled in the bizarre and fantastic. By calling geometry to our aid certain types of curves may be plotted; yet in practice we are thrown back upon our curve sense, if it mav be so expressed. Our equipment may be increased by the purchase of a number of the "French curves," so called; but the best advice is—don't. In these mechanical aids there is no clue to the why, when and where of curves. It were better to cultivate a curve sense through diligent study and practice, and then place dependence upon that most remarkable of all instruments, the human hand.

Mr. Ruskin in "Modern Painters" calls the circle the "finite curve." Any section of a circle, if completed, returns unto itself; a segment from one portion is the same in shape as a segment from another portion. The circle has unity, but lacks variety.

Now, there is another kind of curve which Mr. Ruskin calls the "infinite curve"—more subtle and with greater beauty than the circle. It is the curve that Nature most loves, which she seems ever striving to attain. Seek where you will, from the blade of grass to the shells on the beach, you will find this "infinite curve." With a T-square and triangle one can be easily plotted, (Fig. 13-B). Draw a series of horizontal lines equally distant one from the other; cut them at one end with a vertical; then from the top of the vertical draw a line, at whatever angle you choose, to the lower horizontal. This gives to the series of lines a rhythmic measure of decrease from the longest to the shortest. By placing these lines in regular order,

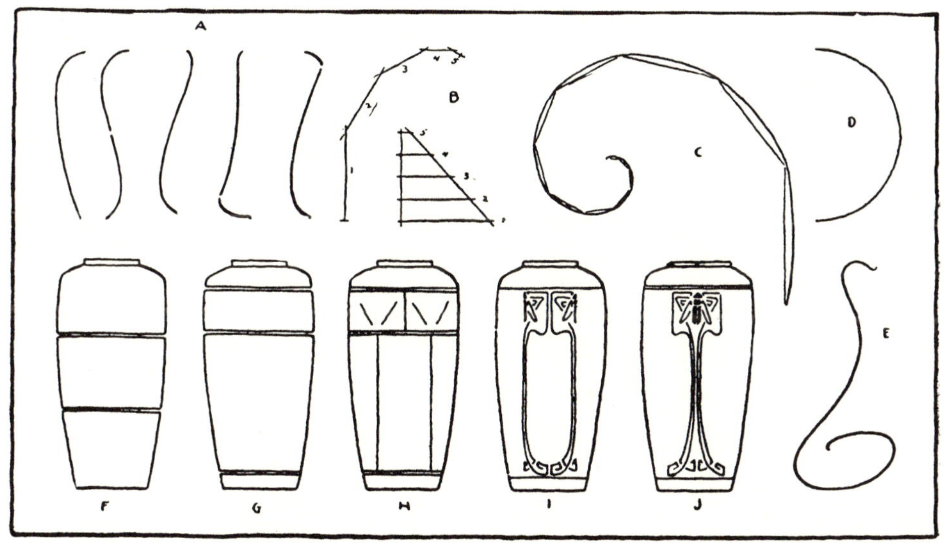

FIGURE THIRTEEN.

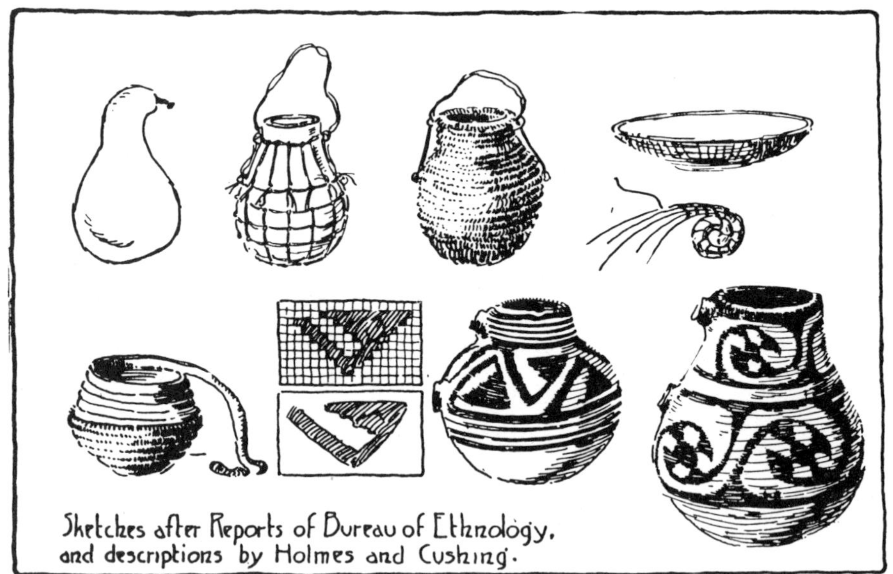

FIGURE FOURTEEN.

end to end, taking particular care that the angles formed by the different lines are the same, we may be sure that a curve drawn through the intersecting points will be a beautiful curve. It is the "infinite curve"; it may unfold itself until the end of time; but it can never return to its starting-point. The lines may be increased in number; a different angle may be chosen, giving to the curve a stronger movement; but the law governing its course is the same. (13-C) In this curve there is variety with unity.

There are various other geometric curves that might be plotted, such as the curve of the ellipse, the oval, and the cycloidal curve; but if we appreciate the reason *why* the "infinite curve," or the "curve of force," is more beautiful than the "finite curve," and can apply the idea in practice, we are making commendable progress toward the cultivation of a curve sense. It is a live curve that interests us most (Fig. 13-A), sometimes approaching a straight line, again swinging full and clear; sometimes reversed, ever subtle and varied in its course. It may become as eccentric as in E; but if it is to be beautiful it must never be uncertain or lacking in firmness. There is no better device for charting its course than the hand, with the eye for a compass and a clear head at the helm.

Draw two lines, two or three inches apart, as a limitation in height, and see if you can swing a series of live, freehand curves, simple, firm, and unmistakably clear in expression. (A) Try reversed curves as in the second one. Which is more interesting, the second curve or the third one? And why? It would be well to trace some of these curves and reverse them in symmetry with the thought of pottery in mind. In this case it must not be forgotten that a piece of pottery has a top, bottom, shoulders and body, and that lines should be related so as to distinguish these elements.

We know too much to be true and simple and spontaneous in our own work. We are burdened by too many conflicting traditions and precedents. In this day of inexpensive casts, pictures and photographs we find the world's work spread out before us. We select for purposes of study those things that are far beyond us in the terms of our own experience. We are induced to imitate and copy those things because of their manifest superiority over our own immature efforts. We are impatient of time and study and experiment. If we are workers in wood or metal or what not, we find, even supposing that we have achieved

the logical solution of the constructive demands of a problem, that in its further enrichment we are hopelessly impotent; we have no ideas to express, so bring forth a formidable array of arguments to prove that there never was such a thing as originality in design; and in the meantime complacently appropriate the work of others to our own ends.

Primitive art comes as a refreshing breeze. Here were people with real needs to meet with such beauty as they could de-

FIGURE FIFTEEN.

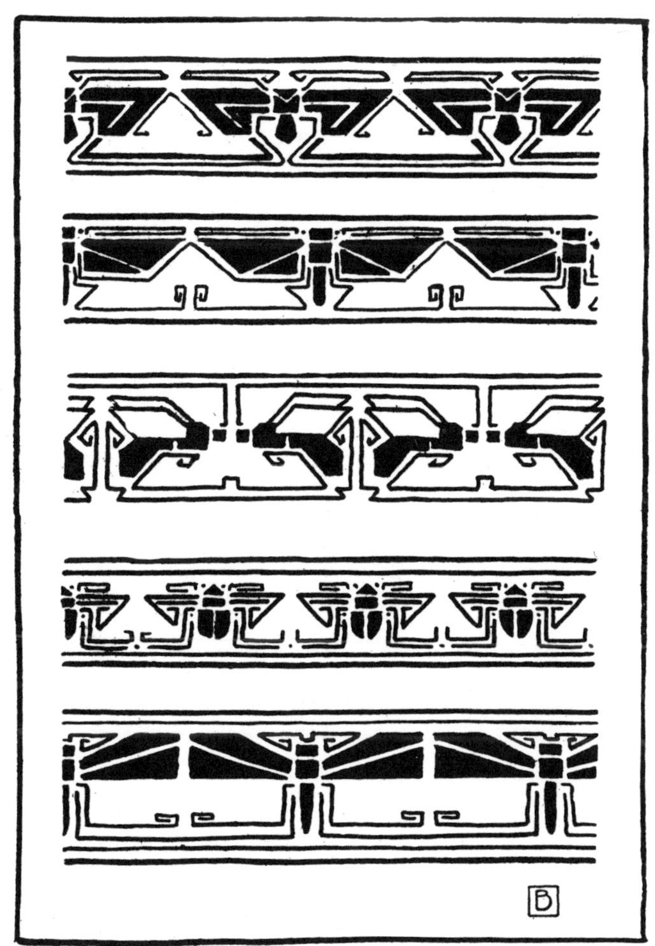

PLATE SIX.

vise. They gathered perforce their own material from the mountain slopes and the river bottoms, made with their own hands all the tools, and wrought a product simple and honest in construction, strong and insistent in its grasp of fundamentals. The work of primitive man comes from his heart; from his nature rather than from his knowledge. He designed beautifully because he could not help it; and the step from his idea to its vigorous execution is so simple that it can be readily studied. In all justice the feminine pronoun should be used; but to simplify matters let us allow man to shine with reflected glory!

The questions of tools, materials and processes are reduced to their simplest elements; we may trace the experiments and influences from one material or process to another. (Fig. 14.) In our own Southwest gourds were common in many sections, and were used as utensils for various purposes. For convenience in carrying the gourd, and possibly for protection, a coarse weave of wickerwork was made about it. There is good reason to believe that this suggested the weaving of baskets, merely by increasing the strands of the wicker covering.

The technique of weaving and basketry inevitably gave rise to a geometric ornament. The growth of pattern was slow, because primitive man, as we have already seen, was a conservative designer in spite of the vigor of his utterance. From one generation to another the simple patterns were passed, with gradual changes tending toward a more complete expression. We cannot appreciate the completeness of the result until we sit down to a careful examination of an Indian basket; count out the strands of the pattern and note how difficult the task becomes.

Into these patterns there entered at an early stage a fresh element of interest. The primitive man looked out upon the world through the eyes of a child. Science had not robbed him of an imagination; the forces of nature, from the forked lightning to the blade of grass pushing upward with the new rains, were explained only in the lore of his mythology. His gods of the wind, the rain, and the sun were real deities to propitiate. He lived close to the heart of Nature. And, as the hand serves the mind, there inevitably appeared in his work earnest efforts to interpret the natural phenomena about him, developing in time a rich symbolism which we can only in part understand or translate.

His pictorial art, like his designs, strikes out boldly for essentials, for lines expressing movement, action, life. He was more intent on recording impressions than in nice distinctions of texture, color, light and shade. He was the first of the "impressionists." He even recorded his ideas through pictographs in lieu of a written language.

There entered then into the technique of his weaving certain nature-derived elements, often arbitrary and unreal. Sometimes we recognize the motif as nature-derived; again it requires the ingenious logic of an archæologist to assure us. The interplay between the two is so intimate that it cannot be said positively; this started in geometry; this in nature. A whimsical twist in a line may have sent a given pattern toward nature; or again the designer may have done the best he could for nature under the circumstances. The point is illustrated in Fig. 15. Is the development from 1 to 8; or from 8 to 1; or from the extremes to the center?

Now, from Fig. 15 there is this to be gained, of immediate application to our own problem: however much of interest there may be in primitive man's pictographs, the value of his designs increases as they approach the geometric. Whatever motif he may use, geometry furnishes the bones.

You were asked, "What do you expect Nature to do for you?" Just this: she may clothe your work with fresh life and interest; but you must furnish the bones; and if the bones are weak or poorly jointed, Nature cannot hide the fault. Nature may indeed arouse latent ideas, and stimulate the imagination; but the organic structure of the design rests with you. In a final analysis its beauty is dependent on line, form, and tone adjustment; failing there, it fails as a design.

When the cartoonist is not correcting the nation or battling for it, then it is his high privilege to amuse it. In his hours of ease he may entertain both king and street sweeper, possibly teaching a little even while entertaining. And as he cannot amuse his own land without appealing straight to the kind of humor which is its national characteristic, then how neatly is it possible to judge of a nation by its cartoons. The subject for laughter of a people is unquestionably the index to the mental and moral qualities of that nation, and so if the caricaturist becomes a national biographer, are we not entitled to infer that *Le Rire*, *Simplicissimus*, *Punch* and *Life* are frank presentations of the temperament of each country in turn? If this is true, there is food for thought at hand.

M. de Zayas

JOHN DREW AS A MATINÉE IDOL.

ALVIN L. COBURN—A STUDY IN CONCENTRATION.

This and the following six paintings of Peasant Scenes by Millet are from a private collection in France; and so far as the editor is aware have never been reproduced in this country.

"THE SPINDLE": JEAN FRANÇOIS MILLET, PAINTER

THE SINCERITY OF MILLET

"A SINCERITY so absolute and convincing as to become at times almost depressing is the secret of Millet's art. He painted that which he knew and understood and felt. In eighteen hundred and fifty-one he wrote, 'The most joyful thing I know is the peace, the silence, that one enjoys in the woods or on the tilled lands. One sees a poor, heavily laden creature with a bundle of fagots advancing from a narrow path in the fields. The manner in which this figure comes suddenly before one is a momentary reminder of the fundamental conditions of human life—toil. On the tilled land around, one watches figures hoeing and digging. One sees how this or that one rises and wipes away the sweat with the back of his hand. In the sweat of thy brow shalt thou eat thy bread. Is that merry, enlivening work, as some people would like to persuade us? And yet it is here that I find the true humanity, the great poetry.'"

ARTHUR JEROME EDDY.

WHAT A WORK OF ART OUGHT TO BE

"THINGS (in a picture) must not have the appearance of being brought together by chance or for a purpose, but must have a necessary and inevitable connection. I desire that the creations which I depict should have the air of being dedicated to their situation, so that one could not imagine that they would dream of being anything else than what they are. A work of art ought to be all one piece, and the men and things in it should always be there for a reason. . . . It were better that things weakly said should not be said at all, because in the former case they are only, as it were, deflowered and spoiled. . . . Beauty does not consist so much in the things represented, as in the *need* one has had of expressing them; and this need it is which creates the degree of force with which one acquits oneself of the work. One may say that everything is beautiful provided the thing turns up in its own proper time and in its own place; and contrariwise, that nothing can be beautiful arriving inappropriately. . . . Let Apollo *be* Apollo, and Socrates Socrates. Which is the more beautiful, a straight tree or a crooked tree? Whichever is most in place. This, then, is my conclusion: The beautiful is that which is in place."

JEAN FRANÇOIS MILLET.

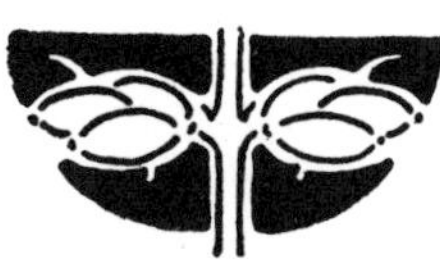

THE CRAFTSMAN

IS THERE A SEX DISTINCTION IN ART? THE ATTITUDE OF THE CRITIC TOWARD WOMEN'S EXHIBITS: BY GILES EDGERTON

AN EXHIBITION of paintings at the Knoedler Galleries, New York, during the month of April, brought forth many extended press notices and a good deal of argument of a kind; not because the paintings heralded a new school of development in American art, or even advancement along established lines (if we except a most unusual and distinguished portrait called "The Miniature Painter," by Ella Condie Lamb), but frankly because it was a women's exhibit. The reviewers apparently entered the galleries with a point of view at once tolerant and sentimental; as if to say, "The poor dears; why shouldn't they play around with their little feminine art? Who are we, the great of the world, to discourage or criticise their harmless amusement?" and then they went away and wrote long foolish notices, praising some work that was distinctly poor and dipping their pens in treacle where criticism was inevitable. After a careful summing up of the different reviews, I cannot see that any man approached the subject with the honest frankness, the open mind, alert brain, the willingness to see in a dignified way the unpleasant thing, if necessary, which he would have taken to an exhibit such as the National Academy, or the Ten American Painters, or any individual studio showing of work, where men and women face the public definitely seeking honest opinion.

This Exhibition of Paintings by Women Artists was presented to the public with a sentimental plea, and the critic, the usual arbiter of the destiny of American art, took a fair new pad and a soft pencil and went forth to it as a knight-errant, with powers of analysis laved in chivalry. The gentler sex should receive no blow at his hands; not if real courtesy knew its place. Now this Chesterfield-Bayard-Raleigh attitude toward accomplishment in art is honestly about the last thing in the world that the genuine hard-working women artists—who are striving just as men are for the best that they can express

about the truth of things—want. On the contrary, they are humiliated by it. They resent a sex distinction in art (not in the variation of art, but in the quality) and they honestly prefer just discriminating criticism to this attitude of tender-hearted masculine protection.

Such painters among the exhibitors as Charlotte Coman, Alice Schille, Rhoda Holmes Nicholls, Ellen and Lydia Field Emmet, are accustomed to face the juries of the Pennsylvania Academy, Pittsburgh, and the National Academy with no more heart palpitation than any good artist must experience. Their work is judged side by side with Sargent's, Chase's, Wiles's and Lathrop's, and they expect and are entitled to the same dignity of criticism. They belong to the art world of America. They are not afraid of a trial by jury, and they are accepted and hung or rejected, as the case may be, without sentiment or chivalry. And this leads us back to exactly the point we wish to make in this article: that a "women's exhibit" is something out of the past. It is Eighteen-Thirty in expression and belongs to the helpless days of crinoline when ladies fainted if they were spoken to with undue harshness; when a sampler, at least in America, was the only field for feminine artistic endeavor.

IT STANDS to reason, if one thinks at all about these things, that there must forever be a wide differentiation between the painting that men do and that women do, because in all the civilized world there is such a tremendous variation in the outlook on life of men and women. As long as society decrees this radical sex difference in the attitude of men and women toward the world and of the world to them, there must follow along the same lines exactly a corresponding difference in the art expression of men and women. Composition, technique, color may be taught by the same master in the same studio to a group of boys and girls, but when these boys and girls have grown up and have gone through the essential experiences of life, they will inevitably paint the same subjects differently, the work of women being so classified by the woman's outlook that inevitably there would ensue comparison, an interesting appreciation of certain qualities that women have expressed and a different sort of enjoyment for the feeling that men have painted into their canvases. Each may be progressive and each great in achievement, but under present social conditions there must be the fundamental difference.

It is not once in a generation that a woman so subverts her essentially characteristic outlook on life to her work that her art impulse becomes universal, as that of the greatest men often is. One feels that Cecilia Beaux has done this in her portrait work, as George Eliot did in her stories. One feels, too, something of the universal quality in the work of Charlotte Coman, but one is not quite sure whether it is the result of achievement greater than personality or whether it is born from a certain attitude of delicate reserve toward Nature, a certain tender courtesy toward all the illusions that cover the land for every season of the year. One cannot tell quite whether it is the universal quality of genius or whether it is just a fine sort of reticence that will not obtrude one's own personality upon Nature.

But grant, as a rule, a compulsory sex difference in art. Look for it; admire it; classify all art by it; all this is just, but it is equally just to go a step farther and rank both the expressions as of equal interest; demanding equal technical excellence, equal standards of perfection in composition, color values and sympathetic understanding of life, and the same courage in facing the attitude of a usually unsympathetic, unappreciative public. No one has a right to ride a steeplechase who cannot keep a quiet saddle for the hurdles. It is fatal that women should accept rejection at the hands of big exhibits with a feeling of hurt vanity, turn about and decide "to have an exhibit of their own anyway, and just hang any picture they want to." Not that Academy decisions are final toward art, for the juries often reject very important and significant work and hang very dull and inadequate pictures. Indeed, at times this threatens to become the rule, and men have this matter to face as well as women. All that is necessary to point out in this connection is that women should never for one moment admit that the rejection is made because it is *women's* work. The somewhat revolutionary young American artists called "The Eight," by chance all men, did not go away from the Academy last fall pouting and fretting. They gathered up their rejected pictures with apparently a light heart, expressed a few pointed opinions as to the stupidity of the jury that *could* reject them; were promptly invited by a very understanding and sympathetic art dealer to hold a little academy of their own, which turned out the most successful art exhibit of the year.

NOW in spite of some very excellent work at the Knoedler Galleries, and a few paintings of exceptional value, the exhibition as a whole would not have secured half a column press notice if it had been a mixed exhibit. It would then have been taken seriously, praised highly in some instances, moderately in others, and vigorously condemned where the work deserved it. And the women who were poor craftsmen would have learned some valuable truths, and would not have been permitted the poor satisfaction of thinking that "a woman's *feeling* in art is so interesting that it does not matter whether she understands drawing, or perspective, or composition, or technique." Fancy an intelligent art critic feeling justified in saying as praise of an exhibit that there was "a soprano note in the work," and that the pictures were "evidently painted for women, with that straight march to the central sentiment which characterizes the 'intuitional' artist."

What utter rubbish that is! In the first place, women do not paint for women, any more than they dress for women or do anything else for women. The genuine woman works for her own self-esteem, or to win out with the world, or, as a by-product of her own effort, to win praise and appreciation from men. And why in the world should not painting "which has tenderness, grace and appeal" (to quote the same authority), interest men as well as women, or men even more than women? But here is the difficulty. The minute that you label any sort of exhibit as exclusively "women's" you have let

loose the flood gates of masculine sentimentality, and an honest point of view apparently cannot obtain. As for instance the phrase "intuitional art!" What could have a more sentimental ring to it? and what possible meaning can it have as applied to women's work? Does it suggest that women are not expected "to mark, learn, and inwardly digest" their craft, that they can *guess* at success, that they may jumble in a heap oxen and a woodpile so that the whole suggests "After an Earthquake" (and this done by a woman who *can* paint), that they may draw a face so impressionistically that it looks as if the model had been interrupted in an operation for the sitting; that an Art Nouveau-Burne-Jones girl can be drawn with a neck a quarter as long as her body and then be exhibited as a siren? If this is "intuitional art," then there was some of it at the women's exhibit, the "art" that moves without care or study or logical preparation to its work. It is hard to know whether this phrase is silly or wise, kind or cruel, or just intended to be pleasantly mysterious, because truth is not usual in such criticism. But it seems to me that this sort of talk, and much besides that was published immediately after the press day of this exhibit, is far more seriously a handicap to any real progress of women in art than the most unjust or prejudiced point of view that an Academy jury could possibly show. We have already granted a difference in art expression for men and women, but these expressions can never move along in parallel lines without identical standards of self-esteem, of willingness to work for success, equal desire for honest and dignified criticism, and the courage to benefit by it.

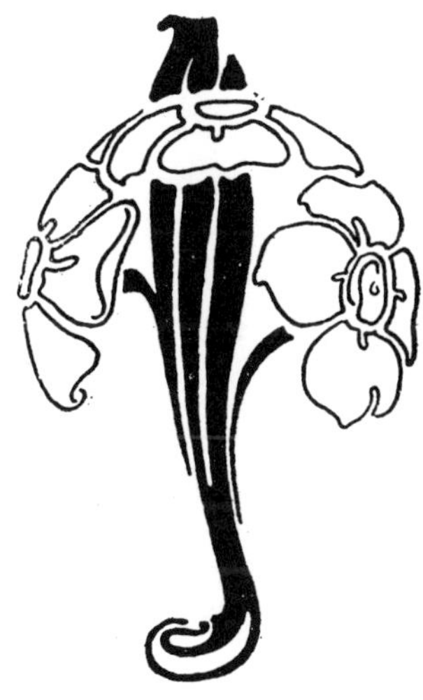

THE DECORATIVE GOURD VINE.

THE MARTIN GOURDS WHERE THE BIRDS NESTED.

IN THE DAYS OF THE GOURD

EVERY COOL SPRING HAD ITS GOURD DIPPER.

A STUDY OF PICTURESQUE ROOF CONSTRUCTION

HOUSE AT KENILWORTH, ENGLAND.

ONE of the evidences that a newer and more vigorous phase of thought in house building is springing up in this country, as well as abroad, is the care that is now being given to the beauty and individuality, as well as the durability, of the roof. It is coming to be recognized that, whatever the plan of a house, the keynote of its character is the roof, for the best design may be ruined by a roof that is not in keeping, and a plan in other respects mediocre may be redeemed by a roof that is beautiful in line and proportion and that gives the impression of a generous, protecting shelter.

So it is that the best of our architects are devoting much thought to the designing of the roof, adapting its lines not only to the building, but planning them with an eye to bringing the whole structure into harmony with the landscape by reflecting in a measure its general characteristics.

HIGH ROOF WITH ONE GABLE.

Several ideas for picturesque lines in roofs are given in the small pen sketches.

HOUSE WITH LONG RIDGE AND TWO GABLES.

CUBAN FARM HOUSE.

JOHN MUIR

HAPPY is the tenant who falls heir to the home of a garden lover who has planted rhubarb or asparagus, fruit trees or grapes. An asparagus bed is a mine of riches in May and June, and old apple trees will benefit an entire generation. There is so little we can do in this world which is at all likely to be remembered to our credit after us that we might at least, like *Johnny Appleseed*, plant fruit trees.

THE VALUE OF A RIGHT APPRECIATION OF WOOD

A well-known writer on Japanese architecture and interior decoration says: "To the Japanese, wood, like anything that possesses beauty, is almost sacred, and he handles it with a fineness of feeling that at best we only reveal when we are dealing with precious marbles. From all wood that may be seen close at hand, except such as is used as a basis for the rare and precious lacquer, paint, stain, varnish, anything that may obscure the beauty of texture and grain, is rigidly kept away. The original cost of the material is a matter of no consequence; if it has a subtle tone of color, a delicate swirl in the veining, a peculiarly soft and velvety texture, it is carefully treasured and used in the place of honor."

We of the Western world are as yet only beginning to appreciate what this may mean. With us, the original cost of the material is a matter of the greatest possible consequence, and we are too apt, when we are choosing wood for the interior of our houses or for the making of our furniture, to put a money value upon it rather than to allow ourselves to appreciate its natural beauty. For it is a fact that the greatest beauty often lies in wood that is faulty and comparatively valueless from a commercial point of view, and that by throwing this aside we sacrifice the most interesting characteristic of the woodwork. When we do strive for the effects produced by crooked growth and irregular grain, we go to the other extreme and instead of studying each particular piece of wood and using it exactly where it belongs with relation to the rest, we hunt out deliberately the most gnarled and knotted pieces, so that the result instead of being interesting in a natural and inevitable way, is eccentric and artificial.

This is the greater pity because, after all, it requires only a little interest, care and discrimination to give to the woodwork of a room just the kind of interest and beauty that belong to it. Instead of that we are apt either to imitate the wealthy man who built a cottage in the Adirondacks and paneled it throughout with spruce so carefully selected that not a single knot appeared throughout the entire house, or else we go to the opposite extreme and deliberately select the wood of irregular and faulty grain for the entire house, instead of letting it appear here and there as is natural.

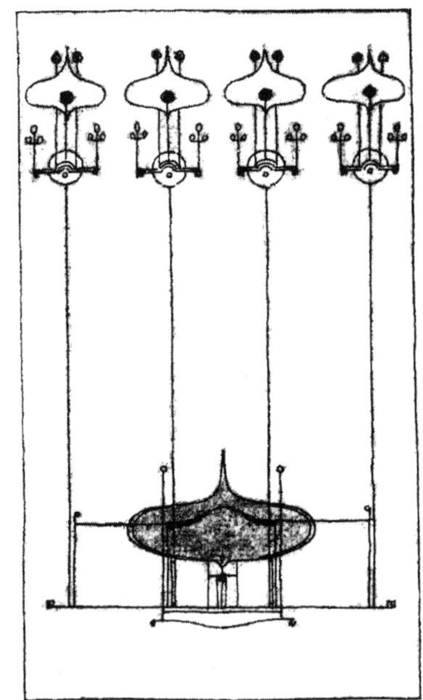

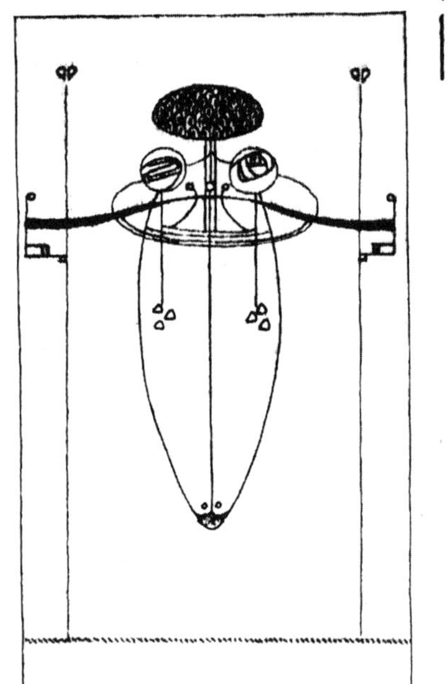

THE ARTS AND CRAFTS MOVEMENT IN AMERICA: WORK OR PLAY? BY ERNEST A. BATCHELDER

IT IS doubtless a matter of common knowledge that the term Arts and Crafts was coined by William Morris and his associates in London some twenty or more years ago for the immediate purpose of defining the nature of an exhibition that differed in one essential point from the conventional art exhibitions offered by the Royal Academy and similar institutions, which for many years had fostered the idea that the practice of art was the exclusive function of painters and sculptors. The unique feature of this exhibition was to be found in the fact that it sought to eliminate distinctions in art and furnish an opportunity for the display of work in wood, leather, glass, metal,—in fact, any material adapted to artistic expression. The term Arts and Crafts as applied to this exhibition stood boldly for three things: It was a protest against the narrow and commonly accepted definition of art; it was a protest against inutilities, the ugliness, the sham and pretense of a great portion of the English industrial product of that day; it was a protest against the deplorable industrial conditions which that product represented. To put the matter into a positive statement,—it sought to demonstrate the value of art combined with honest workmanship when applied to useful service; while it deplored the ugliness of the industrial product, it sought, not to withdraw art from it, but to bring art to it under the belief that an enduring basis for the appreciation of art must be established in the home rather than in the picture gallery; it sought to make manifest the dignity of labor and the individuality of the worker. On the strength of the ideals of which this exhibition was a concrete expression was formed the first society of arts and crafts.

A seed from this parent tree fell upon American soil; it flourished, and has spread into a growth of remarkable proportions. There is scarcely a city or town in the land that is without a society of arts and crafts with more or less clearly defined ideals. The interest and enthusiasm have been widespread; of this there is ample evidence, but does this movement rest upon a secure basis of real worth and true understanding? Is present enthusiasm any gauge to future stability?

The seed fell upon fertile soil, long fallow. We are undergoing a period of reaction along many lines. We have been, and are now, experiencing an awakening of our moral and political conscience. On all sides one hears a persistent demand for civic beauty, for a more sane, more vital expression in architecture, for furniture that shall be simple and well made. Away with unsightly billboards! Down with the hideous telephone poles! Give us parks and playgrounds! These are all familiar cries. And as another indication

of this reaction for better things has come the arts and crafts movement.

TO SPEAK of anything as a "movement" naturally leads one to inquire: To what end is it moving? For what purpose are its many units working? We may properly assume for the terms arts and crafts, and, by the same token, for the societies organized under that term, the clearly defined aim adopted by those responsible for the beginning of the movement. In fact, the term is its own definition,—art applied to craft, thoughtful design expressed through good workmanship. With this idea in mind it is pertinent to ask just where many of our societies stand in relation to this movement. To make it lasting it needs a stable market, a just appreciation of standards, an insistent demand for good things that will enable men and women to earn a decent living without surrendering their individual initiative. What are we doing to strengthen the convictions of the consumer, to give incentive to the mind and hand of the producer?

It is undeniable that many busy, thinking men and women in America assert, in words that admit of no misinterpretation, a belief that this movement is a fabric of unrealized expectations, that the term arts and crafts is in danger of becoming a synonym for amateurish incompetence; that few of its workers possess either real ability in design or skill in technique; that the larger portion of our product rests upon a basis of false values, and, to complete this direful toll of pessimism, that the ideals of the movement are out of touch with modern life and thought.

It must be admitted that such criticism as the above is not without provocation. For, lo! these many days we have been casting stones at machinery and machine-made goods, have been decrying the industrial products and methods about us. We have planted over our heads a banner inscribed with a term that would seem to indicate that our wares are not of the common sort. And it may be that we are living in glass houses. It is quite proper that we should be asked to bring our goods out into the open market-place, far from the hypnotism of studio teas, and leave them to demonstrate their own superior merits. It is true that the Arts and Crafts movement was started as a protest against the monotony of machine-made things and the dreary level of mediocrity to be found in the English product of a generation past; but protest without remedial action is of little avail. From small beginnings one may find today in England a comprehensive system of industrial art training extending its influence into all the skilled crafts of the land. Moreover, it must be remembered that the work of William Morris, who probably contributed more than any single individual to the stability of the "protest," furnished very tangible evidence of the value of his precepts. The books produced at the Kelmscott Press are displayed in the British Museum close beside the work of the master printers in the palmy days of the craft, and they lose nothing by comparison. The stained glass, tapestries, carpets and chintzes that came from the

Merton shops represented splendid achievements in the combination of good design and thorough workmanship. They also stood the test which Morris applied to industrial work; they gave pleasure, solid, enduring pleasure, to those who made them as well as to those who purchased them.

THE justice of the criticism that our work is amateurish and our workers incompetent depends largely upon the point of view of the critic. No doubt many of us in America are playing at arts and crafts. We take a few lessons in an art school, and hasten forth to set up shops of our own, produce wares to sell, and teach others the fascinating pastime of "expressing" themselves in hammer-tracked copper, tooled leather or pottery. In the days when the Mediæval craftsmen plied their trades, seven years of apprenticeship, followed generally by another period as a journeyman worker, were necessary before a man was privileged to call himself a master, hang out a shingle and teach others the details of his craft. But we of a more enlightened age do not hesitate to call ourselves bookbinders, metal craftsmen, potters, jewelers or what not, on the strength of a few simple processes hastily acquired. We hint mysteriously of shop secrets, seek to impress the innocent visitor with our accomplishments and thereby bolster up the price of immature workmanship. In such practice of the arts and crafts the skeptic finds a weak spot in our armor and gleefully prods it.

On the other hand the work of the genuine amateur holds forth much of promise. From the ranks of the amateurs come many who are tempted beyond mere busy work for idle hands, who develop persistence and staying qualities, who come to realize that the study of design is quite as serious and arduous a matter as the study of music or medicine and who learn through their own efforts to appreciate a good thoughtful piece of craftsmanship, and thus acquire a real appreciation of relative values in productive work.

That much of the product of the arts and crafts rests upon a market of false values is a just criticism. Quantities of things are being sold or are offered for sale at prices far in excess of any substantial merit represented in the design or execution. To justify a price in excess of commercial work a product must stand unmistakably for two things. It must possess unusual merit in design; it must possess in its execution qualities that stamp it in every way superior in workmanship and finish to similar things that may be purchased in the stores. A piece of work that is truly beautiful and distinctive in design, thoroughly and earnestly made, painstaking to its last detail, is entitled to a higher price than a thoughtless, commonplace, mechanically made article. But the fact that an article is made by hand does not necessarily reflect to its credit. That it should command a higher price for no other reason than that it is hand-made is absurd; it may be that the worker has misspent time in trying to do by hand many things which may be quite as well accomplished through other processes. We have long made a virtue of the "little irregularities," the "artistic accidents" of hand work.

Such things may very readily become an affectation, a convenient excuse for unskilled technique, at the hands of a worker of immature practice and experience. There is neither art nor craft in a battered piece of copper, a lamp shade it may be, picturesquely colored with spots of green from an acid bath. Art demands sincerity of purpose; craft demands skilled workmanship. The irregularities or "accidents" in the work of a master craftsman are of the kind that come unsought, that he cannot help, that he seeks diligently to overcome. The present strength of the arts and crafts movement is to be found in the work of a comparatively few who are earnestly striving day and night through study and practice to improve the standards of their work in design and execution, who see clearly the difficulties ahead, the necessity of putting into their product the qualities that count for true worth. When we talk about this movement as a real, live issue it must be on the basis of the relation which it bears to industrial activity, to the bread and butter problems of life. To discuss it on any other basis is to deny it a serious part in modern life and work and regulate it to the narrow confines of a studio pastime.

TO CRITICIZE the movement as being out of touch with modern thought is to misinterpret its best ideals. It seeks to bring a better standard to industrial work, establish a permanent demand for better things, and furnish an adequate livelihood for those who are competent to give beauty to hand work. It does not necessarily antagonize machinery, nor does it hope to achieve its ends through a reversion to primitive methods. The glaring inferiority of the present average commercial product when compared with, for example, the work of the Mediæval craftsmen, needs no comment. Any movement which aims to encourage an improvement of this product deserves intelligent support and action. It might be well to devote some of the time and money spent in lobbying for protection against the "pauper labor" of Europe to the training of our own workmen in the skilled crafts that we might make our goods more beautiful, hence more to be desired. Machinery is not in itself an evil; we need more of it. Frankly, we have to believe that if the Mediæval craftsmen could return to the world they would welcome machinery as a means of tiding them over much of the drudgery of their work,—and there is still a vast amount of drudgery in the world for machinery to overcome, innumerable sweatshops for it to clean out and turn men and women back to the land. There are men in the "Black Country" of England still forging nails and cutting files by hand. The evil of machinery is largely a question of whether machinery shall use men or men shall use machinery. There are certain skilled trades such as cabinetmaking, gold and silversmithing, the book trades, etc., which have always in the past offered an opportunity for individual thought and initiative, for a young man to learn a trade, not merely some trivial part of a trade. To the extent that the invasion of machinery into these trades has undermined the independent manhood of the skilled artisan and left him as an unthinking hired "hand" to feed raw material into a hopper, it is indeed an

evil, one to be combatted. The dignity of labor is of the mind and heart, not of the hand alone. When a man is robbed of the last vestige of human interest in the work that necessity compels him to do for a living, it is time to scan the credentials of our commercial standards. It is not remarkable that protection is needed for the product of a carpet mill employing two thousand "hands" but not more than a dozen heads, and not a single designer of carpets among them. The mill bids on designs good, bad and indifferent, mostly bad, just as a contractor bids on the construction of a pipe line. And the "hands," with few exceptions, could be replaced on a month's notice with others equally efficient.

The surest way to turn an evil stream from its course is to dig another channel for it through educational work. If the shops and factories deny a young man a chance to learn a trade, can furnish him with no standards of excellence in design or workmanship, it would seem to be within the province of our educational institutions to supplement the shops with schools of industrial art training where all that is best in the elements that have contributed to give dignity and beauty to a trade in the past may be fostered and strengthened. Our art schools as now organized with arts and crafts studios annexed, can do little more than bite pieces from the edges of the real problem. Their traditions have too long been of another sort to enable them to approach the question of industrial training with any sympathetic understanding. They cannot furnish either the practice or the experience that will draw men from the trades to their doors, or that will place the craftsworker of the future squarely on his feet and enable him to meet fairly the competition about him.

Education, to bear fruit, must extend to the consumer as well as to the producer. In our factories is an army of men and women engaged in the production of inutilities, or in filling the demand due to the appalling waste and extravagance of modern life. Many of the things we buy are of an impersonal nature, keyed to some passing fad or fashion. They gave no one pleasure in making; nor does their possession give pleasure to anyone. Things are broken or consigned to the scrap-heap without a pang of regret; there are more at the store. When purchases are made with the thought of permanent possession rather than of temporary convenience,—a few good pieces of furniture, a few rugs, a few thoughtfully chosen ornaments and pictures,—why then the best ideals of the arts and crafts movement will be realized; for such things cannot be fed into a machine by unskilled operatives. Fewer things carefully made will give employment to quite as many workers as a vast quantity of things thoughtlessly and carelessly made.

This question of industrial art education, and the many avenues for discussion which it opens, is a matter of paramount importance. It is one of the few big questions demanding intelligent and concentrated action; it is right next to the bony structure of our industrial life. Our societies of arts and crafts might demonstrate their usefulness, as some have already, by bringing definite influence and action to bear upon this problem.

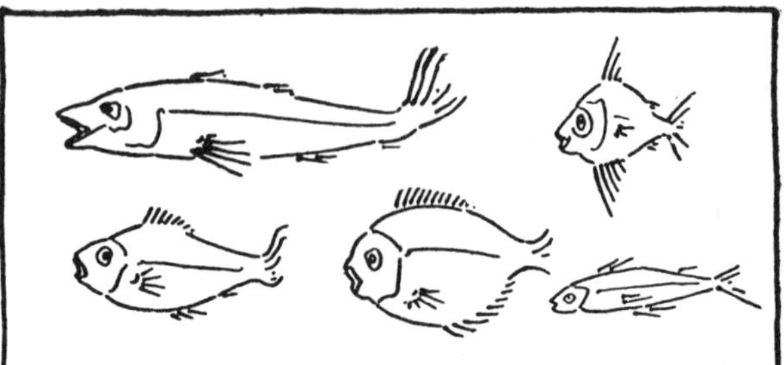

THE TRUTH ABOUT WORK

"I HAVE thought of fitting the interior of my home with walnut wood," a woman recently said to an artist-builder. "Do you advise me to use it? For I do not want to put too much money into anything that is likely to go out of fashion." And the artisan shuddered. "To think," he said, "that there should be such a thing as *fashion* in a wood so beautiful and durable as walnut, that a woman's interest in it should hinge on whether or no others would think it in style or pronounce it the fashion, and that she should stand ready to discard it whenever their ignorant opinion should change! How can a woman," the man continued, "fit up her own home other than in accord with her own taste, her own personal appreciation of beauty and comfort? And having achieved this, or even the vision of it, how could she let her purpose hinge on whether someone else agreed with her, or fancied something different? What relation have other people's houses to hers? She would not permit anyone to dictate to her a fashion in children or husbands or religion, then why in a home, which according to her theory should be the blessed abode of all three? It is difficult to imagine a more artificial or absurd idea than that fashion could create or destroy anything intrinsically beautiful, and fashion cannot even exist where there is an appreciation of the value of work. Walnut wood, for instance, is an appropriate, permanently beautiful fitting for a room, or it is the reverse. Its beauty cannot be intermittent."

And the man's argument in regard to wood applies with equal force to architecture, furniture and every final piece of handicraft which enters into the process of home fitting. It is, in fact, true of all of life. If you understand the truth about beauty and then labor to express it, you have discovered the secret of right, happy living. And what one or a dozen people think about some new trivial departure along eccentric lines can no more affect the life of the woman who has learned to see clearly, to live consistently, than the gay chirp of a spring robin would make her decide to model her home after the cross section of a nest. The achievement of beauty in architecture, in home fitting, is too fundamental and vital a matter to be affected by the chirping of robins, or neighbors. It is the expression, or should be, of all the supreme impulse toward reasonable beauty which a human being is capable of. Imagine a fashion about the material symbol of spiritual development,—and a home is this or nothing. But to appreciate beauty fully one must labor to produce it. It is not enough to recognize it. It is necessary to coöperate with Nature in making it possible.

AS WE have so often said, it is the work which creates to meet a need, creates sincerely and as vitally as possible, that is responsible for practically all permanent beauty, outside of that in which Nature herself is the craftsman. But there is much to be understood in connection with the word work, which most of

us have never taken into consideration. Work, especially in America, has come to mean the ignominious, arduous performance of duty, to be accomplished in a state of coma, to be finished swiftly, to be forgotten. And of itself, without purpose or interest, work can, as a matter of fact, become not only a deadly menace to development, but a system of personal demoralization for commercial results, so that, as is often done, to recommend work in a wholesale way to take the place of play, and this to people who do not know how to work, or to insist that work intrinsically is of value without relation to results, is to lessen the appreciation of the right use and beauty of labor, and to render any argument in its favor open to just criticism.

The plea which The Craftsman wishes to make is for intelligent labor which meets a practical need and which is also productive of beauty; which is wiser than play because it includes the element of play and yet leads to results; is more lasting in effect than work unrelated to life because it is the result of enlightened purpose, and thus is a part of general progress. What we plead for is discriminating labor, not mere slavery or unthinking play. It is productive work beyond mere financial returns that we believe will carry the final benefit for the human race. And in the products of this sort of work there is not likely ever to enter the question of fashion; for fashion is born of the swift-moving, unthinking machine which produces for sales only; it has no relation to life; it has no desire to have such a relation; its purpose is to hypnotize intelligence for financial returns. But the woman who has woven her own rug and the man who has built furniture suited to his own home will not be apt to take seriously the dictates of fashion. These people have gone beyond such artificial discriminations. They have created beauty through their own effort, and the handiwork which is the result they regard as a permanent asset in the interest of their lives.

At present in this matter of work American people rest under the great disadvantage of having permitted themselves to take a somewhat artificial unthinking point of view. We have lost the knowledge of what a stupendous force work is and should be in the development of the individual, and we have forgotten the great lessons of restraint, concentration and discipline which work, and work only, can teach the youth of a land. We have established among us that awful blight, the non-working aristocracy, actually far worse than any European aristocracy; for in Europe, at least the idle people have duties to state and estate, to army and navy, and in a feeble way to Society, duties which apparently do not exist for the wealthy class in America. Thus the rich man in this country who has neither profession nor business is idle; and all that is left is to substitute play for work. The almost inevitable result of this artificial existence is a scorn for labor, because there is an absence of understanding of its vital significance to nation and individual.

Not only have we created this futile idle class and allowed it to flourish, but we are continually exploiting it in our literature and in our press, until throughout our civilization there is springing up a totally false point of view toward the intrinsic value of work. The

girl in our factories, in our shops and in our village homes largely has one standard of gentility (tragic word), and this is idleness. The mother may work, but not the daughter. Pretty widely throughout America our young women are ashamed of housework, ashamed to cook or to sew or to care for the small members of the family. A girl may be weak and silly, even unamiable, but somehow she establishes herself satisfactorily in her own mind as a social success if she is also *useless*. An ignorance of vital domestic conditions and her own inability to cope with them she somehow characterizes in her own mind as "being a lady."

AND with our boys it is not so very different. To do errands, to help in any way about the house, to perform any kind of manual labor, at home or in business, is esteemed unmanly and vulgar. The mother says of her daughter, perhaps to her, "Anna is so refined; she does not like work." And the father says of his son, or perhaps to him, "My boy wants to make something of himself besides a common workman." Thus we encourage our children to regard labor as "common," beneath their consideration, when in nine cases out of ten intelligent work would be the one method by which daughter and son would secure essential mental, moral and physical growth.

But as yet mothers and fathers in this nation do not see clearly the tremendous truth about work. As a matter of fact, they are not quite thinking it out; they have perhaps in their own youth slaved too much, worked too hard without a purpose other than a livelihood. Their only memory of work is in connection with hardship and as an unsatisfactory process of earning food and reaching old age. Not having stopped to consider the fact that there is always the use and abuse of good, they reason from their own unfulfilled experience with labor that it will be better for their children to live idle lives (which in truth is a thousand times more disastrous). Where they have been poor their children shall be rich; where they have worked for themselves, others shall work for their children. And it proves how little they really think that they are willing to pass on to any other than their own what has seemed to them the slavery of labor. They have not reasoned out that the essential thing is to better conditions which have hurt them, rather than to merely spare their own children from suffering. Of course, it is all selfish, illogical and unthinking, and yet this attitude of mind obtains all over our country, in the average middle-class American household, and spells disaster both for parents and children. For to release children wholly from their obligations to life is to breed lack of discipline, lack of sympathy, a desire for success without effort, for achievement without purpose and a scorn of realities. This tendency must eventually kill romance, degrade affection and create false ethical standards.

The beauty of service, which the truly great of all ages, from the time of Christ until today, have realized, is lost sight of in this atmosphere, and there is no recollection apparently of the fact that to serve others without money and without price was once reckoned

a fundamental of Christianity. Today the supercilious attitude toward labor and toward those who labor has become one of the most stupendous disintegrating forces in all Protestant religion. While we pursue the worship of our idle rich, we fail to realize that in the first place it was service without money which was really the foundation of all aristocracies. Those who ranked preëminent in a community achieved the distinction because they served others and refused all compensation. In the very beginning of kingdoms the king himself was made the chief of the people because he had chosen to serve them, to think for them, perhaps to battle for them without reward. Today, even, the crown worn by the King of England bears the motto *ich dien* (I serve), a pathetic echo from those faraway times when the workers were exalted and the drones forgotten or obliterated. But so perverted have we become that today it is the drones who wear the insignia of achievement, while those who serve truly and unselfishly are often without honor.

AND yet if the mothers and the fathers of this country would look the matter squarely in the face, work would once more become a title of dignity, associated with beauty and happiness. The very children themselves would see to this if left unhampered, for when not restricted with undiscriminating rules children know, or crave to know, the delight of work. The very plays of natural children are invariably adaptations of real things to their own little ways and means. Normal little girls adore being in the kitchen and are enchanted to wipe real dishes or pat an actual pie into shape, while to make one side of a grown-up bed or sweep, with a baby brush in hand, a real room where grown-up people live, are among the real joys of childhood. The smallest tots will work for their dollies, dressing them, putting them to bed, making their tiny clothes and arranging busy practical lives for them. All this is the very normal instinct of childhood which gets its joy out of actualities. It has no modern standards for separating its little life into work and play, frowning at one and happy in the other, and is only hurt and grieved when the average mother, as is usually the case, heedlessly but persistently endeavors to kill this instinct for play-work, and to offer instead instruction in that fatal estate of "being a lady." The busy, happy little personality must be taught that it must sit still, keep away from the kitchen, take no part in the daily routine of making the home pleasant, have no knowledge whatever of the value of mutual service, in order to grow up into a stilted, artificial, undisciplined person without much happiness or usefulness in life.

Picture what a child would gain if taught that all the small home tasks had a relation to real joy in life, that it was a significant pleasure to do some work for mother or father, brother or sister, until unconsciously the duties and tasks of the ordinary household became a symbol of the sympathetic dependence of the family and their need of mutual service. Of course, a child would not be taught these things in words; indeed, it would not be necessary. It would all be evolved by the wise attitude of the mother in developing the child's

natural instincts and in fostering a love of simple home conditions.

And the boy who wants to build a house or paint a fence or "play pretend" in a shop, he, too, should be allowed all possible freedom for the development of these instincts and for the turning into right channels his joy in the play which relates to interesting work. It seems reasonable that such a boy would have a better physique, a wider intelligence, a saner understanding of real happiness than the one whose chance in life is back of a bank window or idling in a law office to acquire that interesting but anomalous position known as the "American gentleman."

In the public schools, where the majority of *city* children, at least, secure practically about all the instruction, spiritual as well as mental, which is likely to come their way, the attitude toward work is even more deplorable usually than in the home. The unacknowledged aim of the average metropolitan schools seems to be, in actual instruction as well as in the personal point of view of the instructor, to insist upon the degrading quality of work and the necessity of belonging to the professional classes to achieve happiness.

WHAT do we intend to do with all these children whose natural instinct for labor we have destroyed and whom we have trained to a false standard of society, in no wise preparing them for success in professional channels, or in the least permitting them to understand the truth about the wide fields of usefulness from which they have been withdrawn? As a matter of fact, we are already beginning to feel the result of our fake attitude toward labor in the state of unrest and idleness in our cities, which is constantly making for an increase of poverty and crime, daily becoming more difficult to cope with, and which is due wholly to our ignorant, foolish attitude toward "common work." And this must continue until we teach our children both at home and in the schools that the ability and willingness of all men and women to earn their own living is the patent of their right to life itself. And they should not only be taught the necessity for each individual citizen to earn a living, but their preparation should be such that their means of livelihood would be the best, most valuable work which their taste and capacity would render possible. Once having passed the barriers of ignorance and resentment, this would be a simple process, and it would do more in actual practical results than all the social betterment workers, the settlement groups, the college philanthropic societies, the sincere socialists and rabid anarchists the world over.

Unhappily for our national pride, America is largely responsible for this unutterably foolish, harmful point of view toward work, which has created in this country a class distinction, based wholly on wealth and idleness. And strange, almost unbelievable as it is, we are cultivating so wide an envy of this class that we are actually placing idleness before our children almost as a national ideal. There is but one remedy for this demoralizing condition, and that is the establishing of a *new ideal of work*. We must set before the youth of our land a standard of labor that realizes the utmost beauty, permanence and

interest. If we have permitted ourselves as a whole to grow to hate or to despise work, we must do our children the justice of rehabilitating labor in their eyes, and this cannot be done without ourselves appreciating all that work means physically and ethically. We cannot hope to create an ideal born out of the present prevailing management of our sweatshops and mines,—a standard blotched and blackened in places by our own greed or lack of honest human sympathy. But from the beginning, before school days are thought of, our children can be taught to understand their intrinsic right to all real beauty and joy which life holds; but which they may only realize through their own individual purpose as laborers.

"EVENING, TWENTY-SEVENTH STREET":
FROM A DRAWING BY JOHN SLOAN.

"A JAPANESE DESIGNER": BY HOKUSAI.

"WHEN THE TWILIGHT BATS ARE FLITTING": BY HOKUSAI.

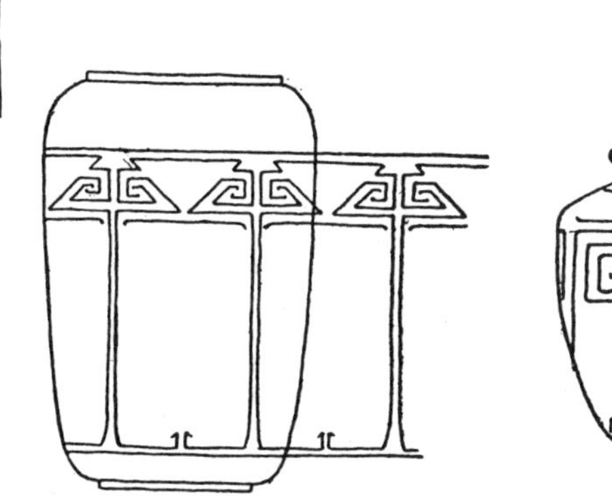

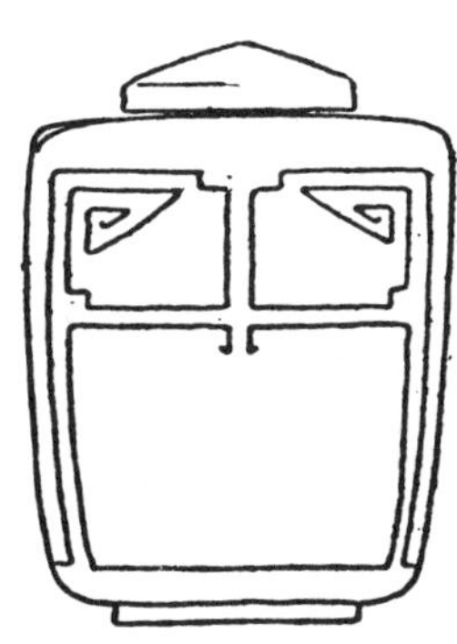

INDIAN BLANKETS, BASKETS AND BOWLS: THE PRODUCT OF THE ORIGINAL CRAFTWORKERS OF THIS CONTINENT

IN connection with the handicrafts which are cultivated because of their artistic or commercial value, and also because there is at the present time a reaction toward hand work that tends to provide a market for the products of the craftworker, the mind turns naturally to the only real handicraft this country knows, that of the Indian. While we admit that Indian products are becoming more or less fashionable, we yet venture to assert that very few people realize their beauty and value from an artistic point of view as well as that which comes from interest we find in them as an expression of the life, customs and character of a fast-vanishing race.

We call the Indian work our only real handicraft because it is the only one we have that is the spontaneous growth of necessity and therefore an absolutely natural expression of the individuality of the maker. No one ever went to the Indian and said: "Make this pattern of blanket or this shape in your pottery, or use this or that design in your basketry or silverware, because it is quaint and artistic or because someone else did it centuries ago and there is a demand among certain people for such things now." The white craftworker can hardly escape from the suggestion of secondhand ideas, but the Indian who is affected by them must have degenerated sadly under the influence of civilization, so that his work as a craftsman is hardly worthy of the name. We are not thinking of the Indians of the younger generation who are taught sloyd and needlework at the Government schools, —these are not craftworkers and never will be,—but of the old men and women of the tribes who have held to their ancient religion and their ancient ways and who still dread and resent keenly the encroachment of the white man upon their time-honored beliefs and customs.

Naturally, in thinking of the Indian as a craftworker, the peaceful and industrious tribes of the desert come first to our minds because they alone make things which can be used in the home of the white man as well as in their own hogans and kivas. The making of needed articles, of course, is common to all primitive peoples, but in the case of the warlike Indians the products of their crafts were adapted solely to their own use and have little value outside except as curios. But the blankets, baskets, pottery and silver work of the Hopi, Navajos and other Indians who live in their pueblos and cultivate their fields from generation to generation, have a charm as well as use which is appreciated keenly by the white man, so that these things are eagerly sought by him. This appreciation has caused extensive imitation of Indian handiwork, but such is the primitive sincerity of the genuine thing that it cannot easily be imitated, and the result of such attempts has been to turn out a mass of trash that no self-respecting Indian would acknowledge as his own work or that of any of his tribe. The Indian craftsman has a sincere

reverence for his art and prides himself greatly upon such skill as he may possess, and, however crude his taste may be in the kind of wares he selects in the trader's shop, he will tolerate no imitation stuff when it comes to his own crafts. A Pima basket weaver would consider himself disgraced if he turned out a basket that would not last a lifetime, and the Navajo silversmiths will work with no metal but pure silver and will use no design that is not an expression of religious symbolism or some natural force or phenomenon. As to the blankets, the difference between the real Indian blanket and the imitation is so marked that only the veriest tyro could be deceived.

The first Indian weavers were the Hopi, who had been weaving for generations when the Spaniards first entered their villages in the year 1540, and found them weaving fabrics from their home-grown and hand-spun cotton. Wool was unknown, for the sheep had not yet been introduced into the country. This art of weaving was one greatly envied by the neighboring tribes, especially the Navajos, who were always the hereditary enemies of the Hopi. After a war between the two tribes had dragged along for years with much suffering on both sides, a treaty of peace was concluded and the principal condition imposed upon the Hopi by the conquering Navajos was that they should teach the latter the art of weaving. The Hopi complied, because they could not very well help themselves, and today their great rivals as handicraftsmen are the Navajos.

It is three hundred years since the Navajos learned blanket weaving by force of arms, yet in the case of both tribes the weaving today is done precisely as it was then, save that wool is used for the blankets and heavier garments, instead of cotton. Great as was the harm done by the Spaniards, their invasion was beneficial at least in one respect, for it taught both Hopi and Navajos the use of wool, which furnishes both warp and woof of the genuine Indian blanket. It is well known that among the Hopi the men are the weavers, but with the Navajos the women do the work, taking months or even a year or more for the completion of a single blanket. The looms are set up in the open,—under a tree if there happens to be a tree sufficiently near at hand,—and the designs are all taken from nature or from the symbolism of their nature religion.

It is the quality of sincerity that gives the Indian blanket its peculiar value when used as a rug, portière or couch cover in a Craftsman room, or in any one of the rooms so characteristic of the West. No form of drapery harmonizes quite so well with plain, sturdy forms in woodwork and furniture and with the mellow tones of the natural wood, as do these Indian blankets, for the reason that they are simply another expression of the same idea. Anyone who has ever been in a typical country house or bungalow in southern California, Arizona or New Mexico will realize precisely what we mean, for the fitness of these blankets for such uses is so keenly appreciated that the craftsmen are kept busy supplying the white man's demand. As the blankets will last for a generation and will stand almost any kind of use, it is easy to see why they naturally belong in houses of a rugged, hospitable character, especially as the primitive forms and geometrical lines of the design are absolutely in keeping with the whole decorative scheme of such a house. An appealing human touch is given by the fact that no two Navajo blankets are ever woven alike and never is one found to be perfectly symmetrical down to the last detail of its pattern. The reason for this is the superstition of the Navajo squaw against making a perfect pattern, which to her mind would imply the perfect completion of her work and consequently the ending of her life. Like most Indian superstitions, this one embodies a truth so universal that it is felt and acknowledged by everyone who has thought much about life and its mysteries, and this touch of sympathy and comprehension is a clue to the bond that exists between all,—white men and Indians alike,—who live close to the unseen.

The same general character distinguishes the Indian baskets. Basketry is a form of handicraft more generally practiced by Indian tribes than any other. From the pueblos of New Mexico to the Pacific coast and extending thence into Alaska, we find a multitude of different types, each one characteristic of its makers. The best baskets, however, are made by the Pimas and the Apaches, who excel in this art as markedly as the Hopi and Navajos excel in the making of blankets. These baskets, showing the same natural symbolism and the same instinctive feeling for

form, color and design, are as much at home in the white man's house as are the much-desired blankets. The real Indian basket is something to bring despair to the "arts and crafts" basket maker, because it is a form of handicraft as nearly perfect as any that exists. These baskets are woven from willow, which is gathered at a certain season of the year by the Indian squaws, peeled and stored. When taken out for use it is placed in water for a certain time to be made sufficiently pliable. The process of making the baskets is exceedingly slow and laborious, and a weaver will often spend more than a month on a single basket. The groundwork is woven in the natural color of the fiber, a light dull yellow, while the pattern, which is made from the peeled bark of a native plant commonly known as "devil's claw," is usually a dull rusty black. The finest of these bowls are waterproof and they are in all manner of shapes

The third great craft of the Southwestern Indian is the making of pottery, which is undoubtedly the oldest of all the Indian arts, for examples of it are found in almost all the ruins that remain as records of prehistoric times. The Indians of the pueblos are the master potters, and their handiwork is of infinite variety both as to form and ornamentation. Each tribe has its own peculiar method of working, and all differ in such details as the methods of preparing the clay, of making the vessel and of firing, while the variety of forms and decorations used is almost endless. The pueblo potter uses no wheel and the forms he makes are his original creations of eye and hand. The clay is ground and mixed with powdered potsherds. The bottom of the new piece is molded on a form such as the bottom of a jug or bowl, and on this the clay, rolled out into a slender coil or roll, is fastened. By process of careful coiling, the vessel to be made is gradually put into its beautiful form, then smoothed with a gourd rind and dried in the sun. After it is dried it is covered with a wash put on with a piece of rabbit skin, and when again dry the exterior surface is given a beautiful finish by being rubbed down with a smooth polishing stone, an article that is frequently handed down from one generation to another as an heirloom. The decorations in natural Indian colors are then applied by means of a brush made from yucca fiber. Finally the piece is burned in a rude kiln or oven and at length comes forth, a remarkable example of the keramic art. The making of a piece of pottery has in it the same mystic element that goes into the weaving of blankets and baskets. While the piece is burning the Indians attribute the hissing sound caused by the heated moisture in the bowl to the spirit which is embodied in the bowl or jar. The break in the lines decorating many Indian pieces of pottery is purposely left there by the maker to release the spirit of the bowl if it should be broken.

THREE ACRES AND CHAINS: BY ALICE DINSMOOR

IT WILL never be known how many people living on a salary or wages in some form, with little or no time undirected by other people, throw up their positions when they read "Three Acres and Liberty,"—such beguiling statements does it make about the possibilities of pleasure, health and profit.

"An acre," says this courageous inspiring book, "will produce in asparagus 3000 bunches at 20 cents a bunch....$600.00
In onions, 600 bushels at 75 cents a bushel............... 225.00
In peas, 50 bushels at $2.00 a bushel................... 100.00"

The income from fruit grown on "three acres" is even more alluring. From an acre of blackberries, sold at seven cents a quart, one may be assured of seven hundred dollars, and from strawberries at five cents a quart, four hundred dollars. As small fruits are common things that everybody wants, what life could be happier, easier or freer than one spent in raising and marketing these products?

Mr. Hall's book came to my notice at the psychological moment. I held my breath while I read it. I knew precisely where to get three acres of land, with a house and barn and old apple trees, and I had the money to buy them. All I needed was "liberty." This I lost no time in obtaining by resigning an instructorship held for many years. And in thus obtaining "liberty" I have known for the first time in my life what chains are.

My newly bought house was so dirty and out of repair that several hundred dollars had to be spent at once to make it comfortably habitable. Wisely or unwisely, I made this outlay, and by the end of the first month my compensation was that the little old house was in order, and things were standing and hanging as nearly as possible where for years I had dreamed they one day should. The wall paper is all of my own selection. In the low dining room—two steps down from the rest of the house—it is a green lattice-work figure with soft greenish brown rosebuds among it. The sitting room on the southeast corner of the house is bright and cheery with its paper of creamy background bespread with pale rose-colored poppies. The kitchen is the only room I have altered much. It was dark and I

have put a good window over the sink, so that when dish-washing is going on, there is plenty of light, and a view of trees along the river that is lovely all the year round. Some sensible woman planned the capacious cupboards, and the drawers and closets make it possible to have utensils, dishes, etc., in convenient places.

My spacious desk from Mr. Rohlf's workshop is my comfort here as it was in my teaching days. The pigeonholes are filling now with receipts for groceries, farming implements, etc. Oh, dear! everything costs so much. And yet I have grown to love every inch of the place—even the loose stones. Some man has told me they are not altogether a detriment to the land, as they keep the moisture in. Perhaps they do. They certainly do not prevent weeds from growing.

September tenth.—Helen and I are picking tomatoes by the wheelbarrow load. I had three thousand plants set out in June, and they are yielding abundantly.

September sixteenth.—I sent eighteen crates of tomatoes to New York yesterday by my neighbor. They sold for only forty-five cents a crate, and how the chains clanked when they were being packed! Only about one tomato in five is fit to sell; one must raise them to realize how perishable they are.

September twentieth.—Helen, a college girl who really does love outdoor things, has been my right hand in everything since I came here. She has planted and hoed and harvested the little vegetable plot; she has wisely put into the flower garden the seeds from which we might have pleasure the first year—and now our reward, such asters and marigolds I never saw; so large and fluffy and perfect the asters, so gorgeous in gold and maroon the marigolds! And we owe them all to Helen. There is almost nothing she cannot do with tools; when a key will not work, or the pump fails, or curtains have to go up, she is always ready.

October fourth.—After much searching I have found a man who has graciously consented to cut my buckwheat. It was sowed late in July on land prepared for tomatoes. The white field has been beautiful through September, and now it is being cut amid groans from the man who wields the cradle.

October tenth.—W. W. here from the city to work. He and I together have packed the shed full of buckwheat and left the rest outdoors in a big pile under a canvas until I can get someone who will be kind enough to thresh it.

November twenty-ninth. I have had two or three men threshing buckwheat at different times, but it is only today that it is finished by the sixth man who has been good enough to do something to it.

December fourth.—Have had fifty pounds of buckwheat flour made to give away and to use myself. The rest, about eight bushels, has been sold at the mill. Reckoning the cost of seed and labor, I have lost between seven and eight dollars. This is a form "liberty" takes with me. It is evident that as a paying crop my buckwheat does not quite equal Mr. Hall's potatoes or peas.

December ninth.—Mrs. H., a kind and cultivated neighbor, has asked K. and me to join a Shakespeare reading class for the winter. We have had our second meeting today in my library. The ladies thought it an ideal room for the meeting.

February tenth.—I am finding out all the hardships of country life. I have been in the city, at L. P.'s wedding primarily, but incidentally to get thoroughly warm—for the weather indoors and out has been bitter since this month began. Coming home I find my maid is ill at her mother's, and I have myself and the pig to feed and the fires to keep going. Pretty strenuous "liberty!" Three fires I must keep up, to make the house half comfortable—two of them will stay in over night, but the kitchen fire goes out regularly. Going away is out of the question—piggie would starve and the plants and fruit would freeze. I must not let T. know that I am quite alone in the house, though I really don't mind it at all. When I have a moment to lay the shovel and dishcloth down, I have the best companionship in the library—and if I feel a shadow of loneliness creeping over me I seize my pen and write to somebody. While the pen goes I have the sense of some dear presence. The days are really too short; the sunsets are glorious, and the nights—how still they are! And I sleep without the slightest fear. Isn't a man's house his castle, and isn't a woman's house hers? And are not my storm doors as good as a portcullis? Then I have the satisfaction of knowing I have not a diamond or a possession of any kind that would tempt a thief. What safety there is in poverty! Who wouldn't be poor on three acres?

February fifteenth.—Still alone. I never thought I should turn to a pig for society, but I have turned. This is my second week of solitude and, lest I forget how to talk, I chat with piggie while I feed him. He grunts quite sympathetically and I have a growing opinion of his intelligence.

March ninth.—The man whom I engaged to begin work today has not come.

March twelfth.—In city to find man for outside work; woman for indoor. Engaged two—brought woman with me. Man promised to come, but didn't.

March twentieth.—Piggie who had grown to seem quite a friend has been taken to the butcher today. He has cost three dollars more than I sold him for at the market price—my first venture in livestock is not what could be called brilliant in financial returns. And if there were a monetary value put on the hours I have lain awake cold nights wondering if the little fellow were warm enough, my deficit would be considerably larger.

March twenty-eighth.—Henry F., who professes to know a good deal about gardening, has come from the office where I engaged the last man who didn't come. Have set him to trimming apple trees and grape-vines, and he takes hold fairly well.

April fifteenth.—Have been to the Department of the United Charities known as Bureau for the Handicapped to look for man. Henry F. is too dilettante. I must have a stronger farmhand. After seeing a good many, I have engaged a man with one eye.

April twenty-second.—New man, Patrick, is taking hold well. Together we set out the five hundred strawberry plants I had ordered from Three Rivers, Michigan. There are seven and one-half rows, one hundred feet long.

April twenty-seventh.—First potato planting begun.

April twenty-eighth.—I have cut potatoes half the day. Anybody who thinks it is easy work had better try it; anybody who hasn't, can't imagine how much care it takes to cut a moderate-sized potato into pieces containing two or three good "eyes," and a fair share of center to serve as nutriment until the new plant is large enough to get it from the soil. Patrick has dug the trenches for them; put on a handful of fertilizer at three-foot intervals, then thrown over a handful of earth, and I have "dropped" until I am tired. Patrick is not sympathetic, he says women always do this work in Ireland. "Irish cobblers" for earliest, and "green mountain" for later use are the varieties I have put in, on advice of the most scientific farmer in these parts.

May fourteenth.—The first planting of sweet corn, "early cory," has gone in today, at marked intervals shown by strings on the line, Patrick and I officiating; Patrick made a shallow hole, put in fertilizer, then a little earth, and I "dropped" from four to six kernels in each depression. Patrick covered lightly and there is nothing more to do until the corn is ready to be plowed. Seventeen rows each, two hundred feet long, were put in for first planting. Meanwhile Patrick and I have been discussing members of the English Parliament whom one or both of us have seen, or, at least, read about. Patrick is a very well informed and a considerably traveled man.

May twentieth.—J. B. is obliged to change companions for her European trip. "Is it possible for me to go?" she writes. Nay, verily. It does cost a pang or two to say so. But the corn just showing its seed leaves, the blossoming peas, the general promise of things, combine to keep me right here. The best of it is that it does not hurt me to say "no," as once it would have done. My home chains are grown too strong.

May twenty-sixth.—The last of the tomato plants have gone in today. Most of them look well. I paid fifteen dollars a thousand last year for plants like these which I have raised in my hotbed.

July twentieth.—Gathered first sweet corn. Neighbors came to buy, as theirs is not yet ready. One man wanted more than I could let him have. Besides sweet corn I am sending to market now potatoes, cucumbers, squash, beans, apples, cabbage and blackberries.

July thirtieth.—Today when I was dead tired I went down to rest under the trees at the edge of the Hackensack. The stream was as smooth as a mirror and above were mountainlike clouds dazzling in their brilliancy, too blinding to look at; but turning my eyes down to the stream, I found their reflections softened, alpine-like, were making a most lovely picture. Then the thought came to me: Our human vision would be quite blinded by sight of the Father above in His matchless Glory—but He grants us the reflection of his own beauty in the lives of gentle, strong souls whom we love.

August tenth.—The plot of ground at the right of the house, well

open to the sun, about seventy-five feet square, is almost all flowers this year; only one of the sixteen beds is reserved for peppers and peanuts. I sowed all the seeds myself and have fought the weeds with the help of a boy and girl hired by the day. The reward is a daily increasing one. The first delight was a long bed of nasturtiums which are now in their second period of blossoming, running the whole gamut of color from lemon to crimson. The great central mass of pink and crimson hollyhocks were glorious in July, and now a little forest of new ones is springing up around the plants, grown from the seeds that must have sprouted almost the moment they touched the ground. The sweet alyssum and mignonette are spreading and blossoming well. The asters and marigolds are just beginning to fulfil their early promise, and a month from now they will be masses of beauty. If *only* I had more time to be among them! My greatest recreation is to fill every available glass and vase with the blossoms and place them where they will cheer us most.

September eighteenth.—The asters,—white fringed, purple and pink—are glorious.

December third.—K. and I have been preparing for a week to leave for the winter, and today turned the keys, and are off to town.

MARCH fourth, nineteen hundred and nine.—Came home in a driving snowstorm. Everything safe. Very happy to be here, though I have a new man and woman to initiate. Not a house I have been in, or a place I have seen, however sightly or elegant, makes me love this less. I am ready to go into another struggle with the elements with good courage.

March twenty-third.—William sowed the seeds in the hotbed: tomatoes, peppers, cabbage, cauliflower, lettuce.

April first.—The report that I want to buy a horse is abroad and horses are coming from every direction. Men go away disappointed because I am not ready to be duped. They tell me good horses are high; that it is better for a horse to have two spavins than one; that a lame shoulder shows his willingness to work, etc.

April twenty-sixth.—Began planting potatoes,—"Irish cobblers." Have cut them only in halves this year, as the Farmer's Bulletin says this cutting yields best results.

My classmates who were here to luncheon last week, have sent me a most charming sequel to their visit,—Grayson's "Adventures in Contentment." On the card that came with it is written: "A contentment expression of our contentment in your contentment." I evidently look and seem as contented as I am. I have been reading some of the "Adventures" to K. tonight. The chapter on "The joy of possession" brings vividly to my mind that May day before I moved out here, when I came from the city to see how the workmen were progressing on the repairs. The lawn was dotted with violets. As I stood looking at a specially beautiful bunch—suddenly the thought came to me: "They are yours." The feeling of that moment thrills me still; the blue of those violets is burnt into my very soul.

May eleventh.—Picked blossoms off the newly set strawberry

vines that all the strength of the plants may go into roots and stems.

May fourteenth.—Set out early tomato plants. The apple blossoms, the neighbors' and mine, are at the height of their glory and fragrance. They give rich promise of fruit, but their present loveliness is large reward for the trimming and fertilizing I have given mine.

May seventeenth. Transplanted from hotbed, twenty-two wonderberry plants—the creation of Mr. Burbank, which I am trying.

May twenty-sixth.—Setting out more tomato plants, with wrapping paper around the stem at top of ground to protect the plants from the cut worms that have taken many of those previously set.

June eighth.—Picked seven quarts of strawberries. The very first ripe one I ate on the first of June. It has rained so much they have been slow in coming to maturity, but these we picked are fine.

June tenth.—William replanted "early cory" corn. On account of the cold, imperfect seed, or something, I shall have a meager crop.

June fifteenth.—William took twenty quarts of strawberries and several heads of mignonette lettuce to E. The berries sold for fifteen cents a box.

June twenty-fifth.—Sent sixteen quarts of berries and three and one-half pecks of peas to E. They all sold well. I am nearly dead with the picking, though K., my constant comfort, has helped.

The bees swarmed. What a sight and a sound it was! The sound was like nothing so much as the tramp of a regiment of soldiers moving swiftly and cheerfully to victory. They lodged in the top of an apple tree close to where they have lived in their old hive. Mr. L.'s man climbed the tree, carrying a box with the bottom improvised of netting and brought them down. He put the eight frames into the box very quietly and was not stung.

June twenty-eighth.—Notwithstanding we carefully took the egg-laying beetles from the potatoes, we have raised a tremendous crop of bugs. I am having them brushed off by the quart.

June thirtieth.—Took last of strawberries to H. Have had two hundred and fifty-six quarts in all of perfect ones. "Grand and glorious," people have called them. They are really the first crop I have had that has paid well on the investment.

July twentieth.—Sent first potatoes to market. They were planted April twenty-eighth and are ready to eat, just a week later than those planted on the same date last year.

August first.—The wonderberry vines are loaded with berries and blossoms. The fruit raw reminds one, in flavor, of a ground cherry; in appearance of a huckleberry. Disappointed by their insipidity when raw, I have tried cooking them, and stewed they are delicious—about this everybody in the family agrees.

August thirteenth.—My faithful Anna came in today with a great bunch of cardinal flowers that she found just below the bushes, skirting my place, on the edge of the river. I did not know they grew there. They are an asset to make me forget I am dead tired weeding lima beans and potatoes. Just now I am in a sort of life and death struggle with the ironweeds, which are fast going to seed, and will

give me a whirlwind reaping next year if allowed to cast their seed where they are. Positively the last peas were picked today. The first were ready June twenty-fifth. Next to strawberries they are the best crop I can raise.

August sixteenth.—The rain, for which every growing thing has been panting, came today in a downpour that lasted from early till late. I had to go out in the worst of the storm to help gather the vegetables for market tomorrow, and was drenched to the skin. This is the sort of experience that makes farmers prematurely old and rheumatic. William did his share of the picking with no word of complaint.

September first.—T. and I went by train to E., then across to Fort Lee and by boat to Coney Island. I felt like a prisoner out on reprieve, or suddenly pardoned—the shackles off. I did not realize before how the chains were cutting into my very bones—but they were. Three months of toil on a stretch I have had with no let up. But wasn't I glad not to be landing at one of the city docks to be stifled in some crowded apartment tonight?

September eighteenth.—T. and I in city to spend Sunday. I allowed Anna to invite her brother and his wife to visit her while we were away. She was most grateful because they had enjoyed the little home so much. It is worth a great deal of struggle to be able to give so much pleasure in one's home. Half the joy I have had in it is in the sharing with others.

October twentieth.—Had three barrels of Baldwins picked from one tree today. The apple crop has been excellent altogether, and the sales have been so good as to offset losses in poor corn, etc.

October thirtieth.—What a month this has been! Soft air; the maples, golden and crimson; the oaks, rich and satisfying; days of brilliant sunshine—days of dreamy haze. One can almost live on such color and atmosphere.

November twenty-third.—Sent buckwheat crop to market. Gathered flower seeds. The garden has nothing left to remind one of the summer loveliness except a few last pansies. The chrysanthemums that in their yellow glory have cheered us all this month are all but gone—last night's cold wind has beaten them out.

November thirtieth.—The apples are sold and the last vegetables worth selling disposed of. The results of the third summer are not better than the second. Three acres for three summers have given me no liberty, have given me only chains, yet I like them.

"And when at last I can no longer move
Among them freely, but must part
From the green fields and from the waters clear
. . . .
Let me once more have sight
Of the deep sky and the far-smiling land,—
Then gently fall on sleep,
And breathe my body back to Nature's care,
My spirit out to thee, God of the open air."

"Bernmoor."

THE STORY OF CHING WONG, THE CRAFTSMAN: BY WALTER A. DYER

NCE upon a time, ever so long ago, there lived in China a little, weazened-up yellow man. It was in the Ming dynasty, whenever that was. My book says thirteen hundred and sixty-eight to sixteen hundred and forty-four. Like most of us in nineteen hundred and ten, his chief occupation was earning enough cash to buy enough rice and fish to nourish his shriveled little body sufficiently to make it possible for him to earn more cash to buy more rice and fish, and so on, *ad infinitum.* His name was Ching, or Wong, or Ching Wong, or whatever outlandish name you will. Somewhere in Ching's disgusting little body there slumbered a soul about as big as one grain of mustard seed. It was an untroublesome soul that let him beat his wife and do many vile things. Ching's possession of a soul was not in itself remarkable. Most of us have them—much like Ching's.

But one day Ching's soul woke up!

Ching earned the cash for his rice and fish by making pots for other people to cook rice and fish in. He made the pots good enough to sell for cash, and no better. Why should he? It would not be prudent to make them so well that they would never break, for then, by and by, his occupation would be gone, and how would he get rice and fish then? And it really didn't matter if they did happen to be scratched and uneven. Folks simply wanted pots that would hold water and not crack in the fire.

But one day Ching conceived the idea of making an especially good pot. It was his soul that told him to do it, but he didn't know that. So he made a good pot. It was a very good pot, indeed. It was round and smooth and graceful. He spoiled many pots in making it, and wasted much valuable time, but he didn't care. When the good pot was done he didn't try to sell it, but cleaned a place for it on the shelf and sat and looked at it. It pleased him greatly, and as he sat and admired it his soul grew—just a little bit.

After a while the good pot ceased to satisfy Ching's soul, and it clamored for another. So Ching made another good pot, better than

the first. Then he made other good pots, and soon he made all his pots good pots, even though they brought no more cash. It pleased him to know that he could make good pots.

One day Ching saw a piece of glazed pottery with blossoms in it in a mandarin's window. It was green, shiny, and very delicate and beautiful. After that his soul troubled him a great deal. Finally he could stand it no longer, and he journeyed to the big town, where he paid a skilled potter much cash to teach him how to make delicate, colored pots with glazed surfaces. Then he went home, and whenever he found time he made delicate vessels with colored, glazed surfaces. These he did not sell, but put them on his shelf and gazed at them when he was tired.

By and by he found himself desiring to make something even more beautiful, and he set forth again to learn what the ages had taught men about making porcelain.

Finally the great inspiration of Ching Wong's life came to him. He resolved to make a vase that would be a perfect vase—the most beautiful vase that had ever been made. He made and destroyed dozens before he found a shape that would satisfy his soul. Then he made and destroyed many more before he hit upon just the soft sky-blue tint that he wanted. At last it was done. It was a very small vase, but it was the most beautiful vase that had ever been made. He had put the whole of his little mustard-seed soul into it. Then he sent it as a gift to the Emperor.

Whether Ching died happy after he had made his vase, or lived to a driveling old age, really does not matter. The vase has lasted for hundreds of years, and now stands on a little teakwood pedestal in the cabinet of a wealthy collector, and is gazed at and admired by many people who do not understand, and by a few who do.

CHING WONG was one of the world's craftsmen. He was as much a craftsman, in his way, as Michaelangelo; for craftsmanship is not confined to any one age nor to any one people. It is eternal and universal. It was a human attribute in the days of Tubalcain. Craftsmanship is the realization of art for art's sake; only that phrase has been worn threadbare until it hardly serves to cover the nakedness of shiftless bohemianism. The reward of craftsmanship is the satisfaction of the soul in the completion of a perfect thing, whether it be a chair or a cathedral, a sentence or an epic. Craftsmanship is one of the rarest of human virtues in its perfection, and one of the oldest and commonest in germ. True craftsmen are rare, but most of us are potential craftsmen without knowing it. Our souls haven't fully waked up. For craftsmanship is not confined to the making of pots and pictures; it extends throughout the whole range of the world's activities, wherever human creative force is at work. Wherever the creative faculty is exercised for its own sake with a high ideal—there is craftsmanship.

There is no higher ideal than that of the craftsman, for it is the soul speaking; it is the divine spark in us. God, indeed, is the greatest craftsman of all. In fact, so far as we may reason from what we

see, craftsmanship is His chief attribute. Love, mercy, justice, wrath—these things we have guessed at. All we have evidence of is craftsmanship. Look about you—look at the curve of a mountain range, at white clouds and blue sky, at a clump of purple asters and goldenrod, at a chipmunk's tail, at a pine tree against the winter sunset, at the flash of the sun on a mountain brook. Isn't it a bit presumptuous to suppose that these things were made for our pleasure alone?

"And the earth brought forth grass, and the herb yielding seed after his kind, and the tree yielding fruit, whose seed was in itself, after his kind; and God saw that it was good."

We are most of us craftsmen in some material or other—some in pots, some in apples, some in marble, some in pie-crust, "Some with massive deeds and great, some with ornaments of rhyme." We must work, whether or no; shall our work make us happy or miserable?

We are workers, you and I, and our compensation is, for the most part, inadequate. How keenly that fact tortures us at times! We work to make others rich, and we deserve appreciation which we do not get. In the ideal of craftsmanship alone may we find due compensation. Do your work well, and your own soul will not fail to praise you. It will be the God in you saying, "Well done, thou good and faithful servant." External appreciation is pleasant, but in the end it is hollow and ephemeral. Self-realization and self-satisfaction are the permanent, valuable rewards. I can imagine that Robinson Crusoe on his desert island had his happy moments. The Mediæval monk in his cell wrought wonderfully for the delectation of his own soul. Longfellow saw this vision when he wrote "The Builders," and Kipling, when he wrote "L'Envoi."

That's all very well, you say, for one with the artistic temperament. Young Rodin nearly starved in the name of craftsmanship, but he was an artist. I am merely a worker, and I dislike to starve. I inhabit a world of cold, hard facts, not dreams.

You are wrong, brother. You are an artist, too, just as Ching Wong was when he made his ugly pots. Perhaps your soul hasn't waked up yet. You are still working for cash with which to buy rice and fish. That's your trouble—not circumstances.

Take courage, weary toiler. It may be that your youthful dreams never will be realized. Perhaps there is no pot of gold at the end of the rainbow for you. But the rainbow is there—a vastly more wonderful and beautiful thing. Commune with your own soul; you will find it jolly company. Open the windows and let in God's sunlight. Then make something that you know is good. Give your soul a chance.

THE SMELL OF PAINT: AN IMAGINARY CONVERSATION: BY CHARLES BATTELL LOOMIS

SCENE:—*An art dealer's show room. Pictures in stacks. Some on the walls, some on easels. Enter dealer with collector. Dealer goes to corner of room and picks up picture which has been placed face against the wall.*

Dealer (with enthusiasm):—This is a very beautiful picture.

Collector (nodding his head):—Yes, it is.

Dealer:—Do you think it more beautiful than most?

Collector:—It is one of the most beautiful I ever saw.

Dealer:—What do you think it is worth?

Collector:—Well, I don't know who painted it, but I would be willing to give a hundred dollars for it without inquiring further.

Dealer:—Man, it's a Homer Martin!

Collector:—You don't say so! I told you it was beautiful. You can't fool me. I now say that it's marvelously beautiful. Who but Martin could have painted it?

Dealer (laughs):—And you said you'd give a hundred dollars for it.

Collector:—Yes, the joke is on me. Well, I'll back my admiration for it and I'll give you a thousand, spot cash.

Dealer:—Not exactly. Not quite that. You can have it for two thousand five hundred dollars.

Collector:—Done. Here is the money and I think I have a bargain.

Dealer (sentimentally):—I don't suppose that poor old Martin got more than twenty-five or fifty dollars for it and he did need the money so. Well, an artist has no business to die in middle age. Art is long and it's up to him to hang on until he's ninety. Then he may be able to get some of the good prices himself. I wish the poor man was alive and I'd invite him out to dinner. Some of those poor devils don't know what it is to eat a square meal.

Collector (looks at the picture lovingly):—I'm a very proud man to be the owner of this which I consider the most beautiful picture I ever saw. I want to take it with me, and show it to my friends. I feel I am getting it cheap.

Dealer (laughingly):—There's a good deal of paint on it.

(*Collector goes out.*)

(*Scene changes to office of friend of collector. Friend seated at desk. Collector comes in.*)

Collector:—Hello, old man. I've got a surprise for you. Here is a picture that I wouldn't sell for fifty thousand dollars.

Friend:—That's going some!

Collector:—It's the most beautiful Homer Martin that the artist of that name ever painted. Isn't it a tone poem? Don't you think it has the art quality all over it? He's just as careful in his painting of the corners as he is of the center of the picture. That's the mark of a genius.

Friend:—I guess it's all right. I don't know much about pictures myself. I know what I like, but I wouldn't call that a shocker in any way. It don't slap you in the face.

Collector:—That's why I like it? When I started in I liked the slap-you-in-the-face kind of picture, but now I'm educated. No offense. You go in for horses and all that sort of thing, but I wouldn't trust you to buy a picture. Just look at that delicate gray quality——

Friend:—I'd call it "green."

Collector:—What did I tell you. You know horses. You'd never mistake a bay horse for a gray horse——

Friend:—Nor a "green" horse for an old horse.

Collector (*ignoring him*):—I know Homer Martin (on canvas—never met him, poor chap), and I love his pictures. I wish I had known him in life because I could have got absolute gems for a hundred or less, and they tell me he needed the money. Poor fellow!

Friend:—Well, it's not too late. There are poor artists painting pictures now, pictures that will be worth their weight in gold before many years are passed. I don't know this of my own knowledge, but my sister-in-law who is up on all those things and who is a most sympathetic soul was telling me. She says there are artists who are tonight wondering where tomorrow's bread is coming from. Why not buy some of their pictures, since you know so much about that sort of thing, and pay living prices for them?

(*Collector scowls.*) Well, we are all prone to make mistakes and I might get badly stuck. I don't pretend to be a philanthropist. I buy because I love pictures and I'm willing to pay generously if the man has a name. This is worth twenty times as much to me as the price I paid for it. It grows on me. I'm as proud of that picture as some men are of their wives. It is called "The Beach at Canarsie." Or that's what I intend to call it. I believe it has no name.

Friend (*picks it up and examines it*): Why, no, the name is on the back of it, here. It is "Mount Desert."

Collector:—Well, I'm glad you found that out. But I've seen sand look just like that at Canarsie. And that sedge grass.

Friend:—It's wonderful to know what things are in a picture. I like photographs better because there I'm at home. I can tell grass from a carpet and no color at that. But this looks good to me no matter whether it's sand or clouds. When did this Martin fellow die?

Collector:—Twelve or thirteen years ago.

(*Friend sniffs*)—Then why does it smell?

Collector:—How smell?

Friend:—Say, have you paid for this? (*Sniffs again.*)

Collector:—Certainly, I gave my cheque on the spot.

Friend:—Wonderful paint to keep its freshness after so many years.

Collector:—I don't smell paint.

Friend:—Well, I do, and there's nothing been painted in this room since I became a partner. Look out for paint! Some of it may come off on your coat.

Collector (touching picture gingerly):—That's so.

Friend:—And then you'd have an immortal landscape or part of it on your sleeve.

Collector:—I believe I'll take this to an expert, although I'm sure it's a Homer Martin. It has all his earmarks.

Friend (drily):—Earmarks are valuable.

(*They take it to an expert.*)

SCENE: *Expert's drawing room.*

Collector:—What is this picture worth, judged by its beauty?

Expert:—It is worth a good deal. If an ordinary spring exhibition picture sells for five hundred dollars this ought to be worth a thousand. It is very beautiful and when it has mellowed it will be more beautiful yet. Who painted it?

Collector (dubiously, with side glance at Friend):—Homer Martin.

Expert:—The deuce he did. Homer Martin's been dead for a dozen years. This is very beautiful, but it hasn't that gray quality that Martin's pictures had.

Friend:—Ah, ah! I told you it was "green."

Expert:—"Green" and young. It was painted yesterday.

Collector (ruefully):—*Literally* yesterday?

Expert:—Well, last week or last month. See the paint comes off on my finger. It is a very beautiful picture and I hope the man who painted it got good value for it.

Friend:—As a rank outsider, may I ask a question?

Expert:—Certainly.

Friend:—If this picture were exactly as it now is and it was proved by an expert to be a Homer Martin what would it be worth?

Expert:—Anything a collector chose to pay for it.

Friend:—And this Homer Martin, I suppose, painted pictures because he had a love for what was beautiful in Nature and wished to express some of that beauty on canvas.

Expert:—That was why he did it.

Friend:—But it is possible that a young man with his fame to get, might paint a picture just as beautiful as any Homer Martin and yet he could not get enough for it to satisfy his landlord?

Expert:—That's quite conceivable.

Friend:—So a picture is not valued for its beauty, but because some factitious causes have forced up prices. May I laugh?

Collector:—Well, I want my money back. This picture is beautiful, but the reason I buy Homer Martin is because I am proud to own pictures by that man who was not valued as he should have been in an art-loving country, and if this was painted by a man in the employ

of the dealer—and it must have been, since the paint is so fresh—not all its beauty makes it worth much to me. Art for art's sake never appealed to me. I want my money back. And the next time I buy a masterpiece, I'll remember to take my nose along. That was a good idea of yours, smelling the picture. (*He smells it again.*) My, but it's painty, isn't it?

Friend:—Just out of the pot.

And Homer Martin, in the Elysian Fields, breaks into Homeric laughter as the collector goes sadly out of the expert's room.

THE STORY OF GOVERNMENT RESERVATIONS FOR WILD WATER BIRDS: BY T. GILBERT PEARSON: SECRETARY OF THE NATIONAL ASSOCIATION OF AUDUBON SOCIETIES

NEW YORK naturalist stood one day on the beach of the lower east coast of Florida, absorbed in watching what appeared to be a gigantic sea serpent disporting itself along the crest of the waves. As the strange spectacle drew near, it resolved itself into a long, undulating line of brown pelicans winging their way homeward from the outer feeding grounds. With alternate sailing and rhythmical beating of wings, the line of great birds was seen to pass on until it settled on an island in the

heart of the Indian River. A field glass revealed the fact that hundreds of other pelicans were already there.

A boat was procured, and the naturalist soon set foot upon the island, which, however, was the signal for the birds to depart. They were alarmed at the presence of the man, and seemed to distrust human intrusion. Fishermen nearby stopped hauling their nets long enough to explain the reason for the birds' hasty retreat. Yachts, they said, often came to anchor in the vicinity and seldom did they weigh without taking with them trophies of their visit, and leaving behind many demolished nests. Birds were often killed for their feathers, or to satisfy the passing desire to possess for a moment a creature of unusual form and size. Sometimes a dozen were shot to demonstrate the skill of a rifleman in knickerbockers, or again a hundred were sacrificed to procure a small portion of the skin of each bird with which to make a cloak of a kind seldom seen along the avenue.

The naturalist's curiosity and interest were now thoroughly aroused. He made a careful survey of the island and found it to cover an area of about four acres. He counted the pelicans' nests, the young birds and the adults, as opportunity offered during the period of several days, and estimated that the pelican population consisted of about twenty-seven hundred full-grown birds. This was in eighteen hundred and ninety-eight. Two years later he again visited the island and found that the bird inhabitants had shrunk in numbers to an extent of nearly five hundred.

This gentleman was a member of the Audubon Society and, being strong in the faith held by that organization, believed that these birds should in some way be protected. True, they were not known to be of any economic value, but on the other hand they were harmless creatures. Then, too, they were interesting—one reason being that they were so large. When one of these pelicans spread its wings and set out for a sail down Indian River, it would have required a tape line six and one-half feet in length to reach from tip to tip of its mighty pinions. The pelican's bill is thirteen inches long, and the pouch suspended beneath it is capable of holding four gallons of water. Even with such a mouth no pelican—not even a lady pelican —was ever known to utter a sound, as in the adult form they are absolutely silent birds. Surely such creatures were worth preserving as living curiosities. If attempts were to be made to guard them, here was the place to begin, for with a single unimportant exception there existed no other breeding colony of pelicans on the Atlantic Coast of the United States.

UPON returning to New York the naturalist unburdened himself to the officers of the Audubon Society, with the result that plans were immediately set in motion to preserve the inhabitants of Pelicanville. There was no law in the State of Florida at that time extending protection to birds of this character, but on January fourth, nineteen hundred and one, the Legislature was induced to enact a statute making it a misdemeanor to kill interesting

or valuable non-game birds. The Audubon Society at once employed a man to see that the law was enforced on Pelican Island.

Then murmurings began to be heard, "Pelicans eat fish and they should not be protected," declared a stalwart Floridian. "We need the quills for the millinery trade," chimed in another one with a keen eye to the main chance. There was talk of repealing the law at the next session of Legislature, and the hearts of the Audubon workers were troubled.

Then someone suggested that as there were Federal military reservations, and Federal forest reservations, why not make this a Federal bird reservation and permit no trespassing. The island proved to be unsurveyed government land and this gave force to the argument, but there was found to be no legal provision whereby this could be done. There existed no law or precedent for such an act. The discussion at length reached the ears of President Roosevelt, and he settled the difficulty at once and for all time by issuing, under March fourteenth, nineteen hundred and three, a remarkable document which ran in part as follows:

"It is hereby ordered that Pelican Island in Indian River is reserved and set apart for the use of the Department of Agriculture as a preserve and breeding ground for native birds."

The gist of this order, bearing the signature of the Secretary of Agriculture, was quickly painted on a large sign which could be seen for miles as it stood on the end of Pelican Island.

Imagine the chagrin of the Audubon workers upon learning that when the pelicans returned in spring to occupy their ancestral breeding ground, they took one look at this declaration of the President and immediately decamped bag and baggage to a neighboring island outside of the protected zone! Signs less alarming in size were substituted, and the pelicans, with their feelings appeased, graciously returned and, much to the joy of the naturalist and the Audubon Society, have since peacefully dwelt and flourished beneath the protecting care of the Government. Incidentally, a lesson was learned in dealing with wild birds.

When this act by President Roosevelt came to the attention of the general public, it was not hard to find men who complained loudly that our national executive had overstepped the limits of his legalized power. "What meat is this," they asked, "on which our Cæsar feeds that he should take to himself such powers?" So the friends of the wild birds had another task before them—the President must be given this power. A bill was therefore drafted and after a short delay was enacted by Congress, giving the President authority to establish reservations of this character on government lands not fitted for agriculture.

This accomplished, and the legal difficulty removed, the way was open for the establishment of other bird reservations and the Audubon Society eagerly seized the opportunity. Explorations were at once started to locate and survey the territory holding important breeding communities of water birds situated on government lands in other sections of the country.

A SOOTY TERN ON HER NEST AT DRY TORTUGAS, A FLORIDA RESERVATION.

TROPICAL NODDY TERNS, NESTING TIME AT THE DRY TORTUGAS RESERVATION.

Plumage hunters and eggers were busy plying their trade wherever water birds were known to collect in numbers, and in consequence several interesting species were rapidly nearing extinction. Ten thousand terns were known to have been shot in a single season on Cobb's Island, Virginia. The ten thousand pairs of wings collected went to the millinery houses of New York and ten thousand baby birds were left to perish for want of parental care. In the same way, during the seven years preceding nineteen hundred and eleven, twenty colonies of gulls and terns along the coast of the Carolinas were utterly wiped out of existence. From the lakes of the Rocky Mountains and the Pacific Coast thousands of grebes' breasts were torn from nesting birds every summer, and shipped East to adorn the hats of fashionable women, while the infant grebes were left to call and creep among the tule until the breath of death should end their cries.

MR. FRANK M. MILLER, now State Game Commissioner of Louisiana, reported a case in which five thousand sea birds were broken on a nearby island inhabited by sea birds in order that fresh eggs might subsequently be gathered by the eggers whose waiting boats lay at anchor off shore. No wonder the friends of the birds were profoundly disturbed concerning the future welfare of the wild water birds, and hailed with delight the accession to their ranks of the daring, precedent-breaking Mr. Roosevelt.

So enthusiastic was Mr. William Dutcher, President of the National Association of Audubon Societies, with the results achieved in Federal reservation work in nineteen hundred and five, that he declared in his annual report that if the Association had done nothing else than secure Federal bird reservations and help guard them during the breeding season, its existence would be fully warranted.

That year President Roosevelt established four more bird refuges; one of these, Stump Lake, in North Dakota, was an immense nursery of gulls, terns, ducks, cormorants and snipe in summer, and a safe harbor for wild fowl during the spring and fall migrations. Huron Island and the Sickiwit group of islands lying in Lake Superior were the homes of innumerable herring gulls, some of which perhaps find their way to New York Harbor every autumn. These were made perpetual bird sanctuaries and an Audubon warden took up his lonely watch to guard them against all comers.

Away down in the mouth of Tampa Bay, Florida, rests the one-hundred-acre island of Passage Key. Here the wild bird life of the Gulf Coast has swarmed in the mating season since white man first knew the country. Thousands of herons of various species, as well as terns and shore birds, make this their home. The dainty little ground doves flutter in and out among cactus on the sheltered sides of the sand dunes, plovers and sandpipers chase each other along the beaches, and the burrowing owls known to inhabit no other point on our Gulf Coast, here hide in their burrows by day and explore the island by night.

When this place was described to President Roosevelt, he immediately declared that a bird must never be killed here without the

consent of the Secretary of Agriculture. With one stroke of his pen, he brought this desired condition into existence. Mrs. Asa Pillsbury was duly appointed by the Government to protect the birds of the island. She is one of the few women bird wardens in America.

These things happened in the early days of Government work for the protection of water birds. The Audubon Society had found a new field for endeavor, which was highly prolific in results. With all the limited means at its command, the work of ornithological exploration was carried forward each summer. Every island, mud flat and sand bar along the coast of the Mexican Gulf, from Texas to Key West, was visited by trained ornithologists who reported their findings to the New York office.

The Breton Island reservation for the coast of Louisiana, embracing hundreds of square miles of territory, and including scores of islands and bars, was established nineteen hundred and four. Six additional reservations were soon created along the west coast of Florida, thus extending a perpetual guardianship over the colonies of sea and coastwise birds in that territory,—the pitiful remnants of the vast rookeries which had been despoiled to add to profits of the millinery trade.

The work was early started in the West, where Malheur Lake and Klamath Lake reservations in Oregon resulted. The latter is today the summer home of myriads of ducks, geese, grebes and other wild water fowl, and never a day passes but what the waters of the lake are fretted with the prow of the Audubon patrol boat, as the watchful warden extends his vigil over those feathered wards of the Government.

ONCE set in motion, this movement for Federal bird reservations soon swept beyond the boundaries of the United States. One was established in Porto Rico, and several others among the Aleutian Islands, where on the rocky cliffs may be seen today clouds of puffins, auks and guillemote—queer creatures which stand upright like a man—shouldering and crowding each other about on the ledges which overlook the dark waters of Behring Sea. One reservation in Alaska covers much of the lower delta of the Yukon, including the great tundra country south of the river, and embraces within its borders a territory greater than the State of Massachusetts. From the standpoint of preserving rare species of birds, this is doubtless one of the most important which has thus far come into existence. It is here that many of the wild fowl which frequent the California coast in winter, find a summer refuge safe alike from the bullet of the white man and the arrow of the Indian. Here it is that the lordly emperor goose is probably making its last stand on the American continent against the aggressions of the destructive white race.

Away out in the western group of the Hawaiian Archipelago are located some of the world's most famous colonies of birds. From vast and often unknown regions of the Pacific, the sea birds journey hither when the instinct for mating comes strong upon them. There are beautiful terns of many species, and albatrosses, those winged wonders whose home is on the rolling deep. Their numbers on these islands were such as to be beyond all belief of men who are unfamiliar

with bird life in congested conditions. On February third, nineteen hundred and nine, these islands and reefs were included in an executive order whereby the "Hawaiian Island Reservation" was brought into existence. This is the largest of all our Government bird reserves; it extends through five degrees of longitude.

At intervals in the past these islands had been visited by vessels engaged in the feather trade, and although no funds were available for establishing a warden patrol among them, it was fondly hoped that the notice given to the world that the birds here were now the wards of the United States would be sufficient to insure their safety.

A rude shock was felt, therefore, when late that year a rumor reached Washington that a Japanese poaching vessel had been sighted heading for these waters. The revenue cutter "Thetis" then lying at Honolulu was at once ordered on a cruise to the bird islands. Early in nineteen hundred and ten, the vessel returned, bringing with her twenty-three Japanese feather hunters who had been captured at their work of destruction. In the hold of the vessel were stored two hundred and fifty-nine thousand pairs of wings, two and a half tons of baled feathers, and several large cases and boxes of stuffed birds, for which, had the Japanese escaped, they would have realized over one hundred thousand dollars.

Not only have Federal bird reservations been formed of lakes with reedy margins and lonely islands in the sea, but they have been made to include numbers of the big Government reservoirs built in the arid regions of the West.

President Taft has shown much the same interest in bird protection as did his predecessor, his last reservation being Hogg Island in Lake Michigan, which was created no longer ago than February twenty-first, nineteen hundred and twelve.

Up to the present time there have been established by executive order fifty-six of these Federal bird refuges which in the aggregate annually shelter millions of water birds at all seasons of the year.

The likelihood that this method of protecting birds will continue and the number of reservations greatly increased amounts to an almost certainty as the Government policy in this direction is now firmly established.

The movement came not a day too late to save for our North American fauna some of our most interesting feathered forms of life. Within the past generation the Eskimo curlew and the Labrador duck have ceased to exist, and the trumpeter swan, the least tern and the long-billed curlew are examples of others that are fast hastening to join the list of wild creatures which through the greed of man are now known only by name.

CALIFORNIA'S CONTRIBUTION TO A NATIONAL ARCHITECTURE: ITS SIGNIFICANCE AND BEAUTY AS SHOWN IN THE WORK OF GREENE AND GREENE, ARCHITECTS

THE value of Western architecture, locally and to the nation at large, and its widening influence upon home-building all over the country are facts not to be estimated lightly. Every day it is becoming more evident that America is writing her own architectural history, and writing it with no uncertain hand. The East, on the whole, has still a good deal to learn—and perhaps even more to unlearn—before it can achieve much practical or artistic significance in the construction of its homes; but the West has for some time been recording on the fair page of the Pacific Slope what promises to be an important chapter in the life of the people.

The significance, moreover, of this Western accomplishment arises chiefly from the sincerity of spirit in which it is being undertaken. The type of home that abounds today in California—a type in which practical comfort and art are skilfully wedded—is no architectural pose, no temporary style. It is a vital product of the time, place and people, with roots deep in geographical and human needs. It has a definite relation to the kind of climate and soil, the habits of the people and their ways of looking at civilization and nature. It is equally rich in historic traditions and in provision for present needs. Based on the old Mission forms, which in their turn drew inspiration from the ideals of Spaniard and Moor, modern Californian architecture has nevertheless made those traditions servants, not masters. And while drawing from that romantic background both the sturdy spirit of the simple old pioneer

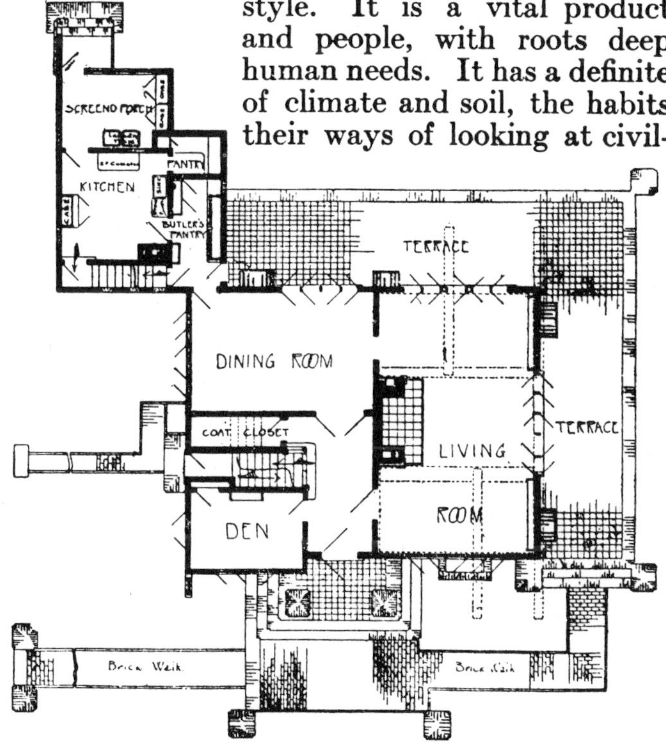

FIRST FLOOR PLAN FOR MR. PITCAIRN'S HOUSE.

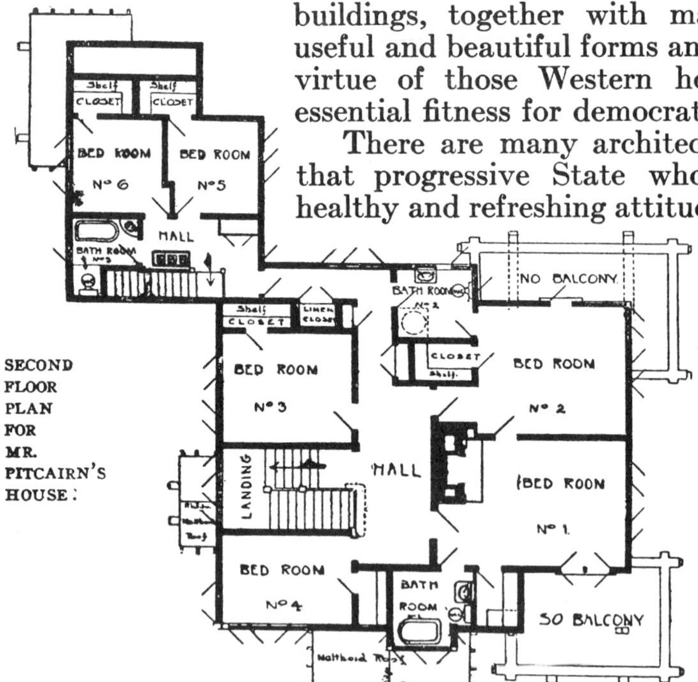

SECOND FLOOR PLAN FOR MR. PITCAIRN'S HOUSE.

buildings, together with many of their most useful and beautiful forms and details, the main virtue of those Western homes lies in their essential fitness for democratic American life.

There are many architects and builders in that progressive State who have shown this healthy and refreshing attitude toward their art, and their work is full of vigorous inspiration and spontaneous outdoor appeal arising from close sympathy with the people and environment. And among those who have helped to make the homes of California proverbial for wise planning and structural beauty, perhaps none has contributed more effectively than the well-known Pasadena firm of Greene & Greene.

Feeling that the work of these men is full of interest and convincing charm and so will be welcomed by all who care about the problems of home-building, from either a national or a personal standpoint, we are presenting in this issue a number of illustrations of houses designed by them, which seem to us especially characteristic of Western ideals and achievement.

Greene & Greene, Architects.

FRONT VIEW OF MR. BLACKER'S HOUSE.

A DETAIL VIEW OF ONE CORNER OF THE PITCAIRN RESIDENCE, SHOWING THE JAPANESE EFFECT OF THE WOODWORK AND THE DELIGHTFUL WAY IN WHICH THE GARDEN HAS BEEN ALLOWED TO ENCROACH UPON THE TERRACE-LIVING ROOM.

One of the first impressions gained from a casual survey of these photographs is the unusually wide variety of the designs. True, there is throughout a resemblance in spirit and purpose, due to the old Mission source and the similarity of the general surroundings. Each building has the typical features of the California home—the low, widespreading roof lines, the solid yet picturesque walls, the frank use of structural beams, the luxurious spaces of porch and balcony and the quiet loveliness of the interior. And yet, so ample has been the range of the architects' imagination, and so diverse the treatment in each particular case, that one feels each house possesses a definite personality of its own, a certain uniqueness both of idea and expression.

The first house, shown on page five hundred and thirty-seven, is

the residence of R. R. Blacker, and is worth studying both for the practical points in its construction and the æsthetic qualities of the whole. The wide overhang of the roofs, the angles of which are so restful and well balanced, the pleasant grouping of the windows, the hospitable breadth of porch and sheltered placing of sleeping balconies, the variety and use of the materials and the attainment of a very decorative effect through the medium of the structure itself—all these things are important units in the final beauty. Not the least of its attributes is the exceptional harmony between the house and its surrounding garden.

FIRST FLOOR PLAN OF MR. HAWKES' HOUSE.

The design of the building is eminently suited to the character and slope of the ground, and the summer house shown in the upper illustration indicates how well the garden features carry out the prevailing architectural theme. As the house occupies a choice site, raised above adjoining streets, fine views are afforded from all sides across the broad valley to the shadowy mountains beyond. It will be noticed that the arrangement of the garden, the walks around the lake and the little stream that trickles over the rocks show the Japanese influence which is felt in so many of our American gardens today.

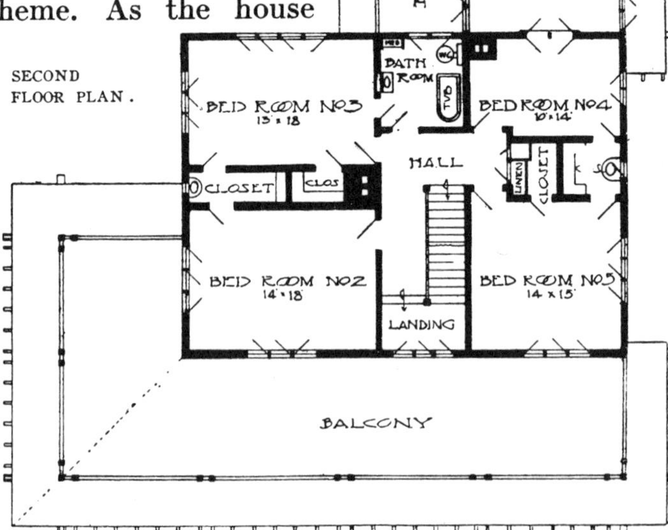

SECOND FLOOR PLAN.

The materials used in the Blacker residence are split redwood shakes and clinker brick. The shakes were dipped in a soft brownish green stain and harmonize wonderfully with the landscape. The architects designed everything—buildings and grounds (including the

main house, a garage, a keeper's cottage, lath house for plants, pergola, lake, etc.), as well as the interior finish, furniture, electric fixtures and hangings. We have not been able to include interior views, but some of the photographs on other pages will give an idea of the homelike atmosphere that pervades rooms which are fortunate enough to owe the beauty of their furnishings to the care of Greene & Greene.

Turning to the views of the Pitcairn residence in Pasadena, we find a general similarity of design but entirely different plan and details. The sides of the building are covered with cedar shingles, left to turn gray by weathering, and the roof is covered with asphalt felt, which is especially suitable to the low pitch. The gutter is designed practically and with good lines, and the leaders are of copper. The casements are hinged to swing inward. The solid timbers used in the construction give a decorative note to the exterior that is delightfully frank and pleasing, and the mortise and tenon joints secured with hardwood pins and wedges are extremely craftsmanlike.

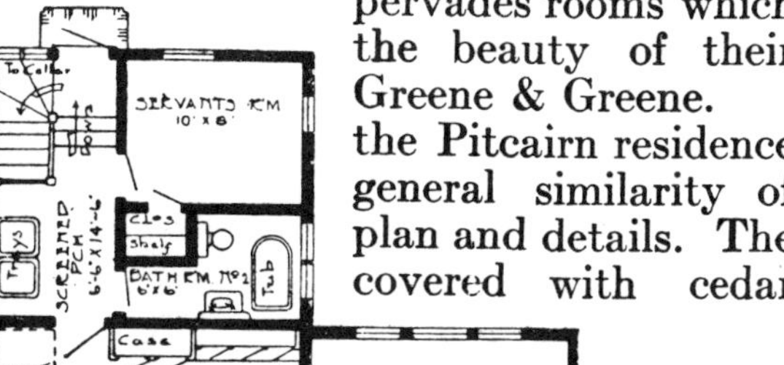

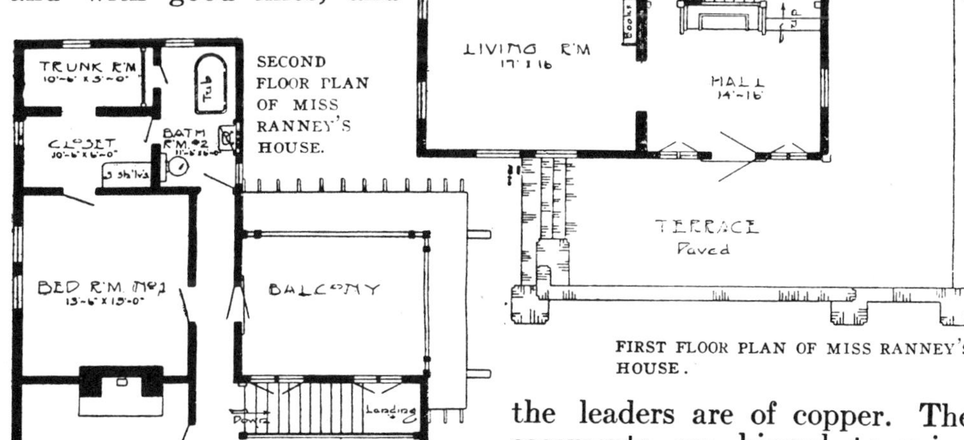

SECOND FLOOR PLAN OF MISS RANNEY'S HOUSE.

FIRST FLOOR PLAN OF MISS RANNEY'S HOUSE.

The terraces are paved with red tile, eight by eight inches, and the steps are of the overburned brick which is used a great deal in that locality for such purposes. The color of the brick is full of interest, and when wide joints and harmoniously tinted mortar are used the finished work is most effective. The same style of brickwork is used in the Ranney house, the photographs of which, on page five hundred and forty-one, show the friendly quality of this construction.

The well-planned interior of the Pitcairn home and the ample provisions for outdoor living and sleeping are shown by the floor plans. As Mr. Henry M. Greene has put it, "the whole construction was carefully thought out and there was a reason for every detail. The idea was to eliminate everything unnecessary, to make the whole as

direct and simple as possible, but always with the beautiful in mind as the final goal." This principle refers equally to the other houses shown, and its successful application accounts for the unusual beauty of the results.

Another house which combines many delightful and typical Western features in a different way is the home of F. W. Hawkes,

Greene & Greene, Architects.

FRONT AND BACK VIEW OF THE HOME OF MR. F. W. HAWKES: ALTHOUGH THE HOUSE IS ESSENTIALLY SIMPLE IN ITS OUTLINE, SO COMPLETELY HAS THE SPIRIT OF THE GARDEN INVADED THE PORCH AND BALCONY THAT THE GENERAL EFFECT IS ONE OF TROPICAL RICHNESS.

shown on page five hundred and forty. Here again the general lines of the building are straight and square, yet so attractively have the various materials been used that the effect is one of almost Oriental or tropical richness. This is heightened by the ingenious way in

Greene & Greene, Architects.

TWO VIEWS ARE GIVEN HERE OF THE HOME OF MISS MARY RANNEY, WHICH ILLUSTRATE MOST DELIGHTFULLY THE CALIFORNIA ATTITUDE TOWARD HOME COMFORT, WITH ITS PERGOLA PORCHES, ITS OUTDOOR SLEEPING ROOM AND CLOSE PROXIMITY OF GARDEN: THE BRICKWORK WITH WIDE JOINTS IS AN ESPECIALLY INTERESTING FEATURE OF ITS CONSTRUCTION.

which the plants and shrubs have been used around the walls and porches, as though the spirit of the garden were trying to invade every balcony and door. As the pictures indicate, the house is satisfying on every side, each wall, roof and angle offering some unexpected glimpse of loveliness. The floor plans are also worth noting, and one can imagine what opportunities they offer for interest of furnishings and interior trim.

The home of Miss Mary Ranney shown next is equally satisfying in its own way. Here again we find the long, rather low-pitched roof and wide overhang that so often characterize California architecture. The projecting beams are repeated in the pergola construction that shelters one corner of the terrace, where comfortable chairs and a swinging seat tempt one from within doors to this breezy open-air living room. The rest of the ample terrace is edged by a parapet of brick, which with its straggling vines forms one of the most attractive features of the place. The quiet harmony of the exterior is further emphasized by the broad, well-placed steps which repeat the brick note of the wall and carry out the terrace effect of the approach. There is an air of unaffected hospitality, of genuine invitation about the place that is particularly winning, and when one stops to consider the very simple way in which this effect has been produced, the utter absence of ornamentation and display, one realizes how much that is beautiful can be accomplished by thoughtful planning, good construction and regard for balance of the various parts.

The floor plans of which this friendly exterior is the result show great economy of arrangement and care for the practical comfort and happiness of the household; not the least important part is the big screened balcony that occupies one corner of the second floor and no doubt makes an excellent outdoor sleeping apartment.

The views on page five hundred and forty-three show the home of Theodore Irwin, which is an old house remodeled. The additions and alterations have been made with such skill and imagination, and the handling of both the building itself and the garden around it is so sympathetic that the ensemble is extremely pleasing. The irregular stonework that walls the lawn has been echoed here and there in the brick parapet, pergola pillars and chimney in such a way as to link the house and its terrace effectively to the surrounding grounds.

While such architectural devices as this are of course the evidences of careful art, they give the place an impromptu and spontaneous touch that is really their chief charm. While stopping short of the eccentric, they add a little sense of the unexpected that relieves the more dignified and conventional lines of the rest of the building. For in architecture, as in every other phase of art, the presence of what may be termed "surprises," when not carried to extremes, may greatly enhance the interest of the work and capture the eye with unexpected and refreshing glimpses.

A study of the floor plans of the Irwin house in connection with the views of the exterior reveals a charming and somewhat unique arrangement. Outside, the living space is extended by roomy terraces and porches, sheltered here by a balcony and there by a pergola roof

supported on massive pillars of irregularly laid brick. Still further love of fresh-air life is evidenced by the interior court, with its central fountain and open galleries above—a most appropriate arrangement in the California climate. Glass doors give access to the court from

DETAIL VIEW OF PERGOLA ENTRANCE TO MR. THEODORE IRWIN'S HOUSE, SHOWING A MOST UNUSUAL AND PICTURESQUE USE OF BUILDING MATERIALS IN THE COMBINATION OF BRICK AND COBBLESTONE: LARGE STONES ARE USED IN THE FOUNDATION OF THE PORCH AND SMALLER ONES ARE SCATTERED THROUGH THE SUPPORTING PILLARS AT WIDENING INTERVALS, UNTIL AT THE TOP SOLID BRICK IS USED: THE EFFECT IS UNIQUE, GIVING A SENSE OF SOLIDITY AT THE FOUNDATION, OF RICH COLOR AND GREATER LIGHTNESS AT THE CROWN: SOLID STONES ARE USED EITHER SIDE OF THE PATH WHICH LEADS TO THIS ENTRANCE AND THE FLOOR OF THE PATH IS COVERED WITH TILES: A GREAT JAPANESE LANTERN IS SEEN AT THE LEFT OF THE ENTRANCE, A MOST PICTURESQUE SUBSTITUTE FOR THE ORDINARY GLITTERING ELECTRIC LIGHT, AND ONE SEEN VERY OFTEN IN WESTERN GARDENS: THE COLOR SCHEME SHOWN AT THE ENTRANCE, IN THE NATURAL-HUED STONE, THE REDDISH TILE, THE BRICK, THE BEAMS OF REDWOOD AND THE SHINGLES OF THE HOUSE, IS ONE OF RARE BEAUTY, NOT COUNTING IN THE GREAT TREE THAT SHADOWS THE ENTRANCE AND ADDS ITS OWN CHARM.

Greene & Greene, ***Architects.***

FRONT VIEW OF MR. THEODORE IRWIN'S HOUSE, SHOWING THE USE OF COBBLESTONE AS A SUPPORT FOR THE TERRACE AND THE COMBINATION OF STONE AND BRICK IN THE CHIMNEYS AND PORCH PARAPETS: THE HOUSE ITSELF IS BUILT OF SPLIT REDWOOD SHAKES.

several rooms, and doors from the bedrooms above open onto the gallery. The rooms with their many windows and cheerful outlooks

DETAIL OF A CORNER OF THE LIBRARY IN MRS. L. A. ROBINSON'S HOUSE: THE VIEWS OF THE EXTERIOR AND TWO SIDES OF THE DINING ROOM ARE GIVEN ON PAGE FIVE HUNDRED AND FORTY-FOUR: THE BRICK-WORK IN THE CHIMNEY AND WALL OF THE LIBRARY IS ESPECIALLY INTERESTING, SHOWING HOW FINISHED AN EFFECT CAN BE GIVEN TO A MATERIAL WHICH IS ORDINARILY SUPPOSED TO BE ADAPTED ONLY TO THE EXTERIOR OF HOUSES, WALLS, STEPS OR PATHS: IN CALIFORNIA APPARENTLY THERE IS NO PREJUDICE AGAINST THE USE OF BRICK FOR THE INTERIOR WALL FINISH OF A ROOM AND IT IS TREATED IN VARIOUS NEW AND PICTURESQUE WAYS TO ADAPT IT TO THIS MORE INTIMATE USAGE: IN THIS ROOM THE BRICK IS A SOFT BROWN, HARMONIZING WITH THE FUMED OAK FURNITURE AND WOODWORK: THE LEADED GLASS IN THE WINDOW IS VERY PALE AMBER WITH CLEAR ANTIQUE IN CONVENTIONAL LEAF DESIGN: ALL THE METAL WORK IS BLACK IRON AND SERVES TO ACCENT THE SOFT BROWNS AND YELLOWS OF THE OTHER FURNISHINGS.

Greene & Greene, Architects.

DETAIL OF THE DINING ROOM OF MRS. BOLTON'S HOUSE, SHOWING THE INTERESTING EFFECT OF CEILED-IN WALLS FINISHED WITH STENCIL FRIEZE: THE FURNITURE IS ESPECIALLY SUITED TO THE ROOM, AND THE FIREPLACE IS SIMPLE AND WELL CONSTRUCTED.

are comfortably planned, and open fireplaces add to the homelike feeling of the interior.

Very different in materials and structure from the preceding houses is the home of Mrs. L. A. Robinson. This is even more reminiscent than the others of the Spanish type. One feels here the influence of the California Missions in the cement walls with their simple lines in which severity and grace are so wonderfully blended, in the massive chimneys, the solid woodwork and the slightly formal touches of potted shrubs and clipped vines. A further decorative note is embodied in the half-timber of the upper walls and the long beams of the pergola roof.

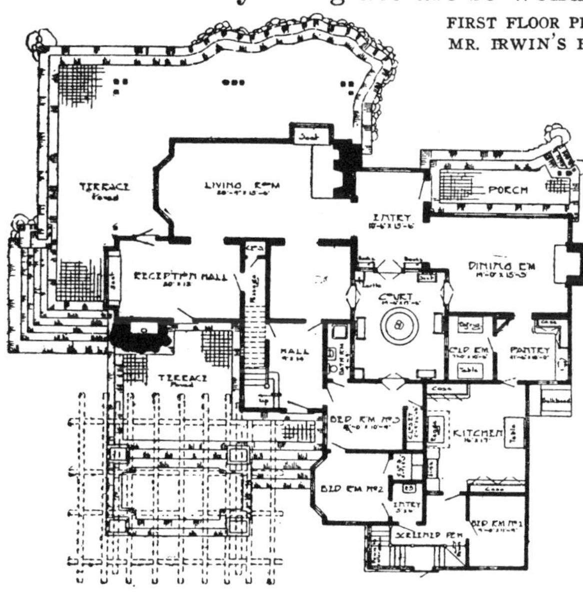

FIRST FLOOR PLAN OF MR. IRWIN'S HOUSE.

It would be difficult to imagine a house more characteristic of this Western State, for it holds the spirit of both the old life and the new, is picturesque from every angle and at the same time is obviously designed for the convenience and contentment of the owners. A home of this type is more than an individual dwelling place; it is a permanent monument of the life of the people and the period.

The two views of the interior (one of which is shown on page five hundred and forty-two and the other on page five hundred and forty-four) fulfil one's happiest expectations. The woodwork and furnishings are sturdy and simple, well made, well proportioned, radiating a real home atmosphere. The glimpse of the fireplace corner, with its brick walls, solid shelf and cozy furnishings, is especially suggestive of the kind of craftsmanship that distinguishes the rooms. Another example of this style of interior treatment is found in the lower photograph on page

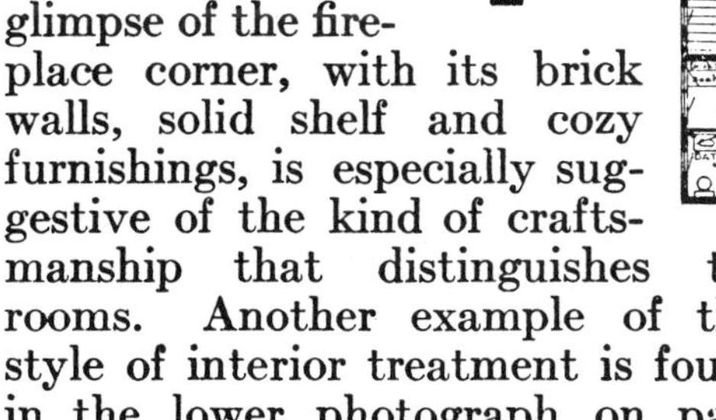

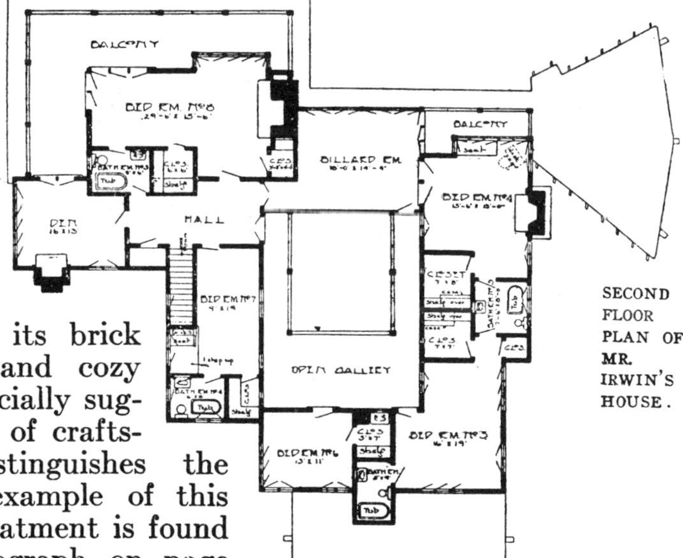

SECOND FLOOR PLAN OF MR. IRWIN'S HOUSE.

five hundred and forty-two, which shows the dining room of Mrs. Bolton's home.

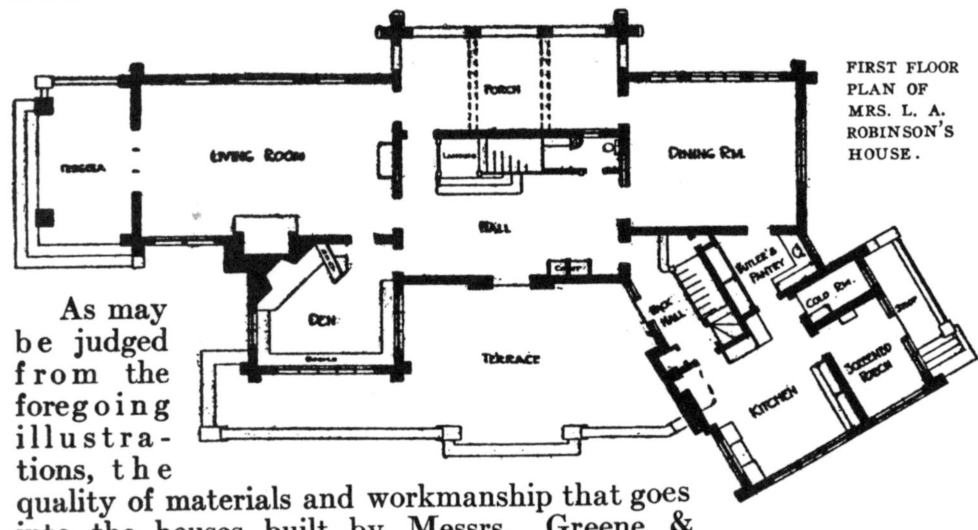

FIRST FLOOR PLAN OF MRS. L. A. ROBINSON'S HOUSE.

As may be judged from the foregoing illustrations, the quality of materials and workmanship that goes into the houses built by Messrs. Greene & Greene renders them of necessity expensive. The construction is always of the best and includes much hand labor—which obviously

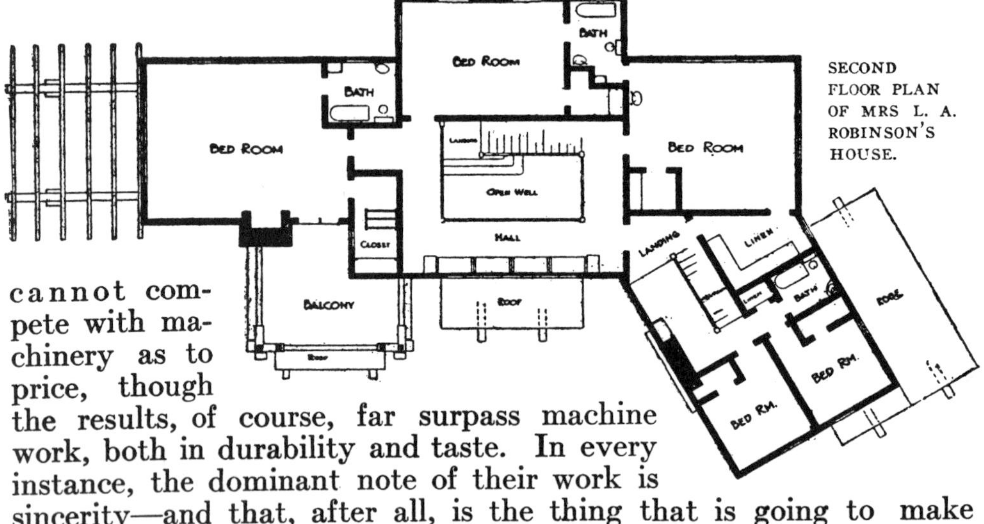

SECOND FLOOR PLAN OF MRS L. A. ROBINSON'S HOUSE.

cannot compete with machinery as to price, though the results, of course, far surpass machine work, both in durability and taste. In every instance, the dominant note of their work is sincerity—and that, after all, is the thing that is going to make California's architecture a vital record in the chronicle of the nation, and help push forward the art of home-building toward our great democratic ideal.

Greene & Greene, Architects.

FRONT VIEW OF HOUSE OF MRS. L. A. ROBINSON, WHICH IS DEFINITELY REMINISCENT OF THE SPANISH MISSIONS, AND FURNISHES AMPLE OPPORTUNITY FOR OUTDOOR LIVING.

CORNER OF THE DINING ROOM IN MR. ROBINSON'S HOUSE, SHOWING WOODWORK, WALL FINISH AND FURNITURE DESIGNED BY THE ARCHITECTS TO HARMONIZE BEAUTIFULLY WITH INTERIOR FITTINGS.

A PEN AND INK SKETCH OF ELLEN TERRY BY PAMELA COLMAN SMITH.

"YOUTH": A SKETCH BY PAMELA COLMAN SMITH.

STORIES OF THE OLD WEST AS TOLD AND PAINTED BY THE COW PUNCHER AND ARTIST, ED. BOREIN: BY A. B. STEWART

HE dream of every tenderfoot who has read of cowboys and Indians, is to sit by a camp-fire and listen to tales of the early West. In the work of Ed. Borein, the life of the cow puncher, the traditions of the Indian, and the stirring fights in the winning of the West find a fresh and permanent expression. These things are part of his life. He has lived among the Indians, and he has herded cattle, not for the sake of telling a story or painting a picture, but as a business. Moreover, in his studio the old camp-fire seems perpetually alight. There all the sons of the West find their way,—Charlie Russell, the painter from Great Falls, Montana, Seth Hathaway, the Indian fighter, Billie McGinty, cow puncher and Rough Rider, Charging Hawk, ex-Sioux scout and U. S. regular—one and all they get the trail as easily as across the plains, the mountains and the desert, and here the old stories are told and retold.

Many a good narrative survives from the buffalo days when the Indian lived off the herds which furnished him meat, clothing, war trappings, hides for his tepee and the material for his religious ceremonial. The Indian buffalo hunt was a model of efficiency and justice. When they needed meat the bucks rode into the herd, killed what they thought they could use, and rode on. The squaws followed with the pack horses; stooping over each carcass for an instant to look at the arrow that pierced it, then going on until each squaw had found an arrow with the mark of a member of her family. Then

"ANY NATIVE WITH HIS LASSO COULD ALWAYS GET BEEF": FROM A DRAWING BY ED. BOREIN.

NAVAJOS, NEW MEXICO: FROM A DRAWING BY ED. BOREIN.

skilfully she skinned the animal, cut up the meat, packed it on the horse, rolled up the hide and made her way back to camp. This custom is the material out of which Mr. Borein has made one of the most interesting of his pictures.

"I once asked an old Indian squaw," said the artist, after describing a buffalo hunt, "what would happen if two different arrows were found in the same carcass. She told me that in that case it belonged to the brave whose arrow had hit a vital spot. If both shots were vital, the meat and skin were given to some old people who could no longer hunt."

It is this form of communism, of primitive justice and kindness, that marked the Indian before his contact with civilization. Borein grows eloquent over the manhood and heroism of the early red man. The old saying, "The only good Indian is a dead Indian," but proves, to him, an ignorance of the history and nature of this primitive race. There were no poor among the tribes. When disaster overtook a family and their horses were killed or their tepees burned and their possessions destroyed in a fight or through misfortune, others who had plenty would start them up again. One would give a horse, another a tepee, another a blanket, and so on until all that was lost had been made up. Once equipped, the unfortunates were thus no longer dependent. Nor did this spirit apply only to those who had more than they needed. If there was but one piece of jerked meat in the camp, the owner would divide it amongst all, for he was trained in kindness, in justice and in honor.

WAR PARTY, TONTO APACHES, ARIZONA: FROM A DRAWING BY ED. BOREIN.

EVERY act of an Indian from his birth to his death was in accordance with his religious belief. No people ever lived up to their religion more thoroughly. Even today the Indians on the reservations, civilized though they may seem to be, cling secretly to their superstitions and traditions. They have their war shirts and leggings hidden away waiting for the "Return of the Buffalo," that Indian millenium which will mark the downfall of the white race and the rise to glory of the red. Indian religion touched all the common things of life with a mysterious wonder. They felt that the Great Spirit had put everything into the world for them and their purposes and that everything created had a soul, personified by its shadow cast by the symbol of the Great Spirit, the sun. The spirit of the grass was no less real to the Indian than his own soul, which he called his "shadow self." Dwelling in his religion as he did, he saw a higher power in every manifestation of Nature, to which he looked with reverent eyes.

The white buffalo was sacred to him. Many a zoologist calls it a myth but the Indian *knows*, and around the rare beast he has gathered hundreds of traditions and religious rites. Here is the story of the last white buffalo known, as told to Ed. Borein by a Sioux half-breed, an old, old man.

Once upon a time, when he was young, he and another half-breed boy lived among their people. One day he was standing looking idly into the distance when he chanced to notice an old woman (who was a relative and lived in his family's tepee) coming down the hillside with a load of wood upon her back. That was commonplace enough. A

moment later he saw her straighten up, drop her burden, look again across the country and then break into a run toward the camp. "Hostiles advancing to attack," was his first thought. But the old woman, reaching the tepee, whispered in his ear, "The buffalo are a mile to the north and a white one is in the herd."

Without a word to anyone, the half-breed signaled his young companion and they caught their war horses, for ordinary buffalo horses were not fast enough for young enthusiasm. The old woman went silently into the tepee. Scouts reported the presence of the buffalo and the squaws went out to catch the horses. The boys did not wait. Stolidly and without curiosity the other Indians watched the departure. Assuredly it could be nothing serious or they, too, would have been told. Only the medicine man, wise in years, experience and tradition, knew better.

The two riders went into the herd but nowhere could they see their prize. They rode far, searching it. At last they saw it, a two-year-old cow, yellow with dust. Even at a distance, they could make out the black horns, the blue eyes and the gray hoofs. They shot at the same moment. The cow fell with two deadly bullets in her white hide. The hunters were young and knew little of the Indian ritual. Before they could dismount to lay hands on the sacred thing, the medicine man waved them back. He had come up with the whole fighting force of the tribe in line behind him. At a word from him, one of the bucks rode back to the camp to fetch forth a maiden. Meanwhile, the rest sat motionless upon their horses while the medicine man uttered his incantations and "made medicine" over the sacred carcass. The messenger speeded back from the camp and the maiden was brought forward, modest and hesitating, wondering that so great an honor should have been bestowed upon her. No one else touched the sacred buffalo as the maiden skinned it and prepared the hide according to the strictest of Sioux ceremonial. She tanned it, embroidered the inside with dyed porcupine quills and then turned it over to be used in the medicine lodge.

The news of the sacred possession spread outside the tribe, in time reaching the Cheyennes. Always eager for war against the Sioux, envy now prodded them on. The Cheyennes came and fought hard; the Sioux defended no less desperately, yet the invader won. With solemn rites the skin was carried to the conquerors' camp. It became a religious duty to fight for the ownership of the white hide. The Blackfeet captured it from the Cheyennes. It passed from one tribe to another, leaving death behind it. For all that it was a thing to covet, to risk life winning and to die losing, it brought no fortune with it. Horses sickened and died, game failed, every trouble overtook the owners, yet the next tribe charged to battle just as eagerly.

Won by bloodshed, lost by death, the white buffalo hide made its journey, the Sioux who shot it ever on its trail. It had passed out of his tribe, but the young half-breed who had heard the first whisper of it at the start, managed to get wind of its changing whereabouts. Possession might never again be his, but he would know its travels, its history and its holy wars. The man grew old. One by one, he had

seen violent death overtake the medicine men who had the skin in keeping, until the Piegans in Canada came into possession of it. After that he lost the trace. It was long ago that he told the tale and he, too, has joined those who fought and died. With him passed away the white buffalo as a reality, to enter the region of tradition and story.

ALL Indian legends, of whatever tribe, are woven through the spiritual fabric of their religion. They are not all concerned with war and death, many are full of sweetness and poetry born of high native imagination. Such is the legend of the butterfly which Ed. Borein learned when he lived among the Navajos, and which he has embodied in one of the most characteristic of his pictures.

The Navajos think that the butterflies are children of the rainbow. When trouble overtakes them, they go out into the sunshine and catch a butterfly. This they put into a little brass or wicker cage and to it they come to tell their misfortunes. They need rain; the grass for their horses is gone; the water holes are dried up; the sheep are dying of the drought. If the butterfly dies, their prayers have not been heard by the Great Spirit. They must catch another. Then the band goes forth carrying the caged butterfly at its head until they find signs of a storm in the distance, for in that country rain may be seen miles and miles away, falling like a black shadow on a tiny spot in the wide sunny plain. As soon as they have seen the rain afar off, the Navajos look for the rainbow in the sunny sky above the rest of the plain. Then they set free the butterfly to soar up to its mother, the rainbow, that she may know the troubles of the poor Navajos, spread the rain cloud over them and keep the drought away in the future.

"THE STRAY BUNCH": FROM A DRAWING BY ED. BOREIN.

ARTHUR RACKHAM, THE ILLUSTRATOR OF FOLK-LORE AND FAIRY TALES

RTHUR RACKHAM, the greatest English illustrator of today, may unquestionably be ranked among such modern master draughtsmen as Daumier, Steinlen, Glackens—who have seen to the heart of the particular phase of beauty that inspired them. Not in the smallest way does his achievement resemble that of any one of these other men. His imagination has been touched by the fairy world, and he responds, brain and soul, to the work of those who have had a vision out into that far land where gnomes and pigmies and imps and all the tiny dreamland folk dwell. And so we find, as we would expect to, that he has elected to reveal to us the innermost spirit of the writers of such fairy lore as Shakespeare in "Midsummer Night's Dream," Washington Irving in "Rip Van Winkle," the wonder tales of the Brothers Grimm, Lewis Carroll in "Alice in Wonderland," J. M. Barrie in "Peter Pan," and then, at last, Richard Wagner in his great revelation of the heights and depths of god life in Walhalla.

A BIRD SKETCH BY ARTHUR RACKHAM.

Arthur Rackham has been compared with our American illustrator of fantastic subjects, Howard Pyle. But it seems to me that as an artist he must take rank among the great rather than among the brilliant and clever, for even though his interest in literature was more nearly related to the interest of a man like Howard Pyle, his composition, his technique, his knowledge of the very fundamentals of art must place him among the really memorable artists of his day. This feeling at least prevails among the art circles of Milan, where he exhibited in nineteen hundred and six, Venice, which presented his drawings in nineteen hundred and nine, Barcelona, where his work was shown in nineteen hundred and ten,

THE ASS AND BOTTOM: FROM A DRAWING BY ARTHUR RACKHAM.

and Paris, where his work is accepted as the final expression possible along his own line by the critics, the artists, the students, as well as the Société Nationale des Beaux Arts, by whom he was invited to exhibit.

Rackham is still a young man. He was born in London in eighteen hundred and sixty-seven, and made a member of the Royal Institute of Painters in Water Colors in nineteen hundred and two. The usual academic training was given him and early in life he began to contribute to the *Pall Mall Budget*, the *Westminster Budget*, the *Graphic*, the *Sketch*, etc., illustrations of real life, of legendary adventure, whatever chanced to come his way or to interest him, but always presented with thoughtful observation, precise and wise drawing, technique swiftly reproducing inspiration and with a touch at once light and fine. Always from the start his great interest seemed to be in relating the animal world to the human world through the fairy adventure that touched each sphere. And although his subjects are nearly always inspired by some fantastic thought, his own or others, his presentation is made with the dignity, the tenderness of real humor, and the imagination that would have made Rackham great in any field of art that had claimed his genius.

His knowledge of the animal world is as great as his understanding of the fairy kingdom, and the play spirit of the people in the trees, in the grass, in the clouds, is a revelation to the pompous human intellect which feels that a humorous attitude toward life is the reward only of its own kind of civilization. Happily enough, we never see what we call real people in Rackham's scenes of fairy life; but practically always their good friends the animals are with them, sometimes in a most neighborly intimate way, sometimes indulging in quaint delicate warfare. We poor dull human beings do not seem to have touched Rackham's interest or fancy. And probably he knows best. He may have left us out of his pictures fearing that the fairy folk and their neighbors of the animal world might not feel at home and happy with us.

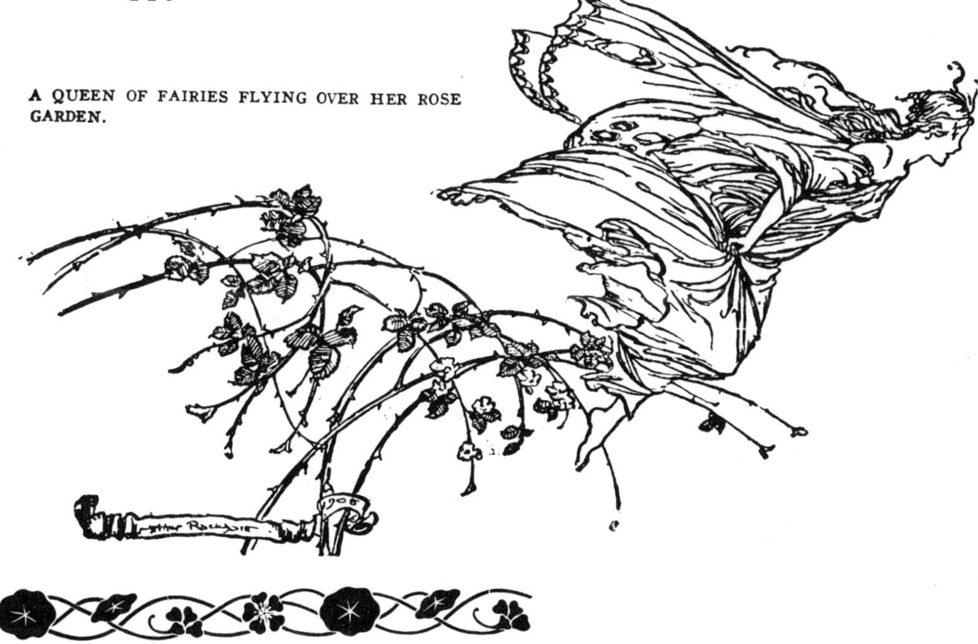

A QUEEN OF FAIRIES FLYING OVER HER ROSE GARDEN.

It is strange how a man, even through the power of his rare poetical imagination, could become so profoundly intimate with the spirit with which Washington Irving has saturated his legendary stories of the Catskill Mountains. Surely no one has so completely realized his impulse, except possibly gentle old Joe Jefferson, who lived over for us the life of this mountain recess many times through his beautiful art. Rackham's pictures seem the very story itself,—the gnomes, and poor old *Rip*, who becomes intoxicated on the juniper gin, his return to the village, interested, young, cheerful, with all of his own generation having passed him by. There is a humor in the types of people Rackham presents in these drawings; there is a true understanding of the hidden world of mysterious people, and there is an exquisite sympathy and appreciation of the old village folk, of *Peter Vanderdonk*, of *Rip's* wife, his daughter and the little grandson.

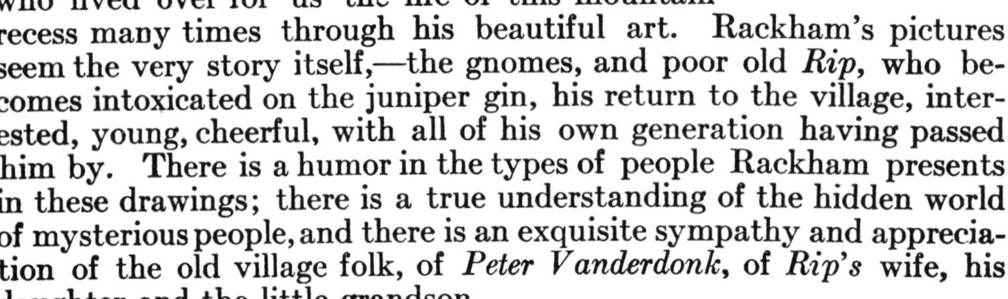

THE BATTLE OF THE FAIRIES AND THE CATERPILLARS.

After this, came "Alice in Wonderland," and anyone who has read "Alice" and loved her in childhood and followed her through the mirror and known her friends, can live this story over again in Rackham's illustrations. For he has seen the adventures of Alice just as *you* saw them, with wonder and delight, and a little fear and a great desire to be admitted without self-consciousness into their marvelous company. And with all his fantastic charm and his grave and gay technique, Rackham never loses for a moment what we are accustomed to call a sense of beauty, in the rather old-fashioned sense. His harmonies of tone are exquisite, and although all in a light key, there is a vividness and a richness that few artists of any time have excelled.

A FRIGHTENED BABY FAIRY.

We are showing one of the most interesting of the illustrations for "Midsummer Night's Dream," the battle in the sky of the elfish children with the gruesome bats. What terror and mystery and strangeness he has put into this picture which is drawn so high up in the air. One only realizes its distance from earth by looking in the lower corner of the picture, to find there a tiny thatched home

QUEEN TITANIA WITH PUCK AND THE FAIRIES: FROM A SKETCH BY ARTHUR RACKHAM.

with a blossoming tree no larger than a pinhead. And yet with all this aerial tragedy, with all the somberness of night and the horror of whirling bats, Rackham never loses his sense of grace, his fine-spun delicacy of technique. We have only to look at his characteristic sketch of *Bottom* and the *Ass*, which he weaves together with wreaths of thorn, to realize the wonderful, trenchant quality of which Rackham's pen is capable when he chooses so to use it. No one surely has ever presented the elfin sportiveness combined with childish glee as Rackham in his sketch which we reproduce here of *Titania, Puck* and the fairies.

With all his love of these tiny folk, of their quaint and wild ways, of their little furies and infantile warfare, there remained, of course, a greater work for Rackham's genius. And this he undertook after his various exhibitions in Europe, and his greater intimacy with the greatest of folklore, the German legends of the Walhalla. Naturally, after Shakespeare, Wagner. After a presentation of the greatest literary mind of England, Rackham turns his attention to the greatest musical mind of Germany, that vast musical storehouse.

And here one realizes, as perhaps the thoughtless may not in seeing Rackham's lighter work, the splendid strength of his imagination. How straight and true his vision is into that part of the soul of every nation which holds the folk-lore, the fairy tales, the songs of the minstrels, the gods of the old faith,—the storehouse of romance, of spirituality, of joy for the art of the world.

Courtesy of Art et Décoration.

"THE ELVES AT WAR WITH THE BATS": AN ILLUSTRATION FOR "A MIDSUMMER NIGHT'S DREAM," BY ARTHUR RACKHAM.

Courtesy of Art et Décoration.

"THE GOD WOTAN": AN ILLUSTRATION BY ARTHUR RACKHAM FOR WAGNER'S "NIBELUNGEN LIED."

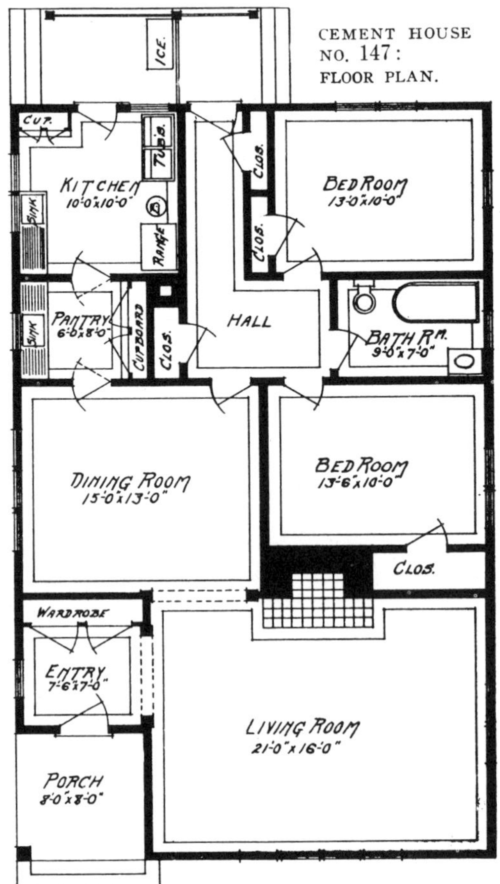

CEMENT HOUSE NO. 147: FLOOR PLAN.

CRAFTSMAN CEMENT COTTAGE NO. 147: THIS VERY SIMPLE CEMENT COTTAGE IS ONE OF THE MOST PRACTICAL AND WELL-ARRANGED SMALL HOUSES THAT WE HAVE EVER DESIGNED, NOT ONLY BECAUSE OF ITS WELL-PLANNED WINDOWS AND PRACTICAL LIVING PORCH, BUT BECAUSE OF THE ARRANGEMENTS OF ALL THE ROOMS IN RELATION TO EACH OTHER, TO THE KITCHEN AND TO THE SERVANT PROBLEM: IT IS A HOUSE IN WHICH A WOMAN COULD WITH VERY LITTLE EXPENDITURE OF ENERGY SO ARRANGE HER DAILY WORK THAT A COMPARATIVELY SMALL AMOUNT OF TIME AND EFFORT WOULD BRING ORDER, COMFORT AND BEAUTY: THE LIVING ROOM IS SO CLOSE TO THE DINING ROOM THAT THEY COULD EASILY HAVE THE EFFECT OF ONE SPACIOUS LIVING PLACE: THE BEDROOMS ARE NEAR THE HALL: THE BATHROOM IS MOST ADMIRABLY PLACED EXACTLY BETWEEN THE TWO BEDROOMS, AND THE KITCHEN WHILE NEAR ENOUGH TO THE DINING ROOM TO SAVE STEPS IS FAR ENOUGH AWAY FROM THE LIVING ROOMS TO LEAVE THEM FREE FROM THE ENCROACHMENT OF SAVORY ODORS: THE WARDROBE CLOSET BACK OF THE ENTRY IS ANOTHER VERY REAL CONVENIENCE, AND THE KITCHEN PANTRY IS PLACED TO SAVE STEPS: ALTOGETHER WE FEEL THAT WE ARE ANSWFRING IN THIS DESIGN A REQUEST THAT HAS COME TO US VERY OFTEN INDEED; NAMELY, TO PLAN A HOUSE THAT WOULD HAVE THE ADVANTAGES WE USUALLY ASSOCIATE WITH WEALTH AND AT THE SAME TIME WOULD HAVE EVEN THE GREATER ADVANTAGES OF COMPACTNESS AND THE COMFORT WHICH IS ESSENTIAL TO THE MODERN INCOME.

DISTINGUISHING FEATURES OF THE CRAFTSMAN HOUSE

THE RULING PRINCIPLE OF THE CRAFTSMAN HOUSE IS SIMPLICITY.

THE central thought in all Craftsman activities is the simplification of life and a return to true democracy. Accordingly the exterior lines of the Craftsman house are very simple and its interior divisions are few.

SIMPLICITY SPELLS ECONOMY.

Elaborate ornamentation is eliminated by our method of interior treatment. Post-and-panel construction replaces useless partitions. Native woods are used liberally. The fireplace is made an ornamental feature. These and other methods are employed in the Craftsman plan to give at a reasonable cost proper decorative effects. The principles of cleanliness and sanitation are recognized in such a way as to make for economy, but possibly the greatest economy of all is the permanent quality of the homes we design. A Craftsman house should stand for 100 years or more without requiring repairs; in fact, for many years a Craftsman house will increase in value and beauty without impairment, and use will give to it a softness and friendliness which will constantly add to its charm.

THE SIMPLE LINES OF THE CRAFTSMAN HOUSE GIVE IT A BEAUTY AND A DIGNITY WHICH REACT MOST FAVORABLY UPON THE LIFE AND CHARACTER OF THE FAMILY.

Growing children reflect their environment. Home-builders who are influenced by the notions of others and who strive to outdo their neighbors in building their home, instil the same spirit into their children, and a home which is the product of weak imitation or freakish straining after originality, cannot have a wholesome effect on its inmates.

BUILT-IN WINDOW-SEAT AND BOOKCASES IN A CRAFTSMAN LIVING ROOM, SHOWING THE DECORATIVE EFFECT OBTAINED BY STRUCTURAL FEATURES.

A CRAFTSMAN HOUSE ANSWERS THE QUESTION—"WHAT ARE THE NEEDS OF THE FAMILY?"

Too large a house with unused rooms breeds a spirit of extravagance. The relation of every part of the interior of a house to the needs of the family should be direct and apparent. A Craftsman house is designed to meet these needs just as simply, comfortably and economically as possible.

CRAFTSMAN FIREPLACE CORNER WITH BUILT-IN SEAT AND BOOKSHELVES.

A CRAFTSMAN HOUSE REPRESENTS NOT ONLY ECONOMY IN COST BUT ECONOMY IN FLOOR SPACE.

Not an inch of space is wasted. Because of this the owner's money is made to go as far as possible, and a small house, properly designed, is generally sufficient for the ordinary family. The general living rooms are thrown together, usually including the entrance hall and stairway, so that the whole lower floor of a Craftsman house has the effect of a great living room. Post-and-panel construction and the arrangement of pleasant nooks and corners give a sense of room division as well as a feeling of semi-privacy.

BUILT-IN FEATURES ARE OFTEN INCORPORATED TO MEET SPECIAL NEEDS.

Like other structural features, built-in fittings add to the interest and beauty of rooms. They are directly related to the life of the household and make for simplicity and comfort.

IN THE YOSEMITE WITH JOHN MUIR: BY CLARA BARRUS

JOHN MUIR, born in Scotland, reared in America, a wanderer in nearly every country on the globe, seventy-four years of age and hale and canny, is doubtless one of the most picturesque figures in our country today. Scot to the backbone, yet America claims him as her own, so earnestly has he studied our trees and mountains, so closely is he identified with the wonders of the great West, so loyally has he labored to preserve our natural beauties when from time to time there have been those of our own countrymen who would have wrested them from us.

It is fitting that the mighty Alaskan glacier he discovered bears his name, and that a noble forest of California redwoods is called The Muir Woods, and it is likewise fitting that a little mountain daisy is his namesake, for with all his enthusiasm for mountain and glacier and noble sequoia, his love for "the bonnie wee blossoms of the wild" is one of his abiding passions.

"To any place that is wild," is the reply Mr. Muir made in eighteen hundred and sixty-eight to a man on the streets of San Francisco of whom he inquired the nearest way out of town.

"But where do you want to go?" the stranger asked. Imagine his surprise on receiving this reply: "To any place that is wild!" But he directed the seeker after the wild to the Oakland ferry, and thence he and another young man made their way on foot through the great flowery central valley of California, walled in on the east by the mighty Sierra range, on through the deep Sierra canyon without knowledge of the topography of the country, and with the snows so deep that the blazed trails were all covered; and after many adventures they reached their goal—the famous Yosemite.

"Any place that is wild" seems always to have been the watchword of this wanderer who started out from Indiana more than forty years ago, journeying alone and afoot to the Gulf of Mexico, then to Florida and Cuba, intending to go to South America. Weakness from Southern fever and failure to get a ship for South America prevented him just then from carrying out his plans, so he took the Panama steamer, arrived in San Francisco, and after one day in that city, set

out, as before stated, for the Yosemite. But, as I heard him say this spring, he usually gets to the place he starts for, and doesn't mind a delay of forty years or more, so long as he can explore other wildernesses by the way. Now in nineteen hundred and twelve he returns from South America and South Africa!

"You see I got there," he said triumphantly on his return.

Recently his book on the Yosemite—the result of ten or more years in the Valley in the early seventies—has come from the press. Assuredly Mr. Muir is not to be hurried. Like the enduring rocks, the slow-moving glaciers, and the many-centuried sequoias, he believes in the amplitude of time. How pityingly he speaks of "time-poor" persons who never spare enough of their scanty store to wander leisurely in some of the world's wildernesses!

IN reading Mr. Muir's book on the Yosemite, or, in truth, any of his books, one gets but a partial view of his character. The enthusiastic nature lover, the tireless student, the adventurous explorer—these characteristics stand out on every page, but to know the man one should camp and tramp with him in the Yosemite, as I did in nineteen hundred and nine, in company with Mr. John Burroughs, Mr. Francis Browne and a few others. There we saw the many-sided Muir—the man one sees in his books, and also the teasing, fun-loving Muir, the arbitrary, the devout, the modest, the assertive Muir—an exasperating, lovable, complex personality.

On first meeting him he fell naturally into telling us about himself; of his boyhood in Scotland, and his early years in the "beautiful wilderness of Wisconsin," where his family first settled on coming to America. He spoke of his stern, soldier-like father, a strict disciplinarian and an enthusiast in religion, with much native intelligence and marked inventive ability, but with little schooling; of his gentle and gentler-bred mother, well educated for her time—she could paint, read poetry and was an ardent lover of natural scenery. He told how she tried to second the father's sternness, and to scold the mischievous lads into decorum, but could never really scold however hard she tried.

If allowed to talk on uninterruptedly, Mr. Muir regales his hearers with a monologue of exceptional range and raciness, but, intrude a question, or venture an opinion, and the smoothly-flowing stream of talk is impeded; and if it happen when a choice bit of description is in progress, the chances are you will never hear that to completion, though you may hear something exceedingly diverting instead. Confess ignorance and seek enlightenment from him, and you will more than likely be met with bantering ridicule; yet he will on occasion volunteer the most minute and painstaking information. I recall how, as we neared the Yosemite, Mr. Muir took great pains to teach me about the different trees in the Sierra, indicating their diagnostic points and the distribution of the various belts—object-lessons in tree-lore one was exceptionally fortunate to have from such a teacher. But when Mr. Burroughs raised some questions about the geology of the Yosemite over which he was

puzzling, and earnestly asked Mr. Muir for a solution, the Yosemite student replied:

"Aw, Johnny, ye may tak' all your geology and tie it in a bundle and cast it into the sea, and it wouldna' mak' a ripple," and that is all the satisfaction one could get out of him.

IT was particularly gratifying to Mr. Muir to show Mr. Burroughs the glories of the Yosemite and make him admit that he had nothing like it in Esopus Valley, or in the Catskills. He had conducted Colonel Roosevelt to his mountains a few years before, and not many weeks after we were there, President Taft saw the Yosemite and the Big Trees under the guidance of Mr. Muir, yet neither the earlier nor later experiences effaced from his recollection the wondrous spectacle as he viewed it for the first time when he and his young companion tramped in there all the way from San Francisco. After crossing innumerable boulder-choked canyons, scrambling through chapparal, and wallowing through snow, they at last stood upon the heights and looked down to the floor of the Valley which lay nearly a mile below them, and across to the opposite wall of the chasm, half a mile distant:

"Great God! have we got to cross *that gulch, too?*" ejaculated his intrepid companion whom Mr. Muir had led at such a lively pace all the way thither.

Thereafter for many years Mr. Muir wintered and summered in Yosemite, tracing the waterfalls to their sources, examining each basin, observing the fauna and flora, making sketches of the rocks, tracing the courses of the ancient glaciers, and discovering the glaciers that still lingered there.

He showed us the site of his old saw-mill, told us how he built it and kept it in repair, and how he used to sit and sketch until he saw the great logs nearing the end, when he would stop and start another log on its way, and resume sketching. He spoke of his inventive ability which showed itself in boyhood, and told us of several ingenious devices which he has patented, which have yielded him tangible financial returns. With engaging frankness he said he was so smart he could not help making money whenever he ceased his wanderings for a spell.

He used to make Sunday raids on the heights above the Yosemite, starting out at daybreak and tracing Pohono or some other wild waterfall to its source, walking all night among the moon shadows, and descending the perilous cliffs in the darkness, reaching his cabin at daybreak to begin work at the mill.

"Ah! how many glorious Sundays were mine!" he mused. And here he roamed, loving the wilderness, glorying in storms, in the roar of waterfalls, even in the thunder of earthquakes and the relentless speed of avalanches. He told of one wild ride on an avalanche: He had been climbing all day hoping to reach a certain summit in time to see the sunset, but stepping inadvertently on the trampled snow, he started an avalanche, and in the twinkling of an eye was swished down to the foot of the canyon, the avalanche lurching and plunging,

the snow particles flying in a blinding mist around him. The next instant he picked himself up unharmed, gloriously exhilarated by the astounding experience.

When his cabin would rock and creak during an earthquake, this imperturbable student would sit unmoved making his notes, registering the desire that some day he could go to South America and study earthquakes. In those days he was so engrossed with his studies that he read the glacial tracings in his dreams, followed the lines of cleavage, and struggled all night with the things that puzzled his waking hours.

He told us how he drifted about the Valley and on the heights above, and said that it was only by resting on the rocks as the ice had done that he was able to absorb and arrive at the truths about them. And when the great geologic truths about the formation of the Valley burst upon him, and he found the proofs piling up as a result of his unwearied research, he was fairly beside himself with admiration of the Power that had achieved such stupendous results. Pushed on by his thirst for more and more knowledge, he became so oblivious to his health and safety that his friends feared for his life; but he laughed at their fears, and only asked that they find him some concentrated food so he could carry a year's provisions and thus pursue his studies in those almost inaccessible heights, without the interruption of coming down the mountains to get bread. Still as a young man he was much more dependable upon friendship than one might gather, and during those years of lonely wandering in the high Sierra he came down from the snow-line to the bread-line quite as often for the nourishment he found in friendly letters as to replenish his bread sack and tea can.

"When I was in college," he said, "I nearly starved; I lived on fifty cents a week, and used to count the crackers and jealously watch the candles, but I didn't mind after I got in here—no bell that rang meant me; I was free to go and come, and here were things that were bread and meat to me—things to fatten my soul, and all free as the air. Ah! but I've had a blessed time in here. But I *did* wish the ravens would come and feed me, so I could keep at my studies."

It was often amusing to hear him recount hairbreadth escapes and in the same breath disclaim recklessness. We wondered to what lengths a reckless person would have gone; but there seem to have been certain rules he observed, such as never taking a step forward when scaling cliffs, unless he was sure that from that point he would be able to take a step backward; and never to gaze about him, no matter how glorious the view, until he had made sure his footing was secure.

That Mr. Muir thoroughly enjoys witnessing one's discomfiture when the distress is only comical was seen when he told us of a well-known lecturer's trip into the Valley many years ago with a body of scientific men. The lecturer having crammed on Whitney's geology, had started out with the intention of worsting Mr. Muir in his arguments in favor of the tremendous importance of glaciers

in the formation of the Valley. Though talking glibly at first, he was soon at a disadvantage, having no well-grounded knowledge of these things; while Mr. Muir was able to prove to the audience that what he affirmed was first-hand knowledge. After the discussion, the lecturer trotted up to Mr. Muir as they were about to start for a walk up one of the trails where he was to show some of the convincing evidences of glaciation, and asked, "If there were glaciers here, Mr. Muir, where are the moraines?"

"You better ask, 'Where could the moraines have rested in the Valley,' " retorted the Scot. Then he explained that if the lecturer had known a moraine when he saw it, he would have recognized a large lateral moraine, covered with trees and underbrush, at the beginning of the Valley. Presently, they came to a place where the old glaciers had made it very slippery. The stout defender of the Ice-gods warned the guest: "Look out here, Doctor, it is pretty dangerous, you better take my hand." But saying airily that he was all right, Mr. A. went his way. The next instant out went his feet and down he fell on the slippery rocks, striking on the ice-polished granite with a force that made him pale long afterward. He sprawled about, and finally tottered to his feet, his clothes dripping. For the rest of the way he was willing to take Mr. Muir's hand.

"*Now* are you ready to accept the glacial theory?" mercilessly asked the stout defender of it.

"Yes, I capitulate to the Huge Miller of the Sierras," humbly answered the dripping disputant.

"I thought you would," added Mr. Muir. "God works in a mysterious way His wonders to perform—He almost has to kill some people to get the truth into them." Then he chuckled as he recalled how comical the stout little man had looked when on returning to the hotel he had walked about in someone's trousers much too short for him, while his own were being made presentable again.

But many a man thinks Mr. Muir goes too far in attributing so much of the formation and sculpturing of the Yosemite to glaciers, though unquestionably they have done their part. Mr. Burroughs had many a tilt with him on this score, and said of his claims: "Muir rides his ice-hobby till the tongue of the poor beast hangs out, and he is ready to lie down and give up the ghost. Ice is by no means the only agency at work here." This much to the scorn of Mr. Muir; but the two men were one in their admiration of the beauties and wonders of the Valley.

Mr. Muir shows a marked indifference to creature comforts, especially to food. After long tramps, when the rest of the party would almost devour luncheon, he would sit and play with a piece of dry bread, and keep up a steady stream of talk. Place a sandwich close to his hand, or shell an egg for him, and a courteous "thank you" is forthcoming, but more often than not a mere nibble is all the attention he pays to your efforts, and the talk flows on. Not that one wants it to stop, but one feels guilty at being so entertained at the expense of the entertainer. He declares that bread

is about the only food that he needs, and insists that through some temperamental quality he can get out of bread more than any chemical analysis can show—if his spirit is pitched in the right key. "Eat bread in the mountains," he said, "and with love and adoration in your soul you can get a nourishment that food experts have no conception of."

THE NEGRO'S CONTRIBUTION TO AMERICAN MUSIC

An unexpected force for better understanding between whites and blacks has been liberated in this conscious admission of the Negro into our musical life. Music has always sprung from people who labor out-of-doors,—simple people who sing as they work and pray and dance. Whether the Negroes, any of them will develop into great artists is not the present question; what we hope is that the Negro of today shall carry into his free industrial life in ennobling form the same love of song that upheld him spiritually in the days of bondage and made slavery bearable. For us, the fact is here, that the untaught Negro has already unconsciously given to this country the elements of a type of music that the people love, while the Negro with a little education now gives us the promise of a development of that type. The folk-song of the Negro has something to give to art,—something that is original and convincing because it speaks directly from the heart. Like all music born of the need of song in a people, it appeals to the listener with that elemental truth of feeling in which race has no part and humanity is one.

If anything can bring harmony from the present clashing of the two races during this difficult period of problem and adjustment, it might well be the peace-giver—music!

As this article goes to press another concert of Negro music is announced to take place in Carnegie Hall on Lincoln's Birthday, when a great chorus will sing in commemoration of the Emancipation Proclamation the beautiful old slave song whose burden runs:

"Oh freedom, oh freedom over me!
And before I'll be a slave
I'll be buried in my grave
I'll go home to my Lord
And be free."

CRAFTSMAN STENCIL DESIGNS

POPPY STENCIL DESIGNS IN RED AND GREEN OR RED AND BROWN.

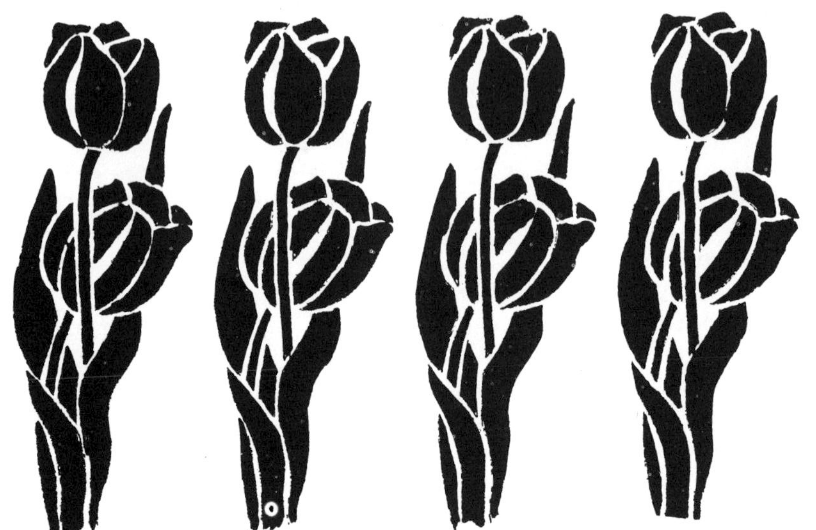

TULIP STENCIL DESIGN IN YELLOW AND GREEN.

CATTAIL STENCIL DESIGN IN GREEN AND BROWN.

THE GARDEN CITY IDEA THE WORLD OVER: WHAT IT IS AND HOW IT GROWS: BY ESTHER MATSON

"That one may see the heavens wide,
And grass, and grass so green."
—*The Bard of the Dimbo Vitza.*

HE magic of property," Arthur Young has said, "turns sand into gold. Put a man into a precarious possession and he will turn a garden into a desert. But put him into a state where he can securely anticipate the fruits of his labor, and he will turn a desert into a garden." This is the essence of the Garden City movement—"*to give to every inhabitant an interest in his holding.*" As we know, alongside with a sense of proprietorship always goes a sense of responsibility. Believing this intensely, the advocates of copartnership housing aim to arouse in tenants a new sentiment which has been aptly termed "estate patriotism," and they consider this a stepping stone to the development of a higher civilization.

In England, where this copartnership plan is being tried, the tenant is enabled, by means of federation, to become a member of the society which owns his house and the other houses of the estate. In other words, he is enabled to participate in the general interests of the whole community as well as to become in greater or less degree his own landlord.

"But," it is objected, "this is all very well and good for the toiling masses, and of course it's sound philosophy. But who's to pay for it? And if somebody does pay for it, isn't he simply increasing the grand army of hangers-on?"

On the contrary, the advocates of the new system hope to decrease it. To be sure, the initial bulk of capital for such undertakings is necessarily supplied by non-tenant capitalists. And to these the societies pay a four per cent. return—which should surely disarm the prejudice against them as "charities." Moreover, the proportion between the number of non-tenant and tenant shareholders is a constantly varying one, the ideal being confessedly that which Godin worked out at Guise in France over a quarter of a century ago: "ultimate ownership by the tenants themselves."

The garden city, it is important to note, is for both the more and the less wealthy. The idea, as exemplified at Hampstead, is to provide homes that vary as much as may be in value, in order, as Mrs. Barnett puts it, "to bring about a better understanding between the classes." Who will dare deny that we need such understanding?

At the Garden Suburb, Hampstead, for instance, accommodations are offered to business men and women, to artists and to artisans. There are single and goodly sized houses, semi-detached houses, groups of small homes; and there are even one or two interesting quadrangular structures where tiny apartments may be rented. If one cannot afford an outlay of more than five shillings sixpence, or about a dollar and a half a week for rental, one can here find some-

thing far better for the money than in crowded London. If one can pay nearer fifteen hundred dollars a year, one may also find here the worth of the money plus immensely more freedom and breathing space.

ANOTHER crucial point for the economic viewpoint is, unquestionably, a basic one; the Garden City Idea must satisfy financial demands or fail. The astonishing fact is that it is making good. It is proving that the speculative real estate scheme with its drearily laid-out sites, hacked-down trees, miles of stolid sidewalks, is not more sure of success than the newer and better plan. It is proving, on the contrary, that well-planned areas, with trees and natural advantages conserved, and houses built for comfort, durability and attractiveness do pay.

We are obliged to give the credit for the working Garden City Idea to England. To be sure, it is not a new thing. France can show its village of Menier and its peculiarly significant Familistère at Guise. Germany can tell a story of her own in the matter of housing her citizens; while in Great Britain certain philanthropist-manufacturers, such as Mr. Lever of Port Sunlight fame, and Mr. Cadbury, who has established the model village of Bournville in connection with his great chocolate factory outside of Birmingham, have long been claiming that the welfare of their workers was a business concern to themselves. But not till about a dozen years ago did the matter receive systematic and scientific attention.

The inspiration for it came from a book called "To-morrow," written by Ebenezer Howard in eighteen hundred and ninety-eight. The second edition of it came out under the more suggestive title, "Garden Cities of To-morrow," and in nineteen hundred and one a little group of idealists gathered together and determined to translate the book into reality. They decided to try an experiment—to create a town that should combine the attractions of city and country, and provide both industrial and social opportunities in an area where there would be "fresh air, sunlight, breathing room and playing room."

The site chosen for the experiment was in Hertfordshire, where, within thirty-four miles of London, a property was bought consisting of about six square miles. The first Garden City, Limited, was there born, and christened Letchworth.

The scheme included the setting aside of a belt of small farm holdings around the edge of the estate, the laying out of various areas for manufacturing and other industrial purposes, of other areas for residential sections that should be kept quiet and free from smoke, and a necessary business section for shops and offices.

In addition to these reservations numerous others were made for open spaces and recreation centers, so that out of nearly four thousand acres of property, two hundred will always remain open.

An interesting feature of the Letchworth plan is the care with which trees and shrubs have been planted. Near the railway station, for instance, no less than two hundred different kinds of plants

have been set out. Another experiment has been tried in certain sections in the planting of fruit trees along the street instead of merely shade or ornamental trees.

Most of the designs for the houses have been made by Messrs. Parker and Unwin (whose work is familiar to THE CRAFTSMAN through a series of articles by Mr. Parker); they are of gray rough cast, with tiled roofs, red brick chimney stacks and green painted woodwork. There are never more than twelve houses to the acre and the rentals run from a dollar and a quarter and two dollars and a half a week up.

Always there is some space in which to cultivate a garden, be it for flowers, vegetables, or for both. The objection inevitably crops up that it doesn't pay to do your own gardening—that it is far cheaper to buy your food at the greengrocer's, cheapest of all to buy it in tin cans. Perhaps it is, in many cases. But it is also cheaper to die than to live. Listen, however, to the words of an essentially practical manager as well as a philanthropist of peculiarly clear vision—one moreover whose own model village at Bournville has set a standard for all future garden towns.

Mr. Cadbury reports that his tenants, with garden plots of about an eighth of an acre each, make a fair profit of twenty-five cents a week. More than this, he says: "The benefit, physical, moral, and even spiritual, is so great that it would have been worth while cultivating the gardens even if there had been no profit for the labor expended. I would also point out that *the adoption of garden cities*

WORKMEN'S COTTAGES IN HAMPSTEAD WAY: EACH COTTAGE CONTAINS TWO DWELLINGS: DESIGNED BY JOSEPH & SMITHEM.

would materially increase the food supply of the country, as one acre of garden ground produces as much food as thirteen acres of pasture land."

We have in this country taken with avidity to tearing down slum districts in order to rebuild in better form. This may be interesting—but it is expensive. They are showing us in England that greater returns can be realized by expending such money and energy on the development of wholly new areas. This in a nutshell is the principle on which the founders of Letchworth have worked.

By starting out with a "clean slate" they have been able to secure their wished-for belt or agricultural zone (consisting of some two thousand five hundred acres, or about two-thirds of the property) around the edge of the town; they have been able to separate the business, industrial, residential and social interests, to secure proper sanitation and modern conveniences, and to preserve and enhance the natural advantages.

The ground being thus prepared, into the new city came persons who were weary of the "awfulness of London;" anon came manufacturers eager for a location entailing less waste of human health than in the great cities. Following the factories and the workers, came shops, churches and clubs.

EALING gives us illustration of the garden suburb project as applied to the outskirts of London—the "dormitory" idea—and it deserves special notice because it was the pioneer in the application of the copartnership principle to housing problems. As mentioned at the beginning of this article, under the copartnership plan, the tenant pays his rent to a society instead of to a landlord. He is able, by investing his savings in the society at five per cent., to become in greater or lesser degree his own landlord. As a result of this he will be fired with ambition to make the utmost possible of his home. The very fact that he does not own it outright, means that if his occupation requires his moving away from the locality, he will not be saddled with a piece of unprofitable real estate.

From the viewpoint of the tenant, then, the project appeals. He here gets for the same or less rent than he would have to pay in town, a pleasanter and healthier place to live in. At the same time that he develops a community spirit, he becomes a capitalist, and by so doing assumes greater sense of responsibility.

On the other hand, from the view of the philanthropic investor who makes the society possible, the cause is good because it "encourages thrift and tends to put capital into the hand of the working-classes."

The pioneer copartnership suburb began in a very humble way by the formation in nineteen hundred and one of a small society. It was not until a year later that it was able to buy sites for about fifty houses and thus materialize under the title, The Ealing Tenants, Limited. In the next year an increase of capital made feasible the purchase of an adjacent estate of some sixteen acres, on which a model village was erected under the supervision of Messrs. Parker and Unwin.

Five out of the sixteen acres were devoted to outdoor life and

recreation purposes, on the rest were built cottages renting from about a dollar and a half a week—"exclusive of rates and taxes"—and upward. Today the association owns a little over sixty acres, twelve in all being given over to recreation purposes and open spaces, while the idea of associated ownership which it projected has spread so rapidly that there are now fourteen societies in the Kingdom where the principle is being tried out. In all of them stress is laid on the creation and maintenance of the social centers. There are cricket field and bowling green, a central hall for indoor games and meetings, both social and educational, and plenty of spaces for outdoor sports and pageants.

It would not be fair to ignore a distinction which exists between the terms garden city and garden suburb. The first would transport the work as well as the worker into the new conditions. The second contents itself with offering the worker a haven beyond the pale of his working place.

No longer insignificant, the Garden City movement now enrolls as many as twenty societies under its wing in England alone.

But as yet the most striking and picturesque illustration of the Garden City Idea is after all that of Hampstead. Some notion of the rapidity with which the idea has spread at Hampstead may be had from the fact that in the short space of two years there were built five hundred houses. Moreover, according to the report of January nineteen hundred and eleven, the demand at the Hampstead Garden Suburb was in excess of the supply, and it was found advisable to add a new area of one hundred and twelve acres.

Nonetheless there is a real unity of purpose through all. Everywhere the visitor is made conscious that here is a new impetus at work and a new meaning being infused into that much maligned word "land development."

As the London Times succinctly put it the garden suburb (and we must now add these other organizations as well),—shows "proof of what can be done when order and design take the place of anarchy and chaos."

New York's Newest Institution for the Service of the Public

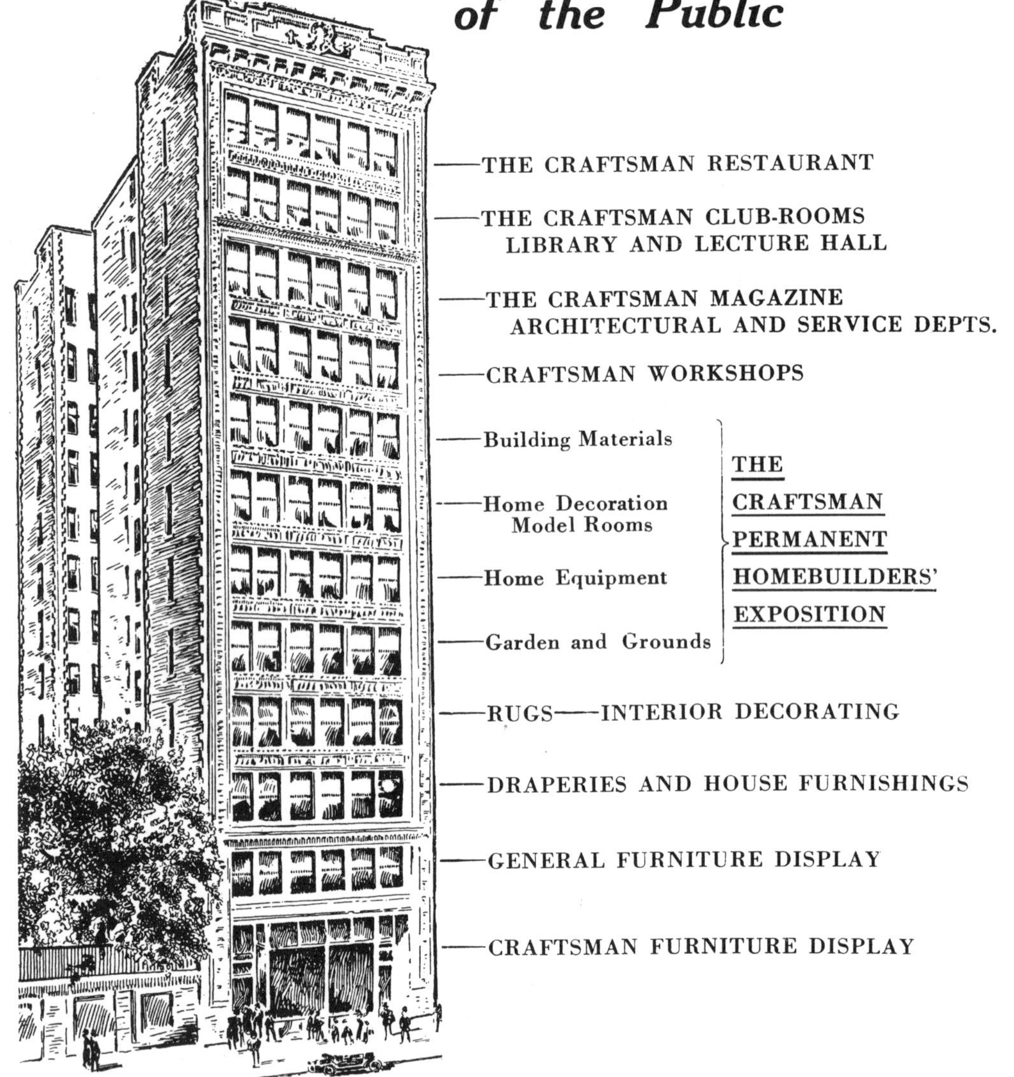

EVERY floor of THE CRAFTSMAN'S new twelve-story building—running through an entire block, 38th to 39th Streets, a step from Fifth Avenue, in the shopping centre of America—is devoted to the service of the home-loving, home-building public, as indicated above.

The display of furniture, rugs, and draperies on the first four floors is full of inspiration for the homelover who is seeking to furnish a home in good taste. The next four floors are given over to the chief feature of the Building—the exhibits in the Craftsman Permanent Homebuilders' Exposition, as outlined on the next page. On the tenth floor, The Craftsman Magazine offers the resources of its Architectural and Service Departments to those about to build or remodel a home. The Craftsman Club-Rooms on the eleventh floor are for the free use of the public; here are charmingly furnished rest rooms for men and women, a reference library, and a lecture hall in which lectures will be given on building and decorating. The Craftsman Restaurant on the top floor is designed to cater to the comfort and refreshment of visitors to the Building.

THE CRAFTSMAN MOVEMENT: ITS ORIGIN AND GROWTH: BY GUSTAV STICKLEY

FEW weeks ago I was showing a friend of mine over the new Craftsman Building, explaining my plans for its development—describing all the interesting things I hoped to bring together there. And after listening to me for a while, he said:

"Tell me, what makes you do this? Why do you want to move into this big place? Do you realize the enormous load you are shouldering, how many more problems you will have to solve, and what a difficult undertaking this will be to carry through? You're getting on in years; you've reached an age when a business man usually begins to think about retiring and settling down to a quiet life. Instead, you are taking on harder work and bigger responsibilities. Why do you do it?"

"Because I can't help it," I told him. "A movement that has grown as this one has, must keep on growing, People need it; they wouldn't let me stop even if I wanted to."

As I think the matter over, it comes to me more and more clearly that here lies the true explanation—that it is a *movement*, and not merely an individual enterprise. It must either grow or decay; it cannot stand still. For a movement is like a tree—if it once gets a firm hold in the soil, if it has its *roots in the ground*, it cannot help growing. Barring accidents, nothing can stop it.

In every vital movement this principle of growth is seen, and the Craftsman Movement is no exception. Its development has been a matter of natural, logical expansion. First it had to be rooted in the soil of actual physical conditions, to be the outgrowth of real spiritual needs. It had to push its way up toward the light of a definite ideal. It sent forth one branch after another, each new development suggesting still wider and more varied growth. And like the tree, each branch had to be hardy, had to weather rebuff and criticism just as the branches of the tree have to withstand storms and insects and other natural foes. Moreover, its growth had to be more or less in line with the thoughts and wishes of the people, for the public tendency, in a general way, is right, and the wind that sways and determines the growth of any democratic movement is always the *zeitgeist*, the "spirit of the times." Because of these things its present stature has been reached.

Fifteen years ago this Movement started. It had its origin in a few simple chairs. Yet such sound principles of craftsmanship inspired their conception, and such popular response did their making invoke, that out of this seemingly insignificant beginning developed all that the word "Craftsman" now implies.

TODAY the Craftsman Movement stands not only for simple, well made furniture, conceived in the spirit of true craftsmanship, designed for beauty as well as comfort, and built to last, it stands also for a distinct type of American architecture, for well

built, democratic homes, planned for and owned by the people who live in them, homes that solve the servant problem by their simple, pleasant arrangement, and meet the needs of wholesome family life. Big, light, airy living rooms that foster the social spirit are a part of its purpose; it holds as essential the open fireplace as the natural nucleus for happy indoor life. The plain yet decorative woodwork and built-in fittings that help to simplify housework and produce a restful, homelike atmosphere are inherent in its plan. The sheltered places for outdoor dining, rest and play, and the healthful sleeping porch which is coming to be recognized as so vital a part of the modern home are inevitably a part of the Craftsman home. It stands, too, for the companionship of gardens, the wholesomeness of country and suburban living and the health and efficiency which these imply. It aims to be instrumental in the restoration of the people to the land and the land to the people. It is always for progress, for scientific farming, for closer coöperation between producer and consumer, and less waste in both agricultural and industrial fields. It stands for the rights of the children to health and happiness, through an education that will develop hands as well as heads; an education that will give them that love and enthusiasm for useful work which is every child's rightful heritage, and fit them to take their places as efficient members of a great democracy. Civic improvement is close to its heart, political, as well as social and industrial progress; it desires to strengthen honest craftsmanship in every branch of human activity, and strives for a form of art which shall express the spirit of the American people.

And now as the Movement reaches the next stage in its evolution, the opening of the new Craftsman Building, it seems only fitting, for the information of those who may not be familiar with its various activities, that I should offer this brief explanation of its origin and growth.

I had always been interested in wood, even before I became interested in furniture, for as a farm boy out in Wisconsin I used to make wooden ax helves, yokes for the oxen, runners for the sleigh—whatever happened to be needed for the task in hand. In fact, in the making of these rough farm implements lay the germ of what I have accomplished in later years.

After the farming I took up stone masonry, and it was the hard daily labor with this stubborn material that made me appreciate so keenly the responsive, sympathetic qualities of wood when I began afterward, at the age of sixteen, to learn the cabinetmakers' trade. It was like being with an old friend, to work in wood again! I began to study its beauty more carefully, to note its varied grains and textures, the way it lent itself to sturdy simple forms and soft finishes, and these things filled me with enthusiasm for the work.

AT FIRST the furniture I made was on the usual conventional lines; but as the years went by and I experimented with the various forms of construction and design, I began to understand better what good furniture and true craftsmanship meant. I tried to make pieces that would be first of all practical and comfortable, that

would last a man's lifetime without being much the worse for wear; the kind of things one could take pride in handing down to one's grandchildren. I wanted them to be beautiful, too, not with the superficial prettiness of applied ornament, but with that inherent decorative quality which comes from good proportions, mellow finish and harmonious coloring. And to these ends I tried always to choose strong, serviceable materials, with the sort of texture, design and coloring that would result in a genuine, homelike charm.

I did not realize at the time that in making those few pieces of strong, simple furniture, I had started a new movement. Others saw it and prophesied a far-reaching development. To me it was only furniture; to them it was religion. And eventually it became religion with me as well.

Thus, unconsciously, a Craftsman style was evolved and developed, a style that gradually found its way into the homes of the people, pushing out a branch here, a branch there, first in one direction and then in another, wherever it met with sympathy and encouragement.

The next thing that naturally suggested itself was the need of a broader medium of expression for these ideas of craftsmanship and home-making; the need of some definite, organized plan for reaching people who, I felt sure, would be interested in what I was trying to accomplish; some means of getting into direct communication with them, of entering, so to speak, into their very homes. And so, in October, nineteen hundred and one, the Craftsman Movement sent forth another branch, full of hope and promise—the first number of THE CRAFTSMAN Magazine.

At the start it was only a small illustrated pamphlet, devoted largely to an exposition of Craftsman ideals. Gradually, however, as the little monthly found its way to sympathetic readers, its circulation, size and interest increased. From Syracuse, where for the first six years it had been published, I brought it to New York; for the metropolis, with its wider interests and activities, seemed the natural place to secure the material I needed, and to get in touch with progressive men and women who were accomplishing significant things in the various fields of work and art.

In the magazine I have striven from the beginning to present the work and opinions of others in sympathy with my ideas, as well as my own suggestions regarding home-making, and point of view about the problems of the day. In as direct, authentic and beautiful fashion as I could, I have set forth what seemed the best and most representative work of artists, craftsmen, architects and other workers in significant fields, both in this country and abroad; reviewing and illustrating whatever I believed would prove helpful to those men and women of America who needed stimulus to spur them on to finer achievement.

But a healthy movement, like a healthy tree, does not grow merely in one or two directions. And while the magazine was sending out its branches and spreading its influence over American homes wherever it could reach throughout the country, the main trunk of the movement was sending forth still other branches.

FOR all this time the original source of the movement, the furniture, had been developing and finding its way to home-loving people who wanted simple, serviceable things. And as the demand grew, I became more and more interested in every detail of the home environment, for I saw that the way a man's house was planned and built had as much influence upon his family's health and happiness as had the furniture they lived with. Besides, such unassuming furnishings as mine were out of place in elaborate over-ornamented interiors. They needed the sort of rooms and woodwork and exterior that would be in keeping with their own more homelike qualities. They suggested, by their sturdy build and friendly finish, an equally sturdy and friendly type of architecture. This being the case, why not build the kind of homes that would be in sympathy with the Craftsman ideal? Thus was evolved what has since come to be known as Craftsman architecture.

I planned these houses with a big living room because I believed in having a comfortable place for general family life, large enough to eliminate that sense of friction which is so apt to invade a cramped and narrow home. In this room I planned a generous fireplace, because I knew that people were longing to return to the oldtime comfort and hospitality that centered so pleasantly around the open hearth. And this fireplace became one of the most characteristic features of my plans—even developing later, after much scientific study and experiment, into a means of heating and ventilating the whole house.

The rest of the space in a Craftsman house I arranged compactly, with as few partitions as possible for the sake of economy and the simplifying of work. More often than not the rooms were all on one floor, to eliminate the trouble of stair-climbing, and special attention was paid to the kitchen and other parts where the maid or housewife would have to spend much time, and which consequently should be light, cheerful and convenient.

Then the question naturally suggested itself—why build homes in the city? Why live in tall buildings, in rows and solid blocks, with a minimum of air and light and garden space, when there is so much beautiful country within reach? Why not live where there is plenty of fresh air and sunshine, plenty of room to grow flowers and vegetables, to rest and exercise out of doors? Why not get "back to the land?"

Thinking and working along these lines, the houses I planned naturally began to take on certain aspects of country and suburban living—big porches for outdoor work and rest and play, dining porches, sleeping balconies, pergolas and other garden features that would link the interior closely with the outdoor life.

The next thing that suggested itself was that people, instead of living in houses built merely for speculation, should plan and build and *own* their own homes—even the people who could afford only a little four or five-room cottage or bungalow. And it seemed to me that if these homes were to be *theirs* in the fullest sense of the word, they must give their own time, thought and energy to the planning of each

detail, and then make sure that the architect and builder carried out their ideas in an economical, practical and beautiful way.

These opinions I naturally expressed in The Craftsman Magazine, where each month I published one or more of my house designs, thus making them available to readers in every part of the world. I published floor plans and perspective views of both interior and exterior, with practical advice as to construction, finish, furnishing and decorating schemes. People began to look more and more to this magazine as a source of encouragement and aid. Men and women who were expecting to build and furnish their own homes would write to me for plans, ask my advice about different methods of construction or different kinds of wood finishes, or want me to make suggestions for interior decorations and color schemes. And out of these inquiries and their answers, Craftsman Service developed—another branch of the constantly growing Craftsman Movement.

As I was continually advising people to build their own homes in a simple, practical fashion, the next thing that inevitably suggested itself was that I should *actually help them to do it;* show them the various building materials, point out the qualities and uses of each, explain the different methods of construction, teach them how to choose the most serviceable and appropriate things, how to plan wisely and build well.

So I began to bring together for their inspection samples of building materials, paints and finishes, miniature models of cottages and bungalows, and household devices of various kinds. But I soon found that three floors occupied by my architectural, editorial and circulation forces were quite inadequate to allow a suitable display or to accommodate with comfort all my visitors. It became necessary to move into more spacious and convenient quarters; hence the Craftsman Movement has branched out into the new Craftsman Building.

This building is now the Craftsman home. Here are the showrooms for furniture, metal work and fabrics made in my cabinet and metal workshops at Eastwood, New York. Here is The Craftsman Magazine with its several departments. Here are the drafting rooms of the Craftsman architects; the bureaus of Craftsman Service—architectural, gardening, agricultural and real estate; the home-builders' library, the lecture hall, the club rooms for Craftsman subscribers, and the homelike Craftsman Restaurant.

More important than all, perhaps, here is the big Craftsman Permanent Home-builders' Exposition, occupying five floors and including in its scope everything that the homemaker might need to see and know, from brick and mortar to wall coverings and stencil designs, from ice-boxes and vacuum cleaners to garden tools and rustic furniture. And all so conveniently and systematically arranged that the visitor may pass from one exhibit to another in logical order, or inspect some particular feature on which information is desired—with always an expert within call ready to give the necessary advice or explanation. Such an exposition as this must surely prove invaluable to the American homemaker; and surely it is a fitting culmination for all the Craftsman activities.

A Craftsman Bedroom

The Craftsman furniture and furnishings shown in the above photograph are as follows:

The Twin Bedsteads are No. 922, single size, inside measurements of each, 75 in. long, 40 in. wide, headboard 50 in high, each **$30.00**

The Bedspreads are No, 909, zinnia design in all-white embroidery on heavy brownish-gray linen each **$20.00**

The Dresser is a special design no longer carried, the nearest approximation being No. 905 (attached mirror), 48 in. wide, 22 in. deep, glass 34 in. x 26 in., height over all 62 in. Copper pulls **$65.00**

The Dresser Scarf is No. 915, ginkgo design in appliqué, rose and green, on Flemish linen, 20 in. x 72 in., $4.00; also done on Craftsman canvas **$4.25**

The Wardrobe is No. 920, 60 in. high, 34 in. wide, 17 in. deep, with four drawers and four other compartments **$36.00**

The Dressing Table is No. 914, 36 in. wide, 18 in. deep, glass 20 in. x 24 in., height over all 55 in. Wood knobs **$26.00**

The Shirtwaist Box is No. 95, cedar-lined, 16 in. high, 32 in. long, 17 in. wide. Hand-wrought lifts **$16.00**

The Rockers are No. 303, spring seat cushion, back 33 in. high, seat 14 in. high, 17 in. wide, 16 in. deep. **Chairs** to match, No. 304. In sheepskin, each, $10.00; soft leather **$11.00**

The Rug is Craftsman Scotch Rug No. 500, all wool, obtainable in three different color schemes and many stock sizes, ranging in price from $4.75 to **$52.00**

The Curtains are of embroidered crape, No. 524, deep yellow with rose and green blossoms and orange leaves. 50 in. wide .... **$1.75** per yd.

Craftsman Furnishings described fully in Catalogue, sent on request.

GUSTAV STICKLEY, THE CRAFTSMAN

29 W. 34th St.	468 Boylston St.	1512 H. St., N. W.
NEW YORK	BOSTON	WASHINGTON

Thus, like the tree, out of what seemed a small and insignificant beginning, has the Craftsman Movement grown. Not because I consciously willed or planned it; not because of great capital or prestige; but simply because it had its *roots in the ground.* It grew out of actual spiritual needs and physical conditions. It drew life from the warm, fertile soil of the people's interest and enthusiasm. And it depends upon their continued love and help, as well as upon my own endeavor, to keep its branches green, to make it grow into still farther-reaching strength and still wider efficiency.

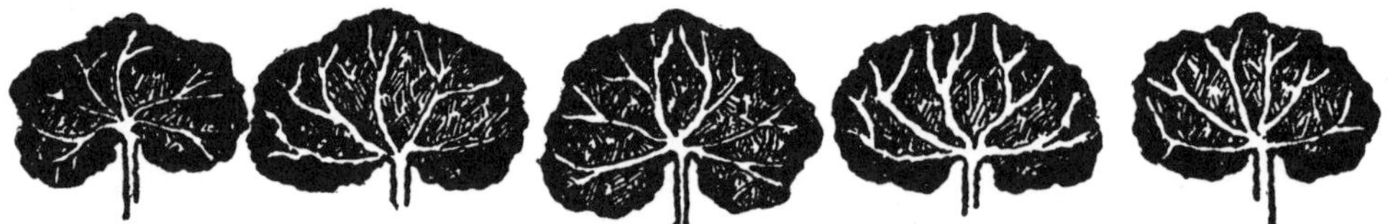

THE FIRE ON THE HEARTH

NOW that the Christmas season is with us again, warming the hearts of young and old, orthodox and agnostic alike, with its message of universal fellowship and good cheer, our thoughts turn instinctively to the genial flame that for so many centuries has been the symbol and center of the holiday spirit. Once more, in our modern and materialistic souls, is kindled the spark bequeathed by our fire-worshipping ancestors; we glimpse again the halo of legend and romance that has ever encircled the altar of the open hearth; we realize with renewed poignancy the vital and far-reaching part which has been played in our individual and racial progress by the fireplace, that "earliest and most influential of schools."

THIS MASSIVE FIREPLACE WITH ITS ANDIRONS AND LOGS AND SIMPLE LIVING-ROOM SURROUNDINGS SEEMS FULL OF THE LATENT SPIRIT OF WARMTH AND HOSPITALITY: HOW READILY ONE CAN IMAGINE IT THE CENTER OF A MERRY CHRISTMAS GATHERING!

THERE IS AN ATMOSPHERE OF SOLID COMFORT AND PERMANENCY ABOUT THIS DINING-ROOM FIREPLACE: THE BUILT-IN SIDEBOARDS, CUPBOARDS AND SEAT ALL EMPHASIZE, IN THEIR PRACTICAL WAY, THE HOMELIKE FEELING OF THE OPEN HEARTH.

It seems difficult to establish relationship between the modern fireplace, with its scientific construction, its beauty of design and decoration and the luxury which civilization has gathered around its hearth, with the primitive form of fireplace that our savage forefathers knew. To them fire was a most precious and cherished possession—a gift from the gods themselves. Each tribe or nation had its own myth concerning the origin of the sacred flame, the best known being the legend of the old Greek Prometheus, half god, half human, who, braving heroically the wrath of Zeus, stole fire from heaven to save the sons of men. Some said he concealed the flame in a hollow fennel stalk—a Grecian mode of carrying fire—others that he held a rod against the sun; but whether gift or theft, the flaming spirit was always an object of veneration.

FIREPLACE IN THE LIVING ROOM OF TWO-STORY BUNGALOW.

NATURALLY, about this important nucleus of the public weal, much sentiment and superstition clung. Religious, social and political customs and rites throve around it, and folklore and history became closely interwoven with this red spirit of the altar and the hearth. It became the symbol of home and country, the synonym for bodily comfort and spiritual gladness, the center of festive gatherings and celebrations of many kinds. In fact, our own Christmas banquet, with its "yuletide log," its mistletoe and holly, its gifts and hospitality, is reminiscent of the feasts given in honor of the gods and goddesses of old, and as Cato said of Rome's luxurious banquets, their fascination is "not so much the pleasure of eating and drinking as that of finding one's self among friends and of conversing with them."

THE CRAFTSMAN FIREPLACE AND INVITING SEAT PICTURED HERE SUGGEST ONE OF MANY DELIGHTFUL WAYS TO BRING AN AIR OF RESTFUL SECLUSION ABOUT THE MODERN HEARTHSTONE.

Thus from those primitive fires of our early forefathers, and the "broad-breasted, deep-chested chimneypieces" of a few hundred years ago, we turn with expectant eyes to the fireplace of the future, picturing, in imagination, its place in the ideal democratic American home. We see the hospitable inglenook, the simple seats, the inviting bookshelves, all those friendly details that enhance the companionship of the blazing logs that rest upon the andirons of the open hearth. We watch the glow reflected in the loving faces of those who gather round, and feel the thrill of warmth and fellowship that expands their hearts. And searching for a fitting motto to inscribe above this simple household shrine, we recall the old tender words, so fraught with Youth's brave hope and Age's garnered memory—"*Where young men see visions and old men dream dreams.*"

Courtesy of Frederick Keppel & Co.

AUGUSTE RODIN, FROM AN ETCHING BY ANDERS ZORN.

"DWELLING HOUSES FULL OF PLEASANTNESS"

Dark Colonial clinker brick was used for first floor and clapboards with nine inch exposure for the second.

House of random width split shingles stained white; silver gray shingles upon the roof: Shutters white on first floor and green on second.

THE JAPANESE PRINT AS A REFORMER: ITS POWER TO INFLUENCE HOME DECORATION

EVERYONE has heard the story of the beautiful salt-cellar, that all unconsciously, merely by the irresistible force of its beauty, transformed the dining table it stood upon and all its appointments, changed the color of the walls, took down partitions, opened up windows, built on rooms, threw out all useless, cluttering objects, planted a garden, educated the young people, and in short revolutionized everything and everybody in the house. This little story, told with many, many variations, persists because there is so much truth in the fact that beauty radiates an irresistible influence. The story meets with responsive sympathy from every home-maker who has tried to create a harmonious room, and therefore knows how difficult it is to do, unless they have some one perfect thing to which the rest of the room may be tuned, some one thing that corresponds to a tuning fork or the piano keyed to correct pitch that all other instruments in an orchestra must be harmonized with.

Many people live willingly and comfortably enough in houses that are a confused jumble of unrelated odds and ends that could furnish a color model for a kaleidoscope. Inharmonious colors disturb them not, nor does a profusion of useless things annoy them in the least. The beautiful salt-cellar would work no miracle in their house, for they are not sensitive to perfection of form or color, creature comforts being their chief concern. But any genuinely fine object suddenly introduced into a room of people with even small comprehension of beauty, will revolutionize it. We know of a woman who put a valuable Japanese print that had been given her upon the wall of a room. She could hardly find place for it among the cheap prints, college banners, gold-framed home-made oil paintings, calendars and family portraits that crowded the walls. But the exquisite colors of that Japanese print soon made the crudeness of its associates apparent by mere force of contrast. One was taken down after another and hidden away out of sight. Unnecessary articles of furniture were banished. The more things that were removed from the room, the larger, finer, more elegant it looked. Red walls were changed to soft gray ones, gay-figured draperies exchanged for plain, finely toned ones, lights were modified, and the room that was a fussy, inharmonious place of no beauty became restful and

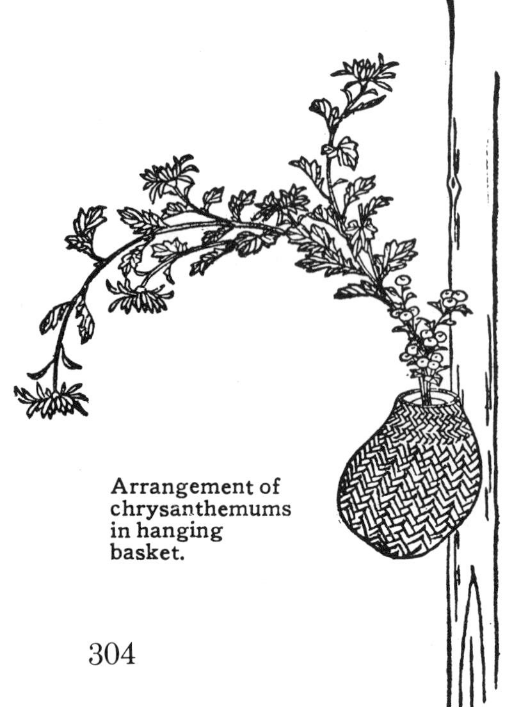

Arrangement of chrysanthemums in hanging basket.

Suggestion for arrangement of flowers and grasses for a summer home.

satisfying. This experience might well serve as a suggestion to other women who are anxious to have a beautiful home or even a single room, but are not sure of their ability to create perfect color harmony. By getting one good Japanese print and keying the room to it, success is sure to come. The Japanese are acknowledged masters of color and color combinations. True, some people do not care for Japanese figure prints, because the fair women and brawny men are drawn with what they call "funny" faces or are dressed in strange-looking clothes; but if these people will look at a print merely as a decorative block of color they will soon come to see its beauty. If the face distresses them then they should, temporarily, hang the picture upside down or sideways or do anything with it that will make them forget the face that they do not like, until they can perceive the marvelous genius of the bold color combinations and the fine, subtle modulations, like harmonics in music, that are brought out in the pattern of a kimona or in the shading of a flower leaf. Some prints are composed in a plaintive minor key, others in a joyous major, some are daring combinations of flat primitive colors, others a subtle blending of shades soft as early dawn. There is every possible opportunity for choice of color in the innumerable flower, bird, landscape and figure subjects that are easy to obtain in America. There are delicious "twilight sky" blues, "plum blossom" pinks, "chrysanthemum" yellows, "wistaria" lavenders and purples, "dried grass" browns, "wild crane" black and whites to which rooms may be safely toned.

It would be a very interesting experiment to introduce a rich Japanese print into a dull, monotonous, characterless room and observe the consequence. The print would, naturally, be too conspicuous, so that the thought would come to add a vase of flowers similar in color or a brilliant candlestick with corresponding shade of wax candle in it or a pillow covered with harmonizing silk. The room would then be brought up to the bright pitch in the easiest, most natural and safest manner. The reverse experiment might also be tried, that of introducing a print of rare refinement into a garishly colored room. Its modifying effect would soon be apparent.

Japanese decorative suggestion for use of vines and basket upon a porch or at a doorway.

For women unable to receive the help of experienced decorators in furnishing their homes or in correcting rooms already badly furnished, we would suggest the aid of a good Japanese print, because it would be a simple matter to bring the room up to it. The print need not be an expensive, genuinely old one. There are many reprints of the old plates to be had at moderate cost that are just as effective in color, although they have but little value from the collectors' standpoint. Of course, America is being flooded just at present with atrocious aniline-dye prints that are more to be avoided than our own Sunday supplement chromos, yet everywhere are to be found very lovely prints that could safely be used

All the pen and ink sketches by courtesy John Lane Co.

PALE YELLOW ROSES arranged as though growing in an antique brass vase make striking color contrast, especially if compelled to take a positive line such as is shown in the peony arrangement in the upper sketch.

BASKET with long handle filled with flowers arranged in swinging line makes a most attractive porch ornament.

as color suggestions for rooms. The tint of the walls, draperies, color of lights and movable ornaments of a room can all be selected from a single good though inexpensive Japanese print.

Before we can make use of Japanese prints in the correct and most effective manner we should have some definite knowledge of the way they were intended to be used. We must have some appreciation also of the ideal of simplicity that is ever before the Japanese mind. Our American tendency is to crowd our rooms with as many costly things as we can get into them, while theirs is to have as few as possible in evidence at one time. They feel that the full beauty of an object can only be gained by giving it a setting that in no way distracts attention from it. By covering a wall with many things they believe none of them have a fair chance of attention. The eye in a restless way glances from one to another with superficial understanding and interest in the subject or its color scheme. Their way is to change the kakemono every day or at different festivals, at the approach of the seasons, when a special guest is expected. Thus their rooms are an ever-changing expression of sentiment and fine, considerate feeling. Foreigners quickly come to like the simple, flat wall with but a single, well-chosen print displayed and the decorative aırangement of flowers that carry out the sense of the season in some subtle way. They find pleasure in the illusion of spaciousness obtained in a simply furnished room, in the dignity and importance that surrounds each object when but a few instead of many are shown at once. They come to see a beauty of color, a charm in neatness, an impressiveness in reserve.

It must be remembered that the aim of Japanese artists is to recall the mind of the beholder to the existence of beauty and to quicken poetic thought. Japanese prints are sometimes mounted on the screens placed before the kitchen fire to protect it from the winds or upon the sliding partition of the walls so that the minds of the workers may be lifted above the monotonous round of drudgery and placed upon the beauties of nature, upon pleasant legend or upon inspiring incidents of history. In selecting the prints for our rooms we should keep this idea in mind and choose a subject that will lift the mind to planes of beauty.

Mary Averill has in a book on the "Flower Art of Japan," called attention to the decorative value of flowers arranged in lines that carry out or emphasize some definite thought. The pen and ink sketches along the margin of this article are from this book.

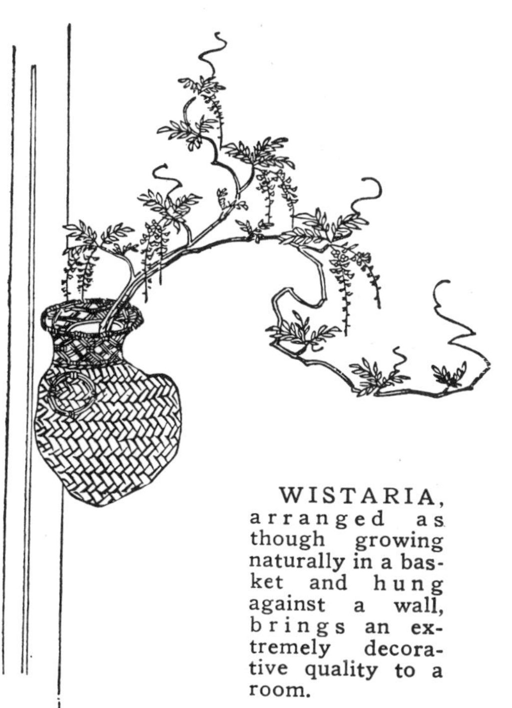

WISTARIA, arranged as though growing naturally in a basket and hung against a wall, brings an extremely decorative quality to a room.

EXTREME SIMPLICITY is characteristic of a Japanese home interior: A reserved refinement in walls and floor coverings makes arrangement of flowers, the coloring of the kakemonos, the fineness of the carvings and the richness of coloring in objects of art, stand out with greater perfection.

In the picture shown below may be seen the manner of displaying a New Year's print of the rising moon with graceful arrangement of flowers at one side.

Residence for Miss Marion Olmsted, San Diego: Irving J. Gill, architect: Typical of the new architecture of the West.

THE HOME OF THE FUTURE: THE NEW ARCHITECTURE OF THE WEST: SMALL HOMES FOR A GREAT COUNTRY: BY IRVING J. GILL: NUMBER FOUR

"An artist is known rather by what he omits."

ARCHITECTURE, Victor Hugo says, is the great book of the world, the principal expression of man in his different stages of development, the chief register of humanity. Every religious symbol, every human thought has its page and its monument in that immense book. Down to the time of Gutenberg, he points out, architecture was the principal, the universal writing. Whoever was born a poet then, became an architect. All arts obeyed and placed themselves under the discipline of architecture. They were the workmen of the great work. There was nothing which, in order to make something of itself, was not forced to frame itself in the shape of architectural hymn or prose. He has shown us that the great products of architecture are less the works of individuals than of society, rather the offspring of a nation's effort than the inspired flash of a man of genius, the deposit left by a whole people, the heaps accumulated by centuries, the residue of successive evaporations of human society, in a word, a species of formation. Each wave of time contributes its alluvium, each race deposits its layer on the monument, each individual brings his stone.

No architect can read his inspired analysis of the place and the importance of architecture in preserving the records of the world's thought and action, without approaching his own part in this human record with a greater reverence and greater sense of responsibility. What rough or quarried stone will each of us contribute to the universal edifice, what idle or significant sentence will we write with brick and stone, wood, steel and concrete upon the sensitive page of the earth? In California we have great wide plains, arched by blue skies that are fresh chapters as yet unwritten. We have noble mountains, lovely little hills and canyons waiting to hold the record of this generation's history, ideals, imagination, sense of romance and honesty. What monument will we who build, erect to the honor or shame of our age?

The West has an opportunity unparalleled in the history of the world, for it is the newest white page turned for registration. The present builders have the advantage of all the wisdom and experience of the ages to aid them in poetically inscribing today's milestone in the progress of humanity. The West unfortunately has been and is building too hastily, carelessly and thoughtlessly. Houses are springing up faster than mushrooms, for mushrooms silently prepare for a year and more before they finally raise their house above the ground in proof of what they have been designing so long and secretly. People pour out here as on the crest of a flood and remain where chance deposits them when the rush of waters subsides, building temporary shacks wherein they live for a brief period while looking about for more permanent anchorage. The surface of the ground is barely scraped away, in some cases but a few inches deep, just enough to allow builders to find a level, and a house is tossed together with little thought of beauty, and no thought of permanence, haste being the chief characteristic. The family of health- or fortune-seekers who comes out here generally expects to camp in these poor shacks for but a short time and plans to sell the shiftless affair to some other impatient newcomer. Perhaps such temporary proceedings are necessary in the settling of a new land; fortunately such structures cannot endure, will never last long enough to be a monument for future generations to wonder at. Such structures cannot rightly be called homes, so do not justly deserve notice in a consideration of Western domestic architecture.

House on a canyon lot designed for Miss Teats, most typical of Irving J. Gill's architectural form.

If we, the architects of the West, wish to do great and lasting work we must dare to be simple, must have the courage to fling aside every device that distracts the eye from structural beauty, must break through convention and get down to fundamental truths. Through force of custom and education we, in whose hands much of the beauty of country and city is entrusted, have been compelled to study the style of other men, with the result that most of our modern work is an open imitation or veiled plagiarism of another's idea. To break away from this degradation we must boldly throw aside every accepted structural belief and standard of beauty and get back to the source of all architectural strength—the straight line, the arch, the cube and the circle—and drink from these fountains of Art that gave life to the great men of old.

EVERY artist must sooner or later reckon directly, personally with these four principles—the mightiest of lines. The straight line borrowed from the horizon is a symbol of greatness, grandeur and nobility; the arch patterned from the dome of the sky represents exultation, reverence, aspiration; the circle is the sign of completeness, motion and progression, as may be seen when a stone touches water; the square is the symbol of power, justice, honesty and firmness. These are the bases, the units of architectural language, and without them there can be no direct or inspired architectural speech. We must not weaken our message of beauty and strength by the stutter and mumble of useless ornaments. If we have nothing worth while to say with our building then we should keep quiet. Why should we chatter idly and meaninglessly with foolish ornaments and useless lines?

Any deviation from simplicity results in a loss of dignity. Ornaments tend to cheapen rather than enrich, they acknowledge inefficiency and weakness. A house cluttered up by complex ornament means that the designer was aware that his work lacked purity of line and perfection of proportion, so he endeavored to cover its imperfection by adding on detail, hoping thus to distract the attention of the observer from the fundamental weakness of his design. If we omit everything useless from the structural point of view we will come to see the great beauty of straight lines, to see the charm that lies in perspective, the force in light and shade, the power in balanced masses, the fascination of color that plays upon a smooth wall left free to report the passing of a cloud or nearness of a flower, the furious rush of storms and the burning stillness of summer suns. We would also see the glaring defects of our own work if left in this bold, unornamented fashion, and therefore could swiftly correct it.

I believe if we continually think more of line, proportion, light and shade, we will reach greater skill in handling them, and a greater appreciation and understanding of their power and beauty. We should build our house simple, plain and substantial as a boulder, then leave the ornamentation of it to Nature, who will tone it with lichens, chisel it with storms, make it gracious and friendly with vines and flower shadows as she does the stone in the meadow. I believe also that houses should be built more substantially and should be made absolutely sanitary. If the cost of unimportant ornamentation were put into construction, then we would have a more lasting and a more dignified architecture.

IN California we have long been experimenting with the idea of producing a perfectly sanitary, labor-saving house, one where the maximum of comfort may be had with the minimum of drudgery. In the recent houses that I have built the walls are finished flush with the casings and the line where the wall joins the flooring is slightly rounded, so that it forms one continuous piece with no place for dust to enter or to lodge, or crack for vermin of any kind to exist. There is no molding for pictures, plates or chairs, no baseboards, paneling or wainscoting to catch and hold the dust. The

HONESTY, FRANKNESS and dignified simplicity mark this house designed to rest upon the crest of a canyon: Seen from the bottom of the slope, this section of the Bishop's School, designed by Mr. Gill, rises like a natural monument of stone.

Why should any message of architectural beauty be marred by the addition of useless ornament when such supreme results can be obtained from an unornamented surface?

All the windows of this unusual house overlook the waterworn caves at La Jolla and the famous blue water of that region: Blue water, golden brown and tawny hills, cream white of concrete and dark green of eucalyptus contribute an almost tropical color beauty.

THE STRAIGHT LINE, borrowed from the horizon, relieved by a succession of arches, is as impressively used on a flat lawn (as is seen in this La Jolla Woman's Club) as when erected upon the crest of a hill.

doors are single slabs of hand-polished mahogany swung on invisible hinges or else made so that they slide in the wall. In some of the houses all windows and door frames are of steel. They never wear out, warp or burn, a point of importance in fireproof construction.

The drain boards are sunk in magnesite which is made in one piece with the walls and all cornices rounded, so not a particle of grease or dirt can lodge, or dampness collect and become unwholesome. The bathtubs are boxed and covered with magnesite up to the porcelain.

By this manner of building there is no chance anywhere in the house for dust to accumulate. This minimizes the labor of keeping the house clean and gives the rooms a sweet, pure, simple and dignified appearance. The money usually wasted in meaningless gables, swags, machine-made garlands, fretwork and "gingerbread" goes into labor-saving devices or into better grade of material. As much thought goes into the placing of the ice-box that can be filled from the outside without tracking through a clean kitchen, or the letter box that can be opened from within the house, or the proper disposal of the garbage can, or the convenient arrangement of kitchens so that meals may be prepared with the greatest economy of labor, as is often expended in the planning of the pergola or drawing rooms.

There is something very restful and satisfying to my mind in the simple cube house with creamy walls, sheer and plain, rising boldly into the sky, unrelieved by cornices or overhang of roof, unornamented save for the vines that soften a line or creepers that wreathe a pillar or flowers that inlay color more sentiently than any tile could do. I like the bare honesty of these houses, the childlike frankness and chaste simplicity of them. It seemed too peculiar an innovation at first to make a house without a large overhang roof, for we have been so accustomed in California to think them a necessity, but now that the first shock is over people welcome the simplicity of the houses built without these heavy overhangs and see that they really have distinction.

IN the West, home building has followed, in the main, two distinct lines—the Spanish Mission and the India bungalow. True, we find many small Swiss châlets clinging perilously to canyon walls, imposing Italian villas facing the sea and myriad nameless creations whose chief distinction lies in the obvious fact that they are original, different from any known type of architecture. It were much better for California if there were less complicated, meaningless originality and more frank following of established good types.

Because of the intense blue of sky and sea that continues for such long, unbroken periods, the amethyst distant mountains that form an almost universal background for houses or cities, the golden brown of summer fields, the varied green of pepper, eucalyptus and poplar trees that cut across it in such decorative forms and the profusion of gay flowers that grow so quickly and easily, houses of a bright romantic picturesqueness are perfectly suitable that would seem too dramatic in other parts of the country. They seem a pleasing part of the orange-belted flower fields and belong to the semi-tropical land. These same houses would certainly look artificial and amusingly uncomfortable and out of place in the East; but they essentially belong to the land of sunshine.

CONCRETE STEPPING-STONE blocks carry the quality of the house into the garden: Vines, shrubs and flowers carry the spirit of the garden up into the walls of the house: The union of these two forces is always insisted upon by the architects, Gill & Gill.

This photograph of the Darst house shows that any deviation from simplicity results in a loss of dignity: Any ornament put upon these flat walls would tend to cheapen rather than to enrich them: If everything useless from the structural point of view be omitted, we will all come to see the great beauty of straight lines, to see the charm that lies in perspective and in contrast of light and shade: Such is Mr. Gill's conviction.

INNER court of this same house is shown at the left: The conspicuous contrast of square line against the sky and the soft curve of the arch never fail to produce a strikingly beautiful result.

The contour, coloring and history of a country naturally influence its architecture. The old wooden Colonial houses of the East, shaded by noble elms, with their attendant lanes and roads outlined by stone walls, perfect pictures of home beauty; the stone houses of Pennsyl-

vania, charming of color, stately, eloquent of substantial affluence and generous hospitality; and the adobe houses of the Arizona Indians formed of the earth into structures so like the surrounding ledges and buttes in shape that they can scarcely be told from them, triumphs of protective, harmonious building, are familiar types of buildings characteristic of their locality.

California is influenced, and rightly so, by the Spanish Missions as well as by the rich coloring and the form of the low hills and wide valleys. The Missions are a part of its history that should be preserved and in their long, low lines, graceful arcades, tile roofs, bell towers, arched doorways and walled gardens we find a most expressive medium of retaining tradition, history and romance. In coloring and general form they are exactly suited to the romantic requirements of the country. It is safe to say that more architectural crimes have been committed in their name than in any other unless it be the Grecian temples. The facade of the San Diego Mission is a wonderful thing, something that deserves to be a revered model, something to which local building might safely and advantageously have been keyed. Instead of this it has been abused and caricatured in the most shocking way. Its charming proportions and graceful outline have been distorted to adorn tall public buildings, low railway stations, ornate hotels, cramped stables and minute private houses in the most irreverent, inexcusable and pitiable way. The arched cloisters of the Missions have been seized upon and tortured until all semblance of their original beauty has been lost. Their meaning and definite purpose—that of supporting the roof or the second story and thus forming a retreat or quiet walk for the monks—has been almost forgotten.

THE arch is one of our most imposing, most picturesque and graceful architectural features. Its power of creating beauty is unquestionable, but like any other great force, wrongly used, is equally destructive. Fire warms and cheers us and cooks our food, but if not carefully handled destroys everything it touches. The Missions have taught us also the beauty and usefulness of the court. Romana's house, a landmark as familiar in the South as some of the Missions, was built around three sides of an open space, the other side being a high garden wall. This home plan gave privacy, protection and beauty. The court contains a pool and well in the center and an arbor for grapes along the garden wall; the archway that runs along the three sides formed by the house made the open-air living rooms. Here were arranged couches for sleeping, hammocks for the siesta, easy chairs and tables for dining. There was always a sheltered and a sunny side, always seclusion and an outlook into the garden. In California we have liberally borrowed this home plan, for it is hard to devise a better, cozier, more convenient or practical scheme for a home. In the seclusion of the outdoor living rooms and in their nearness to the garden, the arrangement is ideal.

ORIGINAL DESIGNS USED FOR THE STENCILING OF THE WALLS AND DECORATIONS

IS THERE A NATIONAL SPIRIT IN "THE NEW POETRY" OF AMERICA? BY AMY LOWELL

E hear a great deal today about "The New Poetry." Magazines and newspapers print long articles upon it, and people take sides for and against in so heated a fashion as to show that poetry is once more a matter of vital interest. Why? What has brought about this changed attitude? For that it is a changed attitude one has only to look back one short decade to see.

A few years ago the idea that poetry, or anything to do with it, could have any interest for the great public, would have been received by editors and advertising managers with a deprecating smile. Everybody professed to consider poetry of importance, a beautiful thing to cultivate, but nobody read it. No active body, that is. It was all very well for lovesick youth and sentimental old age, but for robust middle life! We lived in a practical era, we were told; and there was a general feeling that all the real poets were dead, and that there would never be any others.

Now there was a good deal of truth in this. There usually is a good deal of truth in anything which is an indubitable fact. Poetry was moribund. Men still wrote it, to be sure, but the kind they wrote had so little in common with the bright, rushing, vivid life other men were living, it is small wonder it seemed to these what the French call *fadé:* tasteless and a little sickly.

All of a sudden there leapt into the world a new poetry. A poetry as energetic, as rapid and full of color as the life it reflected. It was not afraid of the scorn of academic professors, it shrugged its shoulders when people made fun of it, and struck out smartly when anybody aimed a blow at it. It was a good-natured vagabond, but a vagabond who intended to make his way in the world, that was clear. The world is a good deal like the proverbial thistle, if you grab it with firm intention it will usually yield. In this case the world yielded, sputtering, deprecating, denying; it yielded its profound attention. It could no more ignore the youngster than it could ignore an East

wind. Stately gentlemen gave it diplomas of faint praise wrapped in the tinfoil of admonition; less stately gentlemen, with anachronistic souls, raved at it and spattered it with mud; a throng of unworthy imitators sprang up and hid it behind them. Still it went on—growing—growing. We, the world, have been obliged to acknowledge its existence; and to admit some merit to that existence. "The New Poetry" is, and is simply because it deserves to be, because it contains the real heart of the race.

WE have never had a definite American poetry before, a definite movement toward it, that is. Only two of our poets, Poe and Walt Whitman, were truly American. By this I do not mean that our poets did not write on American subjects, but that they did so in the true English fashion, and a little less well than the poets of the parent stock. Critically, they should be considered rather as English provincial poets than as American poets. We were colonials in everything except Government. Our ideas in all the arts came from England, we acknowledged England to be "home" in all things spiritual. No Australian or Anglo-Indian was more convinced of the parentage of England than those Americans who elected to be poets. This vassalage was unconscious, of course, but it was none the less real.

Two great American poets we did have: Poe and Walt Whitman; but neither of them received the honor which was his due in his lifetime. Whitman was an innovator in form and a pagan moralist in substance, and stately, cultivated New England (the literary tribunal of those days) misunderstood and was scandalized, while the vigor of Poe's imagination was so foreign to its placid, incurious temper as to remain unrewarded until its possessor had died of the combined effects of drink and despair.

Gradually the attitude of our country changed. Latin and Celtic immigration began to show its influence. We may deny it; we may say that the immigrants were of so low a class that their effect upon the world of ideas must be *nil*. The fact remains. Constant contact with these people had its effect. Then Americans traveled and lived abroad. And it was not in England with its fogs and gloomy skies that they lived. It was in Italy; it was in France. "All good Americans when they die go to Paris," is an old saying in my part of the country. They read French, they came in contact with French thought. Insensibly they were modified away from purely British influences.

At the same time, the great wave of change was sweeping over all the arts. Wagner came, created a perfect maelstrom of revolts, and smoothed a way to the placid flow of daily life. Our young men studied painting in Paris, came under the influence of Manet and Monet, and brought home new ways of seeing things to astonish the native *bourgeoisie*. Americans demanded music, and outgrowing home talent, demanded the imported best. The best came, and the public was fed upon the latest musical excitement from countries where music is an exciting and vital thing.

THEN the poets took fire and began writing as they felt, as all the influences about them had caused them to feel. People who had not come under the artistic influences I am speaking of were surprised. This was iconoclastic; it was dreadful. But it was not dreadful, it was not iconoclastic; it was merely growth. For the first time in its history, America was having an artistic upheaval; it had grown up enough to develop a sincere artistic life, chosen because it cared for it, no longer in leading strings.

It is small wonder that people brought up in the old conventions, blind and deaf to the great changes going on all about them, should find themselves nonplussed by the originality and strangeness of the New Poetry. It is an old platitude that nothing is so strange as truth. If a man looks into his own soul and writes down what he finds there, he himself will be startled by its unlikeness to what he expected. To be absolutely sincere about one's reactions is as difficult in art as in life. For a country long in leading strings to break them and possess itself of its own extended orbit requires high courage and a great impulse and necessity. That we have so many entirely American poets today is a proof of that courage and that impulse.

Art is a progression; a marching from the known into the unknown. It must start from the conventional and fare forth on its quest for truth. It is truth for an artist to present himself, with his own thoughts and his own likes and dislikes. One can no more attain to the position of a great national poet by thinking about it, than one can add a cubit to one's stature. But what is in the soul comes out, perforce. If an artist is the product of an environment, it will saturate all his work. And as a country produces many kinds of men, so it must produce many kinds of artists. The richer and more varied the national life, the richer and more varied is found to be its artistic output.

Nobody denies personality to the American people. But how hard it has been to get that personality into the higher forms of art! Until recently the higher forms of art have been compressed in the bonds of theory. This, and that, and the other, were to be done, and different things were emphatically not to be done; and for the simple reason that our English cousins, expressing themselves, had never done them. That we were no longer like these same cousins in our lives or our thoughts was not taken into consideration.

BUT the mold has broken and the new product stands out in the clear light. Take the poets of today. Where, in English poetry, do you find the prototype of Edgar Lee Masters, or Vachel Lindsay, or John Gould Fletcher, or even Robert Frost, whose content is purely American although his form is more nearly akin to tradition than that of the other men I have mentioned.

Now why have these men chosen to desert the traditional English forms? The answer is simple. It is that form is merely the outer garment of substance. What these men had to say was different from what any English poet has ever had to say. We may not realize it, but slowly, before our eyes, the American race is being born. And one of the evidences of it is that we are beginning to hew new pathways for ourselves in this most intimate thing—Poetry, and to free ourselves from the tutelage of another nation.

An English weekly, "The New Statesman," recently published a paper which contained this passage:

"Until recently it used commonly to be observed that American poetry was, as a whole, the most old-fashioned in the world. Even Whitman, a native product and a genuine poet, came and went without apparently exercising much influence on the more intelligent of his fellow-countrymen. He had an influence in France and in England; but the most popular, and indeed the better American verse-writers still preferred to write quatrains like Matthew Arnold's, or, at most, villanelles like those produced in England in the 'nineties. Recently there has been a change both in manner and in matter. There are still swarms of extraordinarily conventional poetasters in the States, but a number of the younger writers show marks of Whitmanian and other modern influences. They write in *verse-libre* (or in prose lines of unequal length, as the case may be); they try to express what they see and feel and not what Alfred, Lord Tennyson saw and felt; they do not confine their attention to objects traditionally admitted to be poetical; they write, in fact, as if they really were our contemporaries."

That needs no comment; I merely cite it to support my contention that we are really beginning to produce an original poetry at last.

"The New Poetry" is often understood to mean "free verse," but that would exclude Vachel Lindsay, and much of my own work. The whole New Movement in poetry is a matter of substance rather than of form. Form is merely an adjunct, but because form is more quickly noticed than content, it is principally on the question of form that people have been moved to argue. I shall come back to the form in a moment. Just now I want to lay down some general rules for defining the substance of the New Movement.

Elsewhere, I have said that its chief characteristic was "externality." By that I mean the interest in things for their own sake, apart from their effect upon the poet. It is the reverse of the old "pathetic fallacy." The New Poet sees a world in which he is passionately interested, but in which he is only one of many factors. To portray that world as he sees it is his concern. It may be the life in the street just outside his window with which he is occupied, or it

may be a historic and æsthetic interest in other peoples and places; but his method of approach in either case is the same. It is a passionate desire for truth, and a dispassionate attitude toward whatever his search for truth may bring him. He records; he does not moralize. He holds no brief for or against, he merely portrays.

"This art is cold," cry the older generation, "it is immoral." It is neither the one nor the other. Because the artist speaks no moral, it does not mean that none exists. Lives carry their own moral with them. The world of "The New Poetry" is like the world of reality, the morals are there, but it is for us, the readers, to pronounce them.

ANOTHER desire of the modern poet is to record his truth, not someone else's. To express what he feels, not, as "The New Statesman" has it, what Alfred, Lord Tennyson would have felt. Now it is very difficult to know when one is thinking one's own thoughts, we have all of us read so much, and imbibed so many thoughts belonging to other men, that one has to go on through the phase of imitation (often unconscious imitation) to reach a clear, personal outlook again. This process is called education and development. But it is strangely distrusted by many people, who wrongly suppose that it kills naturalism and originality instead of fostering them. As a matter of plain fact, only two kinds of people can be perfectly simple and perfectly direct. Those who have had no education, and those who have had a great deal. It is a little education that is dangerous—a fact which is seldom denied except when we are speaking of "The New Poetry." Now in this country of educational institutions which do not educate, it would be exceedingly difficult—nay, impossible—to find the man, poet or other, who is in a state of primitive simplicity. So it is safer to hunt for directness among those poets who have earnestly studied their art. And the New Poets, whatever else you deny them, must be acknowledged to have worked hard and mastered the technique of poetry, even to the discarding of much that many people still hold precious.

Every young writer begins by imitating his predecessors, as is quite right and proper. For an individual reproduces in himself the gradual evolution of the race. As the writer develops, he sloughs off

this subserviency to other men, and produces an art in which he can express himself unhampered. Now, originality is not very well understood by the world at large. In nine cases out of ten, it is distinctly antipathetic and disturbing. The man of original mind is called every kind of thing: idiot, hypocrite, charlatan. He is accused of tearing down art, of dragging it through the mire, of shutting it up in an insane asylum. When he puts down the visions of his imagination on paper, he is accused of having spent days seeking for an unusual image, and denounced as a mere hunter after the bizarre. When the truth of the matter is that those thoughts are his every-day companions.

It never seems to occur to anybody that the greater the poet, the less he is like the run of ordinary men. Every one in cool debate will admit that a poet must be different, but when he puts down his differences on paper, the "man in the street" cries out that these ideas are not his and that therefore the poet must be artificial and insincere.

POETIC movements go through regular stages. First is the era of change, of stepping out to conquer new territory; then is the era of accomplishment, when the ground conquered is developed to the utmost extent of its resources; last comes the era of decay. Those poets born to the first era are always treated to contempt and hilarity. But never does the contempt and hilarity stop the march of events. "The New Poetry" in America today is in the era of change. It fully realizes this, however much other people may doubt it. And you will admit that it is facing its task with high courage.

This courage is one of the distinguishing marks of modern poetry. I have said that the "new" poet did not shrink from whatever the search for truth might bring him, and along with many sad and painful realizations experienced mentally, comes the buzzing of the gnat-like mob teasing him and allowing him no rest.

There is much discussion today as to whether "The New Poetry" is democratic, and one of the favorite clubs against it is that Miss Jones, the stenographer, and Brown, the hod-carrier, do not care for it. Being a democratic country, we are much concerned to have all our activities democratic. There is a pathetic side to this; it is such a straining after a loved ideal. The truth is that we are confusing two kinds of democracy, and confounding the greater with the less. For, in one sense, no art can be democratic; in another, art is the most democratic thing in the world.

Democracy as applied to government means the ruling of all the people by a majority of the people. Politics is an affair of the present; art is an affair of centuries. So we may say that democracy as applied to art means the consensus of opinion enduring for long periods of time. And it is certain that only by appealing to this consensus of opinion can art live at all. Only those things for which mankind thirsts will be retained from year to year. The ephemeral, the meretricious, will soon disappear, because the democracy of the ages has no use for them.

I am quite aware, however, that this is not the sense in which the

touchstone of democracy has been applied to "The New Poetry" to confound it. In this sense I say unhesitatingly that "The New Poetry" is not democratic, because no art can be democratic. Is it possible that there is anybody so blinded by a beloved theory as to think for a moment that the great mass of people has any artistic desire, any real artistic taste. If our painters really wished to follow the majority of public taste, their pictures would be endless variations of the smart American girl; if our composers were to be awarded a prize by a *per capita* vote, Irving Berlin would go wreathed in laurel. No, as Mr. James Oppenheim very justly said in an excellent letter to the "New York Times" a few months ago:

". . . When shall we call style democratic? When it appeals to the kindergarten age, the primary age, the high school age, or the university age? And having found our standard, let us ask whether all poetry must conform to it; whether, then, we must throw out such rather cryptic works as the Book of Job, Revelation, and 'Ring and the Book,' 'Hamlet,' and 'Faust'—to mention a few.

"It seems to me, however, that even in a democracy education is deemed of importance. That is to say, that it is not taken for granted that a child can directly absorb the knowledge of the world, but has to be taught. . . ."

Few things require more education than taste.

I THINK of three poets who have been absolutely with the people; who by all rights should be the people's poets. They are: Walt Whitman, Edward Carpenter, and Paul Fort. But I doubt very much whether the people care a straw for any of them. Even today, there is no doubt that any universal suffrage would give the palm to Longfellow over Whitman, to Tennyson over Carpenter, and to Rostand over Fort.

That there are men in every walk of life with real poetic feeling in their hearts I do not for a moment deny, and it is to these men that poets with the welfare of the people at heart should address themselves. For poetry should try to lift men to its level, not sink itself to theirs. And does this new and widespread interest in poetry tell the objectors nothing? Do they not see that this "New Poetry" is reaching a large class of people who were numb to the older types of poetry, because in them they found nothing which made them feel at home? This life of the poets was not the life they were living, these thoughts were not in the least like those which dogged them from sunrise until sunset. But the New Poets live in the same kind of cities that they do, the flux of current events washes over them as it does over the man who reads. Their points of view are native, familiar. They write in the syntax of every-day speech, and open wide doors of vision with a key at every one's disposal. And there comes the old cry which means success to the artist: "We have always thought that, but we have never seen it put down in black and white before."

This is no contradiction of what I said a moment ago about the artist being an unusual man and his thoughts therefore unusual. The conventional minded do not like originality, but there are many people

who are only conventional because they have not the mental vigor to find a way out. These are not the creators, they are the appreciators. They find in "The New Poetry" the freedom they have longed for. They find that beauty is not chained upon the other side of the Atlantic, that it is here at their own doors. That the Singer Building is an achievement to be proud of and one need not sigh because we are not evolving Parthenons; that the Yankee farmer is as interesting as the Wessex yokel; and that sun, and rain, and cloud are as lyric here as over the orchards of Normandy.

It is a great deal to have discovered that. And the New Poetry, the New Painting, the New Music are making such discoveries every day. The artists of the older countries have always written about the things among which they lived, in the way that best suited them. Our artists are only just beginning to dare to be themselves. And the New Poetry is blazing a trail toward nationality far more subtle and intense than any settlement houses and waving of the American flag in schools can ever achieve. I might say with perfect truth that the most national things we have are skyscrapers, ice water, and the New Poetry, and each of these means more than appears on the surface.

BUT to be saturated with the spirit of nationality does not mean that a poet writes only upon national themes. In that case Milton would not be English because the scene of "Paradise Lost" is not England, and Dante would not be Italian because Heaven and Hell are not provinces of Italy. The spirit of a country is a very subtle thing. It is of the essence of a man's being, and betrays itself in a thousand ways. But so little is this understood that people are constantly criticizing the nationality of literature from the standpoint of subject. There is a constant cry for the great American novel, the great American poem, the great American play. And yet, if it came, and chose to deal with Fifteenth Century Italy, it would probably go unrecognized for at least a quarter of a century.

When critics have learned to distinguish the real, abiding qualities which make the American character and differentiate it from all other characters whatsoever, then we shall be nearer an understanding of the movement which is now in its infancy.

Let us examine a few of these characteristics and see how exactly they are expressed in the New Poetry.

The American is a highly nervous race, quick, impatient, energetic. Do we not find all these qualities in a marked degree in the New Poetry? It is bright with color, as befits a people living under so sunny a sky as ours. But this is a dry climate, our skies are a bit sharp and hard, so our poetry has not the languorous charm of those other sunny countries: Italy and the East. We are a sober and a temperate people, a people of ideals and reticencies, therefore we find here very little of the voluptuousness which is so marked a trait of the poetry of all Latin peoples. That we are losing some of these reticencies as we gain in power of expression is, of course, true. But even so, voluptuousness is hardly a quality of American poetry.

The American race is a profoundly unsentimental one. Hard-

headed, money-making, our enemies call us. But there is a difference between sentiment and sentimentality. Of sentiment, strong, almost stern, the New Poetry has an abundance, but the sentimentality of Longfellow's "Children's Hour" is gone. The modern American does not express himself in that way because he does not feel in that way.

AGAIN, we are not a race prone to religious hysteria; we shall search in vain through the pages of the New Poets for devotional poetry as such. We are materialists in a strange, joyful way—loving the things we can see, and hear, and taste, and touch, and smell. So these verses are full of scenes and objects, of beauties —Nature's, Art's—of preoccupation with the things all about us.

The American is a decidedly clear and logical thinker, hence so many instances of uncompromising realism in his verse. Also, the poet is human, and is ahead of his time, for which reason this "dour" realism is the natural reaction of an active, probing mind from the "Glad Book" tendencies evinced by a large portion of the American public.

The American is as quivering with life as a taut bow, and this lack of repose is one of the reasons why his "forte" is clearly not the sensuous, undulating line of pure melody. We shall seek in vain in the New Poetry for the smoothness of the Tennysonian manner. But the American is naturally extremely sensitive to rhythm. He could not have invented (or adopted) the intricate syncopation of ragtime had this not been so. The New Poetry gives us this marked beat and syncopation in the work of several poets, to mention two: Vachel Lindsay and William Rose Benét. But we have this *flair* better exemplified in the more subtle rhythms of the *vers libristes.* Only a poet with a strong sense of rhythm can cope with the difficulties of *vers libre,* simple as it may appear to those who have not studied its laws.

This poem by the American who writes under the pen-name of "H. D." well illustrates this subtle rhythm, but also illustrates some others of our national characteristics, for instance, our vividness and color, our logical thinking, our unsentimental delight in nature.

PEAR-TREE.

Silver dust is lifted from the earth.

Higher than my arms reach,
You have mounted, O silver,
Higher than my arms reach,
You front us with great mass.

No flower ever opened
So staunch a white leaf,
No flower ever parted
Gold from such gold.

Flake on flake,
Your white scale has fallen on earth.
You have dinted petal and leaf.
The narcissus is dark
By your rare grains.

Another poem, by Jean Starr Untermeyer, exemplifies admirably the strong, almost stern sentiment I have spoken of. How different this love poem is to those which have filled our magazines for the past twenty years, and how much truer it is to the idea of love which is ours in America today.

POSSESSION.

Walk into the world,
Go into the places of trade;
Go into the smiling country—
But go, clad, wrapped closely always
Shielded and sustained—
In the visible flame of my love.

Let it blaze about you—
A glowing armor for all to see;
Flashing around your head—
A tender and valiant halo.

I think there will be many to wonder
And many to stand in awe and envy—
But surely no one will come too close to you,
No one will dare to claim you,
Hand or heart,
As you pass in your shining and terrible garment.

I could multiply these examples through many pages. Suffice it therefore if I have but pointed the way to a better comprehension of that body of work which for the nonce we have christened "The New Poetry."

A number of poems have been selected by Miss Lowell to expound her theory of the new poetry of America. They will be found on pages of this issue of THE CRAFTSMAN.

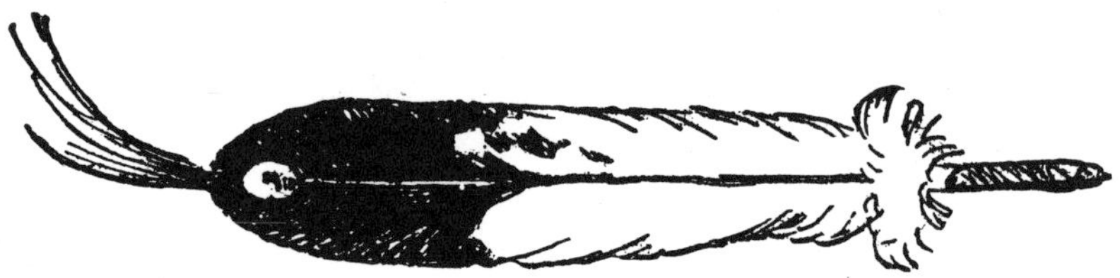

THE VANISHING RED: BY ROBERT FROST

HE is said to have been the last Red Man
In Acton. And the Miller is said to have laughed—
If you like to call such a sound a laugh.
But he gave no one else a laugher's license.
For he turned suddenly grave as if to say,
"Whose business, if I take it on myself,
Whose business—but why talk round the barn?—
When it's just that I hold with getting a thing done with."
You can't get back and see it as he saw it.
It's too long a story to go into now.
You'd have to have been there and lived it.
Then you wouldn't have looked on it as just a matter
Of who began it between the two races.

Some guttural exclamation of surprise
The Red Man gave in poking about the mill
Over the great big thumping, shuffling millstone
Disgusted the Miller physically as coming
From a person who the less he attracted
Attention to himself you would have thought the better.
"Come, John," he said, "you want to see the wheel pit?"
He took him down below a cramping rafter
And showed him through a manhole in the floor
The water in desperate straits like frantic fish
Salmon and sturgeon lashing with their tails,
Then he shut down the trap door with a ring in it
That jangled even above the general noise,
And came upstairs alone—and gave that laugh
And said something to a man with a meal-sack
That the man with the meal-sack didn't catch—then,
Oh yes, he showed John the wheel pit all right!

WINTER'S TURNING: BY AMY LOWELL

SNOW is still on the ground,
But there is a golden brightness in the air.
Across the river,
Blue,
Blue,
Sweeping widely under the arches
Of many bridges,
Is a spire and a dome,
Clear as though ringed with ice-flakes,
Golden, and pink, and jocund.
On a nearby steeple,
A golden weather cock flashes smartly,
His open beak "Cock-a-doodle-dooing"
Straight at the ear of Heaven.
A tall apartment house,
Crocus-coloured,
Thrusts up from the street
Like a new-sprung flower.
Another street is edged and patterned
With the bloom of bricks,
Houses and houses of rose-red bricks,
Every window a-glitter.
The city is a parterre,
Blowing and glowing,
Alight with the wind,
Washed over with gold and mercury.
Let us throw up our hats,
For we are past the age of balls
And have none handy.
Let us take hold of hands,
And race along the sidewalks,
And dodge the traffic in crowded streets.
Let us whir with the golden spoke-wheels
Of the sun.
For tomorrow Winter drops into the waste basket,
And the calendar calls it March.

The Indian sings:

"May it be delightful, my house;
From my head may it be delightful;
To my feet may it be delightful;
Where I lie may it be delightful;
All above me may it be delightful;
All around me may it be delightful."

"In the house of long life, there I wander.
In the house of happiness, there I wander.
Beauty before me, with it I wander.
Beauty behind me, with it I wander.
Beauty below me, with it I wander.

"Beauty above me, with it I wander.
Beauty all around me, with it I wander.
In old age traveling, with it I wander.
On the beautiful trail I am, with it I wander."

We also sing that same song, though with different words. On the trail of beauty we also wander and of our houses as with our lives we should be able to say with them, "It is finished with beauty."